BISON
BOOKS

STUDIES
IN THE ANTHROPOLOGY OF
NORTH AMERICAN INDIANS

The Lakota Ritual of the Sweat Lodge
History and Contemporary Practice

Raymond A. Bucko

Published by the University of Nebraska Press
Lincoln and London

In cooperation with the American Indian Studies Research
Institute, Indiana University, Bloomington

First Bison Books printing: 1999

Library of Congress Cataloging-in-Publication Data

Bucko, Raymond A., 1954–
The Lakota ritual of the sweat lodge: history and contemporary
practice / Raymond A. Bucko.
p.   cm. — (Studies in the anthropology of North American
Indians)
Includes bibliographical references (p.   ) and index.
ISBN 0-8032-1272-0 (cl: alk. paper)
ISBN 0-8032-6165-9 (pa: alk. paper)
1. Dakota Indians—Rites and ceremonies.   2. Dakota Indians—
History.   3. Sweatbaths—Great Plains—History.   I. Title.
II. Series
E99.D1B88   1998
299'.74—dc21
97-47504   CIP

Contents

Illustrations

Orthographic Key

Because many diverse systems have been used to write Dakota and Lakota, words cited throughout this volume have been systematically retranscribed to conform to the orthography of Rood and Taylor (1996). Special symbols are:

ą   nasalized *a*

c   voiceless alveolar affricate, pronounced as *ch* in English *watch*

ǧ   voiced velar frictave, pronounced *r* in Parisian pronunciation of *Paris*

h   indicates aspiration when following a consonant; thus, for example, the sequence *th* in Lakota is pronounced strongly as *t* in English *toe,* and not as *th* in English *thin*

ḣ   unvoiced velar fricative, pronounced as *ch* in German *ach*

į   nasalized *i*

š   voicless alveolar fricative, pronounced as *sh* in English *ship*

ų   nasalized *u*

ž   voiced alveolar fricative, pronounced as *z* in English *azure*

ʼ   glottal stop, as in English *oh-oh!*

ˊ   accent mark that indicates stress

Entering the Lodge

The Lakota Sweat Lodge: A View from Within

Late one fall afternoon in 1989, a Lakota friend called to tell me he was putting up a sweat[1] and that it would begin around sunset. He asked me to come and join the group. When I arrived at the site, just as the sun was setting, I saw neither smoke nor fire down in the draw where the sweat lodge was located. In fact, the fire had not been lit, and the individual who invited me and was to run the sweat was not there yet. As I sat around with some others who had come for the sweat, we told jokes and caught up on the news. No one was in a hurry or concerned that the leader had not arrived. Nor was anyone anxious to start the fire or remove the rocks left in the lodge from the last sweat.

The door of this sweat lodge faced west. A few yards in front of the door there was a large fireplace with a low, crescent-shaped wall made of earth and spent sweat rocks. Closer to the lodge, a few feet from the door, was an altar, situated in line with the entrance to the sweat and the fireplace. A three-foot-tall staff with white and red cloth offerings attached to it had been erected on the altar. Four short red sticks with tobacco ties attached to their ends stood single file on the altar, forming a north-south line. The sides of the altar were lined with spent sweat rocks. A pipe rack rested in front of the four red sticks on the sweat lodge side (east) of the altar. The lodge was near a creek and set against a backdrop dense with the cottonwood trees that flourish along the creek bottoms of the Pine Ridge Reservation.

When the leader arrived, we sat around visiting a while longer. Finally, we helped the leader assemble material for the fire. He first swept out the fireplace while someone else tossed out the rocks left in the lodge from the last sweat. The leader laid two logs about four feet apart in the fire pit on an east-west axis and put four logs on top of those on a north-south axis to form a low platform. Next he placed four rocks on this bed in the four cardinal directions and then piled three rocks in their center to represent the zenith (Grandfather or Great Spirit), the nadir (Grandmother or Mother Earth) and the center. About twenty rocks were then loaded on the platform in no particular order. Long slats of wood were leaned against the pile of rocks to form a tepee-shaped structure. The leader prayed silently, holding some tobacco (a broken cigarette), and offered it to the cardinal directions, the zenith, and the nadir. He sprinkled the tobacco on the rocks and logs and lit the fire with newspaper, and then we all visited a few more hours. A brilliant evening star appeared in the west of the now dark sky. The fire cast bright light and flickering shadows on us as we conversed softly and watched more stars appear. The air was cool and still. We drew a little closer to the fire for warmth. For a while I lost myself in the sounds and colors of the fire, the soft speech, and the quiet tranquility of the night.

As the fire burned down, two participants each took a short stick out of bundles they had brought with them (one used an old briefcase), to which they attached an abalone shell and an eagle feather. They then stuck the sticks into the altar. The same individuals, one of whom was the leader, removed pipes from decorated pipe bags. They knelt close to the ground, and each one offered six pinches of tobacco toward the four directions, the sky, and the earth, placing each pinch into the bowl of his pipe. When the pipes were filled, they used sprigs of sage to seal the bowls. One individual stood and prayed silently, pointing his pipe toward the west, the north, the east, the south, the sky, and the earth. Those with pipes then placed them on the pipe rack on the altar in front of the sweat lodge, stems pointing west, away from the lodge. They did these things quietly, off to the side, not as a public ceremony.[2]

The lodge was already well covered with the tarps when we arrived. The interior was carpeted, and sage was strewn over the carpet. Someone went inside, shutting the door behind him to make sure no light entered the lodge. He yelled and struck the covers here and there so we knew where they needed to be adjusted. After the lodge was secured, he emerged. As the rocks were heating, the leader took a shovelful of coals and sprinkled sage on them to incense around the lodge and its interior, moving in a clockwise direction. The fire burned down, and the weight of the rocks collapsed the burning platform on which they rested, sending a shower of sparks into the air. We were told to get ready. The women participants, who were already dressed in ankle-length loose dresses made of calico cloth, went inside clockwise and sat along the perimeter of the pit while the men went to the back of the sweat lodge and stripped to gym shorts as they continued joking. Everyone brought towels into the lodge.

The leader entered the lodge first of all the men, moving to the right to take his seat at the south end of the circle, followed by the other participants, one by one. Each said, "Mitakuye oyas'in" [*Mitákuye oyás'į* 'all my relatives']³ as they entered. One individual spun around clockwise before entering. We moved toward the left (north), proceeding clockwise, filling in the area around the pit. One man remained outside to act as *thiyópa awáyąke* 'doorkeeper'. After we all were inside, we talked and teased until everyone settled down. Sage was passed along the circle, and we each took some. The doorkeeper passed in a smoldering braid of sweetgrass, which everyone used to smudge his or her body as an act of purification.

Then the leader asked for his pipe. The doorkeeper handed it to him, and the leader passed it to the man sitting at the north end of the circle. This individual had an excellent voice and acted as the lead singer throughout the ceremony. The leader asked the doorkeeper to bring the rocks. The doorkeeper brought one rock on a pitchfork and placed it just inside the entrance. The man holding the pipe touched the bowl to the rock and said, "Mitakuye oyas'in." A third individual, asked to perform this task using two antlers brought into the lodge for the purpose, picked up the rock and placed it in the west end of the pit. A woman was asked to sprinkle dried cedar on each rock as it was placed in the pit. The cedar crackled and popped a little, then sent up a column of fragrant white smoke. This procedure was followed for the next six rocks that were placed one by one to the north, the east, and the south, with three in the middle for the earth, the sky, and the center. After the rocks were in position, the pipe was passed all around the circle, and the leader handed it out the door to the fire keeper. The participants began speaking softly, quietly joking and laughing. More rocks were passed into the lodge and placed in the pit with antlers. No particular order was followed, but everyone jokingly encouraged the man with the antlers to place the hottest ones in front of somebody else. The heat gradually increased as the rocks in the center glowed softly. The fragrant aroma from the cedar filled the lodge.

When the leader indicated that there were enough rocks, the antlers were passed around the circle and given by the leader to the doorkeeper. A drum was passed into the lodge, incensed with cedar smoke, and handed to the lead singer, who sat to the left of the door (as one enters). The leader called for water, which was brought in a large white plastic container. A metal ladle hung within the bucket. More cedar was placed on the rocks, and the water bucket was quickly passed from hand to hand in a clockwise direction. Most participants knelt to better support the weight of the water. Then the bucket was held over the smoke and touched to the rocks by the individuals on either side of the door. As this was done, the leader said, *"Mní wichóni* 'water of life'," before placing it in front of the door.

The leader said, *"Natháka yo!"* ['Close it up!']. The doorkeeper closed the flap, tucking the base of the canvas door flat and tight against the ground. We were enveloped in total darkness except for the soft red glow of the rocks. Heat rising from the rocks struck me on the knees, shoulders, and face. I could hear people stirring a little as they settled down, one person rubbing himself with sage, another clearing his throat. Sweat trickled off my body.

The leader began to speak. He welcomed each of us to the sweat, thanking us for coming. He said this was an ancient and good way to pray and that we were all praying to the same God. He told us that in the lodge we were suffering for the sake of others, but if the suffering became too much, we should say "mitakuye oyas'in" and they would open the door. This was not an endurance contest. Nevertheless, he reminded us that the Lakota ways are difficult and that sacrifice is necessary and assured us that our prayers are heard when offered in this way. The leader said that he ran the sweat because he was the head of this family and that he had also gone on a vision quest and had been a Sun Dancer, but he insisted that he was not worthy to run a sweat and hoped that any mistakes he made would be forgiven. He told us that water was the first medicine given to the people.

He prayed, saying that the west is the direction of the thunder beings and asking that they bring life, purification, rain, and renewal. He prayed that all our prayers that night would be answered and that we would be protected from harm. Repeatedly he stated that he was poor, humble, and nothing, and begged that his prayers be heard and that he be helped. He prayed for the old, the young, the unborn, and the crippled. Because not everyone in the lodge was fluent in Lakota, the leader first used Lakota and then repeated what he said in English.

After concluding his prayer with "mitakuye oyas'in" he asked the singer for a four-directions song, sung in Lakota, as are all the songs in the sweat:[4]

Wiyóȟpeyatąhą étųwą yo!
Nithųkašila ahítųwąhe yelo!

Chékiya yo! Chékiya yo!
Heyáhe ṭuwáhe yaké lo!

From the west, look there!
Your grandfather arrives looking there!
Pray! Pray!
Looking around sitting there he says that!

Wazíyatạhạ étụwạ yo!
Nithúkašila ahítụwạhe yelo!
Chékiya yo! Chékiya yo!
Heyáhe ṭuwáhe yaké lo!

From the north, look there!
Your grandfather arrives looking there!
Pray! Pray!
Looking around sitting there he says that!

Wiyóhiyạpatạhạ étụwạ yo!
Nithúkašila ahítụwạhe yelo!
Chékiya yo! Chékiya yo!
Heyáhe ṭuwáhe yaké lo!

From the east, look there!
Your grandfather arrives looking there!
Pray! Pray!
Looking around sitting there he says that!

Itókağatạhạ étụwạ yo!
Nithúkašila ahítụwạhe yelo!
Chékiya yo! Chékiya yo!
Heyáhe ṭuwáhe yaké lo!

From the south, look there!
Your grandfather arrives looking there!
Pray! Pray!
Looking around sitting there he says that!

Wąkátakiya étųwą yo!
Nithųkašila ahítųwąhe yelo!
Chékiya yo! Chékiya yo!
Heyáhe tųwą́he yąké lo!

Look to the above!
Your grandfather arrives looking there!
Pray! Pray!
Looking around sitting there he says that!

Makhátakiya étųwą yo!
Nithųkašila ahítųwąhe yelo!
Chékiya yo! Chékiya yo!
Heyáhe tųwą́he yąké lo!

Look to the earth!
Grandmother Earth arrives looking there!
Pray! Pray!
Looking around sitting there he says that!

The leader poured water on the rocks as this song was sung with intense feeling. Everyone joined in the singing. The water hissed loudly and the heat became almost unbearable. The lodge filled with steam. I put my head down and just hung on. Others shouted, *"Háu, háu,"* as the heat increased terrifically. Finally, when the song was done, the leader said, *"Mitákuye oyás'į. Yuğą́ yo!"* ['All my relatives. Open it up!']. The door was opened from outside, and there was a burst of moonlight and fresh air as the steam wafted out of the lodge into the night. Everyone was hunched over or lying down. The mood shifted from solemn and serious to casual and even humorous after the door opened. People joked about how hot it was during the round and how they had been cooked. One man claimed he shrank two sizes. Others sat silently, and some lay down as soon as the door opened. One had already assumed this position sometime during the first round. The first round lasted about twenty-five minutes.

The sweat leader asked if anyone wanted to drink water and there was a chorus of yeses. The doorkeeper passed in a pail of water. The lead singer drew the water from the bucket with a ladle, touched the ladle to the rocks, and drank it. He then drew another ladle, touched it to the rocks, and passed it to the person on his left. He repeated these motions for each person, moving around the lodge clockwise. After each person drank, he or she said, "Mitakuye oyas'in." Some drank a little of the water and poured the rest over their bodies. Others poured what was left of their water into the pit. The empty ladle was passed back around the way it came (counterclockwise). Everyone was attentive to the process. Last of all, the doorkeeper was handed out a ladle of water. The leader then asked if people were ready for the second round, and everyone sat up and found a comfortable position. The leader asked the doorkeeper to close the door.

In the second round, the leader prayed toward the north, the place, as he stated, of the Buffalo Nation.[5] He prayed for healing for the people, especially for victims of drug and alcohol abuse and of domestic violence. A Sun Dance song was sung as the leader sprinkled water on the rocks with the ladle:

Wakhą́ Thą́ka ų́šimala yo!
Waníkta cha lechámu welo!

Great Spirit, have pity on me!
So that I continue living I am doing this!

The leader used an eagle wing fan to distribute the steam around the lodge, increasing the heat, which quickly became almost unbearable. Someone next to me advised me to put a towel over my head if it got too hot in the lodge. The leader invited people to pray, beginning at the door where the lead singer was seated and going around clockwise one by one. In this round, three people prayed. The prayers were intimate, about struggles in their own lives, failures, successes, and the difficulties of interpersonal relationships.[6] Each individual prayed for the needs of the leader, the singer, the people present in the lodge, and the doorkeeper. Most were able to mention each participant by name and say something encouraging about that person. There were also prayers for individuals not present at the ceremony. Spiritual leaders and those preparing for Sun Dances and vision quests were mentioned, as well as relatives and friends. When one participant began crying during her prayer, the leader started a soft song to shield her sobbing. Public displays of emotion are rare on the reservation; the sweat provides a space that is both a public and a private opportunity for emotional openness.

The heat increased and, heart racing, I was overwhelmed by the beauty of the prayers, the intense heat, and the stifling steam. At times I could see sparks flashing among the rocks in the pit. The leader explained at the end of the round that some people see spiritual things during the sweat ceremony, whereas others might not. Sparks and sounds are considered manifestations of spirits who come to the lodge.

My appreciation for the people with whom I was praying increased as the ceremony progressed. The darkness dissolved boundaries, and the prayers formed profound links with people voicing deep feelings. I felt closer to these individuals because I understood them better and, in a way, joined in their suffering, both physically and emotionally, as the ceremony progressed.

Each individual ended his or her prayer with "mitakuye oyas'in." They addressed their prayers to Wakan Tanka and Tunkashila, although there was no attempt to define these terms. Throughout the prayers, the image of individuals as suffering beings, poor and pitiful, was reiterated. The participants, both verbally and through the rigors of the ceremony, placed themselves in a humble and pitiful posture and then explained what was needed for their people, their families, and themselves. Those prayed for who were absent were sometimes identified spatially. Thus, one might pray for a relative to the south who was having troubles or a good friend to the north who had visited a few weeks ago.

After the third person prayed, the leader poured more water and called for another song, again a Sun Dance song:

> *Thųkášila ahítųwą yo!*
> *Lé chąnúpa ki le iyékiya yo!*
> *Hé mitákuye ób waníkta cha*
> *Lé echámu yelo!*
> *Thųkášila iyótiyewakiye lo!*

> Grandfather, come looking!
> Recognize this pipe!
> So that I might continue to live with my relatives
> I am doing this!
> Grandfather I am suffering!

The leader poured water on the rocks during the song, and by the time it was completed, the heat and the steam were almost overwhelming. The leader skillfully regulated the intensity of the heat to match expressed emotions, but at the same time he was careful not to scald anyone. He shouted, "Mitakuye oyas'in," and everyone joined in the cry with gusto. The doorkeeper opened the door as we were shouting.

During the second break, someone asked if he could speak. The leader consented, and as water was being passed, this man spoke in detail of a very personal situation in his life. He asked the others to help him by praying for him. He was trying to change his life and walk "the good red road." The ceremony was really helping him to do that. He thanked everyone inside for praying with him and helping him along. While he was speaking and again when he finished, the participants indicated their assent by softly saying *"Háu, háu."* The phrase allows for a wide range of emotional expression: assent, concern, questioning, encouragement. It is used frequently while others pray or speak. This form of back-channeling is especially used by the leader, who is particularly attentive to everything that transpires in the lodge.

After water had been drunk, the leader called for more rocks. The bucket of water was placed outside the door and the remaining rocks were brought into the lodge. They were placed on the pile of rocks in the center, using the deer antlers. After the leader passed the antlers out to the doorkeeper, water was brought in again and we all drank. When we finished, the doorkeeper was given the water, he closed and sealed the door, and we began the third round. This time the leader prayed mentioning the south, the land of the winged creatures. He prayed for the dead, who are believed to travel toward the south. He remembered all mourners. He prayed that the people be kept safe from accidents. Yet another Sun Dance song was sung as the leader poured water on the rocks with a ladle:

Wakhą́ Thą́ka ų́šimala yo!
Ómakiya yo! Makákiže lo!

Great Spirit, have pity on me!
Help me! I'm suffering!

Then he invited the last of the participants to voice their prayers. Each ended his or her prayer with "Mitakuye oyas'in." One omitted this phrase, but no one corrected him. Not sure if he had completed his prayer, after some silence the leader asked if he was finished. He said yes and the leader then said, "Next." More water was poured after everyone had finished his or her prayer. The heat now was so intense that I could feel sweat and water pouring off me and I was light-headed. I was wondering whether the door would ever open, when the leader shouted, "Mitakuye oyas'in" and everyone joined in with him as the door opened. Crisp moonlight illuminated the steam as it emerged from the lodge in billows. Everyone was flat on the floor now, using towels as protection against the heat.

The leader explained that the third round was the pipe round, so after the door was opened, he asked the doorkeeper to bring in one of the two pipes from the altar. The pipe was handed in and the individual to the left of the door lit it with a butane cigarette lighter, smoked, and then said, "Mitakuye oyas'in." The pipe was passed to the left, beginning with the song leader at the door, and each person smoked in succession. Some spun the pipe after smoking; others held the pipe over their heads and prayed softly. All said "mitakuye oyas'in" after smoking. The leader smoked, and then the pipe was held out for the doorkeeper, who also smoked, finishing the pipe. He emptied it and replaced it on the altar. The leader asked that the door be closed again.

In the darkness, the leader said that if anyone wished to pray again or had forgotten anything, now was the chance. There was silence. So the leader began praying, invoking the east. He said this was the direction of the black tail deer. He prayed for enlightenment and wisdom for tribal leaders and families. He prayed for government and religious leaders—that they might be faithful to their commitments. He invoked Grandmother Earth, asking for protection and sustenance. Next he directed his prayers to the above, to Wakan Tanka, thankful for bringing the group to the close of another day and requesting that we receive what we each had asked for. He also prayed for every person in the lodge by name, mentioning the various things each had prayed for and assuring us that these things would be accomplished. He accurately and compassionately summarized each person's prayer, speaking words of encouragement and consolation based on the prayer and his personal knowledge of the individual. Finally, he prayed for the old, the young, the unborn, the poor, and those in hospitals. He called for three songs, and while we were all singing, he again began pouring water:

> Thųkášila ahítųwą yo!
> Lé chaŋúpa ki lé iyékiya yo!
> Hé mitákuye ób waníkta cha
> Lechámu welo.
> Thųkášila iyótiyewakiye lo!

> Grandfather, come looking!
> Recognize this pipe!
> So that I might continue to live with my relatives

I am doing this.
Grandfather I am suffering!

Chąnúpa wą yuhá hoyéwaye yelo!
Oyáte ki nípikta cha
Lechámu welo.
Thųkášila ómakiya yo!
Ómakiya yo!

With this pipe I send a voice!
So that the people might live
I do this.
Grandfather help me!
Help me!

Thųkášila philámaya yelo, philámaya yelo, philámaya yelo.
Wichóząni wą mayák'u cha philámaya yelo heeeeee.

Grandfather thank you, thank you, thank you.
You have given me health so I thank you.

The heat intensified, but the songs kept on, so I sat and sang along with the others. If I moved, the heat seemed even worse. When the last of the songs came to an end, the leader shouted, "Mitakuye oyas'in." We echoed this with great fervor, and the door was opened. We left the lodge one by one, counterclockwise, so as not to cross in front of the leader, who was the last to leave. When we were all out, the leader emerged. There was steam coming off my skin and I felt absolutely washed out. We all stood in a circle around the altar. The leader lit the second pipe, and we smoked in the cool night air, passing the pipe from person to person, each saying "mitakuye oyas'in" as he or she finished smoking. When the pipe had finished circulating, the leader smoked the rest of the pipe and then emptied out the ashes. The individuals who brought their own pipes took them apart and packed them away. After we all shook hands, the women went up to the leader's house to dress, the men dressed behind the lodge, and then we went to the leader's house for a dinner of soup, crackers, and pie. My vision was blurred from the heat, and as I slowly walked up to the house my legs were unsteady at first. But though I felt spent, I also was invigorated. We left the sweat fire ashes glowing and the lodge itself steaming. At the house

I was asked to lead grace, and then we all ate. There was lively conversation and joking, much as there was before the sweat. As I left, I was told to be sure to come back for the next sweat.

Tradition and the Sweat

Although the ceremony just described may be characterized as a typical sweat, having an essential form that is repeated again and again, each sweat is unique. It is the unique nature of the sweat, from both its experiential and its structural aspects, that makes the ceremony so compelling. But, despite the uniqueness of each sweat, there is a significant continuity among sweats historically and on the reservation today. Sweats proliferate on the reservation, both in multiplicity of lodge structures themselves and in the frequency of use of each lodge. The sweat represents a transformation of the past as understood by participants in the present, which they designate as *tradition*. The participants in the sweat bring the past into the present, not as a whole, but according to current under-standings, needs, and circumstances.

I propose the model of a *dialectic* as a useful way to describe and analyze this process of creating tradition by combining an understanding of the past with the needs of the present. The dialectical process holds that two opposite propositions (the thesis and the antithesis—in this case, the past and the present) come together to create a unique synthesis (in this case, tradition). Note that the dialectical model is taken from Western social science and does not necessarily represent the way a Lakota (unless trained in the social sciences) would formulate this process. Note too that these opposite poles (past and present) are ideal types—constructs for the sake of a model—and that in practice the two poles are not always analytically distinguishable, either in descriptions given by practitioners or through ethnohistorical analysis. In this work I examine the poles of the dialectic to show how past and present come together in current Lakota ceremonial practice (and indeed in Lakota life itself) to produce contemporary configurations that participants mark as traditional.

From my observations of contemporary Lakota practice and from the ethnohistorical literature, it is clear that, although these two poles are distinctly formulated by individuals, different people apply the labels "truly past" and "truly contemporary" differently. Lakota ceremonial practice is rather charismatic, fluid, and based on individuals' ongoing spiritual experiences. It is true that early ethnography (for example, the Walker texts) points to a system of mentorship and collective interpretation by elder spiritual practitioners, but individual inspiration and interpretation was and continues to be highly valued within Lakota religious practice.

Some native practitioners are familiar with much of the ethnohistorical literature, particularly the Sword material and such contemporary Lakota ethnographies as those by William K. Powers. Others rely on what they have learned from older people or peers, and still others use a combination of these routes to access the past. Those who are new to traditional practice frankly confess their alienation from the past as they seek various ways to regain their heritage and establish a specific identity. What brings all these people together is their quest to behave in what they conceive as "a traditional manner," and thus they engage in this dialectical process as individuals and as groups to produce a satisfactory rendition of tradition. Each person's circumstances in the present differ from those of others. Some are Lakota speakers, some are new to Lakota belief systems, and others are rising in the ranks of ritual leaders. Thus, the resultant production of tradition is unique or nuanced depending on specific individuals and groups. The dialectical *process* in each instance is identical, whereas the *understandings* of the past and the present, as well as the results of the process, are unique and subject to contestation. Thus, there is a consistent form (the dialectic) with variable matter (construction of the past and the present, as well as their combination into what is termed tradition), resulting in a variety of formulations of what might legitimately be designated as tradition. Because of this variability, certain individuals or groups contest particular outcomes designated as traditional.

In order to understand the meaning of tradition, we must look at the two poles of the dialectic, the past and the present. We need to examine the documentation concerning the early use of the sweat and understand how contemporary participants conceptualize and represent their past. Most contemporary participants in the sweat recognize changes and unique adaptations in the ritual, but they also believe that the core of the ritual faithfully recreates the very ancient past. This examination of continuity and change, conservation and innovation, past and present, is not merely an academic exercise that I have proposed to structure this book. In fact, the question of what constitutes legitimate practice in the sweat lodge is vital to the practice of individuals who participate both on and off the reservation, for they ultimately legitimate or disqualify practice by deciding whether or not a ceremony is traditional and therefore acceptable and effective. My task is not to establish what is legitimate contemporary practice, but rather to demonstrate how this legitimacy called tradition is in fact arrived at.

Tradition itself is a vital term in contemporary Lakota discourse and constitutes a key symbol in Lakota culture. Tradition is used on the reservation today both as a term to authenticate a legitimate link to the past and as a mark of legitimacy itself. People, behaviors, and ceremonies are often called traditional. Once we have examined the two poles that are used to constitute tradition, we will look at the variety of meanings the term has in contemporary Lakota practice.

Chapter 1 is a historical analysis of the sweat lodge ceremony, beginning with its earliest written documentation. Chapter 2 continues that analysis, focusing on contemporary documentation, little of which was written by social scientists. Those two chapters examine the essential continuities and changes in the ceremony and provide important insights into the dynamics of contemporary Lakota ceremonial practice and culture in general; they provide a basis for the examination of continuities and transformations in the form, contexts, and content of the sweat as portrayed in scientific and popular literature. Understanding the changed place of this ritual in the social life of the people of Pine Ridge also allows for insights into continuities and innovations in the late-twentieth-century interpretations of the sweat lodge by both Lakotas and whites—the topics of the third and seventh chapters. These continuities and innovations, analytically the basic stuff of the dialectical process by which tradition arises, are essential to understanding both the persistence and the flourishing of the ceremony today.

Chapter 3 contextualizes and evaluates the various historical documents used in the first two chapters and examines the specific purposes of each group of recorders: missionaries, civil servants, anthropologists, and popular chroniclers who presented the Lakota world to a larger audience through their writings. The implications of choosing both consultants and sources are discussed. Chapter 3 also examines the implications, both for the Lakotas themselves and for the outside world, of creating a representation of culture. Ritual can be seen as a series of contentions over the right to determine and regulate how the sweat lodge ceremony is represented within and across social groups and, in this study, both within the groups involved in the sweat lodge and among interested outsiders.

Chapter 4 examines the importance of language and the different types of communication that take place in a sweat. Chapter 5 is primarily biographical; it considers individuals' introduction to the sweat lodge, frequently described using the language of conversion, and the wide variety of symbolic interpretations of the sweat provided by participants. Chapter 6 looks at the social dynamic of the sweat within the larger context of social exchange and interaction. This chapter demonstrates how both consensus and contention over ritual work out pragmatically through group formation, incorporation, and fragmentation. The final chapter considers how the sweat lodge is used to incorporate people into Lakota groups, with an emphasis on the implications of incorporating whites in Lakota ceremonies and the independent use of the ceremony by non-Indians.

Context for Research

Despite predictions of their disappearance by early missionaries and anthropologists (Lynd 1864:166; Macgregor 1946:103), traditional religious practices remained viable among the Dakotas (Santees, Yanktons, and Yanktonais) and the Lakotas (Tetons) and have markedly increased in the contemporary era.[7] This is particularly true for the sweat lodge.[8] The sweat lodge is part of a larger ritual system consisting of Sun Dances, vision quests, different kinds of healing and spirit-summoning ceremonies, and naming and adoption ceremonies. The reservation today is a site of great religious pluralism; some individuals participate in various Christian and Bah'ai churches exclusively, some combine church-related beliefs with Lakota beliefs, and still others identify themselves as strictly Lakota in belief system.[9]

The Pine Ridge Reservation is located in southwestern South Dakota. It is the home of some 11,200 Indians.[10] Most of the inhabitants are Oglala Lakotas, with small numbers of peoples from other bands of the Tetons, Northern Cheyennes, and Navajos, as well as white landowners, reservation employees, and other native groups.[11] The reservation comprises 2,778,710 acres of land; 372,243 acres are tribally owned, 48,231 acres are owned by the government, 1,089,077 acres are allotted, and 1,269,159 acres are owned by non-Indians (Dent 1976:498; Confederation of American Indians 1986:255).[12] The people of Pine Ridge have faced a series of crises in the past and today must deal with economic marginalization, substance abuse, and violence. But individuals take an active role in their destiny—political, social, economic, and religious. This is accomplished more and more through asserting their political and cultural sovereignty while, at the same time, seeking allies on other reservations in the United States and, indeed, in Europe and across the globe.

Historically, the Lakotas have carefully interpreted their ceremonies and rituals for missionaries, agents, anthropologists, and a continually growing group of nonprofessional "seekers." Interpretation is linked to another salient feature of Lakota life, incorporation. The earliest written records show the Lakotas (whose name literally means 'allies') actively incorporating outsiders into the core of Lakota culture: kinship groupings. Such incorporation, always selective, nevertheless can be traced historically as a consistent phenomenon. It occurred with captives and members of other Indian groups and later with white traders and missionaries.

This desire of the Lakotas to present their culture to outsiders in an understandable and acceptable way is not strictly passive—they are not willing to compromise principles and beliefs simply to be understood and accepted. Their interpretive stance sometimes shifts from making analogies to making oppositions. Thus, Lakota practice is sometimes interpreted as being the opposite of and superior to what is disagreeable in the white world around them (Schwimmer 1972; Simard 1990). At other times, Lakota culture is interpreted as complementary to practices that surround them. So, whereas some Lakotas explicitly eschew Christian interpretations for their rituals and others compare their religious system to Christianity to highlight their separate but equal status, still others freely use these analogies so that their ceremonies and their intents can be better understood or, in some cases, so that the two sets of beliefs can be reconciled.

These strategies of inclusion and exclusion do not represent an either/or choice. Different strategies are sometimes employed by the same individual at different times. Nevertheless, the importance of understanding the differing strategies is vital. Because different groups position themselves differently along this axis of accommodation and resistance, there is a heterogeneity in belief and action on the reservation. Opposition and incorporation represent two poles of an oscillating reality. Elements of all available strategies are used by individuals and groups at different times. The key metaphor that encapsulates these various movements and evaluations is *tradition,* which is generated by the dialectical combination of elements of the past and the present. A crucial question today is whether this constituted tradition is universal and thus open to all or specific to Lakota practitioners.

Personal Statement

My involvement with Indian people began in 1973 as a Jesuit novice on the Fort Belknap Reservation in eastern Montana. I began working on the Pine Ridge Reservation in 1976 when I was a camp counselor at the Catholic mission in Porcupine. I returned in 1978 to teach at Red Cloud High School for two years. I also spent several summers on the reservation and returned for two years of full-time fieldwork and teaching at Oglala Lakota College from January 1988 until December 1989. I went to these reservations because of my own interests and because of the long relationship the Jesuits have had with Indian people.

Since my dissertation was about the sweat lodge, I approached the study by frequent participation in the ceremony. Initially, when I went to sweat with someone, it was simply to pray with him or her. Most everyone on the reservation knows me as a Catholic priest, a person who has been around on the reservation for some time, and a person who makes an attempt to speak the Lakota language with often humorous results. It was a little more delicate matter to introduce myself as a student of anthropology. The "A" word quickly elicits vocal mistrust or disdain, so I softened the blow by saying I was working in "cultural studies."[13] People, whether or not they were Christian, were far less accepting of my role as an anthropologist than they were of my role as a priest. Ultimately I was welcomed into sweat lodges not because of my religious and academic roles but because of my personality, my desire to participate sincerely in the ceremony, and the fact that I had been involved on the reservation for a considerable number of years and had built solid friendships. I had also been adopted into families: three families I had grown to know well during my research later adopted me. This series of adoptions intensified my relationship with the people on the reservation but kept me from being identified with any one particular family, allowing me more freedom to participate with a multiplicity of groups in using the sweat lodge ceremony. I did not use adoption as a wedge for research, nor do I use it to legitimate any of my own work. Adoption is very important to me spiritually, emotionally, and socially. My adoptive relationships intensified and expanded when my father died in 1988, leaving me an orphan, as the Lakotas quickly recognized despite my self-disqualification because of my age (my mother died in 1983). These relationships continue to hold an importance in my life.

Inviting a person to sweat is an important decision and statement both to the one invited and to the surrounding community. I was not necessarily welcome at every sweat lodge; my study is limited for this reason and because I simply could not be present at all the lodges on the reservation. The fact that some lodges were restricted gave me significant insight into the lodges to which I was invited.

Without falling into ethnographic narcissism, I should put my research interests and experience in context. In 1978, when I was teaching at the Jesuit high school in Pine Ridge, I was invited to a sweat by a priest at the mission. When we arrived, I noted that the leader of the sweat asked the priest to purify the lodge with sweetgrass and to make several prayers during the ceremony. I was made to feel welcome and there was a (literally) warm feeling of camaraderie quickly established among all the participants. This was the first of a long series of sweats with acquaintances and friends on the reservation.

Unlike earlier ethnographers who learned the Lakota religion from recognized holy men, I was interested in sweats carried out by a wide range of people, from ordinary participants to recognized leaders, and in their under-standings of what transpires during those sweats. I worked with people new to the sweat as well as those who had participated in Lakota ceremonies throughout their lives, with bilingual Lakota speakers and exclusively English speakers, with those considered spiritual adepts by their peers and those recognized as neophytes, with a full range of ages and religious beliefs and both genders. I moved around the reservation quite a bit, attested to by the four sets of Toyota struts that Brother Mike Zimmerman, S.J., graciously replaced.

I was also interested in the larger social contexts of sweats and the manner in which individuals in these ceremonies generate meaning and appropriate religious and social positions. I did not seek out consultants based on norms of genuineness, either from within the group or according to adherence to past anthropological representations. Thus, I delimited my field geographically and socially, restricting research to individuals and groups who operated within the borders of the Pine Ridge Reservation and sweats where my interest was acceptable, rather than targeting "expert" individuals or "pure" sweats. I realize that this abandonment of expert informants and my inclusion of all available sweat lodge texts in my work (although I am critical of some of the included texts) is a unique anthropological decision. I do not set myself up as an author-ity, nor do I filter out voices with something to say about ceremonial behavior on the Pine Ridge Reservation. There is an important shared conversation among the Lakotas and across Lakota-white boundaries about ritual and tradition, although the rules and terms of this sharing are being reevaluated and redrawn (see chapter 7). Naturally, this text does not include every word by every voice, but I have made a sincere effort to make it as inclusive as possible while respecting people's privacy.

Present-day enactment and understanding of the sweat lodge ceremony cannot be interpreted without a full knowledge of the history of the practice. Contemporary Lakota concern with the sweat includes various estimations and interpretations of past practices. Insofar as ethnohistorical studies shed light on the contemporary ceremony, I use them, precisely because they are of interest and importance to those who practice the ceremony today. When I explained what my research was about, one Lakota consultant commented that it would be valuable to the Lakotas to have access to everything that was written about the sweat in the past. I do not, however, attempt to reconstruct the sweat lodge practices of the past as a single idealized homogeneous ceremony as Walker (1917) did with the Sun Dance.

During my studies in anthropology, I was questioned several times by colleagues who doubted that I could gather objective information, given that I am a Catholic priest. Surely the information would be biased. I have a clear sense of what my theological, philosophical, and anthropological biases are. Contextualization, while imparting knowledge, is always a key element in Oglala discourse with the "outer world," whether with another individual, a family member, people from another district on Pine Ridge or another reservation, or an ethnic outsider, whether from New York, South Dakota, or Germany. Like any other field-worker, I would receive a certain portion of the information, presented in certain ways, that would be unique to my own and to my consultants' social and historical circumstances.

One of Dakota ethnographer Ella C. Deloria's consultants noted (in Jahner 1983b:20) that a certain tale was altered when told to the early ethnographer James Walker to make it more suitable for the audience.[14] The same thing happened to a story told to the Jesuit missionary Eugene Buechel.[15] The adjustment itself is interesting and is key to the dialectical process in producing tradition. Such alteration does not represent duplicity on the part of the Oglalas but rather exposes the core of Oglala discourse and ceremony as contextualized representation from within and appropriate translation for outsiders. One adapts stories to the hearers; one provides descriptions that the audience can understand and with which they can identify. In chapters 1 and 2 of this book, I discuss how certain beliefs and practices related to the sweat lodge fell out of public discourse as represented in texts, only to reappear later. I do not assume that these elements necessarily fell out of actual practice and belief. The historical record is silent in that regard. I personally believe that information about these elements was suppressed because it was perceived as unintelligible or unacceptable to the recorders at that time.

The Uses of Ethnohistorical Texts

I have gathered for this work every text on the Lakota and Dakota sweat lodges that I could locate. These texts were consistently produced for white audiences, and none of them are free of the agenda of their authors. By including them I neither validate nor invalidate any of the texts. Whether they are authentic, partially authentic, or wholly fraudulent, contemporary practitioners, Lakota and other, may take them as representative of sweat lodge practice, and as such, they are important.

During my field research, I did not absent myself from sweats that I or others perceived as invalid or problematic, although Lakotas will often do exactly that. My condition for attending sweats, and eventually documenting the views of various participants, was simply that they agree to work with me; I did not set out to discover *the* authentic sweat on the reservation. Similarly, I present all of the ethnohistorical texts as they are. I try to make some generalizations about trends in textualization of the ceremony, but I do not delude myself or my readers into thinking that written records are or ever were definitive for actual practice among the Lakotas. The authenticity of some of the texts is plainly suspect. These texts, however, particularly those published by Joseph Epes Brown, Richard Erdoes, and Thomas Mails, are ubiquitous on and off Pine Ridge, so I present them as part of a shared discourse. From the nineteenth century on, authors read previous authors in order to amplify their own texts. This is sometimes acknowledged and at other times concealed, so it is rarely clear when similarities represent borrowings of earlier textual material or a genuine continuity in oral transmission. In the later texts of the 1960s, parallels are so glaring that borrowing has obviously taken place. I am also aware that I myself am constructing a textual narrative of the sweat lodge with its own inherent limitations.

Constructing This Text

To maintain confidentiality, I never report actual dialogue that took place during sweats I attended, although during interviews for this work, consultants often reiterated prayers and discussed concerns articulated during a sweat. That interview material and the specific songs, which replicate much of what I have experienced in sweats, are true to the spirit of the sweat but have been recontextualized in the ritual I have constructed in this introduction. I have been careful to conceal specific details to protect the identity of individuals. There is a wide range of opinions about what can properly be recorded concerning ritual practice among the Lakotas. Some hold that these ceremonies should be recorded so that they will be preserved and so that fraudulent variations will be suppressed. Others insist that absolutely nothing should be written about Lakota religion. Still others take the middle ground, stating that only certain things are appropriate to write about. The people willing to help with my work carefully explained what they thought would be inappropriate to report, and I have honored their decisions.

I maintain confidentiality to protect people from conflict within their own communities, even though the material I present may not seem particularly controversial. When I interviewed people, I took close notes so that I could reconstruct the narratives as accurately as possible when I returned home that night. To avoid anthropological stereotypes, and for the comfort of my consultants, I did not use a tape recorder. Instead, I read back to individuals what I was writing, particularly if I was confused on a point. When my dissertation was completed, I sent copies of it to my major consultants and to libraries on the reservation.

In reproducing conversations I had with people, I have placed translations of Lakota words in single quotes, as in *tháka* 'large', if the speaker provided the translations. At times people spoke to me in Lakota or mixed Lakota and English. When no translations for Lakota words were provided for me, I have added the gloss to the text using the convention of bracketing the gloss, as in *tháka* ['large'], to indicate that it was not present in the original narrative. Lakota words and phrases quoted from other sources are treated the same way. Frequently used Lakota words and phrases, such as Wakan Tanka and mitakuye oyas'in, after first usage, are given in roman type.

When I began sweating with groups, I came simply to pray with them, at their invitation. It was only after some months that I explained what work I was planning to do and asked if they would help me. I was generally more reluctant to shift the relationship to academic discourse than were those who helped me. My project was greeted with some enthusiasm: everyone recognized that I sweated with a large range of people and that I would have a perspective that single individuals with whom I sweated did not. Several people also stated that

I would "tell it like it is," having confidence in my ability to record and report accurately. When I interviewed people or even had casual conversations, they would sometimes remark that I already knew more than they did about the sweat lodge. I would counter, "But I don't know how *you* understand the lodge, nor *your* history and involvement in the lodge, and that is what I'm interested in." At one lodge I was jokingly referred to as "Father Sweat Lodge," and I was reputed to have the best sweat lodge tan on the reservation!

Sometimes during interviews people would tell me things I was reluctant to record because the material seemed sensitive to me. The narrator always insisted that I write it down because it was essential to understand what was going on in the lodge. Some narrators would stop at certain points and tell me not to write certain things down because they wanted only me to know them. I honored this. In the lodge also, people say things that are meant only for the lodge. I respect this restriction too, neither placing such material in my field notes nor repeating it verbally. Generally, however, participants would repeat such material in the course of describing their involvement in the lodge, and I was then free to enter it into the notes and into this book.

When I asked people questions about the ceremony, I was often told simply to come and observe their sweat and learn that way. One couple invited me to live with them for as long as I wanted until I learned what I needed. Some Lakotas are reluctant to answer direct questions. One woman explained that when she wanted to know something she would just listen to her father and eventually he would get around to it. A pedagogy of patient listening and observation is the norm on the reservation.

The results of my work are a dissertation and (after considerable rethinking of the material, several summer visits back to Pine Ridge, and astute readings by colleagues of various versions of my manuscript) this book. I am grateful to those who have helped and encouraged me. Raymond J. DeMallie offered unfailing guidance, and Raymond D. Fogelson shepherded me through the dissertation with sage advice about putting my feet up and thinking about things. The two Raymonds as well as Paul Friedrich and Sharon Stephens generously served on my dissertation committee. The late Sol Tax remains an inspiration for me, and his daughter Susan and her husband, Les Freeman, provided constant moral and culinary support. The Jesuit community on Pine Ridge housed, fed, and encouraged me for two years. Dave Shields, S.J., let me stay in his little house on the prairie, his friends Ben and Judy Perszyk gave me high-tech computer equipment to assist with my writing and research, and Oglala Lakota College gave me a place to teach. Jim Green provided invaluable language help. Brother Simon, S.J., director of the Heritage Center, provided a wealth of bibliographical and experiential knowledge as well as encouragement. Le Moyne College's Committee on Research and Development gave me a grant to return to Pine Ridge for a summer and provided a course reduction for a semester while I worked on this manuscript. Larry Nesper was most helpful and encouraging in this process; we spent many an afternoon jogging along Lake Michigan discussing matters of ethnographic importance and contemplating our next foray into high-cholesterol Polish cooking. Dan Plunkett helped with the tedious chore of checking bibliographical citations. Kay Koppedrayer gave helpful comments on the manuscript, as did Robin Ridington and Ernest Schusky for versions submitted to the University of Nebraska Press. Mary Russell, a friend from the Internet, served as text editor and cheerleader. John Langdon provided a final proofreading. I naturally take full responsibility for the actual work. I am grateful also to the non-Lakotas on the reservation who helped me by sharing their own spiritual journeys and struggles.

Recently I was back on Pine Ridge helping out at a parish. After Mass one Sunday, as folks were shaking hands, an elderly man said, "So, you're a doctor now." He then paused a bit and said in true Lakota deadpan, "But that's not the kind of doctor that helps people." My deepest gratitude goes to all the Lakotas whom I have met and who have patiently taught me so that I could construct this text. My hope is that this work will be of some small help, not in resolving controversies or defining proper forms of tradition, but in stepping back, examining, analyzing, and most importantly, appreciating the intricacies of the sweat lodge in the lives of its practitioners.

1

Ethnohistorical Accounts of the Sweat Lodge

This chapter and the next examine the ethnohistorical data concerning the sweat lodge as practiced among both the Dakotas and Lakotas. This examination is necessary for the assessment of change and continuity. Also, some of this material (for the Lakotas also rely on oral tradition) is used today as part of the dialectic that constitutes tradition; more and more Lakotas as well as others are examining these historical records.

First I review the early Dakota material and then provide early descriptions of the Lakota sweat lodge ceremony.[1] The Dakotas, located to the east of the Lakotas, were described in texts earlier than the Lakotas were. The two groups are closely related both linguistically and culturally.

When considering the ethnohistorical material in chapters 1 and 2 as a totality, it is important to note the obvious: almost all of it exists in published texts, thus making it accessible to a broad reading public. Almost all of it, particularly the early material, was intended for an exclusively white audience. Even texts produced by Lakotas, with the exception of school texts, were produced for a largely white audience. The recorders of these texts, with rare exception, have been Western observers rather than Lakota practitioners. Most of the texts are mediated in the early period through interpreters and compilers; later, when English became more common, more "as told to" accounts appeared, though these too are mediated.

Texts represent one form of Lakota cultural representation. Albeit limited, they provide one basis for the historical reconstruction of Lakota practice.

Textual interpretation and production are less and less alienated from the Lakotas themselves. As we shall see, since the production of the Black Elk texts, they are used by more and more Lakotas as a resource, just as Densmore's wax cylinder recordings have been transferred to cassette tapes and are played today on Pine Ridge. I present this material as an available representation—one whose influence is clearly growing, just as the production of this text will provide another route into past materials.

Another aspect of culture is the daily reality of Lakota existence. Reminded of change by these texts and by living memory, many people, Lakota and non-Lakota, bemoan the "loss" of Lakota culture, because the lived reality changes while texts remain as a reminder of past practice. Some Lakotas with whom I sweated clearly did not rely on texts for the operation of their ceremonies. Others had a lively interest in how the past was recorded and what they could glean from texts, although I do not suggest either that Lakotas utilize texts as liturgical guides or that they were consulted much before the contemporary era.

Contemporary chroniclers generally draw on memory, texts, and lived realities in producing accounts of the Lakotas, thereby confounding historical and contemporary practice—realities that interpenetrate in ritual practice itself but nevertheless have an independence in time and space. Thus, the representation of tradition has been assumed, in part, by non-Lakotas. Lakotas themselves may inject aspects of this alienated transcribed culture into the reality of their lived culture, joining history and tradition by way of the mediation of texts and oral history through the actions of contemporary ritual practice. The dialectical process of combining past with present to create tradition may therefore utilize a variety of resources and produce a variety of results. The question then becomes, Which traditions are indeed "authentic," and who may make this judgment?

Crucial to examining these texts is the task of evaluating the legitimacy of each as representative of the culture. The written word has greater legitimacy in academic circles and mainstream American culture than on the reservation. Texts are often accepted uncritically by students of culture and increasingly by Lakotas themselves (particularly those alienated from the historic reservation community through adoption outside the group or those who claim "some" Lakota ancestry), who employ them in order to revive or, in the case of non-Lakotas, recreate certain practices.

Both within and outside of anthropological circles, it is essential to ascertain the authenticity and centrality of the particular native consultants who are the sources of these texts. A key contemporary criterion for the non-Lakota is that of genetic authority. This arose in part from the nineteenth-century government policy of establishing Indian identity according to blood quantum—"how much" Indian ancestry one had. This highly problematic definition endures today and has been adopted by many native people. Texts are evaluated by the authority of the full-blooded consultant as a competent representative of the culture and by the assumed neutrality of the non-Lakota recorder. Thus, the Lame Deer texts have avoided the scrutiny of scholarship for quite some time (Rice 1994). The sine qua non of authenticity is a biological rather than a historical link to that cultural group. Today, at times, blood quantum takes precedence over historic connection with a living community or scholarly research into the culture. This represents a shift from the view of extrinsic authorities as unbiased and able to see the whole picture to truth claims residing in individuals by virtue of an assumed biological quality (being Indian is "in the blood"). Thus, the issue becomes, Is the person actually a Lakota? rather than, Is the person telling the truth?

I present these texts in chapters 1 and 2 "as is," asking the reader to keep in mind the problems of each text but also to listen to the representations, for these are clearly important to contemporary reconstructions of the past despite their ambiguous nature.

The Dakotas: Early Accounts

The earliest description of the sweat lodge among the Dakotas is in Louis Hennepin's *A New Discovery of a Vast County in America*.[2] Hennepin, along with two companions, was captured by the *Issati* (Santee Dakotas) around April 12, 1680, at the mouth of the Rum River.[3] During his captivity he was introduced to the sweat lodge when he fell ill:

> Father; this new Father of mine observing that I could not well rise without two or three to help me, order'd a Stove to be made, into which he caus'd me to enter stark-naked with four Savages; who before they began to sweat, ty'd their *Prepuces* about with certain Strings made of the Bark of a white Wood. This Stove was cover'd with the Skins of wild Bulls, and in it they put Flints and other Stones red-hot. They order'd me by Signs to hold my Breath, time after time, as long as I could, which I did, as well as those what were with me. As for the Privy Parts, I had only a Handkerchief to cover me.

As soon as the Savages that were with me had let go their Breath, which they did with a great force, *Aquipaguetin* began to sing with a loud and thundering Voice; the others seconded him; and laying their Hands on my Body, began to rub it, and at the same time to weep bitterly. I was like to fall into a Swoon, and so was forc'd to quit the Stove. At my coming out, I was scarce able to take up my Habit of St. *Francis* to cover me withal, I was so weak: However, they continu'd to make we [*sic*] sweat thrice a Week, which at last restor'd me to my pristine Vigour, so that I found my self as well as ever. [Hennepin 1903, 1:256–57]

This very early record documents several significant elements of the sweat lodge as it is preserved today. First, the ritual was used for its curative power. The sweat lodge itself, in the shape of an oven, was skin-covered and probably dome-shaped. Hot stones were brought into the sweat. The ritual was repeated until Hennepin was well. There was loud singing, which was "seconded," a style still prevalent among the Lakotas. There was also weeping within the sweat. Hennepin does not record whether prayers were said in the lodge, nor does he indicate whether the sweat was a religious ritual.

Nicolas Perrot was a coureur de bois (fur trapper) in New France among the western tribes from about 1665 to 1705. Although he dealt primarily with Algonquian groups, he did have contact with the Dakotas. His ethnographic writing tends to generalize the customs of "the savages" with whom he dealt, so it is difficult to assign customs to specific groups. Nevertheless, his description of "savage" hospitality expands the range of documented uses of the sweat:

A stranger as soon as he arrives [at a cabin] is made to sit down on a mat, of the handsomest [that they have], in order to rest from his fatigue; they take off his shoes and stockings, and grease his feet and legs; and the stones are at once put in the fire, and all preparations quickly made, in order to give him a sweat. [Perrot 1911:133]

The Dakotas: Nineteenth-Century Accounts

Except for these brief early glimpses of the sweat lodge offered by Hennepin and Perrot, the historical literature is silent on the subject until the early nineteenth century, when white contact with the easternmost Dakotas intensified.[4] These accounts are provided chiefly by missionaries, but there are also some materials from military and civilian sources.[5]

Structure and Ceremony

Like Hennepin and other nineteenth-century chroniclers, the missionary Samuel Pond describes the sweat lodge as a "hemispherical framework" of pliable poles covered with skins or blankets where vapor was created by pouring water over hot rocks brought into the structure (1908:103; see also Prescott 1852:182; Pond 1866:250–51). Pond acknowledges that this was a religious rite, although he confesses ignorance of the ceremonies used in connection with the bath. He also points out that stones identical to those generally worshiped in other contexts were employed in the sweat lodge (1908:104). These stones were ritually painted and decorated, and they were petitioned to avert disaster and gain success in war, much as they would be petitioned within the lodge itself.[6]

The most complete description of a sweat lodge ceremony for this period was written by Stephen Riggs:

> He [Simon, the sponsor of the lodge] took *eight poles* about the size of hoop-poles, of any wood that would bend readily, and putting the large ends in the ground, at proper distances in a circle, bent them over and tied them together at the top. This framework he then covered with robes and blankets, leaving a small hole for a door at one side. It was a little higher than a man's head, when seated within. Before the door he built a fire, and having selected four round stones (or nearly round) about as big as a man's head (size not essential), he placed them in the fire. He called Wamdiokiya to be high priest on the occasion. The high priest then ordered him to call so many to be his helpers—the number determined by the size of the tabernacle—from two to five. With these he entered into the *wokeya* ['bower, hut'], all entirely naked.
>
> Simon stands at the door without, by the fire, to attend the stones. He has made two paddles about twelve inches long and painted them red. These are to be used by the man within to move the stones with. He covers the ground between the tent door and the fire with nice feathers and cut tobacco. When the stones are heated, the chief within calls to him to roll in the first one. This he does, with a brand, putting tobacco upon it and praying to it—"Tunkan wah pani mada wo, toka wakte kta wacin [*Thuká wahpánimada wo, thóka wakté kta wachí* 'Stone, have pity on me. I want to kill an enemy']." So he rolls one after another of the stones over the tobacco and feathers and prays to each one. The men within receive them and roll them to the middle with the painted paddles—singing, hi, hi, hi, hi.[7]
>
> Then they commence their songs; each one has a song. They all pray to the *Tunkan* to give Simon help in the day of battle, to make him strong and

furious and successful. The chief then says to his fellows: "Have mercy on me, I will cool these stones." And he proceeds to pour water on them. The steam fills the tent, which had been closed entirely after the stones were rolled in. Then they pray to the *Taku-skan-skan* [*Tákuškąšką*] or to the *Wasicun* [*Wašícų*]. All their gods are called *Wasicun*.

Simon, this while, stands without, crying and praying. The chief *wakan* man receives an encouraging communication from the stone god which he delivers to Simon. When the stones are cold, they all cry and come out of the booth. So ends this sacrifice to the stone god. [quoted in Pond 1889: 250–51][8]

Stephen Riggs also noted the contextual variation in the Dakota sweat lodge ceremony: "Sometimes a number engage in it [the vapor bath] together, and unite their prayers and their songs. Then the hut is larger, and more ceremony is observed" (1869:82–84). The phenomenon of ritual variation is noted quite early by several observers of these ceremonies.

James Lynd, an educated son of a Baptist missionary, lived among the Dakotas from 1853 until he was killed in the Minnesota Uprising in 1862. He points out the centrality of purification, and the sweat lodge as the key purification rite:[9]

It is remarkable that the idea of purification should be so deeply rooted in the mind of the Dakota. It is as strong in them as it was in the ancient Hebrews. Their entire religion is pervaded with it. In all sacred ceremonies, where fire is used, they kindle anew, for purification, with flint and steel, or by friction. The body, too, must be prepared for interview with deity; and for a Dakota to commence any religious ceremony without having first purified himself by the inipi, or steam bath, and by fasting, would be the height of iniquity. [Lynd 1864:171]

Lynd further states the religious importance of this ritual:

If a Dakota desires to be particularly successful in any (to him) important undertaking, he first purifies himself by the *Inipi* or steam bath, and by fasting for a term of three days. During the whole of this time he avoids women and society, is secluded in his habits, and endeavors in every way to etherealize himself, preparatory to the performance of his religious rites, in order that he may be pure enough to receive a revelation from the deity he invokes. [165][10]

Gideon Pond (1866:251), Samuel Pond's brother and a Congregational missionary among the Dakotas from 1834 until 1851, corroborates the frequent use of the sweat lodge.[11]

Early observers of Santee Dakota religion found great variation in both practice and belief, in contrast to their own rigidly defined and carefully documented systems of ritual and belief:

> Indeed, there were few things concerning which the religious teachers were themselves agreed; and it is probable that their superstitious notions and ceremonies had from time to time been subject to many innovations, for there was nothing to prevent such changes. [Pond 1908:90][12]

The early missionaries to the Santee Dakotas considered variation in ceremonial practice and heterogeneity of belief indicative of religious degeneration. They held that some practices were "very ancient and may have been little changed for generations" (92). Although recognizing both innovation and continuity in Dakota ceremonial practice, the missionaries were unable to see these as essential to the native religious system. Dakota ceremonial practices were both bound by custom and enlivened by innovation, a condition that endures today for the Dakotas and the Lakotas.

Use of the Sweat

The centrality and importance of the sweat in the nineteenth century is seen in the variety of contexts in which it was used.[13] The sweat lodge, or vapor bath as it was commonly called then, was used before performing other ceremonies such as the *ḥamdépi* 'vision quest' and the *wiwą́yag wachípi* 'Sun Dance', before initiation into the mysteries of the society of the sacred dance (mdewiwin), before the raw fish feast, and before all other sacred ceremonies. It was also used as a general religious rite to secure the favor of the gods, as a "sort of sacrifice" to the god *Tákuškąška* in worshiping the *Heyókha* "giant," to cure sickness, for success in endeavors, and to communicate with spirits through the leader in order to learn the outcome of future events. The sweat was used to achieve ritual purity after killing someone or touching a dead body, and after killing a royal eagle. The sweat also had martial uses: to prepare oneself for the warpath, to consecrate weapons, and to prepare for stealing horses.

Health and Healing

Although the missionaries to the Santees consistently disdained most native religious practice, their opinion of the sweat lodge ceremony was more ambivalent. The hygienic effects of this practice were considered laudable, but its religious dimensions had to be expunged (Pond 1908:104). Unfortunately, the missionaries and other observers of the Dakotas never recorded how the Dakotas understood the medical efficacy of the sweat lodge beyond curing itself. Clearly, the Dakotas saw healing as part of a spiritual process, since the missionaries are consistent in their evaluation of the ceremony as essentially religious in nature. Thomas Williamson (1851:250, 1869:446), a doctor as well as a missionary, who labored among the Dakotas from 1835 until his death in 1879, was particularly interested in the salutary effects of this ceremony. Using his own medical categories, he held that the Dakotas used the sweat for rheumatic pains and possibly for other diseases.[14]

Stones

What concerned the missionaries in dealing with the sweat lodge was neither the physical cleansing in the bath nor its salutary effects, but the spiritual power attributed to the Sioux divinities invoked and accessed through the ritual, particularly through the medium of stones.[15]

Samuel Pond and Stephen Riggs believed that the sweat was, at root, a religious rite, and they clearly connect stones used for worship with those employed in the sweat lodge (Pond 1908:104; Pond 1866:250–51). Stones were considered the symbol for and sometimes the dwelling place of *Tákuškąška*, "that which moves" (Pond 1908:87).[16]

Summary of Nineteenth-Century Dakota Sources

Early observers make it clear that the sweat lodge ritual was a flexible ceremony whose structure and usage depended on circumstance. Its goals were purification in preparation for contact with spirits, curing, and seeking aid for a multiplicity of needs. The missionaries dismissed Dakota religious practices as pagan and benighted; much of their writing is therefore intended to discredit native practice in favor of Christianity. The missionaries drew a sharp line between native and Christian belief systems, as did some of their converts. When Dakota practitioners chose aspects of both ritual systems according to need and circumstance, it was viewed by the missionaries as backsliding; for the Dakotas, this mixture of beliefs would probably be no different from choosing different competencies among several medicine men. Because the missionaries believed that the sweat had a separable dual nature, spiritual and curative, they were more tolerant of it than of other practices. Thus, the sweat lodge remained an important ceremony during the early, and generally unsuccessful, missionization of the Dakotas. Nevertheless, missionaries sought to regulate what went on inside the lodge, particularly with regard to what they considered the worshiping of stones.

The Dakotas: Twentieth-Century Accounts

The amount of material on the Dakotas in the twentieth century declines in volume but remains an important source for tracing transformations in the written understanding of the sweat. The Dakotas were dispersed from Minnesota in the 1860s, and ethnographically they are eclipsed by their Lakota relatives to the west.

Structure and Ceremony

Charles A. Eastman, a Santee Dakota born in 1858, educated in American schools, and a convert to Christianity, provides a twentieth-century description of the sweat lodge (C. A. Eastman and E. G. Eastman 1909:125–37).[17] A shelter is made of willows and green boughs. Water is poured four times onto the hot stones in the lodge. According to a story related by Eastman, an individual who had been killed was fully revived when water was poured on the hot rocks for the fourth time. The core ritual action in this account remains the creation of vapor by pouring water (see also Wallis 1919:328).

Contexts for Use

In an early-twentieth-century apologia for mission work among the Santees, Alfred Riggs (son of the missionary Stephen Riggs) shows a continuing ambivalence about the sweat lodge. He himself worked for forty-two years among the Dakotas and understood the language, but although he admitted that, like herbs and other curative techniques, the sweat was employed with some efficacy, he felt it was "used without judgment" (Riggs 1912:8). This indicates the continued suspicion of the ritual and the relegation of medicinal cures to special circumstances on the part of missionaries.

It is Eastman who contextualizes the sweat ceremony within then-contemporary American thought and life. According to him, the *"eneepee"* [*inípi*] or vapor bath was universal among American Indians. Consistent with the nineteenth-century reports, he states that it was used to purify and recreate the Indian's spirit, for both doctor and patient, for any spiritual crisis, for possible death, for imminent danger, and before and after the vision quest (1911:79–81,

9). The sweat represented part of a health regimen that kept the Indian in superb physical condition (1915:138).

Concerning the use of the sweat lodge within the context of the Sun Dance among the Dakota exiles in Canada, anthropologist Wilson Wallis (1919:327) states that the sweat bath is used before and after the Sun Dance by both the individual performing the dance and whomever he wishes to assist at the dance:

> The sweatbath is taken both before and after every performance. This is to tell the stone first of all that the devotee is about to perform the sun dance. The stone had said it was the first thing made on earth, and, no matter what enterprise one was about to embark upon, the person was to pray to the stone first, and the stone would give him strength for the undertaking.
>
> After the stone is heated, water is poured upon it, and it is asked to wash the performer clean for the sun dance which he is about to undertake. When the performance is over, another sweatbath is taken in order to wash the paint off hands, face, and body. The ground on which the devotee has been standing is *wakan* and all the earth from it must be washed from his feet. He asks the stone to grant him long life, adding that he will be ready at any time to do whatever he is asked to do. [328]

Wallis's material is much more in line with nineteenth-century Santee practice (at least as recorded by the missionaries) than are the accounts provided by Eastman. There is a similar stress on the antiquity of stone. Lynd points out in an early-nineteenth-century document: "The *Tunkan,* the Dakotas say, is the god that dwells in stones or rocks, and is the *oldest* god" (1864:168).

Symbolic Interpretation

Charles Eastman provides an interpretation of the sweat lodge ceremony that introduces his own broad conceptions of Western philosophy and theology. He holds that in preparation for the hambeday [*hạmdé*] the quester must cast off "human or fleshy influences" (1911:7). Exercise, diet, and the sweat bath can also assuage "undue sexual desires" (92). Eastman provides the first written example of equating the sweat lodge with Christianity: "For baptism we substitute the 'eneépee' [*inípi*], the purification by vapor" (84). This is in keeping with Eastman's belief that "the spirit of Christianity and of our ancient religion is essentially the same" (24; see also C. A. Eastman 1916:138).[18] His exposition is part of the tendency among some Native Americans to present cultural information to whites using European institutions as parallels. This tendency to compare native practice with Christianity is an attempt to legitimate the very practices condemned by the Christian churches by comparing or conflating native symbols and ceremonies with Christian ones.

Summary of Twentieth-Century Dakota Sources

In the early twentieth century Santee Dakota material is scanty, except for the prolific writings of Charles Eastman. With what we have, we can see that the wide use of the sweat lodge persists, along with continuing adaptations in both its use and its interpretation. Eastman fits his interpretation of the lodge to a rigorous Puritan ethic of moral and physical cleanliness. Further, the missionary response in the early twentieth century continues to acknowledge possible physical advantages of the lodge while denouncing its spiritual import.

The Lakotas: Nineteenth-Century Accounts

The Oglala Lakotas, the main focus of the contemporary research of this work, are part of the Teton Lakotas, a group that moved farther and farther west, away from their Santee relatives, in the eighteenth century. While information on the Dakotas wanes at the turn of the century, information on the Lakotas waxes. The Lakotas eventually become the focus of both anthropological writing and the archetypal Indian in the American imagination.

Structure and Ceremony

As among the Dakotas, there are broad consistencies in descriptions of the Lakota sweat lodge during the nineteenth and early twentieth centuries.[19] The shape of the lodge is round, willows tied together at the top form a frame, skin coverings are used, the rocks are heated outside and transported with special implements into the lodge, and prayers and songs are employed in the ceremony. The anthropologist James Mooney mentions that sage is placed on the ground in the sweat. He also writes that the curer remains outside and prays while the afflicted individual is within the sweat being healed and that the door should face east, as in all ceremonial structures (1896:822–23). Florentine Digmann, a Jesuit missionary on the Pine Ridge and Rosebud reservations, and George Sword, James Walker's most prominent consultant, both mention a hole dug in the center of the lodge to receive the rocks (Digmann n.d.:11; Sword in Mooney 1896:798).

According to Mooney (1896:822), the dirt removed from the hole in the center of the lodge is used to construct an altar in front of the door. A buffalo skull is placed on this altar facing into the lodge. In front of the lodge participants erect a tall pole on which sacrificial offerings of brightly colored cloth, tobacco, and other materials are hung. James Walker, a physician stationed on the Pine Ridge Reservation from 1896 until 1914, mentions that women usually serve as assistants. Walker explains that the "spirit-like [*wakhála*]" of the water [steam] is propitiated with the smoke from a pipe that is brought into the lodge. The number of participants ranges from one to as many as can fit into the lodge. Songs are sung, cedar incense is used to eliminate evil powers, and sage incense is used to draw in the good influences (Walker 1917:67). Thunder Bear, one of Walker's consultants, mentions that infusions of herbs could be substituted for water in the lodge.[20]

Walker (1917:78, 1982:23) states that the sweat lodge (and any lodge not used for habitation) has to be located outside the camp circle.[21] Such structures are not included in the circle because they "were not conical or of formal shape" but rather rounded or dome-shaped (1982:23).

As among the Santee Dakotas, there is considerable variability of ritual practice among the Oglala Lakotas. Sword states, "If this [sweat lodge ceremony] is done for an important ceremony a shaman should conduct the *Inipi,* and he may perform as much ceremony while doing so as he wishes" (in Walker 1980:79). Sword also contends that a shaman could change any custom or ceremony (81).[22] The structure of the lodge had to conform to a specific pattern, but the ceremony within could vary: "The *ini ti* [*iníthi* 'sweat lodge structure'] must be made according to Lakota custom. If it is made in any other shape the ceremony will do no good. . . . *Ini kaga* [*Iníkağa*] may be with only a little ceremony, but there may be much ceremony in performing it" (84). Sword also mentions that nothing should be permitted in the lodge itself except what is necessary for the ceremony (79). Elements can be added and subtracted only when they are validated through a respected individual's vision or shown to be effective through practice.

Uses of the Sweat

As among the Dakotas, the importance of the sweat lodge for the Lakotas is borne out by the variety of contexts in which it was used.[23] Indeed, the records show that the Lakotas' sweat lodge was used in even more contexts than those mentioned for their relatives to the east. The Lakotas used it before undertaking anything of importance, to ensure success in the chase and abundance for the people's needs, so a holy man could locate a buffalo herd through a vision, and to find lost items. Like the Dakotas, they used it as a preliminary to any ceremony pertaining to the Wakan Tanka, so that prayers would be fulfilled, to prepare throughout the winter those who vowed a Sun Dance, during the Sun Dance itself, before and after a vision quest, as part of the buffalo ceremony held after a girl had her first menstrual flow, to purify the medicine man before doctoring a patient, and to counsel, console, and purify mourners. Unique in the Lakota material is reference to the sweat's ability to purify a person morally.[24] Medically, it was used to refresh oneself,[25] to cure illness, to promote longevity, to strengthen the life *(ni)* or ghost, and to purify the body.[26] The sweat also had martial uses, such as for aid in killing an enemy, but it could also be used to ask for protection in peace. In contrast to the early Santee Dakota material, the Lakota sweat had malicious uses as well.[27] For the Teton Lakotas it could be used to inflict illness, to redress unrequited love, and to compel someone to marry through causing illness and the threat of further illness. Finally, it was used to release a person from a vow to taboo *(theȟíla)* something.

Health and Healing

No native explanation of how the sweat effects cures was recorded for the Santee Dakotas. Walker recorded this explanation, given by the Oglala George Sword, which focuses the efficacy of the sweat on a physiological process:[28]

> A man's *ni* is his life. It is the same as his breath. It gives him his strength. All that is inside a man's body it keeps clean. If it is weak it cannot clean the inside of the body. If it goes away from a man he is dead. . . . *niya* is that which causes the *ni*. It is given at the time of birth. It is the ghost. . . . The white people call *ini kaga* taking a sweat bath. The Lakotas mean all the ceremony when they [say] *ini kaga* ["to make *ini*"] or *inipi*. When they say *ini* or *inipi* they mean that it is to make the ghost strong. . . . *Inipi* makes clean everything inside the body. . . . *Inipi* causes a man's *ni* to put out of his body all that makes him tired, or all that causes disease, or all that causes him to think wrong. . . . *Ini kaga* must be done according to the customs of the Lakotas. It must be done in an *ini ti*. This is what the white people call a sweat lodge. [in Walker 1980:83–84, see also Sword in Walker 1917:66, 156]

Sword, in keeping with Lakota physiology, represents illness as an intrusive phenomenon. When the *niyá* is weak, harmful elements can enter the body. The inipi helps to remove these harmful intrusions by strengthening the *niyá* or ghost through the invigorated *ní.* The spirit of the water, trapped by the *iníthi,* is breathed into the body, strengthening the *ní.* The spirit passes through the body and emerges as *themní* 'sweat', washing the body of its interior impurities (Sword in Walker 1980:100). Medicines could also be added to the water sprinkled on the rocks so that their "potency, or spirit-like" can be released and enter the body (Walker 1917:66). Sword also stresses the power of thought, essential in Lakota cosmology and physics.[29] He says that the participant must think about making his *ní* strong so that it will purify him.[30]

A variant on Sword's explanation is provided by One-Star, another of Walker's Oglala consultants, in an interview interpreted by Elmer Red-Eyes on July 8, 1897:

> A *Sicun* [*šichú*] is a man's spirit. A man's real spirit is different from his *Sicun* spirit. *Ni* is also like a spirit. It is a man's breath. It is the spirit of smoke. It is the spirit of steam. It is the spirit of the sweat lodge. It purifies the body. The bear taught these things to the shamans. [Walker 1917:159]

As in Sword's explanation, the *ni*—breath—is the agent of bodily strengthening and purification. One-Star's statement that this knowledge was taught by the bear to religious leaders indicates a unity of medical and religious practice in Lakota thought clearly exemplified by the sweat. There is a marked difference between this description of the action of the sweat and that provided by Wallis for the Dakotas. In Wallis's version the steam washes the outside of the body, and it is the stone itself, not the strengthening of the *ní,* that provides the vivifying power.

Walker elaborates Sword's analysis of the efficacy of the sweat in curing disease in his work on the Sun Dance. The *mniwátu* are water spirits, material beings who enter an individual's body to cause illness by pinching the bowels, pulling the cords of the joints, or beating upon the brain: "They ever war against *niya,* or ghost, and if they prevail the ghost leaves the body. But they may be exorcised in a vitalizing lodge by a Shaman or medicine man" (Walker 1917: 89).[31] Here the physiological effect of both ceremony and ceremonial practitioner are stressed.

Tyon (in Walker 1980:154) suggests an alternate explanation for the efficacy of the sweat: unhappiness causes coldness in the body, which the heat of the sweat lodge corrects. No Flesh provides another theory, which holds that disease is purged through sweat itself:

All diseases are things which get into the body and do violence to it in some way. The thing to do is to get these things out of the body.

If the sickness is of long duration, then someone should seek a vision and learn what to do. It is always the best to *iwani* (take a vapor bath with ceremonies). It is best always to make smoke of sage and then smoke of sweetgrass. This will drive away the evil spirits and please the good spirits.

The medicines drive the disease out in the sweat, in the vomit, in the defecation, in the urine, and in the breath. To drive disease out in the sweat, is the best and easiest way; in the breath, is the next best and easiest way; in the defecation, is the next best way; in the urine is a good way; and in the vomit is a very hard way, but some diseases will not come out in any other way. [in Walker 1917:163]

Illness is viewed as intrusive, to be purged through fluids emitted from the body as during a sweat. Evil spirits instigate all disease by causing "worms" or other foreign objects to enter the body (161). In contrast to Sword's contention that the strengthened *ní* cleanses the body, No Flesh holds that effluvia emanating from the body remove the offending matter.

Stones

As among the Dakotas, sacred stones are important both in the sweat lodge and in Lakota worship in general. In 1914 the Oglala Finger stated (in Walker 1917:155) that rock has a special prominence because it is the oldest and grand-father of all things.[32] George Bushotter, a Lakota born in 1864 in Dakota Territory, connects the worship of stones with their activities in the sweat:[33]

Sometimes a stone, painted red all over, is laid within the lodge and hair is offered to it. In cases of sickness they pray to the stone, offering to it tobacco or various kinds of good things, and they think that the stone hears them when they sacrifice to it. As the steam arose when they make a fire on a stone, the Dakotas concluded that stones had life, the steam being their breath, and that it was impossible to kill them. [Dorsey 1894:448]

Thomas Tyon reports that sweat lodge rocks are *wakhála* 'powerful, sacred' but of a different kind. They act differently, effecting a cure rather than finding lost items. Tyon is the only consultant from this period who distinguishes rocks by types of abilities. He also records a speech a holy man might make in the spirit language. The holy man begs pity of the sweat lodge stones, the sun, the moon, darkness, water (steam), and grass. He also asks that the poor

be pitied. By doing this he causes the sweat lodge stones to "frantically per-
suade the Spirit of the Sky" (in Walker 1980:154). In this way the stones act as
intermediaries to *Tákuškąška,* the animator. Captain William Philo Clark, a
commander of Indian scouts among the Plains tribes from 1876 to 1881,
mentions that within a sweat lodge the Lakota chief Sitting Bull indicated that
he would talk to the stones and make requests of them (Clark 1885:365).

Digmann and other early Jesuits, like their missionary predecessors among
the Santees, took a dim view of the religious system they encountered. When
Digmann first came among the Lakotas on the Rosebud Reservation, he stated
that they were "steeped yet in their old superstitious belief and practices,"
including sweat baths and praying and singing to painted stones (Digmann
n.d.:8, 11–12, 23):

> The attendants crouch around the walls of the booth, howling and singing
> sacred songs, and praying to the red painted stones. Here the superstition
> comes in. We told them, they could have their sweat-baths and also sing a
> song, but not pray to the stones and ascribe to it a superhuman efficacy for
> healing sicknesses of non-participants in the bath, or obtaining other
> favors. [11]

Like the missionaries to the Dakotas, Digmann drew a distinction between
"conjuring" and healing, telling a potential convert, the medicine man Black
Thunder, that he could continue to give medicine after he was baptized but had
to give up conjuring and superstitious practices (Digmann n.d.:28). Note that
Digmann did not doubt the salutary effects of the sweat but condemned the
notion that someone not actually taking the bath could be healed by it.

Summary of Nineteenth-Century Lakota Sources

The nineteenth-century sweat lodge is an essential component of wider Dakota
and Lakota ceremonial practice, healing, and social life, as indicated both by its
frequency of use and by the multiplicity of contexts in which it is used. The
structure of the lodge and the use of stones as the central focus of the ceremony
are consistent for both groups in this period. Both groups emphasize the
efficacy of the lodge for marshaling spiritual powers, focused in the rocks, to
perform specific tasks.

A later trend, promulgated by missionaries, was to separate the lodge's
salutary physical effects from its spiritual functions. Concomitantly, native
descriptions from the nineteenth century, such as Sword's, de-emphasize the
spiritual import of the ceremony and stress its physiological mechanisms. I

believe this splitting of health from the spiritual functions represents a native effort to present the ceremony in a more acceptable manner to a hostile outside world of government agents and missionaries.

The second trend that consistently appears in nineteenth-century accounts is the acknowledgment, both by outside observers and by participants themselves, that sweat ceremonies, although variable, still must be carried out in a prescribed manner. It is impossible to recover the nature of the prescribed manner from textual evidence to see whether it represents a single consistent set of rules for uniformity and acceptable variation. This ambiguity of ritual precision carries over to present practice, for there is no single oral representation of the prescribed manner of the past, although various people offer their opinions or beliefs about what is essential to the sweat. The native recognition of a split between acceptable past formulations and innovation, historical practice and contemporary needs, is evident in the earliest Lakota literature. These two poles, which constitute the essential elements of the dialectical process that constitutes tradition, have long been manipulated by participants, Lakota and outsider; their authenticity and acceptability remain important and debatable issues today.

The Lakotas: The Ghost Dance Era

Mooney (1896:823) points out that, except perhaps for the Shoshones and the Northern Cheyennes, the Lakotas were unique in incorporating the sweat lodge into the Ghost Dance from 1889 to 1890. The physical structure of the lodge was expanded to accommodate the larger groups of participants who gathered for these dances (823). Mooney's report of people sweating in a standing rather than a sitting position is also unique, and probably represents a scriptographic error.[34] Indian Agent James McLaughlin on the Standing Rock Reservation states that, in Sitting Bull's camp, participants used the ceremony each morning before they began to dance (1910:204).

Moorehead points out that women constructed the lodges and that they sweated in a separate structure from the men. Although this account is unique in reporting on the sweat lodge ceremony during the Ghost Dance era, we will see that the sexual distribution of ritual participation is an important issue today and that the past is often cited in this regard as part of the dialectic constituting tradition. The ethnohistorical data generally ignore the issue of gender in the sweat lodge.

Sword indicates that during the Ghost Dance holes were made in the swea lodge floor. He gives no explanation for these holes except to say that water was supposed to come out of them. Sword's assertion may refer to the apocalyptic predictions made by the Sioux that water, fire, and wind would kill all the whites or Indians who helped the chief of the whites (Mooney 1896:798).

Another unique feature of the Ghost Dance sweat lodge, reported by one of Ella Deloria's consultants, was that the sweat lodge was open on both ends. The same consultant, then a boy, reports his own experience: "They stripped our ugly clothes from us and sent us inside [the sweat lodge]. When we were well purified, they sent us out at the other end and placed sacred shirts on us. They were of white muslin with a crow, a fish, stars, and other symbols painted on" (E. C. Deloria 1944:81).

The sweat, like the Ghost Dance itself, serves as a cultural purification. The Ghost Dance represented a return to the power of the past. At the same time it was a reponse to immediate social, political, religious, and economic needs of the time. Ugly "American" clothes were removed, and the individuals were cleansed from alien cultural contact. The sweat lodge today retains both of those features: a return to the power of the past and an addressing of present needs, which are combined to create tradition.

The Lakotas: Early-Twentieth-Century Accounts

Structure and Ceremony

The next published account of a sweat lodge ceremony was recorded in 1908 by the famed photographer Edward Curtis and provides an elaborate description of an Oglala sweat lodge ceremony used for a vision quest. Curtis (1908:65) states that the vision quest had not been performed within recent years, so his account is most probably a reconstruction from the memory of former participants. Because of its detail and Curtis's attempt to capture the feeling of the ceremony, the description bears quoting in full:

> At sunrise the sweat-lodge is erected, facing the east. In the centre is a small pit to hold the heated stones, and behind this the ground is strewn with sage. Ten paces from the entrance the turf is removed from a spot designed to receive the fire and is heaped up just east of the cleared space. Firewood and twenty-five smooth round stones are gathered, and the latter, painted red by the faster, are thrown into the leaping flames. The priest

enters the sweat lodge, and, sitting in the place of honor at the rear, lays before him the bundle containing red robe, calf-skin, tobacco, and kinnikinnick. These articles he unwraps, while the faster enters and sits down at his left. He next commands the Sweat Workers to procure four young cherry stocks, in length seven or eight feet, untrimmed and not cut with axe or knife, but twisted and broken from the roots. Two buffalo-chips are laid side by side back of the stone-pit, and behind them a glowing ember, carefully borne on the prong of a fire stick, is deposited by one of the young men. With the never-omitted motions of raising the hand to the four world-quarters, the sky, and the earth, the priest makes sacred smoke by dropping a bit of sweet-grass upon the coal, and passes the tobacco through the incense four times, to make it sacred. Having thoroughly mixed tobacco and kinnikinnick, he sanctifies the pipe by running his hand downward on each of its four sides, before each movement placing the hand on the earth as if to draw its essence from it. Then with ceremonious deliberation he fills the pipe, seals it with buffalo-tallow, ties a stake of sage about each extremity of the stem, and hands it to the faster, who places it, bowl to the westward, on the heap of turf outside.

The priest is now to prepare *waó"yapi* [*wa 'ǘyǥpi*], offering to the Great Mystery. The principal *waó"yapi* consists of a quantity of tobacco tied into a corner of the red robe, which is attached to a branch of one of the cherry poles. For the others fifty smaller portions of tobacco tied up in pieces of calf-skin are fastened to the twigs of the other three boughs. All four are then deposited in a row to the east of the pile of turf, the principal offering being farthest removed. Beyond this is placed a buffalo-robe, previously purified in sacred smoke. During the portion of the ceremony thus far per-formed—*Waká"-kághapi* [*Wakhá kágapi*] (making sacred)—no one save the two young men is permitted to approach the sweat lodge, which is *waká"*.

Priest and faster now step outside and remove their clothing, while one of the Sweat Workers calls for worthy men to come and take part in the sweat. Those who respond disrobe to the loin-cloth and follow the two principal actors into the sudatory. None may touch the faster, for he is holy. When all are seated, the priest chants a song and speaks:

"This is my rite. This man has given me many presents and asked for *Ha"bělé-cheapi* [*hǥblécheyapi*]. I have worshipped the Great Mystery many times, and I now ask Thunder for a blue day. The Mystery has created many animals, some of which are like men. This young man will see them."

Continuing, he instructs the faster:

"This sweat removes from your body all evil, all touch of woman, and makes you *waká"*, that the spirit of the Great Mystery may come close to you and strengthen you. When our sweat is over, you will take pipe and buffalo-robe and go to some high mountain where the air is pure. On your return you must be careful to speak the truth in telling us of your visions, for should you deceive us, we might work you great harm in trying to aid you in interpreting the revelations sent by the Mystery."

The stones, glowing white with heat, are placed in the pit. The priest offers to the Great Mystery a small piece of dog flesh and another of dried buffalo-meat taken from a bowl of each brought by the faster's relatives, and after marking with charcoal two stripes across the inner surface of a wooden cup, he fills it with water and gives both meat and cup to the faster. The attendants close the entrance, the priest chants another song, and, bidding the faster cry, dashes water twice on the stones. After a time air is admitted; then follows another song, and more water is thrown on the stones. After a time air is admitted; then follows another song, and more water is thrown on the stones. Twice more this is repeated, and the faster, never ceasing to cry aloud, comes forth, puts on his moccasins, takes the pipe in his left and the robe in his right hand, and starts out on his sacred journey. Behind him follow the two *Iní-wowashi* [*iní wówaši* 'sweat lodge helpers'] bearing the offerings. [1908:66–68]

Much of this structural detail closely matches accounts given by Walker and others during the nineteenth century. Both Walker (1917:67) and Curtis indicate that a pipe was used within the ceremony when it pertained to a vision quest.[35] No mention of pipes is made in connection with the sweat lodge in the Dakota material. In Curtis's description only, there is no mention of any altar or sacred path. The practice of throwing rocks on the fire rather than piling them on the wood and then lighting the assemblage is also unique to this description.

There are two distinct rites, according to Curtis's account. The first is a rite of purification. The materials used for the individual preparing to fast are first purified by the leader and supplicant: pipe, cherry poles, tobacco ties, buffalo robe. Then the leader and the supplicant emerge from the lodge and reenter with other supporters. The second rite is the sweat itself, also presented as an act of purification, cleansing the supplicant's body from all evil and from the touch of woman, so that the great mystery may approach more closely and the seeker may understand the speech of the animals, the birds, and the supernatural beings. Curtis does not make it clear whether the "evil" is material (as in Sword's idea of removing impurities from the body) or moral (as in removing the adverse effects of past conduct).

The leader legitimates his role in the rite through a speech, a common feature of past and contemporary Lakota ritual. The workings of the sweat are also explained within the ceremony, possibly a literary device in this description but one practiced today, particularly when neophytes are present. This ceremony purifies the seeker and allows the great mystery to approach. Interestingly, people do not enter naked in Curtis's account, as seems to have been the early custom. This may reflect either Christian mores or the presence of a photographer.

Songs and Utterances within the Lakota Sweat

Ethnomusicologist Frances Densmore worked on the Standing Rock Reservation and at Sisseton, South Dakota, from 1911 until 1914, collecting songs and ethnographic material concerning the Lakotas and the Dakotas. She was the first to record songs and lyrics connected with a sweat lodge ceremony (Densmore 1918:98, 103).

In September 1919 Brave Dog dictated a description of the sweat lodge in the Lakota language to Ivan Stars in behalf of Eugene Buechel, a Jesuit missionary who worked on the Pine Ridge and Rosebud reservations. He gives the first account of back-channeling used in the sweat. Back-channeling is the affirming of statements by the hearer(s) through various emotive sounds. It is used on the reservation today in oratory and during conversation in both secular and sacred settings. According to Brave Dog, whenever someone says anything in an ordinary sweat, everyone affirms it by saying háu. He adds that when the first four rocks are brought into the sweat, there is silence, and that a pipe is offered and smoked within the sweat lodge. Finally, he says that water is both sprinkled and drunk by the participants (Buechel 1978:271).

Health and Healing

Goose, a seventy-six-year-old Teton who worked with Densmore, was the most respected practicing medicine man on the Standing Rock Reservation when Densmore was there. He told her of a dream in which he acquired the power to cure consumption. In his dream he was shown four healing herbs:

> In the air, in front of the sun, was a booth made of boughs. In front of the booth was a very bright object and between this and the booth was a man, painted and wearing an eagle-down feather, while around him flew all kinds of birds. The bright object was a sacred stone, and it was heated red hot. [Densmore 1918:251]

Concerning the dream, Goose states:

> One of the greatest things it taught me is that the first thing a sick person
> should do is to take a sweat bath, to take out all the impurities, so that the
> body will respond to remedies. The booth showed how the sweat lodge
> must be constructed, and the hot stone showed the use of heated stones in
> the lodge. The hot stone is taken into the lodge, and water is sprinkled upon
> it. The oftener this bath is taken, the healthier a person will be. In case of
> illness, the sick person must take this bath the first thing, and as often
> afterward as the medicine-man directs. I always prescribe the sweat bath
> the first thing. I also claim that a sick person can not recover unless the diet
> is changed. Certain kinds of food and of wild fruit are bad in certain
> illnesses, and certain kinds of game or venison are injurious to a sick per-
> son. The food must be lighter than usual, and the person must avoid un-
> necessary exertion. My requirements are the sweat bath, light diet, and rest.
> I have treated consumption, and if the disease is not too far advanced the
> person usually recovers. The treatment depends on the seriousness of the
> case. All three herbs which I saw in my dream were prepared in a certain
> way and were intended for use in consumption, which is caused by im-
> proper circulation of the blood. I do not want the patient to make any undue
> exertion, but I try especially to keep up his circulation. The sweat bath
> makes the circulation better. In the old days a person did not take cold after
> a sweat bath. The sick person did not jump immediately into cold water, as
> is sometimes stated, but was covered with furs and allowed to cool off
> gradually. [251–52]

That passage is interesting for two reasons. First, we see a shift in the concept of disease, Goose making no mention of disease as intrusion yet retaining
the idea that the sweat extrudes harmful matter. He does not speak of the *ni* as
the agent that cures disease. Second, there is an explicit reworking of earlier
beliefs. Goose specifically states that the body should not be shocked with cold
water and that those who say this was the ancient practice are incorrect. He
validates his version of this ceremony (described as purely medicinal rather
than spiritual) through a dream rather than by inheritance or transmission
through a teacher or a tradition.

Context for Use

Because Densmore was working in memory ethnography, she does not record
her own observations of contemporary sweat lodge use, other than noting that

Goose still used it for healing. She does note that the sweat was used in conjunction with the vision quest and the Sun Dance.[36]

Brave Dog's account (in Buechel 1978) states that the sweat is used when a child or some relative dies and for a vision quest. When a mourner is brought into the lodge, those in the lodge give him wise advice and have him drink water. One also prays for one's relatives in the lodge and for good acts and straight doings. In this vein, a prayer for a sweat is recorded: "Grandfather, pity us. All the bad things I have done, we'll escape from here and leave them behind. Don't let anything bad come to us and give us a good day." This stress on moral cleansing is new in the Lakota textual material. We cannot conclude, however, that the moral vision was unique to this period or merely a result of nineteenth-century missionary influence. Missionaries certainly did not introduce ethics to the Lakota people. There is a shift within the recorded literature, however, from a more utilitarian understanding in the early period, when sweats were used to achieve concrete objectives, to a more spiritual and moral orientation. This tendency, as we shall see, becomes progressively more pronounced in the later twentieth century.

Summary of Early-Twentieth-Century Lakota Sources

In these early-twentieth-century accounts we see a move away from the pragmatic and toward the symbolic and moral efficacy of the sweat. Cleansing is directed toward moral behavior, and the role of healing is attributed directly to the actions of the sweat rather than to the spiritual powers working through the rocks and their breath. The role of spirits is scarcely mentioned in these accounts; the power of the sweat is in the ceremony itself. It is essential to keep in mind that this does not necessarily mean the actions of spirits are no longer considered part of the sweat lodge, at least among some individuals—the plurality of belief and practice observed by the Ponds and other early missionaries continues. We can say, however, that the presence of spirits is not stressed in information given to outsiders. Nonetheless, it should be noted that in this period of intense missionization among the Lakotas, the missionaries were quite vocal in their condemnation of Lakota spiritual reality. This was also a time of official governmental repression of native religion.

The Lakotas: Middle-Twentieth-Century Accounts

There is little published material on the sweat lodge from the 1920s to the 1950s, a period of diminished interest in Native American studies on the part of the government and the academic community. During that time focus shifted from reconstructing the precontact world of the Indian to assimilation studies, which emphasize change rather than continuity.

Structure and Ceremony

Robert H. Ruby, a physician stationed at Pine Ridge in the 1950s, provides a valuable description of the principles of the sweat:

> Inikagapi [*iníkaǧapi*] is the Yuwipi [*yuwípi*] ceremony that "renews the body to life." It is the sweat bath. It is conducted in a special structure, separate from and outside the home, made of long, flexible willows [*sic*] saplings, which are struck into the ground and bent inward to form an igloo-shaped hut. These supports are covered with blankets and canvas. Long ago, these structures were covered with leaves and branches to hold in the steam. There are many sweat baths on the reservation.
>
> The diameter of a sweat bath, at the ground, is about six feet. In the center is a hole in the ground, about a foot deep. Rocks heated until they are red hot, in a fire outside the hut, are placed in the hole. Water is then poured over them, and steam is produced. Years ago, a special kind of rock was used, which would not break or chip, when cold water was added.
>
> The participants in the ceremony enter the sweat house naked. The medicine man offers tobacco to the Great Spirit in return for continued health or for a cure. Outside the sweat house, the "rosary," a string of small pinches of tobacco tied in cloth, hangs permanently.[37]
>
> The ceremony is much like the usual service. Songs are sung. The medicine man talks to the Great Spirit. The peace pipe is offered up. Medicine men make a substantial living from their services. They receive money, food, and other articles.
>
> Sweat-bath meetings are held in the dead of winter as well as the summer months. The "bathers" work their emotions to a fever pitch. At one time, sweat baths were located near a stream, and after the ceremony the Indians would jump into the water, even in sub-zero weather.[38] After the ceremony the body is dried with a cluster of sage leaves.
>
> The sweat bath is recommended both for prevention and cure. The Great Spirit may be asked to prevent illness from coming to some home, or to heal some old man who is afflicted or to save the life of an ill child. A

person in pain or showing other symptoms of illness may expose his weakened body to the hot steam and then quick cooling, in hope of a cure.

The sweat bath today is used for other purposes, to find something that has been lost, for instance. If the requests are not granted, it is the fault of the individual, not the Great Spirit. Apparently, in some way, he has displeased the god. [Ruby 1955:48–49]

Ruby here states that the sweat is primarily medicinal, stressing both the invocation of the Great Spirit and the salutary effect of the bath itself. Although there is no mention of the presence of spirits in this account, spirits *are* present in the yuwipi ceremony that he subsequently chronicles. Ruby's classification of inipi as a type of yuwipi (a term he employs for Lakota religion in general) is evidence of a persistent involvement with spirits in Lakota ceremony at this time.

Ruby points out that there were many sweat lodges on the reservation when he was writing. He mentions that sweat lodges were formerly covered by leaves and branches, as do Charles Eastman and his wife Elaine (C. A. Eastman and E. G. Eastman 1909:125–37).[39] Riggs describes Simon's sweat as a *wókheya,* which is more properly a bower than a skin-covered structure (Pond 1866:250–51).[40] There is no mention of sweats covered with leaves in any later writings.

Ruby mentions that emotions are worked to a "fever pitch" during a sweat. This phenomenon is present throughout the ethnohistorical literature. Emotional discharge remains a significant factor in contemporary practice.

Ruby also describes a sweat held with George Plenty Wolf (a well-known medicine man) and Elk Boy. This valuable report represents a record of an actual ceremony rather than an ideal account of appropriate procedures, as provided by Curtis and others. During this ritual Ruby (1955:60–62) mentions that spirit noises could be heard as the sweat progressed, thus indicating the presence of spirits. The fire keeper scooped a bunch of hot rocks into a pail and dumped them into the center pit. This casual attitude toward the rocks is, as we shall see, quite at variance with Brown's and Black Elk's highly determined description (in the same decade) of ritually placing rocks in the four directions. In this particular sweat, the medicine man prayed for the health of the participants. First, Plenty Wolf constructed his altar outside the sweat lodge with four tin cans, two of them having sage leaves on top. This offering, according to Ruby, was to cause Wakan Tanka to come to the earth. Ruby points out that the sweat opening faced the east. The ceremony lasted two rounds. After the second round all emerged and a puppy was ritually strangled, cooked, and consumed.[41] Ruby also notes that the steam from a pail of hot rocks was used at yuwipi ceremonies to purify the implements to be used in the ceremony (63).

According to Elias Elk Head and Ernest Two Runs, who discussed the Calf Pipe with H. Scudder Mekeel at Green Grass on September 7, 1931, "The Sweat Lodge of the Keeper was always outside the circle of the tipi, as were the other Sweat Lodges" (Mekeel 1931–32:45). This is consistent with the descriptions in Walker's material (1917:78, 1982:23).

Contexts for Use

William Bordeaux (1929:107), himself a mixed-blood Teton Lakota, states that sweats were used when someone returned from seeking a vision. Martha Warren Beckwith recorded stories among the Oglalas of Pine Ridge. On July 15, 1928, her Lakota consultant Left Heron told about life as an Indian. He mentions that when the Sun Dance began, men would paint themselves various colors as part of the ceremony. He then states: "Just about this time the sweat-house was inaugurated. They clean off the paint in the sweat-house. If you can stand a little suffering, if you drop a little blood, you get what is promised" (Beckwith 1930:378). Left Heron associates the suffering of the sweat lodge and the Sun Dance with reciprocal benefit.[42] This association of suffering with the sweat lodge was not made explicit in any of the previous accounts, nor was it emphasized as the essence of the performance. It is clear, however, that because of the very nature of the sweat ceremony, suffering is a part of it as well as other Lakota ceremonies. The general trend in Lakota worship is to offer self-induced suffering for specific favors from the spirits. As we shall see, that idea is still important in contemporary sweat lodge practice.

Anthropologist H. Scudder Mekeel conducted fieldwork in Oglala, South Dakota, in 1930–31. He provides some interesting, although brief, insights into the contemporary religious life of the people there. His field notes indicate that Tom White Cow Killer and his father "still use the sweat bath—Tom about once a month—only way of getting clean. This came only after I had approved of sweat baths" (Mekeel 1931–32:7). Charlie Bear Face also still used the sweat lodge, but only away from his own house "because regularly he lives with Wallace Running Eagle, his son-in-law and a minister of the Presbyterian church" (48).

In these passages we see a Lakota reluctance to mention using a sweat lodge because neither the churches nor the government approved of such practices. I heard several times in my own field interviews the comment that native clergy were much harsher critics and suppressors of traditional ceremonies than outside clergy. Thus, the sweat ritual was performed discreetly if not secretly in the 1930s. Mekeel supplies evidence that some had not forsaken traditional ways, saying of White Cow Bull, one of his consultants, "He has a sweat lodge outside [of his cabin], and seems to be a good Pagan Indian" (1931–32:63).

Writers continue to cite the sweat as preparation for the Sun Dance and vision seeking. Standing Bear says that this ritual makes a person clean in order to find lost property, to capture eagles, and to seek a vision to become a medicine man.[43] Except for Ruby's material, no mention of the sweat as a place to encounter spirits is made in any of these accounts. In fact, a general trend continues in the written literature to despiritualize the ritual while emphasizing physical and moral healing.

Health and Healing

Medicinal use of the sweat does continue through this period. Oscar One Bull, speaking to Inez Hilger, stressed the health aspects of the sweat lodge as opposed to viewing the structure as a place for spiritual encounters: "The men of our tribe have always taken sweat baths to keep well; they do so today. They sweat in tepees near the river, and right afterward they plunge into the cold water of the river. I often take a sweat bath; it keeps me well and strong" (Hilger 1946:168).

William Bordeaux expounds on the medicinal value of the ceremony: "The sweat bath method is used by all Wa-Piye's [*waphíye* 'curer']. These vapor baths are taken to open up the pores, enabling the poison to escape. Following the vapor process, proper herbs and roots are administered" (1929:108). This medical explanation of the sweat is in line with that of Goose, who also stressed physiology over spiritual intervention, and Sword's idea of disease as intrusive. Bordeaux provides a description of the sweat lodge structure consistent with those of the nineteenth century, noting that sage was used to wipe off the sweat and that all the water had to be used before the participants could exit (154–55).

In the 1940s Gontran LaViolette, a Catholic priest who worked among the Santee and Teton exiles in Canada beginning in 1934, stated: "The old Indian doctors (medicine men) do not claim any preternatural powers. In their art of healing they make use of the sweat bath, (originally a religious rite), and they prepare their remedies with bark, roots and herbs" (1944:127).

Summary of Late-Twentieth-Century Lakota Sources

As mentioned in the previous summary, we must keep in mind that the majority of these writers are outsiders and thus had access only to certain information. Lakota consultants selectively revealed information about the sweat lodge and other religious matters acccording to their audience. Mekeel gives evidence that these rituals were hidden because of potential criticism from outsiders and from Lakotas who had converted to Christianity. Two strategies seem to have been employed: shift the emphasis in the ritual from interaction with specific spirits to a generalized physical and moral cleansing, and practice the ritual in secret or with outsiders who were sympathetic to this form of spiritual encounter.

We continue to see in these accounts a distinct continuity in the structure and performance of the ritual as described by the earliest observers. Narratives about the ritual, like the ritual itself, continue to address both the historical forms of the sweat and the contemporary needs of the participants. Those needs extend from the pragmatic daily needs of individuals to the need to be understood by the outside world, a world perceived to be hostile at the time to certain Lakota beliefs.

Robert Ruby's account is unique for this period because it represents a participant observer's view. Spirits have become subsumed by the Great Spirit, who is now addressed in the ceremony by the leader, retaining the tradition of accessing spiritual power through the medium of the sweat, its content, and its procedures, while adapting the belief in diverse spirits to one more acceptable to an outside monotheistic world.

Joseph Epes Brown, John Neihardt, and the Black Elk Accounts

A significant shift in the nature of material on the sweat occurs in the 1950s, when Joseph Epes Brown published *The Sacred Pipe,* based on interviews with Nicholas Black Elk.[44] It represents the first extended account of Lakota ritual by a single practitioner and is also the first detailed record of a symbolic interpretation of the sweat lodge.[45] Many of the interpretations used by Black Elk have been carried over to contemporary practice. Whether they originated completely with Black Elk or were suggested or interpolated by Brown is impossible to determine. Nevertheless, Black Elk's description (as recorded by Brown) is the first narrative by a native person whose emphasis is the interpretation of symbols used in the ceremony rather than the efficacy of the lodge in obtaining favors from the spirits or in generalized healing and moral cleansing. Black Elk was first introduced to the American public in an initially unsuccessful but later immensely popular work of John Neihardt, *Black Elk Speaks,* in 1932.

Reginald and Gladys Laubin, professional dancers who went around the country performing Indian dances and ceremonies, also published a book, *The Indian Tipi,* in 1957, which contains a chapter on the sweat lodge, specifically the Lakota sweat lodge. They were in personal contact with Black Elk and cite *The Sacred Pipe* in their bibliography. This begins a line of interpretive works on the sweat, and Lakota religion in general, which depends upon the Black Elk material. It also begins a trend in which non-Lakota writers represent Lakota voices in text, increasing the authority of these texts to outside readers but, at the same time, creating ambiguity as to whose interpretation, the Lakotas' or the editor's, is actually being put forth.

Because of this I choose to examine Black Elk's views of the sweat as a whole and let them serve as a link between past (chapter 1) and contemporary (chapter 2) practice. The Black Elk material has had a vast impact because it has been widely distributed and read both by native and nonnative people in order to understand, interpret, and in some cases enact the sweat ritual. Both Black Elk works have had an immense effect on a wide readership, but *The Sacred Pipe* describes more of Lakota ritual, whereas *Black Elk Speaks,* in its sections on religion, focuses primarily on Black Elk's own visions. The transcripts of Black Elk's narratives, *The Sixth Grandfather* (DeMallie 1984), contain both enthnography and autobiography.

Black Elk lived in a period of great change for the Lakotas. He was a young man when the massacre at Wounded Knee occurred. He was well traveled and became a Catholic catechist beginning in his midthirties. It would not be surprising for such an individual to incorporate universal elements in his worldview, for he was immersed in his own culture, experienced rapid change and innovation in his own lifetime, and dealt with the universalizing tradition of Catholicism as a catechist.[46]

It is difficult to know whether this new level of interpretation in the Black Elk material represents an oversight by earlier recorders or whether it is a new way of regarding the sweat. Clearly, the early missionaries, with their adversarial stance toward traditional religion, could easily have missed this element, or it could have been hidden from them. In any case, these detailed symbolic interpretations are omitted in Walker and other early material. The Black Elk material continues the shift in emphasis that we have noted earlier from personal physical regeneration and success (in the early accounts) to moral and social regeneration.[47] The belief in physical healing available through the sweat is never abandoned; neither is the belief that spirits that come into the sweat have power to act on the world. Black Elk's material, however, universalizes the imagery of the sweat: the role of spirits is downplayed and a focus is placed on one God. Whether this change in emphasis derives from Lakota tradition, Christian teachings, Black Elk's own spiritual insights, or his position as a sincere Catholic catechist or as an individual under the thumb of the Jesuit missionaries may be argued endlessly.[48] Black Elk certainly became a symbol of the "converted" Indian for the Jesuits and their missionary effort. In the 1960s Black Elk, as represented by Joseph Epes Brown and Neihardt, became a symbol of the traditional Indian resisting white domination. T-shirts worn in militant marches at the time bore the inscription "Black Elk Is Speaking." The Black Elk material continues to have an enduring influence both on and off the reservation.

Black Elk's description of the sweat lodge in *The Sacred Pipe* implies that sacred ceremonies were, but no longer are, part of Lakota life. Black Elk states at the conclusion of his description of the sweat lodge ritual: "Now that we have neglected these rites we have lost much of this power; it is not good, and I cry when I think of it. I pray often that the Great Spirit will show to our young people the importance of these rites" (in Brown 1953:43).

Context for Use

Black Elk states that the sweat lodge is used "before any great undertaking" to make oneself pure and to gain strength. The sweat was a source of much of the power of the Lakotas, and both men and women used the ritual. It was also performed in conjunction with other ceremonies, such as the Elk ceremony, the Horse dance, the vision quest,[49] the Sun Dance, to prepare a girl for woman-hood, for men after a period of mourning, to cleanse murderers returning from exile, and to receive warnings of danger from the spirits.[50] According to Black Elk (in Brown 1953:7), the sweat lodge and vision-seeking ceremonies predate the coming of the White Buffalo Cow Woman.

There is an unprecedented multiplicity of effects in the ritual as presented by Black Elk. He held the ritual to be effective for the individual participants, for the nation (I assume he refers to the Lakota people), for all peoples, and finally for all the universe. Through the sacrifice of an individual, all the people are aided. The purpose of the ritual is restorative; marked by prayer and symbol, it is to help the participants and, by extension, the whole universe to live again.

This result is secured by humbling oneself in prayer ("I'm nothing, help me") and in posture (one bows to enter the lodge as a sign of humility). There is a shift from fulfilling specific needs of individuals to generalized cosmic benefits brought about by the ceremony.

Structure and Ceremony

Black Elk (in Brown 1953:31–43) first gives a description of the sweat lodge as a ceremony in itself. The first phase of the ritual is in the ceremonial construction of the lodge and the fireplace.[51] The door, according to this text, always faces east.[52] Next, the leader enters the lodge, fills the pipe in a ceremonial manner, and exits. Finally, all enter the lodge and rocks are introduced in a ceremonial manner and laid to the center, to the west, to the north, to the east, to the south, and for the earth. Four rounds are then performed, beginning with the west and proceeding sunwise to the north, the east, and the south. In each round a pipe is pointed toward the appropriate direction. The basic ceremonial structure includes closing the door, praying, pouring water, singing, opening the door, and then smoking the pipe. Water is drunk and used for anointing the head and the body during the break between rounds when the door is open. Black Elk neglects to mention whether the last pipe (for the south) is loaded. Although there are a few other inconsistencies in the account, the basic structure is apparent.

Symbolic Interpretation

Black Elk offers both factual explanation and interpretive prayers to construct the meaning of the sweat. He holds that "the power of a thing or an act is in the meaning and the understanding" (in Brown 1953:32). For Black Elk, the sweat employs all the powers of the universe: water, earth, vegetation, air, and fire.[53] The water that is used represents the Thunder-beings and Wakan Tanka, who is flowing and gives life. The water is also a symbol of humility, for it is the lowest and yet the strongest of elements. The mound outside the lodge represents *uci* 'grandmother' earth. The earth is referred to both as mother and as grandmother. Human beings are born from earth and return there. The human spirit returns to Wakan Tanka. The willows are a symbol of man's death and rebirth in that they die each fall and come alive each spring. The rocks represent Grandmother Earth, the source of fruition. They also represent Wakan Tanka, who is indestructible. The rocks collectively represent the substance of the universe, whereas individual rocks placed in the cardinal directions specifically represent those directions. Black Elk does not associate the rocks with spirits, as earlier Lakotas and Dakotas did. Fire represents the power of Wakan Tanka. It also represents a ray of the sun, which is also Wakan Tanka in a certain aspect. The fire that heats the rocks represents the *phéta owíhakešni* 'eternal fire'. Finally, the fire has the power to purify. The fireplace within the lodge represents the center of the universe, the home of Wakan Tanka. The path outside the lodge represents the path to Wakan Tanka, according to Black Elk.

The structure of the ceremony continually marks direction: rocks, participants, and the pipe are symbols for the cardinal directions, the zenith, and the nadir. Black Elk states that there is a winged creature in each of the four directions. The west is the source of purifying water—the place where the *Wakíya Tháka* 'great Thunder-beings' control the water and guard the sacred pipe. North is the source of the purifying wind, making participants as clean as snow. Here live *Waziya* the 'Giant' and the bald eagle. From the east come wisdom and light, as opposed to darkness and ignorance. The morning star is in the east. The south represents both life and death and leads one on the sacred red path. Black Elk stresses that, despite the differentiation of powers in symbols, they are in fact all one power, Wakan Tanka.

Finally, the pipe is used to remember the White Buffalo Cow Woman and serves as a medium of purification and prayer. The sweetgrass is an offering to Wakan Tanka and also is a medium of purification. In addition, it is used to make someone a relative and thus secures the relatedness of all things in the universe. The steam, the heat, and the sweat lodge itself are media of purification. There is no overt interest in the physiology of the ritual or its physical effects, only its spiritual and moral ramifications. Health is mentioned only once in the context of a prayer, when the beings to the north are asked to guard the health of the people.

Black Elk's detailed description (in Brown 1953:48–56) of a sweat lodge ceremony used in conjunction with a vision quest is presented as a narrative of an actual event with prayers and speeches. In basic structure the ceremony substantially replicates the sweat lodge ceremony just described. There are some significant additions to the ceremony, however, which are unique to the vision quest sweat; these additions indicate the adaptive quality of the sweat lodge ritual. Two points of ritual precision are insisted upon in this account. One is that all the tobacco cut for the ceremony must be placed into the pipe. The second is that no water may be spilled within the lodge or placed on the lamenter's body. In both instances the consequences of mistakes are cosmic, incurring the displeasure of the Thunder-beings. Black Elk reiterates the propriety of addressing participants by kinship terms. A final propriety is that no one is to pass in front of the lamenter.[54] In this account all participants say "mitakuye oyas'in" in unison. Brown glossed the phrase 'we are all relatives'. This phrase, always repeated in the sweat today, was not mentioned in the initial description of the sweat lodge given by Black Elk, nor is it mentioned in the ethnohistorical literature concerning the sweat lodge up to the 1950s.

In this account Black Elk provides two styles of sweat lodge songs, solo and communal. He presents two communal songs:

> Grandfather, I am sending a voice!
> To the Heavens of the universe, I am sending a voice;
> That my people may live! [Black Elk in Brown 1953:54]

> Grandfather, behold me!
> Grandfather, behold me!
> I held my pipe and offered it to You,[55]
> That my people may live!

> Grandfather, behold me!
> Grandfather, behold me!
> I give to You all these offerings,
> That my people may live!

> Grandfather, behold me!
> Grandfather, behold me!
> We who represent all the people,
> Offer ourselves to You,
> That we may live! [65–66]

A solo is sung in the second round:

> They are sending a voice to me.
> From the place where the sun goes down,
> Our Grandfather is sending a voice to me.
> From where the sun goes down,
> They are talking to me as they come.
> Our Grandfather's voice is calling to me.
> That winged One there where the Giant lives,[56]

Is sending a voice to me. He is calling me.
Our Grandfather is calling me! [55]

Black Elk provides additional symbolic interpretation in describing the sweat lodge used prior to a vision quest. Added to the symbols marking directionality in the first description are *Wạblí Gleška* the 'spotted eagle', highest of all creatures, who both represents Wakan Tanka and is a messenger to Wakan Tanka. A series of birds are added to the six powers (the cardinal points, heaven [father and grandfather], and earth [mother and grandmother]). According to Black Elk, the birds make sure that all the peoples of the world are symbolically included in the pipe. The pipe, like the lodge itself, is an inclusion symbol (Black Elk in Brown 1953:51–52).[57] The last of the tobacco offered represents the individual lamenter, who himself is an offering to Wakan Tanka.

The second description of a sweat lodge ceremony used in conjunction with another ceremony concerns the Sun Dance (Black Elk in Brown 1953:82–84, 99–100). The structure of the ritual is basically the same, with the following minor variations.[58] In the first round sweetgrass is put in the water and touched to the participants' mouths. At the end of the third round, each receives one mouthful of water. In the fourth round they have all the water they wish. The Sun Dance leader both prays and says words of encouragement in each round. There is one communal song sung in this final sweat during the fourth round that Black Elk records:

I am sending a voice to my Grandfather!
I am sending a voice to my Grandfather!
Hear me!
Together with all things of the universe,
I am sending a voice to *Wakan-Tanka*. [100]

Black Elk's descriptions of these sweat lodge ceremonies support the impression that the ritual continues to be variable and adaptable within the set frame of opening and closing the door, pouring water, and praying through words and song. There is a pool of symbols, selectively employed by the leader, according to the context of the ritual and the needs of the participants. This adaptability of the rite, though described as early as the nineteenth century, is difficult to document from within because earlier reports concentrate upon the form rather than the verbal content of specific ritual instances. That is not to say that Black Elk's account exactly represents a sweat lodge ceremony "on the ground." It has been my experience during field research that leaders' descriptions of sweats vary from the actual ceremonies they perform and which I have attended.

The material examined in this chapter represents an attempt on the part of various authors, both native participants and white observers, to record for posterity aspects of a culture that many believed was disappearing and would eventually be gone forever. Most of the works were exercises in memory ethnography—an attempt to preserve rituals as narrators recalled them from the past.

Black Elk's highly detailed descriptions represent a transition in this process and a problematic in the confusion of voices. Whereas earlier material focused on the many pragmatic uses of the sweat lodge, the narratives in the Black Elk texts diffuse efficacy into universal benefits. Is this authentic to Black Elk, or is it a formulation by Brown? I present the texts without critique because they remain an influence in the literature; I counsel caution in interpretation rather than wholesale rejection or acceptance of the texts.

The Black Elk texts sparked a florescence in symbolic interpretation of the lodge, which continues with vigor to the present day. Black Elk also represents a transition in textual production—the beginning of "as told to" accounts in the Lakota literature. These accounts may appear more reliable because Black Elk is supposedly speaking, but they are also laden with ambiguity because it is not always clear when or whether the editor is speaking through the Lakota narrator.[59] We shall see in the second chapter that this continues to be a problem with "as told to" literature.

Subsequent accounts of the sweat depend to a greater or lesser extent on the Black Elk texts, particularly Brown's work, as a source for interpretation. *The Sacred Pipe* received a wide and popular circulation and has become a primary source for later explications and analyses of the ritual. The Black Elk material also represents a shift in domains, moving from military, anthropological, and missionary accounts to works in the history of religion, poetry, and popular literature and, later, to New Age interpretation. The more recent material that we will examine in the next chapter continues the symbolic interpretation first presented in the Black Elk texts.

1. Sweat lodge frame with sacrifice pole (1892). Photo by James Mooney, Pine Ridge Reservation. Courtesy National Anthropological Archives, Smithsonian Institution (negative number 3711-A-1).

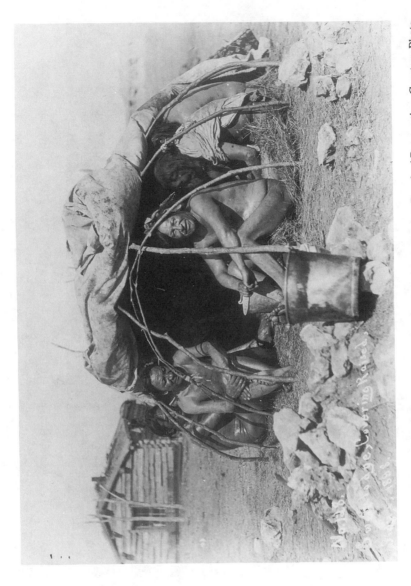

2. Sweat lodge with cover raised (1898). Photo by Jesse Hastings Bratley, Rosebud Reservation.

2

The Contemporary Lakota Sweat Lodge

This chapter traces documentary accounts of the sweat lodge into the contemporary era. There are four sources of information: (1) participant observers: Lakota and non-Lakota individuals who wrote descriptions of their experience of the sweats; (2) "as told to" accounts: Lakotas who provided oral descriptions of their practice for a non-Indian transcriber; (3) anthropologists; and (4) missionaries. I begin with a summary of contexts for contemporary use based on all four groups and end with my own observations.

Context for Use

Contemporary observers provide lists of uses of the sweat that closely parallel those of the past.[1] It continues to be a religious rite carried out for its own sake and prior to other ceremonies. It is used for purification, petitioning, and thanksgiving. The predominant ceremonies preceded by a sweat are the Sun Dance, the vision quest, praying with a pipe, and the yuwipi ceremony. Uses of the sweat lodge ceremony continue to reflect contemporary needs: it is used after international military conflicts, to regain one's power as a spiritual leader or to change one's heart or intention, for protection of young and old, to petition for material help and blessings, and, finally and most importantly, for healing. The healing focus has extended to new diseases such as AIDS and fetal alcohol syndrome.

According to my observation, the sweat lodge continued to be used in the late 1980s and early 1990s for all of the functions just mentioned. It is also used frequently to aid in recovery from drug and alcohol abuse, addiction being seen as a disease. The sweat is used by armed service veterans to purify them of their distress, to affirm their traditional role as warriors (in the case of Lakotas), and to find positive recognition for their warrior status (for non-Lakotas). The sweat lodge is sometimes used as the locus for an adoption ceremony, though this is rather rare.[2] Sweats are, finally, social events that solidify groups around a common set of practices and provide mental, spiritual, and physical enjoyment and refreshment for the participants.

Contemporary Accounts: Participant Observers

Structure and Ceremony

Beginning in the 1960s, descriptions of the sweat lodge appear with increasing frequency in popular literature. These accounts are significant because they have further popularized the ritual among non-Indians, as did Joseph Epes Brown's very successful work with Black Elk, and they clearly depend, at least in part, on earlier textual sources, particularly Brown.

The description of the sweat lodge ritual provided in Reginald and Gladys Laubin's text, based on their personal experience, closely parallels Black Elk's description, outlined in chapter 1.[3] Although their book cites both Brown's and Neihardt's work, they make no direct reference to either publication within their descriptions. The Laubins (1957:106) state that the contemporary sweat is essentially the same as it was in earlier times, although some sweat ceremonies were more complicated and lasted longer in former days (115). Formerly, there were sometimes immense lodges of more than one hundred willows, using a like number of rocks (116). The Laubins' description of the construction of the sweat lodge and the fire (106–8) is essentially the same as that provided by Black Elk, except that they recommend using between twelve and fourteen sticks, whereas Black Elk specifies, in Brown's work, either twelve or sixteen. The construction of the fire and the placement of the door (always facing east) are identical as described by the Laubins and in Brown's version of Black Elk. One unique feature, according to the Laubins, is that four virgins were sent by the medicine man to gather sweat rocks (108).[4] Twelve or more stones were used in the sweat.

The sweat ceremony they describe consists of four closings and openings of the lodge. They did not record any prayers, so it is unclear whether directionality was expressed in that manner. As in Black Elk's account, tobacco is placed in the four corners of the pit, and a coal in the center is used to burn purifying incense. Directionality is expressed when pinches of tobacco are offered to the heavens and the earth and the four directions, starting with the west, before being placed on the ground in its corresponding direction. Black Elk expresses these directions through motions while filling the pipe rather than by placing tobacco in the pit. Placing the hot stones into the sweat lodge pit also stresses directionality, since they are placed in the center and toward the west, the north, the east, the south, and the earth, just as Black Elk described. A seventh stone is also included, representing the seven council fires of the Sioux Nation (Laubin and Laubin 1957:109). The meaning of the seventh stone is not expressed, except that it makes up for the missing council fire. Black Elk offers no such interpretation, although he was aware of the seven council fires of the Tetons. This consciously expressed national symbolism is unique to the Laubins' description.[5]

One minor variation in the Laubins' description of the ritual is that everyone smokes the pipe before the rocks are brought into the lodge. Black Elk places the smoking of the pipe after the rocks have been brought into the lodge. Both sources state that the pipe is touched to each rock as it is introduced. The Laubins do not say whether the pipe is reintroduced to the sweat after each round or whether the exterior pipe is pointed toward each cardinal point as the prayers shift direction with each round. No one speaks when the first four stones are placed into the pit in the lodge. People are to concentrate their thoughts on good things (Laubin and Laubin 1957:114). This represents a continuity from earlier accounts of the importance of mind, thought, and concentration; a period of silence is still practiced today.

The Laubins (1957:111) mention sweat techniques that are rather utilitarian. Water is poured on the rocks before the door is closed to clear the smoke from the lodge. To avoid the intense heat, one can turn on one's side, put one's face to the ground, and in dire circumstances, open the bottom of the covering a little to breathe (112).

In an account published in 1961, Stephen E. Feraca, an anthropologist studying Lakota culture who was then employed by the Bureau of Indian Affairs, described a sweat lodge ceremony held before a yuwipi meeting in 1956 on the Pine Ridge Reservation. Adult males take part in the sweat lodge ceremony before a yuwipi meeting. The sweat lodge structure is generally found "near the houses of older full-bloods" (Feraca 1961:156).[6] He associates the ceremony primarily with the older generation and then with those who are "real Indians," at least by blood quantum and behavior.[7]

Feraca points out some interesting features of the sweat ceremony he documents, in which he participated. He says that colored cloth offerings (*wa 'úyapi*) and Bull Durham tobacco sacks from previous baths were hanging on the frame of the sweat lodge. The door of the lodge faced west, but "contrary to much that has been written about this rite, there is no pattern for the position of the sweat lodge, i.e., for the orientation of the entrance. The owner or builder may favor a particular direction or orientation, this being an expression of Sioux individualism" (Feraca 1961:156–57). Feraca also indicates that there was no ceremony connected with the building or lighting of the fire; trash, broken boxes, and paper were simply piled up against the stones and wood.

Feraca provides the first textual reference to humor in the context of the sweat lodge.[8] Unfortunately, he fails to record any of the jokes. When the first six rocks were brought into the lodge, one of the men requested that all be silent. Despite this request, some of the participants persisted in joking through this part of the ceremony. There seem to have been no repercussions, social or cosmic, for this breach of protocol.

Feraca states that people prayed for the fire tender, the promoters of the ceremony and their families, the wild animals, birds, children, and servicemen, specifying those within the United States, those in foreign countries, and those traveling across the water. Each topic was proceeded by *"Hói Thukášila, "* and the participants answered with *"Háu, "* representing another instance of back-channeling.[9] Feraca mentions that *Thukášila* refers to "a great many of the figures known to Sioux cosmology" (1961:157). The yuwipi 'spirits' are desig-nated in this way. Wakan Tanka was also addressed in the ritual, but Feraca does not translate this phrase.

Although Feraca does not describe the ceremony round by round (it is clear that there were at least two rounds, since he enters after the first round is com-pleted), he does mention some features of the actual ceremony. Rhythmic prayers in "an archaic language" were said by the leader, the participants rubbed and slapped themselves, there were songs using both words and vocables, and prayers were voiced, apparently by the leader only. The leader accompanied the songs by striking the water bucket with a dipper, and a pipe was smoked after one round. The pipe was passed clockwise and each participant said "Mitakuye oyas'in," which Feraca glosses as 'my relatives all', after smoking the pipe. A large stone was introduced, and the last of the water was used up in a final round. The pipe was reintroduced and smoked again after this round. No one doused himself or herself with water, a practice that Feraca states has been largely abandoned.

Symbolic Interpretation

The Laubins' interpretations of symbols associated with the sweat lodge closely parallel those presented by Black Elk as reported by Brown. The fire is lighted on the east side because the east is the source of light and wisdom. The mound represents the earth. The path to the mound is the good road. A painted buffalo skull recalls the herds of buffalo that once wandered the lands and represents abundance.[10] The skull also represents long life and the idea that all things come from and return to the Great Spirit, a concept employed by Black Elk.

The Laubins continue their symbolic analysis of the ritual:

> According to the legends of the Sioux, the small, dark lodge represents the womb of Mother Earth. The darkness is the ignorance of men's minds. The hot stones represent the coming of life; the hissing steam is the creative force of the universe coming into action; the cover is raised to the east, the source of life and power, the dawning of wisdom upon the minds of men. The elements of earth, air, water, and fire are all represented in the sweat lodge, which is called *initipi,* the "new life lodge," by the Sioux. The fire which heated the stones, *peta owihankeshni,* is "the fire that never dies," the light of the world, eternity. [1957:113]

Although Black Elk says (in Brown 1953:40) that one is reborn in the lodge, he does not directly associate the lodge itself with a womb, although this seems obvious.[11] The association of the rocks and their hissing with the coming of life and movement is unique to the Laubins' account. The rest of the analysis is consistent with Black Elk's, save that Black Elk adds plant life as the fifth fundamental element of nature. The Laubins' account strongly accentuates the regenerative quality of the lodge, a feature that is present, we shall see, in many ancient and contemporary stories about the sweat.

The Laubins' account is important because, though it closely parallels Black Elk's published account, it also provides unique procedures and symbolic interpretations, indicating the continued flexibility, adaptability, and innovative tolerance of the sweat lodge. It also represents a set of interpretations voiced if not actually created by non-Lakotas without specific reference to their sources. The confounding of sources is typical of most contemporary descriptions of the ritual.

Contemporary Accounts: "As Told To" Accounts

Structure and Ceremony

Thomas Mails, Protestant minister, author, and artist, is interested in Native Americans in general and contemporary Lakota ritual in particular. He provides a detailed explanation of the sweat lodge, elicited from the Lakota William Schweigman (Mails 1978). Schweigman, also known as Eagle Feather, was a mixed-blood born in 1914 on the Rosebud Reservation (Mails 1978:45), who had studied to become an Episcopal lay reader. In 1957 he had a dream that he would restore the full Sun Dance to the Lakotas, including piercing. He states that he dreamed this, yet did not know much at that time "about my Indian religion and culture" (46).

Schweigman's account of the sweat lodge, told in connection with the performance of the Sun Dance, is enlightening both because of its obvious connections with the Black Elk material published by Brown and because of the variations and innovations that appear. Although the Black Elk texts have become increasingly influential, Brown's documentation of Lakota ritual never gained the status of a liturgical text to which practitioners strictly adhere, because continuity with the past is also established orally, through the personal relationship of teacher and student. Most Lakotas practicing the sweat lodge today learned specific procedures from their teachers, usually relatives. Whites who practice the sweat lodge inevitably trace their ceremonies to an Indian leader or an adopted Indian relative who has in some way "authorized" them to perform the ceremony. Some Lakotas also cite texts as one of the sources for their ceremonial knowledge, but others strongly eschew the use of texts, stating that those who employ such material "get the whole thing wrong." Thus, continuity here consists in oral passage of information and, for some, the use of printed materials from the ethnographic record. Although oral transmission obviously cannot be textually documented, it should not be discounted. The difference from transmission in the nineteenth century, however, is that continuity is, in part, encapsulated in a new medium: the written word. In this era segments of Walker's materials were published, first by Holy Rosary Mission between 1971 and 1973 intended as texts for Lakota school children and later in a more complete form (Tedlock and Tedlock 1975; Walker 1980, 1982, 1983; Dooling 1984).[12]

Eagle Feather related the details of "his" sweat lodge on July 11, 1974. There are many striking similarities with Black Elk's account. Both refer to the pit as an altar (Black Elk in Brown 1953:33; Mails 1978:87), although Eagle Feather also refers to it as the "rock cradle." In prayer, both stress purity and living by the will of Wakan Tanka (Black Elk in Brown 1953:33; Mails 1978: 88). When individuals enter Eagle Feather's lodge, they pray, "All my relatives thank you," whereas for Black Elk this prayer is recited after each individual has smoked the pipe during a vision quest sweat (Black Elk in Brown 1953:53; Mails 1978:90). Bowing low in order to enter the lodge is a symbolic gesture of humility, according to both sources. Eagle Feather includes nakedness of the participants as further intensifying this symbolic humility (Black Elk in Brown 1953:35; Mails 1978:90). Black Elk equates nakedness with poverty, an analogous image (57). Both state that a woman may act as the fire keeper (Black Elk in Brown 1953:35; Mails 1978:91).

These repeated images may represent a central symbolic continuity within Lakota symbolic tradition. Presenting oneself as poor and needy in order to garner the aid of supernatural beings is salient throughout the ethnohistorical data. The continuities may, however, reflect the author's (Mails's) or Eagle Feather's amplification of his own material using some of these sources. The prayers that Eagle Feather says paraphrase those recorded for Black Elk so closely that one can attribute them to a direct reading of Brown's text on the part of either Eagle Feather or Mails. For instance, as part of the preparation for the sweat lodge ceremony, a pipe is introduced and smoked. This is recounted by both Eagle Feather and Black Elk. According to Black Elk:

> The person at the west now offers the pipe to heaven, earth, the four directions, and then he lights it, and after a few puffs (rubbing the smoke all over his body) he hands the pipe to the one at his left, saying: *"Ho Ate,"* or *"Ho Tunkashila,"* according to their relationship. The one who takes the pipe says in turn: *"How Ate,"* or *"How Tunkashila,"* and in this manner the pipe is passed sun-wise around the circle. When the pipe comes back to the man at the west, he purifies it, lest some impure person may have touched it, and carefully empties the ashes, placing them at the edge of the sacred altar. [in Brown 1953:36]

Eagle Feather says:

> The helper now offers the Pipe to the six directions. Then he lights it, takes a few deep puffs, and blows the smoke out so that he can rub it all over his body. Then he hands the Pipe to the man at his left saying, *"Ho ate"* or *"Ho tunkashila,"* depending on his relationship to the person.
> The man who receives the Pipe responds by saying, *"How ate"* or *"How tunkashila."* *"How ate"* means "my father," and *"How tunkashila"* is "my

grandfather." The Pipe is sent sunwise, which is clockwise, around the circle until it comes back to the leader. He generally purifies it with burning sweet grass in case some impure person has touched it, carefully empties the ashes, and deposits them at the edge of the Rock Cradle. [Mails 1978:92]

The only difference between the accounts is that the helper offers the pipe in Black Elk's account and the leader offers the pipe in Eagle Feather's account. Black Elk states that the man to the west of the lodge prays at the beginning of the first round:

> *"Hee-ay-hay-ee-ee!"* (four times)
> (This we say whenever we are in need of help or are in despair, and indeed are we not now in darkness and in need of the Light!)
> "I am sending a voice!" (four times) "Hear me!" (Four times). [in Brown 1953:37]

Eagle Feather explains the opening prayer in these words:

> The leader now prays to *Wakan-Tanka,* saying *"Ha-hey,"* four times. This is what we say when we are in trouble; when we are in darkness and in need of enlightenment. We send Him our voice four times because we want Him to hear us four times, which is the sacred number He has taught us to observe. [Mails 1978:92]

Black Elk continues the prayer:

> *Wakan-Tanka,* Grandfather, You are first and always have been. You have brought us to this great island, and here our people wish to live in a sacred manner. Teach us to know and to see all the powers of the universe, and give to us the knowledge to understand that they are all really one Power. May our people always send their voices to You as they walk the sacred path of life! [in Brown 1953:37]

Eagle Feather states that the leader prays at the beginning of the first round:

> *Wakan-Tanka,* Grandfather, you are first and always have been. You have brought us to this land, and here our people wish to live in a sacred manner. Teach us to understand and to recognize all the powers of the universe, which is really one power. We pray that our people will always send their voice up to you as they walk the sacred path of life.
> *Tunkashila,* you are here with us at this moment. You made the earth, and we pray that our generations will be able to walk in the days ahead without falling. [Mails 1978:92]

Black Elk continues the prayer:

> O Rocks, you have neither eyes, nor mouth, nor limbs; you do not move, but by receiving your sacred breath [the steam], our people will be long-winded as they walk the path of life; your breath is the very breath of life. [in Brown 1953:37]

Eagle Feather continues the prayer:

> O rocks, you have neither eyes nor mouth nor arms nor legs. You do not move about as we do. But by receiving your sacred breath, the hot steam here in the sweatlodge, we and our people will have the breath and strength to walk the difficult path of a holy life. [Mails 1978:92]

Black Elk continues the prayer:

> There is a winged One, there where the sun goes down to rest, who controls those waters to which all living beings owe their lives. May we use these waters here in a sacred manner! [in Brown 1953:37]

Eagle Feather continues the prayer:

> We know there is a winged power in the west where the sun goes down who controls the water all life relies on, so help us to please him by using these waters in a sacred manner. [Mails 1978:92]

Black Elk continues the prayer by referring to the tree people who were selected to construct the lodge. This is not included in Mails. Black Elk concludes the prayer from the west with these words:

> To every earthly thing, O *Wakan-Tanka,* You have given a power, and because the fire is the most powerful of Your creations, since it consumes all other things, we place it here at our center, and when we see it and think of it, we really remember You. May this sacred fire always be at our center! Help us in that which we are about to do! [in Brown 1953:37–38]

Eagle Feather concludes his prayer at the beginning of the first round with these words:

> To every earthly thing, *Wakan-Tanka,* you have given a power, and because the fire is your most powerful creation we have placed it here at the center of the sweatlodge. Help us in the purification we are about to undergo. [Mails 1978:92–93]

Eagle Feather states after he describes the sweat lodge ceremony that he always prays this prayer:

> "O Grandfather, *Wakan-Tanka,* you are and always were, I have done your will on this earth as you have taught us by placing the sacred rocks at the four quarters of the altar. We understand that it is really you who is at the center of the sweatlodge where the rocks are being placed. O sacred rocks, you are helping us to do the will of *Wakan-Tanka,* Almighty God. [Mails 1978:93]

Consistent with the above parallels, Black Elk has a similar prayer in his account of the sweat lodge. His prayer is said as the fire for the sweat is being made:

> "O Grandfather, *Wakan-Tanka,* You are and always were. I am about to do Thy will on this earth as You have taught us. In placing these sacred rocks at the four quarters we understand that it is You who are at the center. O sacred rocks, you are helping us to do the will of *Wakan-Tanka!"* [in Brown 1953:32–33]

At one point Eagle Feather quotes Black Elk himself in stressing that Wakan Tanka is the center of everything (Mails 1978:91).

There are two possible explanations for these striking similarities. The first is that Mails took down Eagle Feather's account and amplified it with Brown's material. The second is that Eagle Feather actually memorized some of Black Elk's prayers. Neither individual (both voices appear in this work) acknowledges Black Elk as source of these prayers. Considering that all Lakota prayers, though they reiterate certain themes, are spontaneous, mere coincidence seems to be unlikely. I believe that the similarity of these two texts exemplifies the importance of the Black Elk corpus as a guide for ritual behavior, both for white authors and for some Lakotas.[13]

As I mentioned earlier, however, Eagle Feather does not rely entirely on Black Elk and, in fact, strongly varies from Black Elk in some of his own practices. The most obvious variation is in directionality. Eagle Feather states that the doorway and the fireplace are to the west of the lodge and that the fire itself is lit on the west side (Mails 1978:87). Medicine men of this era are rather definite about the direction of the door of the sweat. Selo Black Crow (in Jackson 1978:96), a contemporary medicine man from near Wanblee, South Dakota, says that for the Sun Dance he has the door face east, whereas the door of his personal sweat at home faces west. He gives no reason for this configuration.[14]

The fireplace used by Eagle Feather is completely different from that used by Black Elk. The pit is called "Old Man Four Generations." It is cut in the shape of a man's head and has four horns representing the four generations.[15] The four generations represent the individual and three descending generations, children, grandchildren, and great grandchildren. Seven rocks are laid out in the pit: two to represent the eyes, two the nose, and three the mouth of Old Man Four Generations. The firekeeper "reads" the fire by the color of the ashes that appear in the pit and can thus determine what is being prayed for within the lodge (Mails 1978:88). The mound in front of the lodge represents a molehill, for moles live beneath the earth and are thus close to Mother Earth (90).

Eagle Feather's color and directional symbolism both reflect Black Elk's explanation and exceed it. Both men hold that the north is the source of purification, the east of understanding, the south of life, and the west of water. Eagle Feather also gives a much more social orientation to the directions. He states that when these colors are found in the fire pit the following is implied: black (west) is for remembrance of our dead relatives, red (north) represents the people who are sick, yellow (east) is for families that are fragmenting and in need, and white (south) is for purification and thanksgiving to God (Mails 1978:87). Eagle Feather also says in a prayer as the pipe is filled, "We are going to tell you of our troubles and our needs" (91). This focus on troubles is essential in constituting tradition appropriate to the present but at the same time consonant with the past.

Eagle Feather states that the leader determines how many times the pipe will be smoked within the lodge, rather than locking this aspect of the ceremony into a set procedure (Mails 1978:93). As in Black Elk's account, silence is required as the initial stones are brought into the lodge. The first rock is placed in the center to represent Wakan Tanka, the next is placed to the west, the next to the north, the next to the east, the next to the south, and the next toward Mother Earth. As each rock is passed in, the pipe stem (Black Elk uses the bowl) is touched to the rock and all inside cry, "Thank you." The rest of the rocks, when assembled, represent the universe, as stated by Black Elk (Black Elk in Brown 1953:31; Mails 1978:92).

Eagle Feather also universalizes the symbols in his lodge to include universal consequences and specific ethnic groups as representative of all humanity. While the pipe is loaded, a prayer is said: "Almighty God I want to thank you for all you have provided for me and my brothers throughout the universe" (Mails 1978:91). He also states concerning the fire pit, "Bear in mind as I continue that the rocks, the sweat lodge, and the outside fireplace are extremely important to all mankind, regardless of what race or nationality an individual may belong to" (88).

Thomas Mails also interviewed Frank Fools Crow for his Sun Dance book. In addition he wrote a popular interview biography of Fools Crow, which was published the next year (Mails and Chief Eagle 1979). This material is useful for comparing Fools Crow's sweat ceremony with that conducted by Eagle Feather. It is clear that each individual used both historical practice and innovation (introduced by vision and dream) in shaping his sweat lodge ceremony. Mails asked Fools Crow about Eagle Feather's use of a symbolic fire pit in his ceremony. Fools Crow replied that his own fireplace was devoid of symbolism and that he did not know where Eagle Feather got the idea (Mails 1978:202). Whereas Eagle Feather employs seven rocks in his ceremony, arrayed to represent a face, Fools Crow consistently uses twelve (Mails and Chief Eagle 1979:202).

Fools Crow is quite explicit about the origins of his ceremonies. He states that although he learned ceremonial practice from the medicine man Stirrup, the particular medicine he employs for his special sweat lodge ceremony came from a personal vision at Bear Butte (Mails and Chief Eagle 1979:86–87).

Despite the variations exhibited across instances of sweat lodge per-formance, Fools Crow, like George Sword in the early 1900s, holds that ritual propriety is important for spiritual efficacy. He supervises how the rocks are laid into the pit, for if this is done incorrectly the ceremony will not work (Mails and Chief Eagle 1979:97). Sincerity of the participants is important for the success of the ceremony, but the ceremony itself must also be properly con-ducted. We shall see in the contemporary era that, although the emphasis is on inner disposition for ritual success, procedure also remains an important focus. Contention over tradition will focus both on the psychological disposition of participants and on correct procedure, including questions about who may appropriately lead and participate in rituals. Propriety remains couched in the dialectical process of satisfactorily combining past and present into an acceptable amalgam.

Fools Crow describes three sweat lodge ceremonies, two involved with healing (Mails and Chief Eagle 1979:95–102) and one for use at the Sun Dance (124–29). The structure of the ritual is consistent with previous descriptions. Four openings are employed, prayers are said by each individual, there is clockwise directionality focused on the cardinal points, and there are songs for each round (a minimum of four songs). No nails, wire, or string are used in constructing the lodge.[16] In Fools Crow's healing sweats, the pipe is smoked after the sweat by the participants, beginning with the patient (99). This allows the pipe to be charged with the power of the spirits. Thus, the spirits are "loaded" into the sweat lodge itself, and then their power is transferred to the pipe. Fools Crow, like Eagle Feather, states that the sweat faces west, although neither gives a reason for this. They both refer to the mound in front of the lodge as the mole hill and the pit inside the sweat as the rock cradle (121).

For the Sun Dance sweat, Fools Crow has each person pray about why he has come to Sun Dance and also offer prayers in gratitude for what the powers have done and will do for him. The individual can also make petitions about such concerns as finance and health (Mails and Chief Eagle 1979:136).

Fools Crow mentions two songs used in the Sun Dance sweat. First there is a song to call the spirits. The words are

You are coming,
you are coming among us.
We have prepared everything for you
and we are waiting. [Mails and Chief Eagle 1979:125]

That song is repeated three times, for Wakan Tanka, Grandfather, and Grandmother Earth. Then he sings this song:

You are all here.
You are among us,
you are with us,
you are in our presence! [125]

Unlike the Black Elk material, which stresses the powers of the universe, Fools Crow calls personal helper spirits into the lodge. When the last song is sung, he calls to the spirits who can be heard all around.

Demonstrating how ritual continuity is important for the Lakotas, Fools Crow says of Good Lance, another medicine man, "He was pleased to discover that our sweatlodge rituals are alike in many ways" (Mails and Chief Eagle 1979:161). Note that isomorphism is not at issue, but rather continuity. The continuity expresses interpersonal harmony, just as Fools Crow's ability to pass on messages from the spirits to others without verbal exchange expresses harmony among participants within the lodge (51). When a quester goes up on the hill seeking a vision, Fools Crow remains in the sweat lodge, a further expression of that sympathetic connection (120).

Fools Crow also provides some insight into the mechanical operation of the sweat lodge. He states that the length of the ritual depends on the duration of individuals' prayers (Mails and Chief Eagle 1979:125). If someone becomes too hot during a round, that person says "mitakuye oyas'in," and the custodian opens the door (96). When Fools Crow wants the singers to sing longer, he requests it indirectly by asking whether they are done. Only if they miss his hint to sing another song will he tell them directly to continue (98). To end a sweat, Fools Crow says the final prayer, telling God and, indirectly, the participants, "I am going to be outside pretty soon" (126). He shouts "Ho" four times, indicating to the custodian that the sweat is completed and that he should open the door. Another indication for the ceremony to end is when the bucket of water brought into the lodge is used up.

Richard Erdoes, an immigrant Viennese artist and author, edited a narrative provided by John Fire Lame Deer.[17] Erdoes's texts have come under close examination, and it is clear that he amplified much of his "as told to" material with previous ethnographic works (Rice 1994). Nevertheless, this material, particularly *Lame Deer—Seeker of Visions,* has been used and continues to be used uncritically by many readers as a point of access to and a guide for Lakota ritual practice.

One chapter is devoted to the sweat lodge (Lame Deer in Erdoes 1972b:174–82). Lame Deer acknowledges variations in the construction of altars on the earth mound: some make pipe racks, others place a buffalo skull on the altar with six tobacco ties on its horns, and still others erect a black and white stick representing day and night. That "up to" fifty rocks can be used in the sweat indicates a further flexibility. At the same time he presents some practices as absolute. Water used in the lodge must be drawn from a stream, according to this account, as it represents the water of life (178). Only cottonwood can be used for the fire because it is the most sacred tree (177). Eighteen rocks are used for healing ceremonies (180). These practices are all unique to Lame Deer's view, despite his apparent universalization of the rules.

Lame Deer (in Erdoes 1972b:179) distinguishes two differences between contemporary and "traditional" practice. First, if someone wants to do the ceremony "right," a forked stick should be used to bring in the rocks. Second, if one wishes to do things the old way, one must use sage or sweetgrass to sprinkle water on the hot rocks. Nevertheless, a ladle can be used. The shift in material instruments expresses alienation from perceived traditional implements and the totality of ancient practice, as reflected in the oft-cited ambiguity of "living in two worlds." Lame Deer laments the fact that they used to use beautifully painted skin bags to hold the water in the lodge, but now pails must suffice (178). This could also be an artifact of Erdoes's desire to construct a pure tradition devoid of white contamination. It is clear that Lakotas from the time of contact utilized European goods; today few notice at ceremonies that sticks are in coffee cans, nor are many concerned that cotton cloth rather than deerskin is used.

A unique Lakota first-person account of participation in a sweat lodge ceremony is found in Arthur Amiotte's description of his own vision quest, conducted by Pete Catches (Amiotte 1976).[18] Amiotte, a Lakota artist from Manderson, South Dakota, on the Pine Ridge Reservation, studied under Joseph Epes Brown. The details of the rite, insofar as they are elaborated in that article, are similar to those given by Fools Crow and Eagle Feather, although variations are present. The door faces west, with an earth altar and a fireplace directly outside the door. Whereas Fools Crow states that he remained in the sweat while the quester was on the hill, Amiotte mentions that Catches left his own filled pipe in the sweat during his quest rather than remaining there himself. All the material to be used on the quest was touched to the hot rocks and purified in the steam at the beginning and the end of the vision quest. Amiotte draws a very sharp distinction between the sacred and the profane. He states that at the end of the vision quest Catches wiped his (Amiotte's) eyes, nose, mouth, and ears, and blew into them "so that they too would be made ready for the common world again" (40).

Catches conducts two rounds in the sweat before the vision quest and two rounds after the quest. Personal narrative is essential to this ceremony. Catches begins each sweat by describing his own visions and experience, thus validating his leadership role. Amiotte explains in the first sweat why he had come to vision quest and in the last sweat what he had seen while praying on the hill (Amiotte 1976:32, 40).

This lodge also involves manifestations of particular spirits. At one point Amiotte (1976:32) feels eagle wings touching him. He also hears the little bird sound of Catches's intercessor, Red Hawk. This spirit acts to validate the legitimacy of Amiotte's experience on the hill as well as Catches's ability as a medicine man (40). What is unique to this description is Amiotte's recording of his personal feelings. He states that while in the lodge "sweat poured from me as I have never known it to do before" (32) and "indeed I felt as though I were newly born" (33). This appropriation of symbols by the intense physical experience of the lodge and the intensification of physical experience itself characterizes the sweat lodge ceremony.

Symbolic Interpretation

From the writings of Charles A. Eastman onward, we see Dakota and Lakota ceremony and symbolism explained by native practitioners using Christian analogies, a trend that continues into the contemporary era. Black Elk (or Brown) states in the foreword of *The Sacred Pipe:*

> We have been told by the white men, or at least by those who are Christian, that God sent to men His son, who would restore order and peace upon the earth, and we have been told that Jesus the Christ was crucified, but that he shall come again at the Last Judgment, the end of this world or cycle. This I understand and know that it is true, but the white men should know that for the red people too, it was the will of *Wakan-Tanka,* the Great Spirit, that an animal turn itself into a two-legged person in order to bring the most holy pipe to His people; and we too were taught that this White Buffalo Cow Woman who brought our sacred pipe will appear again at the end of this "world," a coming which we Indians know is now not very far off. [in Brown 1953:xix–xx]

This justification of faith by analogy is carried on in Eagle Feather's description of the sweat lodge:

> The Peace Pipe, or Sacred Pipe, is a very important part of the ritual and is used because the Traditional Sioux of modern times sincerely believe that it is our Jesus Christ, or our Savior, and that He is still here on earth in the person of the Pipe. The non-Indians have killed and crucified their Savior. This is why traditional people do not celebrate Easter at all. [Mails 1978:88]

> In the Sioux mind there are many similarities between the Christians' Jesus Christ and the Sioux Sacred Pipe. For example, when Calf Pipe Woman brought the Pipe to the Sioux people it was like Christ being brought into the world by a woman at Christmastime. Christ was wrapped in a bundle, and the Pipe is wrapped in a bundle also. [Mails 1978:88, 90]

Eagle Feather also directly uses this comparison of Judaism and Lakota practice specifically for the sweat lodge ceremony: "Moses went to the top of the mountain to receive the Ten Commandments, written on the tablets of stone. And on these stones we use in the sweatlodge there are scriptures, too" (Mails 1978:93).

Equating traditional Lakota religious practice with Judeo-Christian ideas represents an attempt to establish Lakota practices as equally valid in a social and religious system imposed through inequality and presumed superiority.[19] The later missionaries begin equating Christianity with Lakota religion rather than rejecting native practice out of hand as did their predecessors.[20]

Fools Crow offers quite explicit interpretations for the symbols used in the ceremony. Although he gives no symbolic interpretation for the sweat lodge supports, which number twelve, he states that the rocks and the order in which they are loaded into the rock cradle represent the west, the north, the south, the east, Grandmother Earth, Grandfather, and Wakan Tanka.[21] Concerning his healing ceremony, Fools Crow focuses on the first six rocks, combining Grandfather and Wakan Tanka into one rock (Mails and Chief Eagle 1979:96–97). The first rock of this series has a small red circle painted on it. With regard to his Sun Dance sweat, Fools Crow says that seven rocks are loaded, the sixth representing Grandfather and the seventh, Wakan Tanka (125).[22] The seventh rock is the one with the circle painted on it in this instance. Just as with Black Elk, variation by circumstance is evident within the practice of one individual. Fools Crow states that the circle on the rock represents the participants' being seated in a circle in the lodge and that their hearts will be as one (124). In all instances there is silence when the rocks to which symbolism is attributed are brought into the sweat and a pipe stem is touched to each of them (125). This action with the pipe, according to Fools Crow, blesses the rocks and fills them with Wakan Tanka's power. Fools Crow reiterates the directionality of the rocks' positions by consciously pouring water in the four directions during the ceremony. Four twisted pieces of sage are laid around the fire pit within the lodge, pointing to the four directions (97). The bowl of his pipe points west (97). Few prayers are recorded in this account, none giving a sense of directionality, unlike the prayers reported by Black Elk. Fools Crow universalizes his prayers to include all "races" of people: "And show us the good road we must all walk in unity and as close friends, whether we are red, white, black, or yellow" (126). The four colors used in his ceremonies represent these four races, all of whom are under the care of Grandfather's spirits (51–52).

Lame Deer provides a series of symbolic associations for various items and actions in the sweat lodge. Many of these images can be found in Black Elk's narrative given to Joseph Brown. The supports of the sweat lodge dome form a square at the top, which represents the four directions and the universe (Black Elk in Brown 1953:32; Lame Deer in Erdoes 1972b). They also represent the bones of the Lakota people, a symbolic association unique to Lame Deer. The lodge itself also represents the universe, containing the spirits of all living things (see Black Elk in Brown 1953:32). Twelve or sixteen willows are used for the frame (see 31). The pit represents both the center of the whole world (see 49) and *wakícaǧapi,* the dead relatives who have returned to the earth (Lame Deer in Erdoes 1972b:178). This association with the dead is also unique to Lame Deer. The circle of the pit formed within the circle of the lodge represents life that has no end, another theme of Black Elk (Black Elk in Brown 1953:32; Lame Deer in Erdoes 1972b:178). The mound in front of the lodge is *uci* 'grandmother' and represents the earth. The extra stones loaded into the sweat represent the trees, the plants, and the animals, which is to say, everything else in the universe (see Black Elk in Brown 1953:36).

The first six rocks are arranged in the sweat lodge pit in silence. The order is shifted from Black Elk, with the first representing Grandmother Earth and the sixth, the sky and the Grandfather spirit (Lame Deer in Erdoes 1972b:179; see Black Elk in Brown 1953:36). Water is poured four times, and the pipe is smoked four times (Lame Deer in Erdoes 1972b:181). When you emerge, you are "like a baby coming out of your mother's womb, our real mother, the earth" (179; see Black Elk in Brown 1953:40).[23] Lame Deer closely parallels Black Elk's words in stating, concerning the rocks, "They have no mouth, no eyes, no arms or legs, but they exhale the breath of life" (in Erdoes 1972b:180).[24] The pipe that is smoked, according to Lame Deer, links participants as brothers. Black Elk indicates that kinship terms are used when passing the pipe, focusing on the relatedness of those participating in this ceremony. Black Elk states that the prayer *Philámaya* 'Thanks' is said during the sweat, but Lame Deer uses it for the introduction of rocks into the lodge (180).

Lame Deer provides other unique interpretations of sweat lodge symbols. The path from the mound to the sweat entrance is the road for the spirits. The fire, constructed as Black Elk indicates, represents a tepee with the Indians inside it. The flame represents the continuity of generations. The door of the lodge faces west. Lame Deer states that although anthropologists claim it should be east, only a *heyókha* sweat faces that direction (Lame Deer in Erdoes 1972b:178).[25] Sage strewn on the floor of the lodge represents the spirits of the trees and the plants, all of which are present in the sweat lodge (179). Crawling into the sweat lodge reminds the participants that they are related to the four-leggeds (178). Whereas Black Elk uses the prayer mitakuye oyas'in to indicate that all who have finished smoking the pipe together are relatives, it is used by Lame Deer, as it is by Fools Crow, both at the end of the ceremony and during the ceremony to signal for the lodge to be opened (180, 181; Black Elk in Brown 1953:53; Mails and Chief Eagle 1979:98). Finally, Lame Deer states that one can read the future in the designs on the sweat lodge rocks, stating that one old man predicted a flood in this way and was quite right (in Erdoes 1972b:177).

Health and Healing

Fools Crow holds that, in healing sweats, the patient's relatives need to make known the patient's ailment and also request that the patient live for the next four seasons. When the patient is not present, Fools Crow conducts the ritual without participants (except, at times, singers) and relies on the spirits to find the patient through their sense of smell (clothing of the patient is put into the lodge) and tell him the proper remedy. The spirits can "doctor" a patient who is not in the sweat because they are mobile and because it is they, not the physical process of sweating, that are essential to the cure. Tobacco ties are used to attract the spirits, one spirit for each tie. The rock spirits communicate only with Fools Crow. Rocks as spirit agents, consistent with nineteenth-century accounts that focus on the power of the rocks, are especially important. Fools Crow acts as the intermediary between the patient and the rock spirits.

Lame Deer's material indicates a shift in understanding of the physio-logical process of healing in the sweat lodge. The nineteenth-century material maintained that the water passed through the body, strengthening the *ní* and eliminating intrusive disease (Walker 1917:66). Lame Deer, however, holds that the steam stops at the skin, but the "earth-power" penetrates the body and the mind, curing both physical and mental ailments (in Erdoes 1972b:181). Sword indicates that the steam was introduced into the body through breathing. Interestingly, Lame Deer does not emphasize individual spirits but rather a generalized force located in the earth. The Walker material (1975, 1980, 1982, 1983), except for the 1917 Sun Dance piece, was unpublished until after Erdoes published his Lame Deer work, so it could simply be that Erdoes was not able to access this explanation. The agency of the *ní* cannot be found in material antedating Sword's descriptions and is only mentioned afterward by a Lakota referring directly to Walker's material (see Amiotte 1982:27, 1987:86–87).

Lame Deer implicitly expands the healing role of the sweat lodge to the level of social interaction. He states: "When two enemies participate in the putting up of the little beehive-shaped lodge, their old hatreds are forgotten. Envy and jealousy disappear. The two men laugh and josh each other; they joke about the fights they have had" (in Erdoes 1972b:176). When incense is burned, "all bad feelings and thoughts are driven out," and when someone emerges from the sweat at the end of a ceremony, that person has a "new mind" (179). Although the social function of the sweat lodge is found in Brave Dog's narrative (Buechel 1978:270–71), the role of the sweat as a healer of interpersonal relationships is very important today. Humor is interpreted by Lame Deer as a vehicle for achieving social harmony.

Selo Black Crow states that the sweat removes the bad things that are done, which are then transferred to the sage.[26] Thus, he calls sage "sinner's grass." With each use of the sweat, the lodge must be cleared of this grass and the incense burned (Black Crow in Jackson 1978:95–96). Purification, in this analysis, is linked to moral rather than physical cleansing and strengthening. Nevertheless, like disease, sin is seen as an intrusive element to be extruded from the body through the agency of sweat.

In a later article on Lakota religion, Arthur Amiotte (1982:27–28) explains the physiological workings of the sweat lodge along the lines of Sword, stating that the *mniwátukala,* which he glosses as 'toxic matter', is expelled through the pores and that the *niyá* is strengthened though union with the spirit world. This is attributed to the efficacy of song and "communion utilizing the sacred pipe" (28). Amiotte here proposes a triple efficacy within the sweat lodge: the action of the steam expelling impurities from the body through the sweat, the efficacy of contact with spirits brought into the lodge, and finally a socially useful union obtained through communal song and the sharing of the sacred pipe.

Stones

The rock spirits are instrumental in Fools Crow's healing ceremony. In Black Elk's account (in Brown 1953:32), rocks used to heat the lodge are presented as symbols rather than spirits or their vehicles. They are animate objects, however, for they are capable of transferring their cleansing power through their breath (56). Again we see a reappearance, at least in the texts presented to the outside white world, of particular spirits in the lodge; the first mention after the nineteenth century was in Ruby (1955). Fools Crow's spirits, which are associated with specific stones rather than the rocks used to heat the lodge, tell him which medicines to use for the patient. Following Fools Crow, Mails calls these stone spirits *"Ivan wasico [íyą wašícu]"* (1978:95) the 'Stone White Men' (Mails and Chief Eagle 1979:49–53). They provide the information he needs to heal the patient. Fools Crow also reports that he has stones within himself that emit sparks during the ceremony. These stones speak Lakota and communicate freely with Fools Crow as the ceremony progresses.

In normal sweats the rocks are said to increase in heat well beyond the temperature acquired in the fire when they are prepared for the ceremony (Mails and Chief Eagle 1979:97). Fools Crow's greatest ceremony consists in loading cold rocks into the sweat lodge and spraying them with his special medicine, which causes them to become even hotter than rocks heated in a normal way. The performance of this feat was once witnessed by Fools Crow's friend and uncle, Black Elk (102). As Fools Crow explains, Nicholas Black Elk (of *Black Elk Speaks,* not the contemporary Black Elk from Rosebud) questioned Fools Crow about the items he used, what they meant, and where they were placed. Fools Crow justifies using new rocks for all his sweat ceremonies by saying that this practice was given to him in a vision at Bear Butte.

Contemporary Accounts: Anthropology

Structure and Ceremony

In his ethnography, *Oglala Religion,* William K. Powers reconstructs the historical ceremonial practice of the Oglalas through ethnographic texts and his own fieldwork.[27] Although Powers (1975:89) acknowledges the role of innovation in ritual practice, his text provides a single structure for the sweat lodge ceremony, based in both past ethnographic writing and contemporary observation.[28]

Powers (1975:89) states that the ritual must be conducted under the supervision of a sacred person. Although all accounts indicate that there is a specific leader in each sweat lodge ceremony, no other account makes this a universal requirement. Ringing Shield suggests (in Walker 1980:113) that an individual finds out from a shaman how to take a ritual sweat bath. George Sword states (in Walker 1980:86) that a shaman should be present when a person prepares to seek a vision but that only in a ritual sweat is this a requirement (79). As we shall see, who may run a sweat remains an important issue in contemporary practice. Walker states: "A single person may vitalize alone, but as many as can get into the lodge may vitalize together. The process of vitalizing is elaborated to the purposes for which it is done and may be a complex ceremony supervised by a Shaman, and prolonged for a day and a night or even longer" (1917:67). Thus, when a sweat is conducted for oneself or without complicated ceremony, an individual can perform the rite himself. Thus, from early on, there seems to be a distinct variety of sweat forms.

According to Powers (1975:90), the door of the lodge faces east (see Laubin and Laubin 1957:107). Mooney also states that the door faces east, as with all Indian structures (Mooney 1896:822). This agrees with Black Elk (in Brown 1953:32), but it contradicts a story told by Black Elk and recorded by Neihardt (in DeMallie 1984:393) as well as the practice of Fools Crow (Mails 1978:202), Eagle Feather (87), Catches (in part) (Amiotte 1976:31), Black Crow (Jackson 1978:96), and Brave Buffalo (Hassrick 1964:278). Sword states that the door can face any direction except north (Walker 1980:79).

Powers also states that women and men both participate in the sweat lodge ceremony, but never together. This is borne out in all the documents that are gender specific, with the exception of one reference made by Black Elk (in Brown 1953:81–82) stating that a woman was present for one of the rounds of a sweat used as part of a Sun Dance. For the structure of the ceremony itself, Powers matches what we have already seen in Black Elk's description, except that he says the pipe is smoked during the third round. Black Elk has the pipe smoked before the actual sweating phase of the ceremony begins and at the end of each round. The ritual use of the pipe represents an element of free variation within the sweat, used in different phases of the ritual according to the judgment of the leader. Powers's account could lead one to believe that the pipe is simply smoked in the third round (see also W. K. Powers 1969:131) if the reader focuses on the account as rule and misses the caveat on variation. Although this often occurs in contemporary practice (the third round is sometimes called the pipe round), there is no mention of this practice in early documentation, nor is there strict adherence to the procedure in contemporary practice.

Powers makes the important observation that, despite the ceremony's serious nature, humor is essential to the ritual. The only previous writer to note this feature was Feraca (1961:157). Today, humor is consistently present at sweats and, as we shall see, it is vital to the conduct of the ritual.

Symbolic Interpretation

In accord with Black Elk, William K. Powers refers to the mound in front of the sweat lodge as *uçí* 'grandmother'. Powers later (1975:182) states that this mound is called *pahá wakhą* 'sacred hill'. Each person prays "mitakuye oyas'in" after drinking water and after smoking the pipe in the third round.[29]

Powers (91) does not specifically say that each prayer is ended in this manner, as is the case today.

I do not propose that Powers is misrepresenting the sweat lodge in his account. All his material can be found in some written source, his own experience, or the narratives of consultants.[30] However, despite Powers's caveat that there is variation, the textual description presents a single (though composite) procedure (the one explicated). Indeed, each description given in the ethnohistorical documents can be read as its author's idea of a correct procedure for a sweat. Note that Sword says the ceremony must be done properly to be effective (Walker 1980:81, 83–84). Authors, including myself, acknowledge variation, but texts tend to codify practice and destroy (or freeze) the ongoing dialectic essential to the constitution of tradition. Furthermore, although variation faces the practitioner and the historian at every turn, participants consistently state that there is a proper way to run a sweat, and individuals today seek the "correct way" of proceeding. This debate over propriety is, as we shall see, an important factor in validating one's practice of the ritual and represents the working out on the ground of the dialectic between history and contemporary need, between continuity and change.

Contemporary Accounts: Catholic Missionaries

The 1980s provide a significant number of works on Lakota religion written or published by Jesuit missionaries.[31] The most salient shift in this modern literature is that it not only ceases to condemn Lakota traditional religious practice; it even documents missionaries' participation in these ceremonies and their appreciation of Lakota rites.

Paul Steinmetz (1980) was instrumental in combining Catholic and Lakota rituals while he served as a pastor on the Pine Ridge Reservation. His doctoral dissertation has been published, as well as several other works (1967, 1969, 1970, 1980, 1984a, 1984b). William Stolzman, a missionary on the Rosebud and Pine Ridge reservations, published two works on Lakota religion: *The Pipe and Christ* and *How to Take Part in Lakota Ceremonies.* The former work was the result of a series of dialogues carried on between Lakota medicine men and Catholic pastors on the Rosebud Reservation from 1973 to 1979. It is often impossible to be sure which explanations of the Lakota rites belong to Stolzman and which to the medicine men; nevertheless, he provides a written account of an interchange that has been going on informally since contact between the missionaries and the Lakota people. His work is important also because it makes available to a broad audience a set of data, symbols, and interpretations of the sweat lodge as well as of other ceremonies. With the exception of Black Elk, Stolzman presents the fullest textual treatment of the sweat lodge prior to this present work.

Stones

Steinmetz holds that spirit manifestations such as sparks and the presence of spirits called stonemen represent the intrusion of yuwipi practices into the sweat lodge (1980:55–56). Although the sweat lodge has historically been a place for encountering spirits, others state that yuwipi occurrences can happen in the sweat. The early ethnohistorical material is silent concerning spiritual manifestations in the forms of sparks or rattles. Nonetheless, the presence of stone spirits is frequently cited in the early rituals, and the missionaries reacted specifically to the spiritual aspects of the ceremony.

Stolzman states that the Lakotas consider rocks to be the first things to exist and believe they will also be the last. He reports that it is often said, "They have no eyes or ears yet they see and hear everything" (1986a:48).[32] Black Elk uses this prayer also, connecting the rocks with the breath they exhale as steam, which, he states, makes the participants live. Black Elk does not connect rocks with spirits. Eagle Feather repeats the same prayer and sentiments as Black Elk. Rocks can be read, telling about the past and future. So, too, in the sweat, "all historic wrongs are brought out and wiped away" (Stolzman 1986a:48). Stolzman compares the sweat lodge with the Catholic sacrament of reconciliation (confession).[33]

Structure and Ceremony

Steinmetz quotes Richard Moves Camp's explanation of why sweat lodge rituals are performed after certain ceremonies: "The main purpose is to untie the knot that connects the person with the sacred ceremony so that he can go from the sacred world to the profane again. He also has to live with the responsibility of his vision and the concluding sweat lodge allows him to purify himself for carrying that out" (Steinmetz 1980:55–56). Steinmetz assumes that this young medicine man's intuition is essentially similar to that of Eliade and Durkheim, without considering that these scholars' classification of the world into sacred and profane may have influenced Moves Camp's understanding.

Each person prays "to God and to the spirits" in the lodge (Stolzman 1986a:25). In my opinion this represents an essential compromise between the two religious systems. Early missionaries were puzzled as to whether or not there was a single God in Dakota and Lakota belief. Most felt that this concept was introduced by the missionaries themselves. Today, almost all Lakotas say that all people pray to the same single God. Lakotas who follow what is professed to be the traditional way hold that there are also spirits that act as messengers to God and helpers for individuals on earth. These spirits are intensely personal, being individuals who have died, animal spirits, natural material such as rock, and cosmological forces and designations (W. K. Powers 1975:136). The spirits, however, have taken an intermediary position between humans and God. Individuals use specific spirits as helpers and protectors, and the power of a person is sometimes measured by how many spirits are under his control. Spirits can also directly perform assigned tasks.

William Stolzman's second work, *How to Take Part in Lakota Ceremonies,* represents a further transformation in mission thought.[34] Whereas earlier the Jesuits convinced others not to participate in Lakota ceremonies, now a Jesuit speaks in an authoritative voice concerning proper ceremonial protocol. Stolzman freely participated in sweat lodges, vision quests, and other ceremonies, as have other Jesuits from the latter 1960s to the present. Stolzman also had his own sweat for a time.[35]

Stolzman dedicates an entire chapter of his work to proper use of the sweat lodge (1986b:13–30). He begins by indicating the proper attitude toward participation. One should act in faith and trust, being both humble and other-directed.[36] This theme of selflessness, performing religious acts primarily for others, dominates in contemporary Lakota practice. Nevertheless, people generally put up ceremonies for very concrete personal needs. The purpose of the sweat lodge, according to Stolzman, is to communicate with the spirits. This is done through intense sacrifice and strong prayer, although the suffering that takes place in the lodge should always be tempered. Sacrifice heightens one's sincerity and pitifulness, which appeal to the spirits.

Stolzman gives specific instructions on how to construct the sweat lodge and how the ceremony is conducted, following the general pattern we have seen in previous literature. In the beginning of his work, he makes an important statement about variation (which he well recognizes) within the ritual system:

> It is important for beginners to be prepared for one rather frequent negative attitude. Young, energetic followers of particular medicine men, and even some immature medicine men themselves, are so self-focused that they

say, "*My* ritual way is the *only* true way. *His* way is different from *my* way; therefore, he is wrong!" Such people know that it is the spirits who are the real designers of Lakota religion but forget that the spirits have the freedom to direct different people to do things in different ways. Because of the total demands of religious fervor, it is easy to become dogmatic and absolutistic about spiritual matters. Since it is the *spirits* who specify the right way, the main question to ask such a person is: "Is the other person perhaps doing everything the way the spirits directed *him* alone to do it?" [1986b:vii-viii, emphasis in original]

Stolzman highlights an important phenomenon in contemporary practice: the conviction that there is a correct procedure for conducting the sweat lodge and other rituals. He emphasizes spirits as the main operants in the lodge, a transformation from the earlier missionary attempt to purge the spirits from the lodge.

Stolzman is careful to present variation within the ritual structure itself. Thus the initial four, five, or six rocks may be designated as "especially symbolic," depending on the medicine man (Stolzman 1986b:22). People may enter nude or covered, as is proper to the moment (21). Today, tobacco ties are brought as offerings, whereas in the past (no doubt a reference to Black Elk's material), a pipe was offered with each round, being filled when the flap was closed (22).

Stolzman differentiates the sweat lodge ritual itself from preparations for the ritual. The ritual "officially begins" when the door is shut for the first time (Stolzman 1986b:24). He holds that there are essentially two types of sweat lodge ritual, one, in which the medicine man calls in *his* spirits, who manifest themselves through sparks, and the other, in which people pray to God and the spirits in general (25). This is an important distinction that does hold up, in my observation. There is, however, a third type of sweat practiced on the Pine Ridge Reservation, run by Native American Church members, in which spirits are neither summoned nor petitioned. These participants acknowledge the ancient roots of the sweat, but they understand it strictly as a prayer to Christ, the Holy Spirit, and God.

Stolzman indicates that "mitakuye oyas'in" is said after any ritual action: on entering the lodge, after praying, after drinking water, when asking for the door to be opened, when passing the pipe, or when emerging from the lodge. Although other authors from the time of Black Elk onward indicate occasional use of this prayer, Stolzman's material provides for the most extensive use of it.

Symbolic Interpretation

Stolzman (1986a:45–48) offers symbolic analyses of several aspects of the sweat lodge ceremony, providing a multiplicity of interpretations, only some of which appear in other writing. The lodge itself, for instance, represents four things: the willow hut made by warriors (as such, a place of strength and protection); a womb as a place of new life and strength; the ribbed back of a mud turtle, representing life both above and below ground and the turtle's qualities of slowness, patience, and strong-heartedness; and the universe with all of creation, rocks, trees, clouds, and earth gathered within. The mound before the sweat symbolizes the hill of vision. The pit represents the depth of the mysteries that take place there. The buffalo skull represents one who has given up his life so that the people would have nourishment. Sweat represents what is not right in a person, physical or mental. This is a notable transformation, from the concept of disease as intrusive and sweat as the medium of removal of the malady to the concept of moral inadequacy as issuing from within (and thus intrusive) and the sweat again as symbolic of removal. Stolzman cites both processes as active in the sweat. Sage, itself a medicine, represents all the medicines available on the earth and repels evil spirits. The fire represents Wakan Tanka, who dwells in the tepee of the universe. In line with Eagle Feather's explanation, the fire also indicates the themes of the prayers within the lodge.[37]

Humility is expressed by stripping oneself of clothing (except when the sweat is for both men and women). So, too, one enters the sweat on hands and knees like a little child. Stolzman (1986a:51) states that one should think only of good things in the sweat and dispel bad, hateful, or angry thoughts. This is in line with the focus on efficacy of thought presented throughout the ethnohistorical data. When entering the sweat lodge or any other ceremony, participants are invited to think about why they are there and what they seek. The cleansing power of the sweat extends to the mind, dispelling evil thoughts and healing the mind. The sweat purifies the mind, putting it into a holy state. One continually guards one's thoughts, because they have the power to effect good or evil.[38]

When the bucket of water is brought into the sweat lodge, it is touched to the rocks, representing union and fellowship (Stolzman 1986a:52). Water is a symbol of strength. Though it appears to be weak, it can wear down rocks. This image is also used by Black Elk (in Brown 1953:31). Water also makes people happy, especially when transformed to soup, according to Stolzman. It is a sign of God's blessing and a sign of the *Wakįyą,* the protector of the sweat bath. The darkness in the sweat represents helplessness, blindness, confinement, and pitifulness. One enters the darkness to represent one's ignorance, confusion, disorientation, and lack of vision. Yet, it also represents hope, since plant and human life gestate in darkness. Visions come to the weak and lowly.

Health and Healing

Stolzman is quite clear that spirits enter the lodge and effect cures. This represents a shift in comparison with the literature from the 1920s to the 1950s, which omitted the operation of specific spirits and stressed general physical and moral healing qualities attributed to the lodge itself or to the divine. Although some form of spiritual efficacy has always been attributed to the lodge, at certain times particular spirits have been either focal or peripheral to the ceremony and its textual representation. Stolzman clearly focuses upon healing as being more spiritual than physical. This is in keeping with my observations. Prayers in the sweat are directed to divine intervention in illness, eclipsing the nineteenth-century view that either the vapor itself or the power of the rocks released through vapor is efficacious in producing a cure. However, contemporary Lakotas also attribute health benefits to the physical act of sweating.

Contemporary Accounts: Personal Observations

Structure and Ceremony

In my experience the physical structure of the sweat lodge (*o'inikağapi* 'the place where individuals sweat') is semipermanent, generally located close to homes but also found at Sun Dance grounds and near vision quest sites. The lodge is usually located in a secluded draw, a short distance away from the home for the sake of privacy. When this is not possible, a screen is built around the lodge. The lodge is sometimes erected for specific events, usually of a perceived religious nature. For example, the sweat was used prior to protests concerning territorial rights as established in treaties, which are considered by the Lakotas to be sacred agreements.

Sweating is a regular event for many families and groups, carried on throughout the year. Some sweats are consistently held on certain days of the week, and one that I know of takes place during a specific phase of the moon. Sunset is often the time chosen to begin a sweat, although they can occur at any time. Life cycle events such as birthdays, becoming an adult, and the death of a relative or a friend are marked by this ceremony. More often, life crisis events such as illness, alcoholism, incarceration, familial conflict, or severe distress precipitate the ritual. During what is called the ceremonial season, from the first thunderstorms in the spring till their cessation in the fall, there is an increased frequency of sweating, to prepare for the Sun Dance or vision quest and to support and pray for others who will participate in these religious events. A sweat is also sometimes used to prepare for a lowanpi (a ceremonial prayer and healing service), a yuwipi (another type of prayer and healing service, during which the medicine man is bound by an assistant and released by the spirits), and Native American Church meetings. Finally, the sweat is sometimes simply a social event, specifically held to draw relatives and friends together and provide refreshment and relaxation in a congenial setting, although all the sweats I have attended have included some element of prayer.

Often a sweat will be delayed for hours when a particular participant or even the leader arrives later than expected. Rarely will a sweat take place earlier than announced. Sweats are unhurried. The time before one enters the sweat lodge is an essential part of the ritual; it is spent relaxing and enjoying the company of those assembled. One may sweat alone, but isolation is rarely a part of a group sweat, although people often report experiencing a comforting solitude during the ritual itself.[39] Participants rarely prepare themselves for a sweat by going off alone. Instead, they sit around talking and joking. A lot of teasing also takes place, particularly between men and their sisters-in-law and between close friends.

Ritual sweating is not confined to adherents of one particular system of belief on the reservation, even though it is universally acknowledged as "traditional" behavior and part of the "old ways." Members of Christian groups and Native American Church members, as well as individuals who consider themselves traditional believers who exclusively practice the "old ways," use this ceremony.[40] Nor is the sweat lodge restricted to Lakotas on the reservation. All lodges welcome Indians of other tribes, and most allow non-Indians to participate. A spiritual disposition rather than doctrinal allegiance is essential for participation.

Contemporary ceremonies, although generally following consistent lines of procedure, are each unique, even when run by the same individual with the same participants. The sweat is by no means secret, but matters broached during a sweat ceremony are considered confidential. One is expected not to speak of what another prayed about or revealed in that context. The ceremony often takes place among intimates—friends and relatives whom one trusts. The deeply personal nature of the sweat can be diminished when individuals who do not know each other well sweat together. Sweats conducted for mixed groups are of a different tone from those held by a specific family or group of close friends. The former tend to feature generalized prayers concerning nature, the social order, and the spirit world. The latter often concern themselves with internal struggles, personal histories, and social conflicts. There are no hard and fast rules, however, and no one would be directly corrected during a sweat for praying or speaking inappropriately.

Although there is a wide variation in ceremonial procedure and verbal content depending upon the leader, the reasons for having the sweat and the configuration of the participants, the construction of the sweat lodge and the physical ritual associated with this structure are, in my observation, strikingly consistent. This indicates the importance of accurate historical reproduction of the sweat as part of the dialectic that the Lakotas use to create tradition.

The lodge structure itself is always circular and dome-shaped with a single entrance facing one of the cardinal directions (today usually west, but sometimes east). The frame of the lodge is always made of pliable saplings, often willow but sometimes cherry. The saplings, bent toward the center and tied together at the top in various patterns, are of a predetermined but variable number, ideally sixteen. The frame is always covered with a combination of available materials such as tarps, blankets, or black sheet plastic, to make it as light- and airtight as possible. A circular pit is always dug in the center of the lodge to hold the hot rocks that will be brought into the lodge for the ceremony. The earth from the pit is generally piled a short distance from the door to form an altar. Most sweat lodges have some form of altar, always round and made of earth, in front of the door.[41] A path from this altar to the lodge entrance is often demarcated. The floor of the sweat lodge is covered with carpet pieces or sage, or both, which make for a cleaner and more comfortable seating area. A fire pit, in which rocks will be heated, is always constructed outside the lodge. Generally, the fire pit is on a line with the altar and the door and some distance away from both of those structures.[42] Rocks are always the medium used to transfer the heat from the pit to the lodge. Water, normally clear but sometimes infused with herbs, is always used in the sweat and is always poured on the rocks to create the steam.

The decoration of the altar in front of the lodge entrance provides for the greatest structural variation. The earth mound is sometimes ringed with decorative stones or fragments of rocks used in prior sweats. Some altars have one or more buffalo skulls or skulls of different animals on them, facing various directions. At times the altar is covered with sage and sage is stuffed into the openings of the skull(s). Other altars have single erect poles of cherry wood, three to six feet high, on which cloth, tobacco, and sometimes flesh offerings are tied, singly or in combination. Short red sticks with tobacco ties [*chạlí waphákta*] (squares of cloth holding pinches of tobacco) on the ends sometimes encircle the altar or mark the four cardinal directions. Some altars also have pipe racks made of two forked upright sticks with a bar across them. Personal symbols, such as sticks decorated with abalone shells, medicine wheels, and eagle feathers, are sometimes erected by participants on the altar for the duration of the sweat. These decorated sticks, called *sagyé*—'canes or staffs'—are generally used in an individual's vision quest or given as special gifts to individuals. Rattles, fans, medicine, herbs to be used as incense, and pipes are also sometimes placed on the altar prior to use in the sweat.

The ritual that takes place within the lodge is also consistent, in broad pattern. The basic form consists of closing the door of the lodge, pouring water on the hot rocks, praying, singing, and then opening the door. This sequence is repeated a set number of times, four being the ideal in most circumstances. Songs are always sung, always in Lakota. The ideal is also to pray in Lakota, but if an individual does not speak that language, he or she will frame prayers with Lakota, generally beginning with Wakan Tanka (generally translated today as 'Great Spirit' or 'God'), Tunkashila 'Grandfather', or *Até* Wakan Tanka 'Father, Great Spirit', an invocation to the divine, and terminating with "mitakuye oyas'in" 'for all my relations', the standard ending of any prayer used in what is considered a traditional setting.

Actions that may be included or that, if normally included informally, may be carried out in a formal manner are purifying the lodge; smudging oneself and certain objects to be used in the sweat, such as drums and rattles; filling a pipe outside the lodge before beginning the actual sweating; bringing in the stones in a ceremonial manner—touching them with a pipe, incensing them, and arranging them in a particular pattern in the pit according to the cardinal directions, the nadir, and the zenith;[43] entering the lodge; preparing or smoking the pipe(s); bringing water into the sweat and passing it around the circle; drinking water; blessing or purifying certain items, such as medicines or ritual paraphernalia; exiting the lodge; shaking hands at the conclusion of the ritual once everyone has emerged from the lodge; praying before a meal after the sweat; giving a name; and sometimes adopting an individual.

The ceremony itself is highly charged. Heat and cold, light and darkness, sound and silence, laughter and tears—all these make the ritual vivid. In terms of participation, the ritual is highly inclusive: the leader delegates tasks such as preparing the fire and the lodge and performing certain ritual actions in the sweat so that all participants perform some task. By and large, everyone is invited to pray and sing within the lodge, and individuals can speak whenever the leader deems it appropriate. Some individuals may bring along a personal pipe to the ceremony. Everyone shares in smoking the pipes, either within or outside the lodge. The physical structure of the lodge, generally no more than ten feet in diameter, places people in close physical proximity. The physical and emotional rigor of the experience focus one's attention on the present and on one's place within the ceremony. As a Lakota friend expressed it, "You cannot not pray and not pay attention in there. It's the only way you make it through."

The sweat is a ceremony through which some participants perceive themselves returning to the past, to a state of original harmony, when the Lakotas were believed to have lived without care or conflict, before the coming of the whites.[44] This return is not considered possible without a harmonious union within the sweat among its participants, no matter how ephemeral that harmony might be in the face of day-to-day conflicts or deep-seated animosities.

Health and Healing

In my field experience, it was clear that healing is considered a vital function of sweats today. In fact, healing is more prominent than purification, although purification and healing are sometimes seen as a single phenomenon. Both states, illness and impurity, represent disorder—the sweat restores order in both cases. It is clear, however, that sweating before other ceremonies, such as the vision quest, is a preparation for an ensuing ordeal. Sweats held apart from other rituals generally focus on healing, whether physical or psychic, individual or communal. Healing is also not restricted to what individuals perceive as physical ailments. People will use the sweat seeking simple peace of mind, renewal of friendships, or a resolution to a difficult problem.

The sweat itself is seen as a place to suffer, to struggle through the difficult ceremony. Prayers and pain not only attract the attention of the spirits, making a person worthy of spiritual intervention, but they are iconic reenactments, verbal and physical, of an existential condition of alienation, pain, and suffering. Healing in the lodge today, as in the past, is directed to physical maladies. The focus has also expanded, as demonstrated in the literature from the 1970s onward, to include social malaise.

It is essential to note that the sweat lodge ceremony is not the only locus of curing power. Individual and communal healing and health are part of all contemporary ceremonies, such as yuwipi, lowanpi, and the Sun Dance. People also use the public health system, recovery programs, local support groups, and off-reservation medical facilities. One individual who regularly participates in sweats expressed his doubts over the total power of this ritual by itself over alcoholism: "Some use ceremonies as an avoidance technique and unless they really confront alcoholism and work a 12 step program, they will not begin recovery." On the other hand, certain individuals report miraculous cures of alcoholism using the sweat alone. In one case, an individual reported that the spirits had given him permission to drink, although most Lakotas would look askance at this claim because Lakota ceremonial practice in general is strongly associated with abstinence and sobriety.

Individuals who are linked closely with AA groups and have been through treatment programs generally hold that recovery is an ongoing process and that though the sweat can help someone in the process, there is no substitute for meetings and following the AA principles:

> In AA, you talk about drunkenness. Guys who go to sweat, they develop a grandiose attitude that they have a direct pipeline to God. They get the idea that they walk alone with God. Lots of that is temporary. They are self-deluded rather than having found the answer. Then it appears that it's an emotional sobriety, they can stay sober on emotions for a while or they can stay sober on a religious high. I believe you can. I have seen some people sober up through these religious rituals. You can't measure their intentions. Most guys Sun Dance, have a pipe, sweat, but they don't integrate it in their way of life.

Although that Lakota narrator does not question the power of the sweat, he believes that to achieve what he considers full recovery, one must "work a program." The sweat for such people is part of an ongoing process of sobriety rather than an immediate cure. Here, the community of sufferers and supporters takes precedence over the immediate effect of the sweat; the sweat, like AA meetings, becomes a focus for the process. On the other hand, some believe alcoholism can be removed through the action of the sweat. This view maintains the disease conception of alcoholism but diverges from AA doctrine in seeing the disease as curable. People often pray for those who suffer from alcoholism (sometimes specific people, sometimes a generalized group) as well as for help with their own struggles. In either case the solidarity of the group is important in effecting the desired end, whether it is a definitive or an ongoing cure.[45]

In the contemporary sweat lodge, different people attribute healing to a variety of sources: intercession of the spirits with God, the power and recommendations of the spirits themselves, the power of Tunkashila or Wakan Tanka, the powers of the rocks (themselves seen as spirits or grandfathers) or the steam, or the physical effects of the lodge itself. Members of the Native American Church attribute ultimate healing power to Christ or to peyote or to a combination of the two. One member of the church who uses the sweat lodge stated: "No medicine man will save your soul. They could cure disease but not cancer, diabetes, alcoholism. Christ saved me from all them. That's why I lived this far."

There is no consensus concerning the source of efficacy within the lodge. In fact, this is not an overt concern among contemporary practitioners and participants. The focus is on the experience provided by the sweat itself and the resultant change in the lives and situations of the individuals.

Another factor involved with healing associated with the lodge is the Oglala Lakotas' contemporary concept of faith. Most practitioners insist that it is the individual's faith that allows for the cure.[46] The precise details of that belief, whether it is invested in God, the spirits, Tunkashila, Wakan Tanka, on one's "higher power" (an Alcoholics Anonymous designation more and more frequently employed in the lodge), the physiological effects of the heat or one's "inner power" are rarely voiced. Individuals present themselves at a lodge because they wish to pray or be cured. Social solidarity is more essential than orthodoxy, and emotional support of the individual takes precedence over agreement with his or her belief system. Even when people clearly have differences of beliefs, no reference is made to this fact. Faith lies in expectation of results, not in adherence to a specific doctrine. At a Sun Dance an elderly Lakota Sun Dance leader said that it did not matter whether all the procedures in the ritual were done incorrectly. Clearly, this allows for variability in the ceremony and is an attitude frequently held by many Lakotas. Note, however, that each practitioner has limits as to what is acceptable, so this is not simply free variation. Both poles of the dialectic must be considered in order to understand the constitution of tradition. It is commonly held that so long as the participants believe that Tunkashila will bless them, then it will be so and their prayers will be answered.[47] Another leader stated that the participants must believe that they are already cured when entering the sweat lodge. Faith is used here not as assent to a body of doctrines but an assurance that the ritual is at least potentially effective and that some undesignated power is capable of effecting a cure.

Accounts of individual practice are valuable, indicating both continuity and innovation in the use and interpretation of the sweat lodge. What early missionaries viewed as corrupt inconsistencies in religious practice, the medicine men in these works see as inspired by individual visions and particular teachers. So, too, in the dialectical process the assembly of individuals gathered around specific purposes determines the structure of the sweats as much as historic ritual procedures do. Thus, a sweat for a Sun Dance is different from one for a healing service, without losing the basic character of the sweat.

Shifts can be observed in this era in the type of healing that takes place in the sweat lodge. There is an expansion from personal and physical to communal and moral conceptualizations of healing in the sweat. At the same time, the sweat remains a place for physical cures for individuals. Healing is extended to new maladies, such as drug addiction, alcoholism, and AIDS.

The influence of the Black Elk texts is evident in this material. Some of that is acknowledged, as in the case of the Laubins' work. In other cases it is evident that authors (and perhaps their collaborators) amplified their "as told to" material, using other textual material. Both in texts and in practice, the past has such a compelling draw as authentic that the more it is incorporated, even without knowledge of consultants who have had their own narratives "amplified," the more these works are viewed as authentic.

I cannot reliably separate genuine narration from interpolation in these texts. Thus, I present each text "as is"; for that, by and large, is how it affects its reading audience. There is a clear trend by some non-Lakota authors to strictly equate authentic with the past in looking at the sweat lodge and to miss or dismiss the other pole of the dialectic as a contemporary aberration. As in the turn-of-the-century material, most researchers look to past performance and echoes of the past in the present rather than accepting simple contemporary performance as authentic (and interesting) in itself, without conflating one with the other. Some ritual performances are thus rejected for others that seem more authentic. Past texts are also conflated with contemporary actors and actions without trying to separate one from the other to attempt to construct an authoritative text.

We see several important new trends established in contemporary publications on the Lakotas. For instance, in Steinmetz's and Stolzman's works, not only has one of the major Christian churches desisted from actively eradicating traditional religion, but leaders of some churches have both participated in

Lakota ceremonies and incorporated Lakota practice into their own ritual system. In addition we see an increase in publications on this and other Lakota rituals, not so much to preserve the legacy of "vanishing races" and forsaken practices (as in the works of Walker, Curtis, and Neihardt), but as guides for contemporary practice. The source of authority has expanded also from anthropological to popular accounts, from analysis to re-creation of ritual forms. Symbolic interpretation of ritual items continues, with readily available texts a source of diffusion for such data. Although those guides are controversial in some circles, they have important ramifications for the process of cultural continuity and innovation as well as for diffusion of the sweat lodge beyond the reservation.

Keeping in mind that we are working only with available texts, which do not entirely represent actual Lakota practice, we can make some tentative generalizations about historical trends. We have seen that the sweat, as a structured set of procedures, has retained a fundamental consistency throughout its 316 years of recorded history. Although the structure remains the same, there are wide variations in the symbolism and in interpretations of the symbolism, both over time and within a single period when enough comparative material is available. Symbolic focus has shifted (at least in how consultants present their knowledge to interested outsiders) from spirits associated with rocks to healing associated with the salutary effect of the sweat, to the one God associated with direct aid to the pitiful petitioner, to spirits associated with messengers providing aid by invoking God or directly intervening in situations at the call of particular leaders. Although these different foci do not necessarily reflect actual practice on the reservation itself, but rather changes in the content of the texts presented by various Lakota consultants, which texts we have examined in these two chapters, they indicate a specific public trend—first, to despiritualize the ritual in the face of missionary opposition, then to repopulate the lodge with spirits, while acknowledging the primacy of the single God whom, according to current views on the reservation, the Lakotas always venerated. Finally, there is a tendency to incorporate the expanding world of the Lakotas in the sweat. The occurrences in the world around the sweat are always the proper subject of prayer and petition; thus, as the world of the Lakotas changes, so does the focus of their prayers. As the Lakotas encountered new and different people, the symbols within the sweat became more universal. This incorporationist tendency is extended to include non-Lakota persons to expand the Lakota system of social alliance and solidarity. Just as information from the outside world is incorporated into the cognitive construction of the sweat ceremony through prayers and symbols, so, too, individuals encountered in the outside world can be incorporated into the Lakota social world through participation in the sweat.

There is a broad continuity in the purposes of the sweat historically: healing, preparation for other rituals, and life crisis situations. But the sweat has also been adapted to new situations, such as the Ghost Dance movement and modern militancy. The interpretation and mobilization of symbols shows a further tendency to incorporate the lived world of the Lakotas into this ceremony. Current emphases on expurgation of sin, restoring dysfunctional families, and moral cleansing represent adaptation to contemporary social and religious realities and interpretations.

Trait analysis is not itself the key to understanding the sweat lodge. The flexibility of these features, however, provides important clues for understanding the continuing importance of ritual on the reservation and the dynamic of the dialectic used in creating tradition. The sweat lodge is broadly adaptable. Its use by those seeking to find or affirm their Indian identity is possible precisely because of this openness. So, too, Christian Indians once alienated from traditional practice can participate in this ritual structure but retain their adopted belief system. The ritual itself has no doctrinal prerequisites. The essential requirement at a contemporary sweat is that one be "comfortable" at the ceremony so that a certain harmony can be achieved. This norm precludes debate in the public forum over ritual propriety or doctrinal correctness. The sweat ceremony can also integrate outsiders into the Lakota kinship structure as Lakotas welcome them to the sweat and as they endure its rigors together.

The symbols employed in the sweat lodge say something about the world while trying to alter that reality through reestablishing a harmonious universe—the world of the Lakotas before contact. Lakotas will often state that religion is the last thing they have left, everything else having been taken by whites. Flexibility both in the structure of the ritual and, as we shall see, in the incorporation of heterogeneous groupings within the ritual, has allowed the sweat lodge to continue and indeed to increase in popularity in the contemporary era. Thus, the dialectic retains two separate and equally important poles—the past, which links the Lakotas to their ancestral ways and preserves a sense of cultural ownership of at least part of the world, and the present, which allows them to survive and adapt in a changing world. Neither pole is sufficient without the other.

Nevertheless, despite the adaptability of the sweat lodge, tensions often arise over its performance. There remains the idea, which is consistent in the literature, that there is a correct way to conduct the ritual. What is correct is a result of a valid operation of the dialectic, not simply a reapprehension of the past. This struggle for harmony in the face of local factionalism and discord contributes to the shaping of the social configuration for sweat lodge participation. With an increasing consensus that religion is the last thing the Lakotas have left, there are more and more movements to regulate and restrict ceremonial access in order to protect this resource.[48] Although the lodge structure itself and the basic ritual expressions of opening and closing the door, pouring water, and sweating with prayer and song, which were first noted by Hennepin in 1680, remain consistent, the motivations and purposes of the ceremony continue to change as the Lakotas struggle to transform themselves and the world around them.

History is joined to contemporary exigencies in a dialectical process to create tradition ever anew. Tradition is neither *creatio ex nihilo,* nor is it an exact replication of the past. It is the debate over the valid combination of these poles by valid interpreters that sparks the variation and core consistency of the sweat lodge ceremony today. The following chapters further explore the construction and consequences of this dialectic.

3

Continuity and Change in the Sweat Lodge

Tradition

Having examined the written accounts of the sweat lodge of the past, we can now consider how the ritual has changed and persisted. Historical analysis is important for understanding contemporary practice, because practitioners of the sweat lodge ritual view and categorize their actions as faithful to past practice. Although no one with whom I have worked would claim isomorphism with the rites of the past, fidelity to perceived tradition is invoked by many to authenticate their practice. The Lakotas' use of their understanding of the past is essential for understanding contemporary ritual in which past and present, continuity and innovation, precedence and practicality are brought together each time a sweat is performed. Even though no Lakota disputes the fact that the sweat has changed, there is a concomitant assumption that the sweat lodge represents a continuous line of practice from precontact times.

In light of the value placed on tradition in Lakota discourse and the way behavior is validated by the use of the word, it is important to look at tradition from two sides, that of Western social science and that of local understanding. These issues impinge directly on the ritual under examination, for the sweat is presented and evaluated by current practitioners and in anthropological analysis as falling under the category of traditional.

The word *wichóȟ'ą* 'tradition' is used in several ways by the Lakotas on the reservation. The first meaning nearly matches the English definition of the word; it implies the handing on of a body of material from the past. The second, more analogous to custom or habit (Buechel 1970:582), refers to actions in the present that represent generalized repetitive behavior. Finally, the English word *traditional* is used to mean "proper, correct, or accurate" and can imply one or both of the two Lakota meanings.

Actions or behaviors consistently carried out by a wide variety of Lakotas in the present qualify as traditional. After a sweat in which I participated, someone showed up with a cooler full of pop. The leader took one and announced, straight-faced, that this was the traditional drink of the Lakota. When I laughed, he said with a grin, "Well, when have you been at a ceremony where they didn't have pop to drink?" Traditional is, in all cases, synonymous with appropriate and valid, which shows the importance of both dialectical elements, past and present, in its construction.

Authors writing about Lakota ritual also use the word *traditional* in a variety of senses. Stolzman's work is a good example. He states that there are "traditional times" for the sweat bath: "In the order of preference: sunset, before sunrise, at noon, at a time of need, and at any appropriate time," referring to a set pattern of behavioral preferences (1986b:18). He holds that it is the "tradition" of some people to lay the initial rocks brought into the sweat according to the four cardinal directions. Here he uses tradition not in the singular sense of how it was done in the past but rather according to linear transmission of practice. When he says that it is "traditional" to sing several songs during a sweat bath, but this need not be done (1986a:55), he uses tradition in the sense of "proper," fitting in with past performance and accepted variation. The word *traditional* is also used as an adjective to describe a usual form of performance. Thus, the leader gives an introduction to the sweat lodge for those assembled, which is "very brief and done in a rather traditional way" (Stolzman 1986a:53).

There has been much ink spilled over the question of tradition and reinvention of culture.[1] According to Edward Shils, "In its barest, most elementary sense . . . it is anything which is transmitted or handed down from the past to the present" (1981:12). His understanding of tradition has been challenged by Handler and Linnekin. Shils acknowledges that unchanging folk societies never existed and insists that tradition changes (19), but Handler and Linnekin (1984:274–75) fault Shils for retaining the notion that tradition consists of an unchanging core. Handler and Linnekin, in examining tradition and innovation, maintain that tradition represents a symbolic construct, an ongoing interpretation of the past in light of the present (274). According to them, social science and common sense incorrectly treat tradition as an objective natural reality, a core of teachings handed down from the past to the present (275). In pressing their view of tradition as interpretive rather than historical, they state that

> traditions are neither genuine nor spurious, for if genuine tradition refers to the pristine and immutable heritage of the past, then all genuine traditions are spurious. But if, as we have argued, tradition is always defined in the present, then all spurious traditions are genuine. Genuine and spurious—terms that have been used to distinguish objective reality from hocus-pocus—are inappropriate when applied to social phenomena, which never exist apart from our interpretations of them. [288]

Nevertheless, they insist that traditions that are naively inherited are "genuinely traditional" (276), whereas those that are self-consciously created, and therefore recontextualized, are spurious (280). By their very definition of tradition, however, there cannot be a tradition that is not self-conscious since, ultimately, tradition is always in the eye of the beholder.

Handler and Linnekin (1984:281) define pristine tradition as that which was unreflectively handed down in unchanging form. Yet, there can be no tradition or culture (or anything else for that matter, according to their view of culture) without reflection and therefore consciousness of some kind. Contradicting their own relativistic stance, they lace into their work such statements as "In many ways, of course, Keanea's traditionality is superficial" (283). They also mention that the kava ceremony was never practiced in Hawaii, yet it was used as a recently revived "traditional" (implying its ultimate spuriousness) ceremony (283). What Handler and Linnekin omit in their analysis is history. For them, tradition is a matter of free interpretation used by individuals with specific interests in the present. Clearly, tradition is negotiated in the present, as demonstrated by currently observable Lakota customs. This is consciously admitted by the Lakotas themselves. Deviance from tradition (or adaptation of tradition) is often explained by practitioners as due to the fact that the Lakotas must now live on the reservation, having been removed from their natural surroundings.

Nevertheless, there is an objective guide, albeit subjectively interpreted, and that is history, recorded in texts or the memories of individuals. Handler and Linnekin state that "historically, Kahoolawe's claim to sacredness is tenuous" (1984:283) (Kahoolawe is an island in Hawaii), but despite their use of history as a criterion for their assertion, they insist that truth claims are relative. They also fail to examine native discussion of tradition. Among the Lakotas there are many voices of tradition, and there are many disagreements over what may properly be designated as traditional. Tradition, like culture itself, is not a homogeneous phenomenon. In the case of the sweat lodge, we are dealing with traditions (plural, not singular) in a very heterogeneous context. Nevertheless, as seen in chapters 1 and 2, there is an enduring historical core of the sweat ceremony, one that affects the dialectical construction of tradition.

Although it is evident both from texts and from practitioners that traditional practice is not a strict and slavish duplication of the past, it is helpful to add another anthropological definition of tradition, one that focuses on contemporary practice. Morris Foster, in discussing the Comanches and using Shils's definition of tradition (1981), states: "The pattern of repeated interaction constitutes the tradition in each community. The modes of subsistence, the social units, the cultural frameworks, even the languages used in any one period are instrumental rather than fundamental to this pattern of tradition" (Foster 1991: 172–73). This returns us to the Lakota definition of tradition as that which is constituted by communal action. I asked an elderly Lakota speaker how to say "traditional" in Lakota, and she was thoroughly puzzled. She said, "We never talked about that in the past," and then volunteered that you could say *Lakhóta ų́* 'do things Indian way' or *líla Lakhóta* 'very Indian'. Thus, contemporary behavior is the ultimate criteria for tradition, albeit behavior that is linked to and evaluated by perceptions of the past.

Legitimacy

The contention that ceremonies went underground during the era of government and missionary prohibition and interference provides a key link for continuity with the ceremonial practice of the past. That underground movement is clear both in the history of the reservation and in the texts we have analyzed where descriptions of such elements as spirits in the lodge "went underground" only to reappear in the 1970s. Secrecy allows for the broad development of what might be called ethnognosticism, which holds that when cultural information was transmitted to outsiders (particularly anthropologists), it was deliberately altered in order to protect the true tradition. Thus, the true past is known only to certain individuals (or distributed among a few individuals who must meet together to reconstruct the whole). Tradition, in this instance, is preserved in secret knowledge, held to be transmitted within family lines. Since there are several groups who propose authentic but conflicting narratives, there has arisen contention among ethnognostics—the true knowers—who claim access to differing recondite traditions. Some Lakotas, not privileged with this secret knowledge, reject this mode of representation as illegitimate.

Like the Jewish and Christian gnosticism that arose, in part, in response to Roman domination around the beginning of the common era (or at least became evident in texts at that time), Lakota ethnognosticism is found both within and outside of Lakota groups. As an internal strategy, it is used to defend its own construction of tradition against the truth claims of outside groups and even competing groups internal to the system. As an external strategy, New Age individuals claim access to legitimate practice from traveling medicine men, from the reading of texts, or from insights gleaned from their own spiritual experiences or former lives as Indians.

Ethnognosticism has the potential to create an internal Lakota canon of orthodox beliefs and rituals to protect itself against the spurious claims of outsiders. Even though individuals may talk about how the tribal council, federations of medicine men, or even the federal government under the Indian Religious Freedoms Act should protect Lakota belief and practice, no unified movement has yet arisen to create a definitive formulation of tradition or rules for ceremonial behavior. Clearly, this would radically alter the dynamic nature of Lakota ceremonial production.

Tradition draws on the past and the present to create acceptable forms of ritual behavior. Argument or dispute arises over who may bring together the two poles of this dialectic and what proportion of each element represents an acceptable mixture. There is here a dual issue of authority and validity of practice. When contention arises over practice, participants split the poles of the dialectic. They may assert a right to adapt as appropriate, they may claim access to the true tradition, or they may reproportion the importance of the two poles of the dialectic. Thus, some Lakotas will say that certain sweats are "more traditional" than others.

Change and variation are just as evident as continuity, both in the ethnohistorical and the contemporary representations of the sweat ceremony. Innovations are incorporated into ceremonial practice through visions and dreams of particular individuals. By appealing to visions, one renounces the onerous role of innovator, placing the source of change in the realm of the spiritual. The religious system of the Oglala Lakotas, as recorded by Walker (1980:131–32), expressly balanced innovation and tradition. When someone went out to seek a vision, that vision had to be brought before older men in

order to validate and interpret the insights gained by the seeker. In Lakota ceremonial structure, no single group has ever gained a monopoly on this authority,
although the situation is changing as some Lakotas become more resistant to the
diffusion of their ritual practice to non-Lakotas, particularly whites.

Another legitimating mechanism in Lakota ceremonial practice is the
appeal to direct access to the past through kinship ("this is how my grandfather
or some other relative did the ceremony") or through pedagogy ("this is how I
was taught by a certain spiritual leader"). Rarely will contemporary Lakotas
appeal to written literature as the source for their practice, despite the fact that
some individuals acknowledge an initial entrance to Lakota practice through
such works. There is no rigorous ownership of Lakota ceremony, as one might
find among the Crows or certain Missouri River tribes. Thus, there is no clear
and consistent source for validation of leadership and participation, making the
question of legitimacy and who may legitimately operate these ceremonies even
more thorny. Some people I worked with stated that only those who were taught
the proper ceremonies and knew the songs could conduct a sweat lodge. Others
claimed that one must perform a vision quest and a Sun Dance before being able
to lead a sweat lodge ceremony. One individual insisted that anyone could lead
a sweat. Most practitioners agreed that anyone who was sincere could participate. Few would exclude whites who were intimate friends, but at the same
time most would exclude whites as a class of people.

When a ritual is not performed according to perceived norms, individuals
conducting the ritual and participating in it are said to be *škátapi* 'they are
playing around'. A correctly performed ceremony is referred to as a *wó'echu*
('doings', in reservation English). Not just anyone may manipulate the poles of
the dialectic to create a generally acceptable form of tradition, nor does every
resultant form of tradition necessarily achieve legitimacy.

Authority

It is important to discuss the question of authority in relation to the creation of
tradition and the enacting of proper sweat lodge ceremonies. The most
important authorities are, of course, the Lakotas themselves. As we have seen,
they do not present a homogeneous viewpoint on matters religious. Contesting
for authority, however, are also historical texts, accounts of contemporary practice written by anthropologists, missionary accounts (and at times missionaries
themselves), as well as, increasingly, New Age practitioners and other prac-

titioners who are not Lakotas and may not be Indian.

Although there are legitimating mechanisms for both continuity and change in Lakota culture, those mechanisms are brought into play, as indeed is the very dialectic on which Lakota ritual is based, by individuals and groups of individuals. As a band society, the Lakotas themselves never have established a single defined body of doctrine and belief, nor have they established single lines of ritual authority. This is due to the very nature of Lakota practice, which is a combination of inspiration and tradition:

> The Lakota religion was not embodied in long series of memorized prayer texts like the Pawnee, Omaha, or Blackfeet, and even the details of ritual behavior varied from ceremony to ceremony. What was esoteric knowledge was not standardized as it was in many other tribes, but was individual. Each man possessed certain types of esoteric knowledge based on his own visions and sacred experiences. These might or might not be shared with other shamans in the sweat lodge. [DeMallie and Jahner 1980:25–26]

This phenomenon is in sharp contrast to what is found in Euramerican culture, particularly the religious culture represented by Catholic and Protestant missionaries. As we have seen, one of the chief criticisms the missionaries held over Santee Dakota and Lakota religion was that the native religion did not have a consistent, systematic formulation. Ironically, the principal systematizers of Lakota thought as presented to the outside world in writing—anthropologists and missionaries—have generally been themselves outsiders.

Authority of Texts

The documents examined in chapters 1 and 2 were created by the authors from observation; conversations; past observations reported by other authors; or participation in ceremonies, preserved in written form. Those texts, which make various claims concerning the representation of past or contemporary practice, influence an ongoing Lakota system of practice. Systematization and theoretical formulation of ceremonies, essential to both anthropologists and missionaries, tended to solidify and codify a rather fluid native system. Particular instances of performance have the potential to become paradigmatic simply because they were put in writing. This is particularly true for potential practitioners outside the Lakota social system, whose primary access to Lakota ritual is through texts. At a Sun Dance two young men from France informed me that its performance was quite incorrect. I asked them how they knew this, and they immediately cited Walker's Sun Dance text! Texts have not taken on this level of importance for the Lakotas themselves, but the potential remains.

Walker's texts, as well as William K. Powers's *Oglala Religion,* are used in college courses on Lakota culture that are offered on the reservations, and excerpts from Walker's material were used at the Catholic and other high schools on the reservation beginning in 1971. Individuals from off the reservation have also been very strongly influenced by this corpus of material. These works are often viewed as "catechisms," particularly the Black Elk texts.[2] This adds a further pressure from the outside to conform to an externally perceived image. One sweat lodge leader told me how a couple from Florida had memorized the final prayer in *Black Elk Speaks* to be recited at their sweat lodge ceremony. Both the couple and the sweat lodge leader were unaware that this prayer was composed by Neihardt and not Black Elk. Much of this material is also epitomized in New Age renditions of Indian religion that are packaged and marketed in books, tarot cards,[3] and seminars. Classic anthropological texts and New Age "how to" books are found side by side in the Indian spirituality section of New Age bookstores and are used as guides to authentic practice.

The use of textualized material is problematic for local practitioners. In some circles such renditions are readily assimilated into current ceremonial practice. On the other hand, written materials concerning the sweat lodge and other ceremonies are sometimes seen on the reservation as stolen goods and sacrilegious treatments. One consultant said of Stolzman's *How to Take Part in Lakota Ceremonies:* "It's all there but he hasn't gotten it right." Ethnognostics reject the entire corpus of ethnographic data, claiming that the old people consistently lied to the anthropologists and the missionaries as well as to certain contemporary practitioners to protect their knowledge. The true recondite teachings were subsequently handed down to only certain individuals, so only these individuals have a true understanding of Lakota ceremony.[4] One Lakota explained to me that Walker's consultants deliberately lied to him about Oglala culture in order to protect the true beliefs of the nation. Ethnognosticism rejects the body of recorded literature, claiming that a true, pure, unbroken tradition exists. The inherent assumption is also that there is a single tradition. The veracity of these recondite teachings is a point of contention on the reservation, where groups and individuals sometimes argue over both who has the accurate tradition and who represents it faithfully. In my opinion ethnognosticism is a symbolic defense against what is perceived as the alienation of cultural property through anthropological and missionary works as well as New Age renditions of Indian spirituality. It also allows for broad cultural creativity, having a built-in form of legitimation (secret transmission), which is more difficult to refute than public explication. As a form of dialectic, ethnognosticism claims sole authority in access to the past, shifting the debate of legitimacy to who actually has access to this legitimate knowledge.

I have seen some practitioners make use of ethnographic texts and even make direct reference to them. One consultant invoked the Walker material several times during one sweat to validate some of his practices as the "real and true" way it used to be. It is impossible to quantify the impact of printed material, but its influence is significant both in the use of the material and in the opposition to its use (or even to its very existence). Some practitioners hold that only those ceremonial instructions and songs received directly through dreams or visions or instructions from a legitimate elder have power and are legitimate. Others self-consciously state that reading books was, for them, an essential and valid entry into Lakota practice. Several consultants explained to me that they had developed their "new consciousness" (as one described it, "I'm a born-again Indian") through the reading of various texts. Consistently, however, they stated that they had moved from this initial textual encounter to learning through oral transmission, spiritual experience, and participation in rituals.

The fact that documentary representations of Lakota practice have an influence on Lakota belief has been consistently recognized (DeMallie 1984; Medicine 1987; W. K. Powers 1990a). The analytical problem for anthropologists is how to separate the direct oral tradition from the "reassimilated" textual tradition in contemporary practice. In addition there is the conundrum of popular writers like Mails and Erdoes who put ethnographic words into the mouths of their narrators. Powers (1975:xv) holds that he can discover the true Oglala religion practiced by the true Oglalas.[5] Nevertheless, this true representation is itself a construct based on the dialectical construction of tradition. Anthropology itself has been crucial in creating and legitimating cultural practice, but fiction, film, art, the New Age movement, and the American popular imagination and culture must be acknowledged as other factors contributing to the Lakotas' own opinions of what is truly valid.[6]

Internal Authority

Today, as in the past, no one individual or group is universally accepted by the Lakota population as final arbiter of legitimate tradition. In fact, the individuals with whom I worked were cautious about presenting their understanding of the sweat ceremony on their personal authority. They generally couched their explanations of the sweat lodge in terms like, "This is how I understand it" or "This is how I was taught." At large gatherings of outsiders, however, I often heard cultural discourse framed with claims like "the Lakota really believe," "we always . . ." or "in the old days everyone . . ." Thus, on the interpersonal level, culture is presented as individualized, bounded and contingent, but on the level of group discourse (especially with the uninitiated) some individuals are quick to speak in universals, generalities, and necessities. A telling joke concerning authority is told on the reservation: "An Indian on Pine Ridge is just another Indian. If he goes off to Nebraska he portrays himself as a local leader. If he makes it to New York, he is a chief. If he gets to Europe, he immediately becomes a shaman."[7]

Anthropological Authority

Within the reservation there is a continual vying for authority, with frequent accusations that individuals are exploiting positions of recognized authority. Even so, many individuals claim civil or religious authority. What is interesting is that individuals from outside the group, particularly white Americans and Europeans, are increasingly enlisted to bolster such claims to authority. Anthropologists and missionaries are also enlisted in this process. My own status as a Catholic priest was sometimes cited by individuals within the lodge as a sign of the authenticity of their spiritual practice. As one friend laughingly said to me during a ceremony, "You make me look good." This is a reciprocal relationship, for without these individuals my own work would not "look" very good.

At one sweat I attended, the leader drew a circle on the sand in front of the door of the sweat lodge during one of the openings. After completing the diagram, he explained that the spiritual energy used by the Lakotas was identical to that of the Egyptians, in that they both went in a clockwise manner. The door was then shut and the sweat continued. On one level I reacted emotionally to the statement, doubting the appropriateness of such a comparison, its historical validity and veracity, and even the aptness of the conceptualization of the sweat as energy, let alone "clockwise energy." On the other hand, the participants at the lodge, a mix of Indians and whites, merely nodded assent as the statement was made. I was caught between the ethnographic fact of this innovative mode of explanation and the disquiet over what I judged as incongruous. Almost reflexively, I evaluated the notion as spurious and foreign, even though I myself could be evaluated as incongruous, spurious, and a foreign element. Later on I realized that the very nature of symbol production and cultural creation consists of constant reassessment and reevaluation of symbols in relation to past and present knowledge. Cultural systems are not frozen as a whole to be defrosted later as contemporary practice. People continually evaluate both new and ancient practices as well as explanations as worthy of preservation and continuation into the future as part of the dialectical creation of tradition.

The tendency to universalize and to seize authority is also reflected in anthropological circles. Arguments over the reliability and appropriateness of specific consultants tend to assume that culture is a homogeneous phenomenon. Heterogeneous explanations are systematized into a single line of thought, or a single version is accepted as authoritative, and variants are dismissed as aberrant. Nevertheless, a wide variety of practices and interpretations coexist in any culture.

Like the Lakotas themselves, anthropologists have entered the debate over the legitimacy of documentary influence on contemporary practice. Some anthropologists (W. K. Powers 1987:164; Kehoe 1990) claim that much of ethnographic description of ritual practice, particularly in recent works, was created by the writers themselves and does not reflect the true tradition. Accomodation is multidirectional. The Lakotas influence and are influenced by the cultures around the reservation. Representation of ceremonial practice is itself a multidirectional phenomenon, particularly in a larger system, where information is commoditized and marketed. Today's practice may become tomorrow's description, and yesterday's description may become today's tradition. I say that not to discount or devalue the process of handing down knowledge directly along a line of participants but to show that other avenues are possible for acquiring ceremonial knowledge. It is particularly crucial to recognize that fact in regard to the sweat lodge, for, as the following chapters show, many individuals characterize themselves as initially outside the tradition, consciously working to place themselves within Lakota culture and practice through ceremonial action. So, too, as we have seen, the U.S. government and, most especially, the missionaries worked deliberately to disrupt this direct line.

The debate over the authenticity of consultants has had its airing in Lakota studies and combines the issues of both local and anthropological authority. For example, William K. Powers, after using much of Walker's work in his earlier writings (1975), later denigrates this corpus of material. First, Powers points out that Walker himself was not a speaker of Lakota and therefore his analysis of Lakota belief is suspect. Casting aspersions on George Sword, the main informant of the workings of the sweat, Powers states: "One wonders why some of

Sword's interviews seem to require an interpreter while others do not. This is of particular interest since George Sword's greatest claim to fame at Pine Ridge was that he was in charge of the Indian police, not that he was a medicine man" (1986:125). Powers implies that Sword and Walker's other consultants were not central to the tradition of the Lakotas because they were not recognized medicine men.[8] They were obviously tainted, in Powers's view, by white culture through both contact and participation. Powers goes on to question other sources: "Since the turn of the century, much of what passes today for Indian culture and religion has been fabricated by the white man, or Indians who have been trained in white man's schools" (1990a:147). The hidden assumption is that there is one single uncontaminated source of truth that can be mined through access to particular consultants. Change and innovation (or what the field-worker contends are change and innovation) are rejected as contamination and spurious or bracketed as aberrations.

Charles A. Eastman is also suspect according to Powers (1990a:147). Although it is quite true that Eastman is writing for a white audience, he does nevertheless represent a significant voice in the development of Indian religious thought.[9] Because of his publications and their recent reissuance, his voice continues to be heard.[10] Powers, while recognizing variation and changes in the Lakota religious system, still searches for an orthodox core. Thus he exonerates, in part, Joseph Epes Brown's work on Black Elk because "there is no pretense in creating a voice, only a culture-history, whose contents include the seven sacred rites of the Oglala in which all Lakota medicine men believe" (1990a: 148). Brown himself claims that he is (as Paul Radin would have all anthropologists be) merely the pen recording Black Elk's words: "Everything the old man told me I recorded during the time that was available" (1953:xiv).

According to Powers, there are two "traditions" on the reservation, one absorbed through books by the "younger generation" and the other "that is the product of an oral tradition handed down by a dwindling number of tribal elders" (1986:126).[11] Thus, Powers sets up the dichotomy of spurious and genuine based on the method of acquisition of knowledge. Although this is one way to proceed, one that marks anthropological practice in general as well as the viewpoint of some Lakotas, my own work takes a direct interest in the "younger generation," some of whom have added textual material to the dialectical process.

The contradictory contention that cultures are rapidly disappearing but that there still remains somewhere hidden the pure untouched culture is consistently found in anthropology and Western thought in general; that supposition motivated much exploration and research in the nineteenth and early twentieth centuries. It also has a currency on the reservation itself. One consultant told me about how a tribe in South America was discovered; it was "untouched by the outside" and had maintained its pure traditions.

I agree that native cultures have transformed radically, but that is the very nature of culture and the production of legitimate ceremonial practice. "Salvage anthropology" inadvertently created cultural high-water marks in an attempt to preserve a very idealized cultural configuration, largely anthropology's own invention. Reconstruction of past cultures is a valid pursuit, done both by anthropologists and by members of particular cultures through texts and oral reporting, but it is only one element of the dialectical process. My own preference is to examine contemporary practice in all its variety rather than to value certain configurations over others in relation to their presumed faithfulness to the past.

Whereas anthropologists once sought isolated locations to discover natives untouched by civilization, Powers implicitly holds that certain individuals on the reservation have maintained a cognitive isolation, passing their teachings, substantially unchanged, on to others. Thus, he sees the true source of Lakota teaching as emanating from "their [the untouched natives'] direct source of inspiration on the reservation" (W. K. Powers 1990a:149). In this charter of authoritative legitimation, textualization of spiritual experience is uncharacteristic of these "true" medicine men and disqualifies pretenders to the title: "The religious zeal of even more romanticists is overshadowed by their total ignorance of a Lakota religion learned first hand from those ritual specialists who are not the subject of books, and who are therefore more nearly akin to the ideal type of Lakota medicine men accepted by Lakota culture" (W. K. Powers 1990a:149).[12] Powers cites Lame Deer as one of these pretenders to the throne, but he states in an earlier work, "Frank Fools Crow is unquestionably the leading Oglala medicine man" (1986:226), even though *Fools Crow,* Frank's narrated spiritual biography, was published in 1985.[13] In his 1990 article no evaluation is made of Fools Crow's legitimacy in light of this aberration, despite the fact that his narrated biography is cited in Powers's bibliography.

Once the field-worker determines that certain individuals are authentic or representative, then he or she has selected a limited range of opinions and beliefs and has declared these and no others to be valid. Thus the field worker, taking on an authoritarian role, legitimates certain voices and invalidates others. The anthropologist establishes an orthodoxy where one might not exist or shifts the weight of authority by elevating one participant's view over another's.

Clearly, the heterogeneous nature of Lakota ceremonial practice is a fruitful arena for such a bias on the part of both observers and participants (and participant observers).

Anthropology in the nineteenth century sought through textualization to preserve a representation of cultures that were destined, according to the thought of the time, to disappear; today, some anthropologists and researchers seek to defend what they perceive and define as the authentic practices of a culture against spurious pretenders, both from within the culture ("city" Indians and apostates to Christianity) and from without (white authors and "wannabes").[14] Other anthropologists, taking the other tack, critique the very notion of Indianness or Indian identity as a spurious construct, part of a long process of Western differentiation of self and other (Clifton 1990a, 1990b; Simard 1990). The hidden assumption is that of Malinowski, who usurped the power to describe and create "*the* native," according to which anthropology has the power to discern the single authentic representation of a culture. Anthropology thus has found itself (and, at times, positioned itself) in the role of defining the genuine and the spurious in native culture. This role was particularly salient in the legal arena during the Indian Claims Commission era. Today, anthropologists continue to serve as expert witnesses as certain groups petition the government for tribal status.

At the same time, there is a continual stream, ever widening, of texts written in what can be called the New Age genre. Those texts (by plain vanilla whites, by adopted-by-a-wise-Indian-grandfather whites, by full-bloods, by mixed-bloods, by pretenders to Indian blood, and by "reincarnated" Indians) have become part of a large commercial market in alternative spiritualities, as have the many seminars, retreats, and spiritual tribal memberships provided by those individuals. They have also been widely contested (Kehoe 1990). I do not question the right or legitimacy for practitioners or analysts to discern authentic practice, but I do want to point out that this process presents a certain result. I am more interested in the process in this work than the result.

Contemporary Tradition in Light of the Past

Although the establishment of validity of sources is essential to anthropological research, the existence of "spurious" accounts is a social fact, and the designation "spurious" itself is dependent on how each text is judged. I believe we must listen to a multiplicity of voices presenting their viewpoints rather than to select out certain voices as more or less accurate and authentic. My consistent experience in fieldwork has been that there is no single "true" position concerning the nature and use of the sweat lodge. Therefore, I do not want to construct a past orthodoxy, nor do I wish to create a contemporary one where I feel no single form exists. If tradition is a process as much as a thing, as I contend is the case with the Lakotas, then no single source or single representation will fully encompass it.

As the historical literature itself demonstrates, ceremonial practice among the Lakotas was and continues to be internally both mutable and heterogeneous. DeMallie states:

> The renaissance of Lakota religious life draws attention to the individualistic nature of Sioux religion and to the role of revelation through visions in shaping ceremonial life. Although the broad forms of ceremonies are set by tradition, wide variation occurs based on individual experiences. Perhaps this gives insight into nineteenth century Lakota religion as well; the forms for obtaining insight—the purification lodge, vision quest, and Sun Dance—remain constant, and there is no reason to assume that the innovation of modern times is fundamentally different from that of the historical period. In this sense, the present resurgence of Lakota religion follows directly the patterns of the past. [1988:17]

Thus, the task of assigning the seal of authenticity to a particular text or consultant is problematic. Continuity, not isomorphism, is essential in Lakota ceremonial practice.

By recognizing the influence of all the textual material, we gain as comprehensive a view as possible of how the sweat is represented by historical sources. We can examine the change in representation of the ceremony, itself an important consideration, and we become familiar with sources, particularly contemporary popular accounts, that are accessible to practitioners of the sweat lodge.

Nevertheless, when all documentary sources are considered and the fullest range of variation in practice acknowledged, there remains a consistent core of ritual for the sweat lodge ceremony that contemporary practitioners believe must be adhered to for the ceremony to be effective.[15] To understand the dialectical nature of tradition, it is essential to consider both the consistencies and the variations in the sweat lodge ceremony itself.

Continuity and Variation in Historical Practice

Concerning the ethnohistorical data, with the exception of the account by Humfreville (1899:145), both the Dakota and the Lakota material concerning the design of the lodge and the basic process of performance within the sweat are highly consistent in form.[16] The physical structure of the sweat lodge has remained strikingly consistent according to literature for both the Dakotas and the Lakotas. The lodge is dome-shaped, constructed of pliable saplings, and, except for one documented Ghost Dance era ceremony, has a single door. Eastern Dakotas may sometimes have used branches and leaves to cover the sweat, but there is a fair consistency in using skins and blankets. Rocks are heated outside the sweat and brought into the sweat. Water is poured over the rocks to create steam. The door is opened and closed several times, four being the commonest number. Participants within the sweat express themselves in some way—praying, singing, crying, or shouting. All this remains valid today.

From the historical texts we can also extract some historical variation (and perhaps innovation), particularly between the Santee Dakotas and the Lakotas. First, the nineteenth-century Santee material makes no mention of altars constructed in front of the sweats, although there is reference to a path drawn from the fire in front of the lodge to the lodge itself. That path was sometimes covered with swan's down and tobacco. There is no mention of altars in the Lakota material until Mooney (1896:822) mentions them in connection with the Ghost Dance. Altars are not mentioned again until the Black Elk material (Black Elk in Brown 1953:34). Today, there are many varieties of altars created in front of the sweat lodges. Only one sweat lodge that I know of has no altar at all.[17]

The early texts do not mention any ceremony connected with building the fire to heat the rocks. The first mention of an elaborate ceremony related to this procedure is by Black Elk (in Brown 1953:32). Today, the construction and igniting of the sweat lodge fire is often done ceremonially. In the nineteenth-century Santee material, pipes are never mentioned as used in conjunction with the sweat. In the Lakota texts, pipes are mentioned in conjunction with the sweat, but the ceremonial use of a pipe within a sweat is not clearly documented until the Black Elk texts. Today, pipes are frequently incorporated into the sweat lodge ceremony and are smoked either during breaks in the round (the third round being the most frequent) or after the sweat is concluded.

The Orientation of the Door

Perhaps the most significant change (or variation) in the sweat lodge structure itself is in the positioning of the entrance to the lodge. There is no specific orientation for the door of the lodge mentioned in the nineteenth-century Santee material, nor does Charles Eastman mention orientation of the ceremonial structure in his turn-of-the-century material. Throughout the Lakota material, however, the position of the door is mentioned by both natives and whites. The consistent interest documented in the Lakota ethnohistorical material is very instructive concerning how rules are constructed and reconstructed through the interaction of written texts and oral narratives. These written rules have a life only insofar as individuals employ these texts and are willing to accept them as authoritative. Within the debate about placement of the door, some practitioners specifically reject textual constructions of rules, replacing them with other rules, which, ironically, are then themselves textualized. Thus, the Lame Deer text voices a position that explicitly challenges anthropological opinion.[18]

From the anthropological camp we have: "Contrary to much that has been written about this rite, there is no pattern for the position of the sweat lodge, i.e., for the orientation of the entrance. The owner or builder may favor a particular direction or orientation, this being an expression of Sioux individualism" (Feraca 1961:156–57).[19] Sword states, "An *Ini ti* should never have its door toward the north" (in Walker 1980:79); Walker presents that statement as a general rule. Black Elk, as represented by Brown, states the first unidirectional rule: "The sweat lodge is always constructed with its door to the east, for it is from this direction that the light of wisdom comes" (1953:32). This contradicts a story told to Neihardt by Black Elk in which a sweat used to purify murderers opens to the south (DeMallie 1984:393). This positioning, like that toward the west, is explained symbolically: the south is the direction in which the dead travel, and the murderers were exiled to wander toward the south. Ruby maintains that the sweat he attended had the door facing the east. He proposes neither a general rule for this positioning nor a reason for it. The Laubins state categorically that all the sweat lodges they had ever seen faced east.

From the literature of the 1960s onward, the door seems to be placed more commonly in the west than other directions. Feraca, Amiotte, Schweigman, Fools Crow, Lame Deer, and Stolzman all state that the door to the sweat faces west. Lame Deer insists on that orientation, although he does not qualify the rule as always the case, allowing for the exception of the Heyokas. History of religions scholar Jordan Paper claims it faces west, "the direction of life's path" (1990:86). Only Powers in his 1975 work states that the door of the sweat lodge faces the east.[20]

Stolzman takes several tacks in analyzing variation in door alignment. He states that the normal alignment, west, may be changed for pragmatic reasons, as when geographic structures prevent proper alignment. He also states that Heyokas, those who have visions of lightning or special spirits from the east, face their "Heyoka sweat lodge" to the east (1986b:15). He invokes this rule in Black Elk's case, providing a consistent logic about alignment—consistent at least in Stolzman's view:

> Why do the doors of sweatlodges on the reservation face West; didn't Black Elk say they face East? Many people have read *The Sacred Pipe: The Seven Rites of the Oglala Sioux.* This is an excellent book written by Joseph Epes Brown from his interviews with Nicholas Black Elk. A few local people have pointed out that most people do not recognize Black Elk's association with the *Wakinyan* (Thunder Spirits) as a sign that he was in some respects an *Heyoka* (Contrary). On the reservation, a sweat lodge which faces the East is called an *Heyoka* sweatbath. [1986a:73]

Black Elk, according to Brown, states, however, that his alignment is to represent wisdom that comes from the east; he says nothing about lodges ever facing west or the thunders being of focal importance in the lodge. Most other descriptions provide no reason for alignment. Feraca, whose representation of the sweat is not symbolic/interpretive, as are Black Elk's and later authors', says it is a matter of individual expression. Black Crow states that he has two sweats, one east and one west. The one for his own personal use faces west, for it is used at the end of the day.

We can see several factors at work in these descriptions. First, there is a tendency to universalize practice. The Sword text begins with the rule "never north," and then the historical literature indicates always east and then to the west. Whereas one anthropologist explains this as individual expression, most other field-workers seek to explain it by symbolic exegesis or structuralist patterning. Practitioners simply state these as rules, often without long explanations. Many accounts are rather doctrinaire about a correct direction, although there is no consistency in the explanation. Today, most sweat lodges I have observed are oriented toward the west. My collaborators maintain that west is the most powerful direction or simply say that this is how they are supposed to orient *their* sweat. Most agree that as long as there is a reason for aligning the sweat in a certain direction, it is proper to do so. Some would also say that west is the right direction and that east is the *heyókha* 'backward' way to face. Others rely on vision or inspiration for the facing of the sweat. Still others attribute the direction to that in which their teacher had his sweat. There is no unanimity on this point among contemporary Lakotas.

A more significant rule, and one that is consistently invoked, is that if you are not comfortable with the way the sweat lodge is facing, you should go find another or build your own. Thus, the final criterion is individual choice—one should not compel others to follow a certain prescribed orientation. Nor should anyone feel compelled to participate in a sweat that he or she considers misaligned. On the other hand, one should not press too hard the opinion that someone else's sweat is improperly oriented. The fact that there are so many sweats operating on the reservation allows for this option to be used effectively. This is not to say that orientation itself is not an issue but that the norm is to not force uniformity of performance.

There were other explanations given to me for orientation of lodges while I was on the Pine Ridge Reservation. One consultant explained: "The east represents wisdom and enlightenment. For that reason, we all come out facing east. The direction moved west because we are in disharmony. I have heard this from the medicine man with whom I worked and others." One sweat I attended had its back to a cliff and could be faced only one way. The owner of that sweat used very pragmatic logic in explaining that this was the case, although he would have preferred to face his lodge the other direction. I have never seen or heard of a sweat on the reservation today facing north or south.

Consistencies in Contemporary Sweats

Although orientation of the sweat has varied across time and space, uses of the sweat lodge have remained fairly consistent. It can be used to purify (in preparation for other ceremonies and in itself), to mark life crisis events (such as war, disease, and death), and to petition specific powers (to achieve certain ends). The ceremony was and continues to be used before and after other important ceremonies, such as the Sun Dance and the vision quest. It is also used for healing. Today the sweat lodge is seen as a locus for spiritual encounter. Even in "cowboy sweats" (sweats held purely for refreshment), some prayers and songs are used. In the past certain sweats were used primarily for sanitary purposes and did not have religious overtones. One elderly Lakota consultant said that when he used to herd cattle in the 1920s, he and his partners would sweat at the end of the day.

The Walker material reveals some malicious uses of the sweat, such as causing illness or compelling someone to fall in love. Contemporary consultants state that the sweat, like any other ceremony, can be used to hurt as well as to help. The spirits are seen as neutral beings, willing to carry out any request of the practitioner if invoked properly. However, it is held on the reservation today that if you use the sweat in an evil way, that evil will return to your family or yourself. The English phrase "What goes around comes around" is often cited to explain this principle. Other practitioners discount the belief that a ceremony can actually be used to harm someone, saying that these ceremonies can be used only for good. Such people acknowledge that others believe they can use the spirits to harm someone but contend that this is false and not a part of the true traditional Indian belief.

Although contexts precipitating a sweat lodge ceremony have remained fairly consistent, the central purpose of the sweat lodge varies both diachronically and synchronically in the ethnohistorical literature. Stephen Riggs points out that, for the Santee Dakotas, the sweat may be used for refreshment and healing, but it is used more often for "getting into communication with the spirit world" (1893:101). That distinction was drawn quite clearly by the early missionaries themselves, who permitted the sweat lodge for medicinal use and but not for spiritual encounters. This was consistent with their secularization of medicinal practice and their claim to the exclusivity of the power of their own religious tradition.

Today, some Lakotas take a scientific view of the effects of the sweat, making generalized statements such as, "Scientists have proven that there are many physiological benefits to participating in the sweat ceremony." They also claim psychological benefit for the sweat.[21] Many state that they "need" a sweat to calm or readjust themselves. Psychological adjustment comes under the category of healing. There is a wide variation in understanding today concerning the presence and importance of spirits in the lodge with regard to healing and other benefits. The Lakotas with whom I have worked see healing as part of spiritual intervention, either by specific spirits who act as intermediaries between God, the medicine man, and the patient or directly by God. No one with whom I worked saw the sweat as a purely secular event. I have never participated in or heard of a sweat in which there were not at least some prayers.[22]

Spiritual intervention is effected in two ways in the sweat lodge. Certain spiritual leaders have access to specific spirits, which they are able to summon into the lodge. These spirits cooperate with the wishes of the spiritual leader and respond to the needs of those whom the leader is attempting to help. Other leaders do not invoke specific spirits, relying on the sweat itself and the concomitant prayers to draw in the appropriate spirits or the power of God. General spirits, such as those of the directions, are mentioned in prayer. These sweat lodge leaders do not claim power as medicine men or women. Individuals who do not claim these powers are very careful to offer disclaimers in their opening talks in the sweat. Along with spirits, if the individual leading the sweat is a Christian, the spirit of Jesus is sometimes invoked. In sweats held by Native American Church members, Christ and the Holy Spirit are invoked exclusively.

Calling the spirits is generally accomplished by song and prayer. The spirits' presence is indicated by bursts of hot or cold air, flashes of light in the rock pit, sounds of rattles or drums, singing, the shaking of the lodge structure itself, pounding under the earth, sounds of deer hoofs clicking as they dance, eagle cries, and the beating of eagle wings. In some lodges none of these phenomena are manifested. In other lodges they provide validation for the presence of spirits that come to help the participants. It is generally believed that some participants in the lodge are capable of seeing or hearing the spirits, whereas others are not.

Historically, there is remarkable consistency in the supplicant presenting himself as poor and pitiful, but the focus of prayers has shifted. As we saw in chapter 2, contemporary prayers commonly refer to social concerns such as broken families, alcoholism, drug abuse, violence, and poverty. This shift is discernible beginning with the Black Elk material. The prayers also have an expanded focus from the individual and the tribe to all peoples of the world. The trend to universalization is first noticeable in Black Elk's work but continues in the present with the inclusion of the four races (matching the four colors for the four directions) in sweat prayers. Specifically ecological concerns, as opposed to invoking powers symbolized through the natural world in prayer, absent from early sweats, are prominent in prayers today.

Historically, there has been a shift from presenting oneself as poor and pitiful so that one's needs might be fulfilled to praying for those who are poor and pitiful, believing that in so doing one's own needs will also be addressed. Today's standard formula includes praying for the poor, children, the unborn, and the elderly. The crippled and the sick may also be mentioned.

The two most significant changes in the sweat lodge accounts concern representation and participation. It is clear from the earliest accounts that the sweat lodge was a place of spiritual encounter. The Dakota and Lakota material particularly stresses the use of rocks that themselves were or contained certain spirits. Appeals were made to various powers. According to Sword, it was the spiritual powers themselves who strengthened the *ni* of the participants. In the early twentieth century, there is a shift away from mentioning actual spirits in the sweat lodge. Black Elk speaks of the spiritual rather than of specific spirits, omitting particular spirits that are at the service of particular holy men. There is a shift back to the mentioning of specific spirits in the late-twentieth-century literature, particularly the narrated biographies of Lakota medicine men. Also, whereas the missionaries once attacked the presence of spirits within the lodge as diabolic, contemporary Christian writings (particularly Jesuit material), attempt to reconcile Lakota belief in spirits with Christian cosmology rather than condemn, suppress, or discredit those beliefs.

It is essential to see changes in the Lakota religious system within the context of historical change on a broader scale. As the twentieth century progressed, the government interfered less and less with the religious practices of the Lakotas. The Jesuits and other mission groups opposed the reforms of John Collier and others precisely because of the new policy of noninterference. Later, with changes in the philosophies and theologies of their own churches, some Christian missions, particularly the Catholic, shifted from a stance of opposing traditional religion to attempting to incorporate it into the larger structure of the churches.[23] This was not without opposition by both Christian and native groups. Today, however, it is uncharacteristic to hear any but fundamentalist Christians condemning traditional belief systems.

Christianity also transformed the understanding of Lakota spiritual tradition through the dual process of resistance and accommodation. Both George Sword and Black Elk spent a lot of time discussing spiritual matters with missionaries.[24] Correlations were made between Lakota belief and Christian belief. Sometimes this was done in order to justify and protect the indigenous system of belief. At other times, comparisons might be drawn to emphasize the difference between Lakota and Christian belief systems.[25] Once in a sweat lodge that I attended, the leader announced, "This ceremony has nothing in Christianity." A few minutes later he stated, "Do this in memory of me." An elderly Lakota friend typed out notes for me from a lecture he gave concerning Indian religion at a local college:

The Lakota people do not have the Bible; however, everything we do is found in the Bible verses, because the Great Spirit gave us the knowledge.

The Lakota people in their vision and dreams had befriended animals and the winged ones, and the Grandmother Earth.

In the Book of Exodus, chapter 33, verse 9, "And it came to pass as Moses entered into the Tabernacle, the cloudy pillar descended and stood at the door of the Tabernacle; the Lord talked to Moses."

This resembles the sweat lodge ceremony. We in the misty vapors talk to the Great Spirit.

In the Book of Job, chapter 12, verse 7, "Ask the beasts and they will teach thee; and the fowls of the air and they shall tell thee": We communicate with the beasts and the fowls of the air.

In the Book of Job, chapter 12, verse 8, "Or speak to the earth and it shall teach thee and the fishes of the sea shall declare unto thee."

We always speak [to] the Grandmother Earth.

Another partial transformation that occurred in Lakota religion is a shift from the understanding of ritual as a text to be followed to seeing ritual as expressive and symbolic.[26] In the first instance, ritual is a set of prescribed actions and utterances that must be duplicated as faithfully as possible in each performance. This is commonly the case in early Lakota ritual, although not strictly so, particularly in comparison with the ceremonies of other Plains groups. Sword insists that certain procedures must always be carried through for the ritual to be effective. Beginning with the Black Elk material, the emphasis is not so much on precision (although there are elements of that in the Black Elk corpus) as on interpretation, on the appropriateness of the ritual to the historical and emotional situation, and on the importance of understanding the inner meaning of the ceremony. At a Sun Dance I attended in 1979, a Sun Dance leader (not the one leading this particular dance) told me that it did not matter if everything done in this dance was performed incorrectly. What was essential was the inner attitude of the participants. Thus, the participants in the ceremony operated out of their intentions rather than from strict adherence to a preestablished course of actions, prayers, and songs. Sincerity rather than acumen was the essential ingredient for participation. Again, this is a matter of degree, for the Sun Dance contains prescribed actions that distinguish it from other ritual or secular actions. This particular dance was no exception, following general lines prescribed for such a religious celebration. There is a general sense, as mentioned before, that all rituals must be conducted in a certain manner. Personal and cosmic misfortune is often ascribed to carrying out a ceremony incorrectly or in an insincere manner.

Interestingly, it is ritual activity that anthropologists and other observers often use to gauge the authenticity and orthodoxy of cultural participants. Thus, acculturation is measured in deviance from ideal typical models of past ritual performance. This also holds for Lakota practitioners. Local participants will sometimes make the claim that certain contemporary rituals are "just as they were" in order to validate a performance. Lakotas themselves gauge ritual propriety in part on its "correct" performance. Certain sweats are considered invalid because they are too easy, they are not set up right, the wrong types of people attend, or they use the wrong songs or prayers. As mentioned above, this is not the sole criterion. Lakotas will also gauge ritual on its experiential impact, usually with such observations as "I was really comfortable in there" or "I prayed really good in there" or "There was a good feeling in there." None of these categories are mutually exclusive, and combinations of the above criteria are often employed in conversations about ceremonies.

The material examined in this chapter demonstrates continual heterogeneity of practice with regard to the sweat lodge ceremony, with a concomitant core of historic continuity. It is the very malleability of this ceremony, along with its enduring structure, that has made it important in contemporary practice, for it represents the dialectic of tradition as it encompasses two elements—something done in the past and something necessary for the present. The ability of the sweat lodge to be both conservative and innovative has accommodated and promoted that dialectic for both conservation and alteration of the ceremony. Thus, the Lakotas have access to their past while dealing with contemporary needs.

Written documents provide but one of many links to the past, one that is treated ambivalently on the reservation. That ambivalence is heightened when the texts are given the status of ultimate arbiter, particularly by people from outside of the culture, for this represents alienated tradition. There are varieties of reactions to this material, which span from free use of the texts to bolster tradition to the total rejection of outside knowledge in the ethnognostic movement. The idea of a single authoritative position on ceremony is also treated with ambivalence, for independence and freedom of action based on charisma remain important on the reservation. Thus, even ethnognostic representations of tradition are argued over, because each gnostic practitioner claims a totality of representation. Finally, ritual authority on the reservation remains diffuse and has not yet become centralized, although a movement in that direction is becoming increasingly popular as a means of resisting New Age appropriation of Lakota ritual.

This is not to say that those seeking to find a correct procedure are them-selves in error, but rather that there is a range of differing but correct procedures that sometimes conflict with each other. Correct procedure is evaluated in light of both historical precedence and contemporary need. In the case of the Lakotas, with their widely democratic and decentralized religious system, this dialectic is in the hands of individuals and extended families—thus, a multiplicity of forms and procedures arise. What is correct ultimately is what is judged correct by those who use particular sweats—adaptation is constantly being intertwined with past procedures. Correctness is also determined by the efficacy of the ritual, the legitimacy of the leader himself, and the rhetoric of legitimation that is brought to bear in cases of conflict, rather than by simple adherence to an accepted canon of procedure such as might be found in documented rituals of the past and in the variety of Christian rituals with which Lakotas have had contact.

It is important to note, however, that both investigator and practitioner seek the correct procedure. The criteria for correctness range from efficacy ("When done this way, the ceremony works") to precedent ("So and so performs the ceremony this way") to historical precedence ("I was taught by a person who did it this way") to textual verification ("I read that it was done this way") to inspiration ("I was told by the spirits to do it this way") to pragmatic considera-tions ("This is the only way we were able to do it"). Anthropological work errs when it eliminates the multiplicity of considerations that form the actual prac-tice or when such texts seem to establish a single extrinsic set of norms and rationales by their very documentation of the event.

The dialectic between historical practice and present needs and capacities produces ceremonial action that is defined as tradition at any given time. The authentication of traditionality revolves around both legitimacy and authority. Contention over authority revolves around who may properly manipulate the two poles of the dialectic to produce traditional practice, and legitimacy con-cerns the final product—whether or not the resultant practice is judged by the participants as truly authentic and thus traditional. This process is dynamic, not accomplished once for all; it is worked out today primarily within Lakota groups themselves but also across ever-widening groups.

4

Language and the Sweat

This chapter will examine the significance of language use within the sweat. It begins with a consideration of the Lakota and English terms used for the ceremony and continues with an analysis of the uses of language within the lodge itself: prayers and responses (backchanneling) while someone is praying, also teasing, joking, speeches, and testimonials. It is important to note again that the Lakotas consider all interaction within the sweat lodge to be confidential. The material I present here on prayers, speeches, and songs was gathered from interviews and conversations with participants outside of the sweat. I was careful in these interviews and during my own participation in sweat ceremonies not to breach the confidentiality of the sweat lodge.

Language, as the vehicle for dialogue and transmission of information from past to present (including the nonverbal language of symbols), is used to interact within the ceremony itself, to describe the sweat, to gauge its efficacy, and to legitimate its practice and practitioners through the dialectic that creates tradition. The Lakota language is important both in itself and as a link to history and identity.

Terms for the Sweat Lodge

Throughout the ethnographic literature, beginning with Lynd (1864:161), the first to refer to the sweat lodge by its Dakota name *inípi,* the term for the ceremony in both Dakota and Lakota has remained the same. Sword is quite clear on the disjunction between the Lakota and the English: "When a Lakota says *ni* or *ini* or *inipi*, or *initi*, he does not think about sweat. He thinks about making his *ni* strong so it will purify him" (in Walker 1980:100). Contemporary Lakota speakers readily acknowledge that 'sweat' is not an equivalent for the Lakota term. Thus, the contemporary Lakota anthropologist Bea Medicine writes: "Even the term 'sweat' has so little significance compared to the Lakota name, *inipi*, which is laden with values in our native culture. It means 'to live again'" (1987:167).

Riggs translates *inípi* as "a steaming, sweating." *Iní* is *"to take a vapor-bath, steam one's self, to take a sweat*—iwani, iyani, uŋkinipi; *to make a kind of* wakaŋ. This consists in washing and steaming one's self four times over hot stones, accompanied with singing, etc. It is done after one has killed an enemy or a royal eagle" (1890:200). Buechel (1970:227) essentially uses Riggs's definition for the word in his own dictionary.[1] William K. Powers offers this etymology: "The ritual is called *inikagapi* (from *i* 'by means of, on account of'; *ni* 'life, breath'; *kagapi* 'they make, cause'). The ritual is held in a sweat lodge, *oinikage* (from *o* 'in' and *inikage*), also called *initipi* (from *ini* and *tipi* 'dwelling')" (1975:89).

On the Pine Ridge Reservation today, the Lakota term *inípi* is most often glossed in English as 'sweat'. This term is used for the act, the name of the ceremony, and the physical structure of the lodge, and *sweat lodge* is used for the name and the structure of the ceremony. In the nineteenth-century literature, it was referred to in English as the stone bath, the sweat booth, the sweat bath, the vitalizing lodge, the refreshing lodge, and, most often, the vapor bath.[2] In contemporary written literature, the terms used most often are sweat, lodge, sweat lodge, and sweat bath. Also used in more contemporary literature are the terms renewed life, reborn-lodge, Grandfather's breath, rite of purification, new life lodge, sacred rite of purification, purification lodge, purification rite, sacred lodge, stone-people-lodge, the ceremony that intermingles and conveys the lifeblood of the world, you-make-your-life, making life, and an interesting hybrid referring to the structure, inipi lodge. Even when the more poetic terms are used, the authors generally revert to *sweat* or *lodge* when talking about the ceremony.

The English and Lakota terms for this ceremony present an interesting dichotomy. The English term focuses on the physical act of extruding water from the body under conditions of extreme heat, one of the most striking physiological effects of the ceremony. The Lakota term, on the other hand, focuses on the *ní*, the breath, spirit, or life force, and its renewal. Although the terms *inípi* and *sweat* do not share implicit meaning, they have a similar brevity of expression, which may account for the persistence of the English gloss. One contemporary connection that bridges the gap between the two terms is the frequent association of water and life made in the sweat. Several Lakota speakers with whom I worked gloss *mni* 'water' as *miní* 'my life'.[3] This association of water with life is generally made in reference to the water that is poured and consumed during the sweat rather than to the sweat *(themni)* itself. An interesting link between the terms used in the two languages is thus forged through innovative etymology.

Given the early European mistrust of Lakota spirituality and spirits, particularly on the part of the missionaries, the use of a "neutral" English word that focuses on the physiological function of the ceremony may simply be strategic. On the other hand, the Lakota term quickly brings together both physiological (*ní* is associated with the breath) and spiritual (*ní* is also associated with the spirit or life force).[4] We will see in the music section that although no song in Lakota makes a specific reference to the sweat lodge or to sweating, many songs are concerned with the *ní* and its continuance.

Prayer

The nineteenth-century presentations of the sweat lodge describe it as a cere-mony of prayer and entreaty. The lodge is a place where an individual meets the divine powers and through interaction and intercession may acquire what he or she needs. The nineteenth-century literature inevitably cites prayer as part of the ceremony of purification. Some of the early literature mentions specific prayers said in the sweat:

> Now the robe is thrown down [to cover the door], and then the holy men speak *(woklakapelo)*. They speak in the spirit language *(he hanploklakapi eciyapelo)*. These are the things they say.
> "Sweat lodge stones *(tonkan yatapika)*, pity me! Sun, pity me! Moon, pity me! Darkness of night *(hanokpaza kin)*, pity me! Water, standing in a *wakan* manner *(mni wakanta najin ki)*, pity me! Grass, standing in the morning *(pejihinyanpa najin kin)*, pity me! Whatever pitiful one is scarcely able to crawl into the tipi and lie down for the night *(takuxika teriya tiyoslohanhan hinyunke)*, see him and pity him." [Tyon in Walker 1980: 154].[5]

Prayer continues to be a key verbal interaction in the sweat lodge. Through oral prayer, participants convey their needs directly to the divine and, at the same time, create solidarity through the sharing of individual struggles and pains among the participants. Although the designated leader is ultimately in charge of the lodge itself, individuals are free to pray as they wish when they are granted a turn. Some contemporary participants hold that in the past the leader prayed in behalf of all present and acted as the exclusive intermediary between the divine and the other participants.

During the sweats I have attended, all participants are called upon to voice individual prayers at one time or another. The prayers are generally made after the door is closed and a set of songs are sung. Prayers are less frequently made while the door is open between rounds. Although there is tremendous variation in the way people are called upon, the most common procedure is for the leader to call upon people to pray one at a time, beginning with the individual sitting on the north side of the door in lodges facing west (to the leader's left—the leader sits on the other side of the door) and proceeding sunwise. The leader frames the verbal elements of the ceremony, beginning the prayer (and the narratives) and saying the final prayer, which often carefully sums up the prayers made by all the individuals.

The expectation is that individuals pray privately throughout the sweat but are called upon to pray publicly at least once during the sweat. After all have prayed, the leader sometimes asks whether anyone has anything to add. If an individual does not want to pray out loud, he or she simply says "mitakuye oyas'in," itself a short prayer for all one's relatives in the universe.

There is quiet when an individual prays, except for verbal assents made in utterances by the participants and particularly the leader. These syllables convey meaning not through words or phrases but by their tonal quality. Lakota is rich in tonal utterances, allowing for intercommunication in the dark, where there is an absence of visible clues such as postures, gestures, and facial expressions. This behavior, referred to by linguists as back-channeling, occurs also while individuals are speaking; listeners use it to demonstrate their attentiveness as well as their empathy with and support for the person praying.[6] Participants also use back-channeling to convey to the leader how hot the sweat is and their relative levels of discomfort or pleasure. Words like *háu, ohą́, hó, tó,* and *hų́ñ,* are heard, as well as various melodic groans, sighs, and exclamations. Sometimes, particularly if there is a strong outpouring of emotions by an individual in a prayer, a song is sung while that person prays. The song covers the prayer and the emotions, providing a modicum of privacy.

Prayers in the sweat are generally framed with as much Lakota as an individual is capable of. Although there is controversy over the "correct" language to use in the sweat, it is clear in practice that Lakota is the ideal language. Some hold that only Lakota should be used; others claim that English is as appropriate. With fewer and fewer fluent Lakota speakers, the language question is becoming increasingly focal. Lakota remains the ceremonial language of Pine Ridge today.

Most often, individuals begin their prayer with *Thųkášila, Wakhą́ Thą́ka,* or *Até* ['father'] *Wakhą́ Thą́ka.* Each term can have a range of meanings: praying to one God, praying to spirits, or praying to spirits to bring messages to the one God. No one stops to define his or her belief concepts. The terms themselves allow unity because they are ambiguous. Prayers consistently are ended with "mitakuye oyas'in." That is the summation of the prayer and the signal for the next in the circle to pray. Generally, individuals will pray as much in Lakota as possible and then switch to English. The leader and some individuals will say the same prayer in Lakota and then in English when monolingual English speakers are present. Lakota is consistently used first in these instances, stressing its priority.

One individual with whom I worked described for me the things that one prays for in the lodge:[7]

> *Wichóząni,* that's the main one they pray for, health. *Wó'okiye* is help with whatever you need. *Wó'ableze* is understanding. *Hukpákšica,* medicine men say it quite a bit, kneeling before you, like the stance in the sweat lodge—bend down kneeling. It means humbleness, not an everyday stance.
>
> Those people who have been on solitary prayers, fasts, been through that—their prayers are more in a spiritual sense—they call on the four directions, certain spirits, animals—call on thanks for rocks, water, animals, thunder being people, buffalo people. You can tell how they pray. Those who haven't been on it will be specific with their prayers—uncle, auntie. Everyone begins with the needs of the people. Then they add what's really in their heart.

Healing, understood both as physiological and social, is a dominant function of the sweat on Pine Ridge today, even when the ceremony is used as a prelude to other ceremonies. Prayers requesting health and life, framed with the phrases "help me" and "I'm poor, pitiful, and suffering," ring out in the sweat. Prayers requesting healing for broken families and victims of suicide, violence, and alcoholism are also frequent in the sweat today.

Another individual who leads sweats made very clear what was and was not appropriate in terms of prayer:

> Something they want that doesn't go with the pipe—a job, a man's wife, another wife, for a person to get into a bad wreck. I look out for that—people really want that—they ask for those things.
>
> They ask for *wó'okiye, wichózani.* They ask for physical, financial, spiritual. You can pray that you will be able to pay your bills. Ask for *wó'okiye.*
>
> *Iktómi* ['spider or trickster'] spirit does bad things. People ask iktomi to do that. You have to give me gifts to get that, *wókažužu.* You'll lose a little one, might be sick. *Okáwįǧe,* it come back on you. That's not communicating with God. Talking with spirit people. Iktomi people will do bad things, not the *heȟáka* ['elk'], *wạblí* ['eagle'], *sįtésapala* ['black tail deer']. *Heyókha* medicine man deals with the bad. They are opposite in life. They can trick you, be both nice and bad.
>
> When you face west the *wakįyạ oyáte* ['thunder-being people'] people are there. Prayers are answered before the sun goes down.
>
> When you use the pipe you have to *wa'ýšila* 'pity' *wachạtognake* 'good hearted people'. When you pray you pray for the spiritual and physical, that's all you pray for. People that pray for bad things, that's theirs. We don't do that.

Individuals vary as to what they deem appropriate matter for prayer, but no one would ever interrupt or publicly criticize a prayer. The lodge is focused on healing and harmony. One is expected to respect what a person says, as well as the person himself or herself. Words, like thoughts, are considered to be both part of a person and effective tools. One must choose words carefully, just as one must think good thoughts in a sweat, for words and thoughts are considered highly efficacious. Praying against someone is consistently condemned.

Songs

In addition to prayers, all sweats include singing. The ethnohistorical literature makes it clear that songs were an integral aspect of the earliest observed sweats. During my fieldwork individuals would sing certain songs for me and help me to record and translate them. Other songs they allowed me to hear but asked that I not transcribe them, since those songs were given to them by the spirits through individual prayer. Today on Pine Ridge, there are songs that are generally considered part of the public domain and others that are only for the use of the individual who received them and those whom he or she grants permission to use them. All of the songs used in the sweat are religious in nature and generally said to be inspired or revealed by spirits to specific individuals.[8] Some songs, particularly those in the public domain, are not attributed to known individuals. There is some controversy over commercial vending of sacred songs and even over the propriety of recording them. One frequently sees individuals recording "secular" songs at powwows. That would never happen today at a sweat or other religious ceremony.[9]

Stressing the centrality of song, Walker states, "One vitalizing in the simplest manner should sing an appropriate song while pouring the water on the hot stones" (1917:67). He is silent on what constitutes appropriateness. Concerning the contemporary importance of song, one of my consultants says:

> Songs to an Indian person, the songs are a basic need. A way of praying, making a humble plea to God through song. It's an emotional release. Song can unite a person with others. It can bring people together. It's real powerful when people sing together—get strength from that. Songs can enhance a person's feelings in the spiritual sense—bring out your spiritual feelings when you pray. This is how I see it; that's what's important, as I see it.

As they do with ceremonial procedure, participants in each lodge regulate their own songs. One Lakota individual discussed his use of songs in this way:

> The kind of songs we sing, when you use the pipe, use the pipe filling song outside when you make the *opáǧi,* offering. More appropriate to do it outside than in the lodge—some people do it in the lodge. They use the four direction and prayer songs and Sun Dance songs in the lodge. This is strictly the sweat lodge ceremony. That's what I use. I don't use *iktómi* or *heyókha* songs or anything like that. The *yuwípi* songs spill over to the sweat in contemporary times. Lots of people use *yuwípi* songs. One leader says why use *yuwípi* songs in there? I stay away from *yuwípi* songs. I might use a four direction song used in *yuwípi* but that's not the context I'm using it in. I've never heard that something is just a sweat lodge song. It's an acceptable practice to use Sun Dance songs in there. Some people try to use too many songs, just one after another—five, six, ten songs. Myself, I don't see any benefit from doing that. Concentrate on prayer—that's the most important thing. Songs are like icing on the cake. So it's kind of confusing about what songs belong only to the sweat. The other songs fit in, like the

four directions because we use four rounds. I myself use that song first. A lot of people do that.

Considering the acknowledged antiquity of the sweat lodge ceremony, it is interesting that there seem to be no songs that are proper only to the sweat. Almost all contemporary participants hold that Sun Dance songs are suitable in the sweat. Pipe filling songs, yuwipi songs, Sun Dance songs, and four-directions songs are used in a variety of rituals, including the sweat.[10] Rules for songs are more focused on who may sing them than on when and where they may be sung. Only once during my fieldwork did I hear someone criticize a sweat ceremony for including what the speaker thought were improper (Sun Dance) songs. The variety of songs sung and their conscious functions are evident in this narrative by one of my consultants:

> As I learned the songs, they became more meaningful for me: *opáǧi* ['pipe filling'], four directions, Sun Dance, ceremonial. There is a *wóphila* ['thanksgiving'] if someone is doctored. If there's a mourner, a *chaté t'íza* ['brave heart'] song is used. Last were the thanksgiving and offering songs. I wondered what they were. Sometimes the physical tobacco ties, we sing for those. Sometimes the grief we take, they sing for that.

Another person who taught me about the sweat explained specific songs included in each round of a sweat that was held during a Sun Dance:[11]

> This is a calling-on-the-spirits song (used for the first round of the sweat):
>
> *Wayágkhiya yo!*
> *Wayágkhiya yo!*
> *Chanúpa ki le wakhá yelo!*
> *Wayágkhiya yelo he haaaaaaaaaaaaa!*
>
> Look at all this!
> Look at all this!
> This pipe is sacred!
> Look at this.
>
> I ask the spirits to look at the pipe. There are lots of other different songs. That's the one I sang. That's the first door.
> Second door is the seventh direction. That's for each individual to say their prayer. Then I sing them a song, a Sun Dance song. That's really

appropriate. They all pray in the second round. They usually reaffirm their prayers from that day that they made in the sacred circle. That's keeping in one mind and spirit all that they do. Usually they dedicate one day for one thing or whatever they're praying and dancing for. The song I sang:

Thu̜káši̜la wa̜máya̜ka yo!
Lé miyé cha nawáži̜ yelo!

Grandfather, look at me!
It's me, standing!

That's the second door. At each door opening that sage juice helps them. If they just had water they would have cramps. When the door's opened they get sage water.

The third round is for all we may have forgotten. Everyone can pray again if they want. If not we sing a lot of Sun Dance songs:

Wakhá̜ Thá̜ka u̜šimala ye!
Waníkta cha lechámu welo!

Grandfather pity me!
I want to live so I do this!

The fourth round is for thanksgiving. We sing the thanksgiving song. All that we have to offer we offer.

Stolzman provides this classification of songs specifically for the sweat:

The Lakota songs fall into four general groups, which are related to the four openings of the sweatbath ceremony. First, there are the "calling songs," which cry out to the Great Spirit, the Four Winds, the medicine man's spirit friends, and other spirits related to the ceremony. In addition, there are "answering" song and "doctoring" songs, which ask the spirits to help and answer the people in their material needs. Also, the leader or medicine man may receive a message or instruction, or a blessing from a spirit at that time. Thirdly, a "Pipe" song may be sung before the Pipe is smoked. Finally, a "thanksgiving" and/or a "spirit-sending" song may be sung as the ceremony comes to a close. While it is more traditional to sing several songs during the course of a sweatbath, they are not an essential part of the sweatbath ceremony and are sometimes omitted by beginners.

In the sweatbath after the pouring of water and the singing of the "calling" songs, the medicine man tells the participants which spirits are present. If there are new people or special needs, more explanation about the ceremony, the spirits, and their powers are given. [1986a:55]

In working with sweat lodge participants on Pine Ridge, it seemed clear to me that there are no consistent rules for the use of songs except that people employ only the songs they deem appropriate. The main criterion is circumstance: people come to the lodge for certain purposes, and songs that fit those purposes are employed. Despite the variations in song, there are many consistencies among lodges. No secular songs, such as powwow songs, are sung. All songs sung during a sweat are sacred. In the sweats I participated in with Native American Church members where all the participants were church members, they used songs from their own meetings, accompanied by a water drum and a rattle. Although they acknowledge that this is an innovation in the sweat lodge, they accept it because of the sacred nature of the songs. When Native American Church members sweat with nonmembers, they freely omit their own form of singing and use the songs regularly sung within the sweat.

Another remarkable consistency is that all songs are sung in Lakota. Sometimes the leader will explain what a particular song means, but the use of English has not yet penetrated the Lakota song assemblage. Also, songs are sung only when the door is closed. The single exception is the *opáǧi* 'offering' song, which is sung while loading the pipe. That song, and the loading of the pipe, generally take place outside the sweat before the participants enter the lodge.

There are no songs used in the sweat that refer to the ceremony itself or to the sweat lodge structure. There are, however, a significant number of songs that refer to *ní* 'breath' or 'life' (keep in mind that the Lakota term for the ceremony is *inípi*). These songs are not exclusively the domain of the sweat lodge (several of them are classified as Sun Dance songs), but they are consistently sung during the sweat.

This song, the earliest in the ethnohistorical literature connected with a sweat lodge ceremony, was recorded in the context of a sweat at the end of a Sun Dance ceremony:[12]

> *hó uwáyį kte*
> *namáȟ'u ye*
> *makhá sitómniya*
> *hóyewa yelo*
> *namáȟ'u ye*
> *waní kte lo'*

a voice I will send
hear me
the land all over
a voice I am sending
hear me
I will live [13] [Densmore 1918:124, retranscribed]

That song specifically refers to continuation of life, *waní kte lo*. In prayers, individuals also seek *wichózani* and *zaníye*. Individuals with whom I worked provided a variety of songs that rely on the key concept *ní:*

> This one is an old song. It is a Sun Dance song but we use it and others in the sweat:

> *Wakháthąka úšimala ye!*
> *Waníkta cha echámu yelo.*

> Wakan Tanka pity me
> I want to live so I do this.

> There are also thanksgiving songs:

> *Thųkášila philáma yelo, philáma yelo, philáma yelo.*
> *Wichózani wą mayák'u cha philámaya yelo heeeeee.*[14]

> Grandfather, Thank You.
> You have given me health so I thank you.

> In the second verse you also can substitute *wichóni* ['life'] for *wichózani*.

> Then make prayers. Sing the *Thų̨ká olówą:*

> *Thų̨ká úši'ųlapi ye.*
> *Thų̨ká úši'ųlapi ye.*
> *Mitákuye ób waníkta cha*
> *Wóchekiya ki lená chicú yelo.*
> *Thų̨ká úši'ųlapi ye* [or *po*].[15]

> Stones pity us
> Stones pity us
> Because I want to live with my relatives
> I give you these prayers.

Stones pity us.

This is a sweat or prayer song:

Thųkášila Wakhą́thąka
Eyá hoyéwaye lo
Mitákuye ób
Wanî kte cha eyé hoyéwayel
Thųkášila ómakiya yo makákiže yo.[16]

Grandfather Wakantanka
I send a voice to you
With my relations
I want to live so I send a voice
Pity me grandfather I am suffering

This is a prayer song:

Thųkášila Wakhą́thąka heyá hoyéwaye lo
Mitákuye ób wanîkta cha hoyéwaye lo
Thųkášila ómakiya makákiže yo

Grandfather Wakantanka I send my voice.
I want to live with my relations so I send my voice.
Grandfather help me, I am suffering.

A variation on this one:

Thųkášila Wakhą́thąka heyá hoyéwaye lo
Mitákuye ób wanîkta cha lechámu yelo
Thųkášila ómakiya makákiže yo

Grandfather Wakantanka I send my voice.
I want to live with my relatives so I am doing this.
Grandfather help me, I am suffering.

Sun Dance song also used:

Wakhą́ Thą́ka ųšimala yo
Wanî wachį́ cha lechámu lo
Ómakiya yo makákiže lo

Wakan Tanka pity me.
I want to live so I'm doing this
Help me for I'm suffering.

One of the main Sun Dance songs:

Wakhą́ Thą́ka ų́šimala ye
Waníkta cha lechámu

Wakan Tanka pity me.
I want to live so I'm doing this.

There are two distinct contexts for the entreaty for life *(ni)* made in these ceremonial songs. One specifies that the individual wants to continue to live.[17] The other specifies that the individual desires to live among his or her people.[18] The majority of songs designate the communal context of continuity of life, and this social context may be implied in the other ("I want to live") songs. It is particularly appropriate that all these songs are sung in a communal setting in the sweat lodge. There is in Lakota prayer and ceremony a consistent focus on the desire for continuing to live (W. K. Powers 1990b:62 n. 4). Finally, just as in prayer, songs also refer to *wichózani* 'health' and *zaníye* 'well-being'. Thus, the physical effect of the sweat focuses on health, healing, and life, as do songs and prayers within the sweat.

Narratives

George Sword connects the importance of song and speech in Lakota ritual healing: "When one has a medicine, he must have a song for it and he must know something to say every time he uses it. If the wrong song or invocation is used, the medicine will do no good" (Walker 1980:91).

We have examined two forms of speech already, prayer and song. We will now look at narratives produced in the sweat. In addition to times for prayer, there are also spaces within the sweat lodge ceremony for individuals to speak. Those narratives generally bracket the rounds of the sweat; that is, they occur before the singing and praying begin or after the praying and singing end.

Narratives can be usefully divided into two types according to source. The narratives given by the leader, the first type, provide the reasons for holding the sweat, validate his or her leadership of that particular sweat, and structure the

sweat itself. The leader also sustains and regulates the general narrative structure within the sweat through his own words and by authorizing others to speak.
The second type of narrative comes from the participants. Those narratives,
highly personalized, contextualize the participation and sometimes the life
situation of individuals. Unlike prayer and singing, which are both addressed to
the divine, narratives are used by individuals to address each other.

Narratives are generally delivered while the door is opened but sometimes
when the door is shut.[19] At the beginning of most sweats today, the leader explains what is about to happen. He or she will tell why the sweat is taking place
and what special things should be prayed for and, if there are people new to the
sweat, will tell a little about the sweat itself. The leader also welcomes people,
sometimes each by name, and thanks them for coming and helping to pray.
Those narratives are in Lakota or Lakota and English. They are rarely exclusively in English unless the leader is a monolingual English speaker, since an
ability to speak Lakota remains a qualification for authentic ritual leadership.
The leader will also give his or her qualifications for running a sweat, in a rather
self-effacing manner.[20] Sometimes the leader will apologize for any mistakes
that might occur.

Dialogue also takes place between the doorkeeper and the people in the
sweat. Those inside the lodge must verbally inform the doorkeeper when they
want to end a round of the sweat and what implements to carry in and out of the
sweat between rounds.

The ethnohistorical literature cites several instances of speech making in
the sweat lodge:

> All those men sitting in the lodge advise the man who will cry for a
> vision with the *wakan* knowledge that they have and so the holy man
> instructs the vision quester, they say. "My friend, perhaps something
> frightening comes to you and you want to run away; stand with a strong
> heart! In this way you will become *wakan.*" Saying this, he instructs him, it
> is said. "Pray to inquire wisely and well into everything! You will be a
> coward if you learn nothing," he says, it is said. [Tyon in Walker 1980:151]

> "This is my rite. This man has given me many presents and asked for
> *Ha^{n}běle-cheapi.* I have worshipped the Great Mystery many times, and I
> now ask Thunder for a blue day. The Mystery has created many animals,
> some of which are like men. This young man will see them."
> Continuing, he instructs the faster:
> "This sweat removes from your body all evil, all touch of woman, and
> makes you *waká^n,* that the spirit of the Great Mystery may come close to

you and strengthen you. When our sweat is over, you will take pipe and buffalo-robe and go to some high mountain where the air is pure. On your return you must be careful to speak the truth in telling us of your visions, for should you deceive us, we might work you great harm in trying to aid you in interpreting the revelations sent by the Mystery." [Curtis 1908:67][21]

Those texts clearly establish the sweat lodge as a place of instruction, a feature that persists today when individuals seek visions and answers to particular questions and problems.

Some narratives serve to establish confidence in the proceedings. Stories of healing predominate and continue to validate the practice of inipi in the present. At the home of a sweat leader, before the ceremony began, the leader and one of the leader's relatives spoke about the many individuals who had been cured within her lodge. Another practitioner explained that he had cured blindness and alcoholism as well as healing cripples, in his sweat. Yet another explained the healing process in this way, consistent with the belief that illness is intrusive: "The sweat takes out worries from your mind. It takes everything out. It can cure you. Take sickness into the sweat with you and you can leave it in there. Don't bring it out. This is the traditional way you believe."

Dialogues may also take place between individuals and the spirits. Sword, Bad Wound, No Flesh, and Tyon, in the context of the secret knowledge of spiritual leaders, stress the intermediary role of the shaman as well as the importance of song: "When a shaman prays, he first sings his song or he repeats his formula and then he tells the God what he wishes. . . . Then he tell[s] the people what the God wishes" (Walker 1980:95). Although spiritual leaders serve as intermediaries between the other participants and the spirits, some non-leaders claim direct contact with the spirits. If the spirits speak in their language, which is intelligible only to the medicine man, then the medicine man is called upon to translate so all can understand.[22]

With regard to the vision quest, instructions are given in the sweat, and the supplicant also describes his or her experience in a concluding sweat. Speeches within the lodge continue to be used as in the past to console and counsel mourners (Tyon in Walker 1980:163; Buechel 1978:270–72) as well as to convey ordinary information among participants. Silence is minimal. When people are not speaking or singing or praying, one still hears the hissing of the rocks, considered to be yet another form of communication in the sweat. Often the amount of heat is analyzed as communication from the spirits—too much heat is often interpreted as displeasure. Exploding rocks are interpreted similarly.

Sweat leaders generally speak before the beginning of the first round after the door is shut. If individuals provide narratives, they usually take place between the rounds.[23] The sweat leader might call on someone and set a theme or simply ask someone if they want to talk. When a specific person other than the leader has requested that the sweat lodge take place, then that individual is called upon to speak about the reasons for the sweat. If someone wants to talk, he or she generally asks the leader for permission to speak or simply begins to speak during a silence. Narratives can be very serious or very humorous. Often the talks between rounds allow a person to verbalize specific experiences, gratitude, problems, or struggles, but the individual may use funny stories to make a serious point.[24] Between rounds, individuals chat with each other and joke. Their conversations usually do not gain the attention of everyone, but there is a great deal of give and take, of teasing, or simply of friends asking each other if they feel all right.

Joking Behavior

Humor is wonderfully common in the sweat, as in all other Lakota ceremonial activity. Humor, itself an extreme in the sweat when juxtaposed with individuals' narratives of suffering and the actual rigors of the ceremony itself, is also the catalyst that allows participants to move between suffering and relief, anxiety and tranquility, sickness and health. Humor within the context of the sweat reproduces the extremes of Lakota existence, both historic and contemporary, and at the same time helps to transform those extreme oppositions into a harmonious whole. Humorous stories entertain and instruct listeners about a full range of life situations: failure and success, defeat and triumph, sorrow and joy.

Humor is employed in a very self-conscious manner in the sweat. Although there is a consensus that humor has a place in the ceremony, disagreements sometimes arise concerning the quality and timing of humor in the sweat. This point is never argued in the sweat, but the leader can regulate the use of humor to some extent by changing the subject, beginning another round, or by starting a song or a prayer. Ultimately, if an individual's actions in a lodge are judged inappropriate, that person can start his or her own lodge or find another: "I respect that [someone who wants the sweat entirely serious], but this is our sweat and Church and it is how we do it. We don't do it out of disrespect. When you get your own sweat you can do it that way. Now respect our ways. Somehow you can tell if laughter is disrespectful. Some sweats are really rigid. I couldn't handle it."

Participants offer a variety of explanations for using humor. Their comments are often proffered when outsiders, particularly whites, participate in a ceremony; they explain themselves in order to curtail judgments of impiety, for Lakotas perceive white rituals as totally humorless. In my experience non-Lakotas tend to behave in a consistently solemn manner throughout the sweat, narrowing the range of emotions provoked by aural and sensory prompts throughout the ceremony. That tendency may be the reason early white observers missed the humor in the sweat. Either they assumed that, as in their own religious ceremonies, humor had no proper place, or participants in the ceremony omitted the humor to more closely match the solemnity of Christian rituals. Walker (1917) makes it clear that humor is a vital part of the Sun Dance ceremony but remains silent on sweat lodge humor.

Individual Lakotas are quite articulate about the function of humor. Note how these two narratives on the place of humor themselves are interlaced with humorous examples:

We believe in laughter. Humor is a good medicine. When a person is on the verge, laughter takes that away. A warrior is one who can laugh at death. Folks also say we are stoic and serious. They are stereotyping. We are humans. There is lots of joking and teasing, even in the sweat, especially with brothers-in-law. Once my uncle was trying to be serious. He wanted to say "Hand me the deer antlers." He said instead "Hand me the antlers, dear." The reply from his wife was, "Honey, you haven't said that in years; we should sweat more often." Once there was a lull in the prayers. *"Hokhá kholá"* ['Let's go, friend'] was what the leader wanted to say, but he said "Coca Cola." He was very serious so we tried not to laugh. We learned that there is a time to be serious and a time to let it out. There's a time when it is not proper to laugh and a time when it is not proper to be serious.

Humor is important. It makes you stick to reality. Don't get too serious. You tease someone who is really serious or down and out. You can nearly feel it. *Hé niyé nitháwa* ['That one belongs to you']; they say that when a big hot rock rolls into the sweat. Humor brought me to my senses. I went in the first time with fear, anxiety, uncertainty. We use it so you don't get too mysterious and holy. Somehow out of this comes humility—we go in serious and afflicted—come out *hécheglala ška* 'not so bad after all'.

The first humor I came across: A mouse crawled all over us in the sweat. Some women even screamed. The leader said in a mixture of Lakota and English that itself was comical: *"Tókhašni* ['It doesn't matter']; that's our sacred mouse. *Ki yelo* ['That sure is']!" I thought, that's absurd; you don't say that here! *Ó niyé cha, ó"* ['It was you'] [I said], thinking a spirit was moving around [when it was just a mouse].

Humor is used both by individuals and by supernatural forces, not only for individual comfort and assurance but also to create social harmony:

> *Kichígnapi* 'respect each other'. That's humor; the good part of you comes out. The spirits do that. You might hate each other, but the spirits make sure you have one mind. They don't intimidate you but they joke. If someone is sick, then everyone is serious. Otherwise just crack up any joke. Go in with shoes on or your glasses on. It happens, they forget. That will make them laugh.

Before a sweat began, one leader stated: "Laughter is the best medicine and it helps you feel comfortable. Jokes are to help you get used to the heat but also to relax and ease you." There is a general consensus that humor is essential for surviving the difficulties of reservation life, and indeed laughter permeates all of Lakota life. In the sweat, humor is intensified rather than being created in a new form.

There are standard jokes told within the sweat, which, like the stories above, treat human action and interaction in the sweat as both sacred and profane. Although a sweat lodge ceremony frequently oscillates between high humor and deep gravity, it is precisely in the serious portions of the sweat that out-of-place occurrences are intensely humorous. Just as humor highlights the seriousness of the ritual, so, too, solemnity highlights the funny parts. Teasing emphasizes individual deficiencies and serves as a leveling device.

One common theme of sweat humor concerns modernizing the sweat. To point out the rigors and simplicity of the sweat (and, indirectly, of reservation life itself), people will suggest that windows, video players, televisions, skylights, fans, and other conveniences be built into the structure. Some will suggest constructing a sweat that is high enough that you do not have to bend over to get in, installing a sprinkler system so you do not have to carry in water and pour it by hand, or adding thermostats to regulate the temperature, rail cars to bring in the rocks, and a shower for when the sweat is over. Once in a sweat there was teasing because an old electric blanket was used as a covering for the door. Someone suggested plugging it into an outlet. People will say things like "Open the window" or "Turn on the air conditioner" when the door is opened and the sweat is cooling down.

All this humor is designed to create a good feeling in the sweat. Although sweats are held for specific needs, the expectation is that harmony, both spiritual and interpersonal, will be established among the participants both during the sweat and after. Humor in the sweat, though often spontaneous, is never random. Joking occurs most often while people prepare for the sweat, as everyone settles into the sweat after the initial silence as the first rocks are brought, when the door is opened between rounds, and after the sweat is concluded, before people emerge from the structure. Rarely does humor occur during a round, but when it does, it has even more profound implications based on what is happening at the moment. Closings in the sweat are reserved for intensely serious matters and openings for light matters. When tensions exist among individuals assembled for a sweat, humor is employed to ease or at least suspend animosities. One is never to think or speak badly of another in a sweat or any other ceremony. Humor transforms any bad feelings through teasing acts and acceptable verbal aggression from opposition into solidarity.

Another common theme of sweat jokes is variations on the prayer mitakuye oyas'in. Some will recount how individuals once said "All my rattlesnakes" or "All in the Family" or "My tacos are done" or *"Mitháwicu oyás'į"* 'all of my wives'. I was told that once, in a sweat, when someone said "Mitakuye oyas'in," someone else replied, "Would you shut up? I'm trying to pray."

Recollection of humorous events also provides comic relief. One man laughingly claimed that he never got burned in the sweat because he was without sin. Another told me that he once sweated with two priests and two medicine men. "I was the only sinner in there," he said. Another told of a lady who fell asleep during one of the rounds. They had to wake her for her turn to pray. They teased her by imitating how she snored: "Zzzzzzzzzzzzzzzzzzzzzz pup-pup-pup-pup-pup."

People also joke about the discomforts of the sweat. Comments about how cramped it is in the lodge, how hot the rocks are (insisting that the largest and hottest be placed in front of certain individuals), how hot it is during a round (exclaiming that their eyelashes are curling from the heat), and how weak they feel are common sources of humor. One man claimed that his shorts melted in the last sweat he attended.

Some participants make jokes regarding alcohol use, but those are less common and generally voiced only among intimate friends who know each other's life struggles well. I was told that in a lodge of people who were former drinkers, the comments "Pass the jug," "I want corners," and "I want the back-wash" were all made. Poverty is also lampooned within the sweat. One person said that once, some people who did not have wood made a sweat fire out of old tires. Another countered that an acquaintance had no wood, so he used items from a rummage sale to stoke his fire. Much humor reflects the difficult social and economic conditions encountered on the reservation.

The leader of the sweat has a particular responsibility to create this good feeling among the participants. Leaders will joke about the duration of their sweat, threatening to go twenty rounds or to sing fifty "push ups" (repetitions) on a song. They also make jokes, often repeated from sweat to sweat, as they ready themselves for the first round. One began singing "Little Drummer Boy" as we were getting ready to sweat. Another suggested we sing the doxology, a Christian hymn to the Trinity usually sung in Lakota on the reservation.

It is not entirely up to the leader, however, to achieve a good feeling. Participants must also do their part. They might tease the leader back. One person commented on how fast the leader could eat dog: meat in one side of the mouth and then bones out the other. Another related how, in one sweat, someone brought in a rock and it turned out to be a burning stump—they had to open both ends of the sweat to get the smoke out of there. A lead singer told of the time he got confused and sang a flag song instead of a sacred song. Someone else asked whether everyone in the sweat tried to stand up, the common pro-tocol for honoring the flag. Even the doorkeeper, who sometimes remains outside during the rounds, will join in the exchange. One doorkeeper casually remarked that he was going up to the house to watch television as he closed the flap. Upon entering one lodge, one doorkeeper said in a very serious voice, "Tickets, tickets please!"

If someone makes a mistake, it becomes a source of merriment for a long time. The leader of one lodge asked me to ask the door man to bring in seven rocks. I was sitting on the other side of the door and stuck my head out and said, in English, "Bring in seven rocks." The leader said that I should have said it in Indian since I can speak Lakota. Everyone laughed. Whenever people from that lodge saw me at a sweat from then on, they would call me "Seven rocks, please."

Participants also make spontaneous jokes during the sweat breaks, especially if the jokes involve brothers- or sisters-in-law, who are fair game for teasing. At one sweat, the leader's sister came and announced herself outside the sweat while the door was opened for a break. Her brother-in-law yelled out,

"Take all your clothes off and come on in." Someone explained that when he was a doorkeeper he once accidentally rolled a hot rock on a man inside rather than into the fire pit. An old man took his grandchildren to his brother's sweat lodge and told them that it was a UFO. A leader said, after a horse neighed outside the sweat, that the horse had a crush on me and was looking for me. One evening as I was sweating with a group out in one of the districts, the police were spotlighting around the area. The doorkeeper told the leader of the sweat about it, and the leader said, "What if they come and spotlight into the lodge and take us away just in towels? When we go to court tomorrow, we will only have one pair of pants for all of us." One fellow went on about how he fought the Japanese in World War II. During the day they would shoot at each other, and then when the sun went down they would put down the guns, go over to play horse shoes, and sweat together. The next morning they would start shooting again. He also said that another man who was present once put on a powwow for Hitler's sister. One group calls their sweat "the Indian Fellowship Church."

Another man told of the time a young man was out in one of the districts and went into a sweat wearing a brand new pair of Levis. The leader told him to take them off, but he did not listen. When he came out, the jeans had shrunk skin-tight and he could not unfasten the top snap! Another time, a group of men were sticking out a particularly hot sweat when finally someone shouted "mitakuye oyas'in!" and as the door was opened someone else said: "Come on now, it's not THAT wakan." Someone else told how he once got some lava rocks. There was a sweat up at Devil's Tower, and he saw that there was a black stick across the entrance to the sweat. He took the stick away and began collecting the lava rocks in the pit. Some tourists started taking his picture and he shooed them away. He did not do this because the sweat was sacred but so that the police would not be able to identify him!

Humor is used both to ease tensions and to create harmony in the sweat. Jokes highlight individuals' shortcomings in order to emphasize equality. At the same time, humor itself can be employed to correct unacceptable behavior without directly confronting the offending individual or causing any public embarrassment. Direct confrontation is seen as disharmonious.

Humor should not be overanalyzed, however. Humor is relished for its own sake, and a good sense of humor is really appreciated. The sweat is a break from routine, a movement into another world, which humor helps to create, a world where lessons are learned by counterexample. Incorporating humor into the sweat enables participants to move totally into that world. The world within the sweat is a world of harmony and joy, power and healing, even if it lasts but a few hours. There is a love of laughter, and jokes and stories are often repeated to create that atmosphere.

A good sweat is a hot sweat, but it should never be too hot. Individuals regulate the heat of the sweat by adding rocks, pouring water, indicating their relative comfort through verbal interaction, back-channeling, and manipulating the door. A good sweat is one in which harmonious relations are established and persist. Harmony is regulated through prayers, songs, narratives, and humor. The intensity of the heat and the quality of the talk vary from lodge to lodge and within lodges. The sweat lodge is most striking for its physical effect upon participants. Closer examination demonstrates that verbal interaction is as significant as the physical experience within this ceremony.

The sweat lodge is a place of sound; silence, although never totally absent, is a rare occurrence within its confines. The abundance of meaningful sound, as we have seen, is significant. The sweat is a place for expression of one's inner thoughts and feelings. Communication is diffuse, from invoking the spirits residing in the four directions to the joking of participants seated around the rock pit. My experience is that people who normally talk very little speak easily in the context of the sweat lodge. The insistence upon privacy is part of the reason for this freeness, but the essential quality of the sweat literally brings it out of people. As we have seen in the ethnohistorical documentation, disease and moral wrong are seen as intrusive to the person. Just as one can exude illness through the sweat, one can also verbally (and mentally) remove problems from within by speaking them aloud.

Although the sweat serves to intensify suffering both symbolically and physiologically, it is ultimately concerned with alleviating that suffering by displacing it from everyday life to the ceremonial realm, where it can be controlled. Humor is used in that process to make suffering easier to bear. Narratives objectify suffering and build solidarity by providing the group with knowledge of a person's hardships. Finally, prayer and song invoke the intercession of divine powers for the alleviation of one's suffering and the continuance of one's life.

As the Lakota term for the sweat, *inipi,* indicates, the ceremony is about life and its enhancement, communally and personally. Verbal interaction is a means of communicating one's petitions through song, prayer, and narrative. All is not function, however, for a lot of play is present. Language itself is part of the point of the sweat, particularly in the case of humor. Finally, the use of the Lakota language returns one verbally to the precontact world of presumed harmony and bliss, just as the structure of the sweat physically returns one to that same world. Thus, participants enact tradition, constructed of notions of the past and needs of the present. Because of the contention over tradition and the stresses of reservation life itself, the participants in actual sweat ceremonies strive to make it a place of harmony rather than contestation. Humor and verbal interaction are key for establishing the goodwill of the participants as they engage in this traditional behavior. There are other places to work out the dialectic that establishes tradition. As we shall see, sweat groups are collections of individuals who have agreed on specific formulations of traditional behavior.

5

Stories of Power and Weakness

Stories serve to both establish and legitimate the poles of the dialectic that creates tradition, for they reflect an understanding of the past and serve as guides for present behavior. A considerable number of stories concerning the sweat lodge have been recorded in both ethnohistorical and popular literature; many of these older stories, as well as new ones, are told on the reservation today. Stories on Pine Ridge are flexible, freely adapted to audience and circumstances. Thus, they not only guide the dialectical process but also become part of the process itself.

Origin Stories

Although both ethnohistorical literature and contemporary practitioners consistently attribute an ancient age to the sweat lodge ceremony, only a few stories self-consciously attempt to account for its beginning.[1] Charles A. Eastman and Elaine Goodale Eastman (1909:125–37) recount the most elaborate one of those origin stories. Boy Man, the father of the human race, came into being when He-who-was-first-created removed a splinter from his toe and tossed it out the smoke hole of his lodge. When the splinter touched the ground, it became a baby, Boy Man. When Boy Man failed to return home one day, He-who-was-first-created went out looking for his bones, assuming him dead. In his search he wounded the great water monster and his wife. After this he went to the water and turned himself into a swallow. The loon taught him several mystery songs and showed him how to treat the sick. He then turned himself into a loon and dived to the bottom of the lake. There he entered the tepee of the water monster, whose flap was made of the skin of Boy Man.

He-who-was-first-created took Boy Man's skin and bones and returned to the dry land. He built a sweat lodge and picked a bunch of sagebrush. Wrapping the bones in a skin, he built a shelter of willow withes over them, covering the lodge tightly with green boughs.[2] He thrust his right arm into the lodge and sprinkled water on the rocks with the bunch of sage. Steam filled the lodge and a faint sound was heard. He sprinkled the water a second time and heard a rustling sound as if the dry bones were gathering themselves together. At the third pouring, as he put his hand inside, he heard distant singing. Finally, he heard Boy Man speak, asking to be let out of the lodge.

Charles Eastman retells this origin story in a later work (1911:79–81), adding the detail that four round stones were heated and inserted into the lodge. In that version he explicitly states that water was sprinkled four times, noting that four is a magic or sacred number for the Dakotas. Eastman emphasizes the sacred nature of the ritual:

> Not only the *"eneepee"* itself, but everything used in connection with the mysterious event, the aromatic cedar and sage, the water, and especially the water-worn boulders, are regarded as sacred, or at the least adapted to a spiritual use. For the rock we have a special reverent name—*"Tunkan,"* a contraction of the Sioux word for Grandfather. [81]

A second origin story is told by the Oglala Brave Dog (in Buechel 1978:270–72). In this story Bear Starts Out is given the sweat lodge ceremony by another people in order to put his people "in order." This story stresses social reform. While I was working on Pine Ridge, an Oglala told me a story concerning the origin of the sweat lodge that was remarkably similar in theme to Brave Dog's account:

> In the old days people were not getting along with each other. Brothers and sisters were abusing each other. Brothers were killing brothers, and children were being abused. It was like Gollem and Sodium [Sodom and Gomorrah]. This one father wanted to make peace among everyone, so he went out for a vision. He brought his pipe with him. In those days, the visions were done in pits, so they staked him down there. He prayed and prayed and then had a dream. In the dream he saw rocks coming into the pit from the side. The rocks were red hot. Then water followed the rocks and

steam was produced. This steam purified him. He looked up and saw a dome-shaped structure over himself. Then he looked outside to the west and he saw a buffalo skull. This represented the ancestors. He was tied on a hill above the lake. So after his vision quest, he told the elders about the vision and they used this lodge and it brought about the cleansing that the people needed.

Walker's "Literary Cycle" proposes another origin for the sweat lodge. Unk, the mother of Gnaski, created the Mini Watu, small creatures living in water, which, when swallowed, drank the blood and ate the flesh of their host, causing fevers and pains. The Ikce (descendents of mankind) became sick from these creatures, and the medicine men were unable to cure them. Tokahe, the superhuman culture hero, sought a vision to relieve this malady:

> The powers of remedies are in the smoke or steam that is of them; that if this smoke or steam enters the body, it will strengthen the ghost so that it can cleanse the body of evil that plagues it; that if this smoke or steam is confined in a dome shaped lodge, it will enter the body of one in the lodge where it is confined and exercise its powers to aid the ghost in maintaining the health of such a one. [Walker 1983:375]

This remedy is further refined so that the steam from rocks rather than the smoke from fire, which is less controllable, is used for its salutary effects. At the end of the story, the narrator explains that this rite is used when the descendants of Ikce are afflicted with disease, fatigue, or depression or contemplating something of importance.[3] No one besides Brave Dog (in Buechel 1978) mentions using the sweat on a societal level until the 1970s.

Vitalization Stories

Other stories attest to the creative, regenerative, medicinal, and protective powers of the sweat lodge, focusing on a crisis that is resolved through its use. One type of story in that category concerns the creative force of the sweat lodge and involves transforming blood into a hero who saves those who are suffering. Blood Clot Boy is the most available story in the literature that illustrates this theme. Stephen Return Riggs (1893:95–104) collected a version of it written in Dakota by David Gray Cloud.[4] In it, Badger is exploited by Gray Bear, who takes all of Badger's family's food. When Badger attempts to get food for his starving family, Gray Bear catches him and pushes him down in a pool of buffalo blood. Badger takes a piece of the blood, kisses it, and goes home crying. The story continues:

> On the way he pulled some grass and wrapped it around the blood and laid it away in the back part of his tent. Then he went and brought stones and sticks for a sweat-house, and *Artemisia* or wild sage, and made a steaming. In the back part of the sweat-house he made a bed of the *Artemisia* and upon it placed the blood, and then he covered the lodge well on the outside. Then he took a dish of water and placed it within, and when the stones were well heated he rolled them in also and fastened the door. Then he thrust his arm alone inside and poured water on the stones.
>
> Suddenly the Badger heard some one inside sighing. He continued to pour water on the stones. And then some one breathing within said, "Again you have made me glad, and now open for me." So he opened the door and a very beautiful young man came out. Badger at once named him Blood-Clot Boy, and had him for his son. [102]

This story provides a rather neat description of the lodge, stressing that it was the power of the lodge itself (which, according to Riggs, accesses the "mysterious power"), not the badger, that created the hero from the blood of the buffalo. This is highlighted by Badger's standing outside the lodge when he pours the water. There is no specific mention of spirits in the story, nor are prayers employed in the rite. It is the direct effect of the steam, seen as a spiritual force, that creates the hero from the blood. Significantly, Blood Clot Boy is referred to as Badger's son, solidifying the spiritual affinity and social alliance created through the sweat lodge ritual.

Also significant is the implicit symbolism of the sweat lodge as a womb and the process of steaming as birth. The boy is formed from a blood clot. The term used for the slain buffalo from which the blood was obtained is *pté,* which can be either the generic term for buffalo or the specific term for buffalo cow. Thus, the blood may be interpreted as female, the stones male, and the lodge itself, by shape and function, the womb. The heat is responsible for gestation, and through the lodge Blood Clot Boy is born. Although this analysis is not specifically indicated in the story, it is compelling.[5] Another striking image, further reinforcing the symbolism of birth, is the symbol of intercourse itself when Badger, thrusting only his arm into the lodge, pours water causing Blood Clot Boy to be born. After Blood Clot Boy emerges, the narrator says, *"k'a hé Hoká cįkšíya"* 'Thus he was the Badger's son,' stressing the essential relationship created through the act. According to this analysis, the water is male, the blood female, and creation is generated from the mixture of the two fluids (blood and water) through the medium of heat.

Two other Dakota versions of the same story are recorded by Zitkala-Ša (Gertrude Simmons Bonnin, a Yankton Sioux) and Wilson Wallis (an anthropologist who worked among the Wahpeton Dakotas at Portage la Prairie and Griswald, Manitoba). Wallis's version (1923:75–78) is similar to that collected by Riggs. It states that the badger was outside the sweat lodge when the transformation took place. In Bonnin's version the badger enters the lodge to purify himself, taking the blood with him. Bonnin's description is interesting, too, for it very consciously reiterates the sacred nature of the lodge, a factor taken for granted in Riggs's and Wallis's renditions. Also, petitionary prayers are used:

> On his return to his family, he said within himself: "I'll pray the Great Spirit to bless it [the blood]." Thus he built a small round lodge. Sprinkling water upon the heated heap of sacred stones within, he made ready to purge his body. "The buffalo blood, too, must be purified before I ask a blessing upon it," thought the badger. He carried it into the sacred vapor lodge. After placing it near the sacred stones, he sat down beside it. After a long silence, he muttered: "Great Spirit, bless this little buffalo blood." Then he arose, and with a quiet dignity stepped out of the lodge. Close behind him some one followed. The badger turned to look over his shoulder and to his great joy he beheld a Dakota brave in handsome buckskins. [Zitkala-Ša 1901:71–72]

A Lakota variant of Blood Clot Boy was recorded by Ella Deloria (1932: 113–20). In that version the protagonist is a rabbit rather than a badger. The plot is essentially the same as in the Dakota versions. The rabbit also remains outside the sweat lodge when the clot of blood is transformed into the hero.

These creation-rescue stories highlight the transformative power of the sweat lodge. A clot of blood is transformed into a hero who then rescues people who are oppressed. The agency of the sweat lodge resolves the crisis in each case. Bonnin's version reflects contemporary sweat lodge practice, in which prayer, participation, and intention are essential components for ritual efficacy. None of the other stories detail rituals within the sweat lodge.

Frances Densmore (1918:72–73) collected a rather anomalous story concerning how corn came to the Sioux. In that story an old couple pray for a child while they are in the sweat lodge. They are told in the lodge that their prayers will be granted and the next morning they will have a child. When the couple go out the next morning they discover a plant. They both go back to the sweat lodge and ask what to do. They are told that their child will be the most beautiful plant they ever saw and that they are to care for it.[6] That story indicates the power of the lodge, through prayer, to achieve desired goals. It also links the lodge to the origin of agriculture for the Lakota people, who were by then decidedly nonagricultural. The sweat lodge is also a place to receive wisdom, insight, and understanding. Before the couple enter the lodge, they do not understand the significance of the plant.

The mystical power of the sweat lodge to ensure success in war is illustrated in the story of the medicine bow, collected by Wissler (1907:204–6). In it a poor boy is given a magic bow in the world of the thunder up in the sky. He is told to construct a lodge for himself and to make a ceremony. He calls in four old men to take part in the ceremony. Sweat lodges are made in each of the four cardinal directions, and the young man invites all who wish to participate to come and purify themselves. Those who come break into four parties, the young man among them. After this the boy makes further preparations and then goes out in the cardinal directions with a war party, defeating the enemy each time. The bow makes him invincible and allows him to win victories and capture many horses. The sweat lodge ensures his success. This is in keeping with the role of the lodge as preparation for significant endeavors.

Stone Boy Stories

The most often recorded story in which the inipi plays a significant role is that of *Íyą Hokšíla* 'Stone Boy'.[7] There are two basic versions.[8] In the first one, four brothers adopt a woman who, turning out to be evil, plans their demise. The youngest brother, *Hakéla,* turns himself into a bird and discovers the woman's evil intent. The brothers trick the woman, who then kills all but *Hakéla.* The latter constructs a sweat lodge and revives his brothers. This story is joined to the more predominant version involving the same group of brothers,[9] which tells of a good woman who comes to care for a group of brothers and is adopted by them as a sister.[10] The brothers go out hunting, each on a successive day, and fail to return. Their adopted sister is grief-stricken and begins mourning. While she mourns, she does something that causes the conception of Stone Boy.[11] Most versions say she puts a pebble in her mouth to allay her thirst and accidentally swallows it.[12] The pebble becomes a child, Stone Boy. In all the stories the boy matures remarkably quickly. He then ventures out to find the uncles.

In several versions the uncles are killed by an old hag who tricks them into rubbing her back.[13] She thrusts a spine from her back (in some versions made of metal) into them and kills them. Stone Boy destroys the old hag by his own weight, crushing her to death. He discovers the bones of his uncles and places them in a sweat lodge. Standing outside the lodge, he pours water on the rocks, and the uncles come back to life.[14] Marie McLaughlin (1916:189) states that the uncles told the nephew to stop pouring after the third bucket lest he scald them to death. Old Man Walker's version also has Stone Boy yelling to his mother to open the sweat lodge door lest they all die inside. In that version others are also brought to life. The lodge thus has the power to restore life, but, used in excess, it can also destroy life. In this story the stones and the bones are seen as life-generative. Stone Boy is created from stone itself, and the uncles' bones are restored to life through the agency of water poured on hot rocks. Again, the symbols of generation, womb, and birth are evident.

Bad Wound presents an unusual version for the Lakotas of the Stone Boy tale (Walker 1983:140–53). Rather than the woman's appearing at the brothers' tent, Stone Boy's mother is born from the oldest brother's toe after something runs into it in the woods. She grows up and cares for the brothers well. As in the other versions, each brother fails to return home after going out hunting. She swallows a pebble and gives birth to Stone Boy. After she gives a feast in honor of Stone Boy, he goes off to find the uncles. Stone Boy is mistaken for a Thund-er Bird by a coyote and a bear, who try to destroy him. Stone Boy kills them both, and then he destroys a rock that rolls by itself and a tree with snakes for limbs. An old woman takes him into her tepee and tries to kill him. She turns out to be Iya [Íya], an evil old man disguised as a woman, who made the uncles into tanned skins after the living stone crushed each of them. Iya says that his only masters are the living stone that Stone Boy destroyed and another living stone, which turns out to be Stone Boy himself as the story progresses. Stone Boy makes Iya tell where the uncles are. The uncles and all who were captured by Iya are still alive, hanging tortured on tepee poles. Iya also explains that he sent an evil woman to trick the uncles, but, because they raised her so well, she became good. She turns out to be Stone Boy's mother. Iya refuses to tell Stone Boy how he can revive those tortured on the poles. Stone Boy begins crushing Iya, and he finally relents. Iya tells him to use the skins of the bear and the coyote as a tepee cover. Because they are too small, Stone Boy has to make the tepee low and dome shaped (an explanation for the shape of the sweat lodge). He uses the living rock in the lodge for sweat stones and revives the uncles by pouring water on the hot rocks. The rocks have special significance, for they are "living rock" infused with power that Stone Boy dominates. Stone Boy then crushes Iya, and cherry stones come out of his mouth—those are transformed into the many people of the earth. Iya tricks Stone Boy and saves himself. That version of the story accounts for the origin of the sweat lodge as derived from the power of Iya and the living rock.

Charles Eastman's version of the Stone Boy story (1902:126–37) is also unusual. After killing a bear, Stone Boy hears a whirlwind, and a man descends from the clouds. While fighting, the warrior sweats, causing a heavy shower. When Stone Boy defeats the warrior, the storm subsides. Stone Boy assumes that this man killed his uncles, so he goes to his country in the sky by blowing on some down. In this beautiful country, the land of the Thunder Birds, he sees many people. In a great tree is an enormous nest loaded with eggs of a remarkable red color. He floats up into the nest, causing the people in the villages to panic. He begins throwing eggs at them, and as each one breaks, someone below dies. They exclaim, "Give me my heart." Stone Boy says these people killed his uncles, so he destroys all but four small eggs. He asks the remaining four small boys where his uncles' bones are laid. When he finds them, he tells the first boy to bring wood, the second water, the third stones, and the last to cut willows to build the lodge. He puts the bones into the lodge, and as he pours water, he hears faint sounds in the "magic bath." The voices begin to murmur and finally sing medicine songs. When Stone Boy opens the door, the ten uncles emerge, thanking him for restoring them to life. The little finger of the youngest uncle is missing, so Stone Boy "heartlessly" breaks the last four eggs and takes the little finger of the largest boy and places it on his uncle.[15]

In another contemporary rendition of the Stone Boy story, Henry Crow Dog claims that the lodge in the story was the first sweat lodge ever built (Erdoes 1976:115– 16). Lame Deer also uses this story to demonstrate that the sweat is the first and oldest ritual. He says that, in addition, it stresses the sacredness of the stones, which were the first things worshiped by the Lakotas. When the five brothers fail to return, the woman has no ceremonial or religious knowledge with which to appeal for divine intervention. Lame Deer states that the spirits tell Stone Boy how to construct the sweat. In Lame Deer's version Stone Boy says: "The rocks saved me, and now they saved you. And from now on this sweat house shall be sacred to us. It will give us good health and will purify us" (in Erdoes 1972b: 176). Barbara Means Adams (1990:11) also treats this narrative as an origin story.

Several people with whom I spoke recalled various versions of the stories of Stone Boy and *Hakéla,* the youngest brother, who rescues his siblings from death. Here is a version I was told during my fieldwork, which accounts for the origin of the sweat lodge as the first ceremony:

> There was a time in early creation when all that existed was a young woman and her seven brothers. All of them were young. Life was well with the seven brothers and sister. They hunted, made a lodge, and they had order in the family. Something was missing with this woman. She felt something more was needed in her life. She went out into the country much like today's *hablécheya* ['vision quest']. While she was out, the spirits came and told her to look around herself. In looking she saw a small stone. The spirits said to put it in her mouth and swallow. She did this and found life in her. Nine months later she gave birth to a child. *Íya Hokšíla* was the name she called it.
>
> The child loved both his mother and his seven uncles. He was a very advanced and talented child. He learned well, was well behaved, and he grew quickly. His uncles taught him all he needed to know about crafts, tools, weapons, and survival skills for living. The young boy and mother were sitting by the fire. The uncles were out hunting, but none of them returned. The two were worried as no one appeared. Next day, no one appeared. This happened for four days. On the fourth day, the young mother was so worried that her son promised to look for them. She respected him for saying that but was concerned for him. She said not to go, but he insisted. She gathered all he needed, and he went out searching for four days. He traveled long distances. Finally he came on an old woman who was cooking over the fire. He approached respectfully, called her grandmother. She was covered with a garment which showed only her face. In the lodge, there were seven bundles. The grandmother said: "Grandson, my back is aching, rub it. But you're so small. Walk on my back." As he did this, he felt something almost prick his feet. She was not a woman but a reptile creature with spikes on her back. He jumped up and broke her neck. He figured that his uncles touched the spikes and died. He asked the Great Spirit what to do. The spirits told him to take sixteen willows, make a pit, fire place, and altar. Then he had to heat up the rocks and get water. He was told by the spirits to take the seven bundles into the sweat. He sang songs given to him. Along with the steam, there were voices. He figured they were the uncles so he unwrapped the bundles and continued the ceremony. They came out alive.

The narrator used this story to explain the supernatural origin of the sweat lodge.[16] Interestingly, I never heard this kind of story told around the sweat lodge itself. One person stated, "You can't tell that type of story during the day or around sweat lodge with other sacred things—if you do you will grow hair all over."[17] One should be careful when and how one tells stories.

Another story that illustrates the power of the sweat lodge to revivify the dead was told by Joseph Eagle Hawk, an Oglala. *Iktó* was to help Blue Jay stay awake, but he forgot his charge and Blue Jay went to sleep. Buffalo cows stamped him to death, leaving nothing but one little blue feather. His son (whom he had conceived with a buffalo calf) "picked it up and cried over it and took it into a sweat-lodge, made medicine over it and Blue Jay came to life" (Beckwith 1930:400).

Stories Contesting the Power of the Sweat

Those stories clearly demonstrate the power of the sweat ritual, but there are also accounts, mostly by missionaries and educators, debunking the sweat lodge. Both missionaries and the government attempted systematically to discredit native practice—social, economic, and religious—in favor of "civilization." One such story is told by Elaine Eastman in her personal memoirs. The multiple (and at times ambiguous) roles of the sweat lodge are highlighted in the account of a Christian convert from Lower Brule named Little Forked Tail:

> It was told of him that on one occasion he had been persuaded by some old friends to enter again the sweat lodge, or vapor bath, on the plea that it was no religious ceremony this time, but solely for health and cleanliness. However, habits are strong and soon the ancient songs began to issue amid clouds of steam from the lips of the bathers.
>
> "Let the Dakotas remember their own gods!" exclaimed one, "and let each man sing to the god he worships!"
>
> The new convert listened aghast to what now seemed to him the impious and diabolic invocations that followed. Recovering courage, he struck up "Jesus, Lover of My Soul" in the native dialect. The effect was instantaneous. Within half a minute the place was cleared and the Christian worshiper found himself alone. [1978:72–73]

That incident happened around 1888. Eastman tells the story to demonstrate Little Forked Tail's orthodoxy. In keeping with missionary ideology at that time, native religous practice was to be abandoned. Here we see a split between native people not over the sweat itself, for indeed it could be used as a bath, but over the specificity of religious practice, the locus of which was, in this case, the sweat. The sweat in this story became an arena for combat over religious ideology. Also, the story portrays Christianity as ultimately inimical to traditional ceremonial practices and, in this particular story, triumphant over them.

Florentine Digmann, a Jesuit missionary on the Pine Ridge and Rosebud reservations, used stories to debunk the spiritual experiences of the sweat lodge:

> Joe Schweigman told me some stories of "Follows the Woman" who himself had related them. He used to be taken for a great *"Wakan"* a medicine man. The way he got his fame was the following: He had stolen from another Indian an otter skin, valued very highly. The Indian had a very bad heart about it. F. the W. goes to him and said: "You kill a dog for me. I'll take a sweat bath and ask the spirit." So it was done. Now he had found a hollow rubber ball which he attached to a whistle, taking it into the sweat booth. The otter skin he was hiding under his cloth around the loins and went alone into the sweat. He began to howl and sing his sacred songs to the stores [*sic,* stones] and at the same time produced whistling sounds with his rubber ball. Those outside could not understand how he could sing and whistle at the same time; sure that [it] was *"wakan."* Coming out he handed the otter hide to its owner.
>
> Another time he had stolen all the ponies of an Indian and driven them to a hidden place. It was short[ly] before the Indians wanted to break camp and move to another place. F. the W. goes to the desolate Indian who could not find his horses and again asks him to kill a dog for him and make a sweat bath. Coming out from the booth he tells him in that and that place you'll find your ponies, i.e. where he had put them. [Digmann n.d.:92][18]

Stories Affirming the Power of the Sweat

Although the missionaries assailed the religious system of the Lakotas with charges of charlatanism, the stories the Lakotas and Dakotas themselves told concerning the sweat lodge speak for an essential efficacy of the ceremony. In my fieldwork I frequently encountered stories that continued to highlight the power of the sweat lodge and the personal power of individuals. Some contemporary stories attribute miraculous efficacy to the sweat lodge itself. A consultant said that in the old days a warrior came back riddled with bullets. He took a sweat by himself, the bullets went away, and everything was healed. He described it as "a miracle surgery." One individual stated that a tornado came through and turned their trailer around, but it never went near the sweat.

The power of the sweat lodge and, by extension, the power of tradition itself to heal social ills is exemplified by this story told over the reservation radio station, KILI. A teacher explained that she had a young boy in her class who was a discipline problem and was uncooperative during Lakota language classes. One day, the boy came to class and asked his teacher if she was ever in a sweat lodge. He went on to say that now that he had been to the sweat lodge, he really wanted to learn Lakota, and he was no trouble in the class after that.

The curative powers of the sweat are also demonstrated by specific biographical accounts, as in this Santee story recorded by Robert Lowie. Lowie refers to a buffalo dance performed among the Santees by those who had dreamed about buffalo:

> One man might dream that he was a buffalo and had been shot by an arrow so that he could barely get home. The arrow continued to whirl round in his body. He dreamt that the only way for him to recover was to go into a sweat lodge. First he asked for one of four different kinds of earth to mix with water, drank the mixture inside a sweat lodge, and then recovered. Such a man painted himself vermilion to represent the trickling down of the blood. . . .
>
> While dancing, dreamers would call on outsiders to bear witness to the truth of their statements about such experiences. Once a heyoka challenged a dreamer's account, saying that no man could recover from a wound of the kind described. Straightaway the dreamer offered to be shot by the clown, who shot a bullet through him. The wounded man staggered off, went to a sweat-lodge, and actually recovered within a few days. [1913:119]

Biographical testimonials about the power of the sweat lodge and its practitioners continue. For instance, stories of the sweat lodge restoring people to life are still told. One person recounted this story: "There was once a boy who died. He was well beloved of everyone, so the parents put his body into a sweat lodge and had an *inípi.* They kept the body in there for three more days. On the fourth day, they had another sweat and on the fourth round the boy was alive again."

I asked if the person was restored through the power of the ceremony. The reply was no, that a powerful person had to conduct the ceremony. "In the old days, people could do that and power was really strong but not anymore." Note again the implicit symbols of the womb and gestation.

Some locate the power of the lodge within the physical structure itself, others hold for supernatural intervention, and still others see specific individuals as powerful. As in this contemporary narrative by one of my consultants, power is often demonstrated through superhuman abilities:

> One participant thought to himself as he entered that if the medicine man was so powerful, he could make sparks fly and gourds rattle. That medicine man just looked up at him and said, "That is easy," and rubbed his hands together and there were sparks all over. The medicine man said that that is magic, and while it may help some people realize spiritual reality, it is not significant. That medicine man also can pick up fire or [hot] rocks without being burned. It is said that he did this three times to heal people with serious illnesses and when he does it a fourth time, he will probably die. Once the doorkeeper was loading rocks into the lodge, and as each hot rock came in, that medicine man held the rock and prayed with it. He was not burned. No one else noticed this. Later he asked the medicine man about the incident, and that medicine man said that if he touched cold rocks then he would have been burned.

Stories Highlighting the Ambiguity of Spiritual Power

Although most Lakotas agree that rituals are indeed effective, there is an ambiguity expressed through stories concerning the ability of particular individuals to access this power. These ironic tales of inefficacy are sometimes told during sweat lodge rituals, especially those attended by family and close friends. They do not suggest that the rituals themselves are ineffective but humorously portray characters attempting to use the rituals as incompetent or unworthy and thus unable to access their power. In terms of our dialectical analysis, they demonstrate that not everyone can construct tradition successfully and that the weakness is in some who try to construct tradition, rather than in tradition itself. The stories also affirm the overriding power of the spirituality accessed through traditional behavior. These two narratives from Pine Ridge offer contrasting examples of efficacious and inefficacious powers:

> It was about 10:00 at night and pitch black because there were thunder storms all around the area. I stood in the center between the lodge and the fire pit and prayed. The storm did not come near the lodge until I was finished with the sweat, and then there was a downpour as I headed for my house. *"Líla wakȟá"* 'That was really powerful.'

A big hail storm came while someone was putting on a sweat. That guy held up his pipe and tried to split the storm. He was hit with a big hail stone and got a bump on the head. He finally said, *"Thykášila,* I'm getting out of here," and he ran into a tent, which collapsed on him.

Another humorous story expressing the ambiguity of power in the contemporary era is this: "My grandfather called our family together and announced that he was the reincarnation of Crazy Horse. There was a clap of thunder and the lights were out in town for quite a while. Grandpa then said, 'Maybe I'm not Crazy Horse.'"

Individuals are powerful insofar as they are able to harness spiritual power. That power can be proven only through effective actions. Individuals' assertions of power, demonstrated by taking leadership positions in ceremonies, are often countered with humorous stories. Individuals can be seen as powerful even though they have demeaning stories told about them to place them on the same level as the rest of the group. Some leaders will even tell such stories on themselves to equalize their position. This juxtaposition of extremes is seen in storytelling in the sweat lodge. Many of the stories told in the past emphasize the power of the ritual or of practitioners involved in them. Humor is used to express the polar opposite of this, the weakness of practitioners. Thus, the contrasting elements of the ritual, its openings and closings, light and dark, cool and heat, find parallels within the participants in their illness and health, tears and laughter, misgivings and confidence, weakness and strength. The old days were powerful, but today is a time of weakness. The sweat returns to the powerful past to recapture that strength through healing and social transformation.[19]

Humorous Sweat Lodge Stories

Within the sweat ceremony, humorous stories may be used by any participant. Each story told about the sweat involves people known to, and named by, the narrator. Often the same story is told, but different individuals are named as characters in the story. No one ever questions the veracity of these accounts. Although these stories promote social harmony and equality by breaking down status barriers through humor, they can also serve to indirectly reprimand or instruct everyone present, thus enacting and validating the terms of the dialectic. The most repeated story I heard was about the bull and the sweat. I use this version for an example:

Once all these guys were sweating and this mean big black bull comes along. As it comes, the woman outside hollers *"Thablóka wą él ú ye!"* ['There's a bull coming!']. She heads out but they don't hear her in there. The bull stops at the sweat and starts sniffing under the covers. The leader says *"Thųkášila hí s'elél—anáǧoptą po! Thųkášila ahí yelo!"* ['Grandfather is here—listen! Grandfather has arrived!']. Then that bull hooks his horns under the sweat and pulls it up. Those men inside were *ithųkala chįcá šála s'elél* ['pink just like baby mice'].

The motif of the overturned lodge revealing its squirming contents is frequently employed. The image of individuals pink, naked, and shriveled like baby mice, an image of helplessness and pitifulness, is also considered the height of hilarity:

> There was once an old guy who late one afternoon was going to sweat with two cousins and two brothers. They all were invited to his place for a sweat. When everything was ready, they all went in and he began with the *hąblóglaka* ['recitation of visionary experiences'], talking about himself first, his visions and things like that. He was sitting on the west side in the place of honor. It was a social sort of thing. He's talking and everyone is listening.
>
> Outside a relative was going to break a team of horses; one was wild and the other was tame. He caught them both and roped them together with the same rope when a whirlwind came up and scared the horses. The rope got out of his hands and they got away, heading for the lodge with the rope between them. The rope took off the lodge cover. The four in the lodge were bowed over listening, so when the lodge cover headed away they were sitting there all pink like newborn mice when you disturb the nest. The old man was sitting upright, so the rope took him along with the lodge over the hill. Pretty soon here comes the old man, all muddy with the canvas cover over him, mad as hell. The women saw this and they all died laughing. He shook his fists at his son-in-law and said that I'm gonna get you for this.

Stories may have an explicit moral and are often used to indirectly confront difficult subjects by buffering the message with humor:

> Once I was over there and he did a sweat with some young guys. His son also went in, but he had been drinking and was still half drunk. There were about eight of them in there. My aunt was sitting in the shade. The drunk one was the last to go in so he pulled down the cover. The bucket was there at the entrance, and he knocked the whole bucket into the pit with the hot rocks in it. Everyone in there shot out in all directions, stark naked. My

aunt really laughed. My uncle crawled out of the door with his son on his
back riding him. Even Casey Tibbs could not ride like that. That's a funny
story. When it is told, my uncle just sits there because it is true. His son was
barred from the sweat.

That story is both humorous in itself and serves an important function, to
level the uncle with his nephew. Stories are told about one another to show that
everyone has weaknesses and so everyone is equal. The story also illustrates the
detrimental effect of alcohol, albeit in a humorous manner. This is common in
Lakota interaction, where direct confrontation is rare and reprimands are presented through careful indirection, shielded through storytelling or transmitted
to the individual through a third party.[20]

Stories like the previous one, concerning the embarrassment of an individual, are numerous:

> Some folks had a sweat in the middle of one of the housing projects. At
> the housing was a big St. Bernard. Well, they were all in the lodge and they
> handed in the bucket and dipper. That dog then ran into the lodge and
> grabbed the dipper and headed out. The leader of the lodge, he wanted to
> be traditional. So he was naked. He ran out after the dog up onto a hill. The
> cops came by and shined their spot on him and the guy froze there because
> he was blinded. He then fell on the grass trying to hide himself. They
> eventually moved the sweat out away from all those houses.

Stories that serve to level religious practitioners with the rest of Lakota
society are frequently told.[21] These men prove to be just like everyone else
despite their high reputation. It is just this reputation, and the desire to level it,
that precipitates the stories:

> This story happened around here, as my grandfather tells it. Long time
> ago, the medicine men didn't get along with one another. When they have
> a ceremonial, they would put down each other. They said the others don't
> have powers. When they do meet up in a sweat, they try to chase each other
> out. *Íya yútapi* ['they eat rocks'], they could stand a lot of heat. There's an
> old medicine man. They said no one could chase him out of the sweat. No
> matter how hot it is in there, he'll sing. Some roughnecks decided to fix this
> man. Long time ago, they had this *yamnúmnuǧapi zi,* ['yellow pepper',
> perhaps powdered mustard]. I don't know what it is—pepper now is less
> powerful. They got hold of some of that. They put it in a bag. The old man
> poured lots of water—they all shouted *mitákuye oyás'į.* They can't stand

the heat. The roughnecks went in and sat right beside the old man. The man with the *yamnúmnuǧapi zi* took it out and put some on the old man's back under his neck. His sweat made it run down his back and it ran into his crack and burned his backside. He jumped up and out of there. The door flew open—he ran towards the creek. The water made it worse when he jumped in. It was just like fire down there. He was jumping up and down hollering. His mother and grandmother were there. He was old, but they were still living. His mother said, *Cįkš, tókha he?* ['Son, what's the matter?']. He said, "Get out of here you crazy old ladies, I'm dying." Pretty soon he's *ȝzé ša so?* ['his butt is red, hey?'], sliding his rear end in the mud trying to cool it off, but even that made it worse. That's the story he told. This happened.

A similar story is told in which the antagonists use iron filings. A third story involves some kids throwing hot pepper into a sweat while everyone is in there. The occupants all shoot out of there buck-naked.

Other Pine Ridge stories lampoon unscrupulous medicine men. Although some medicine men are considered frauds (a lively aspect of Lakota conversation is who is and who is not a legitimate medicine man), these stories are not employed against medicine men as a class of people; they concern specific individuals. The most often told story is that of suspicious spirits:

Once a medicine man invites nuns [sometimes "women"] to go to his sweat. He asked some singers to sing at 4:00. When he sees all the nuns, he told them to take off all their clothes. The nuns did this. When the singers saw this, they wouldn't go in the lodge. So they sat outside and sang for him. Well, the medicine man's wife comes over the hill and the leader sends his wife away before she sees anything. The sisters just sit in there quietly. The medicine man told them that the spirits might touch you. After the sweat, they commented on how the spirits were doing that. The nuns were saying that the spirits had big hands, and one nun said, "That one spirit sure had big lips, too."

Another story about a medicine man shows him to be rather cunning: "Once some *thóka* ['non-Lakota'] women were taking a sweat with one medicine man. He said to them that they were born naked so they should come into the sweat that way. He also sat in one place so that the girls had to crawl over him. He's *Iktómi* ['a trickster'].'" In yet another story, a medicine man outsmarts his own family:

This one medicine man once had all his boys prepare a sweat lodge. He knew that some girls were going to sweat, but he pretended that the boys were preparing the sweat for themselves. He then told the boys when the girls showed up that he would sweat with them the next day, so let the girls and him use the lodge now.

There are also stories about outsmarting the priests who were against native practice:

There was a sweat lodge at my grandma's place, but it was kept secret. One day they had *a'íleha* ['lit the fire' (for the sweat)], and up the hill comes the priest in his blue pick-up truck. The family wanted to hide the sweat from him, so they put the fire out as quick as they could. Meanwhile someone went into the sweat lodge itself and lifted it out of the ground and ran down the hill with it. I was a child at the time, playing outside. I remember it looked so funny, like a giant spider running down the hill. The priest never did find the lodge.

In another story, a priest is in a sweat lodge with some nuns who are wearing their habits. As the priest begins pouring water on the rocks, one sister remarks: "Father, would you please pour some more of that cool water on the rocks. It's sure getting hot in here."

When Digmann pointed out that someone deceived people in the sweat lodge, he assumed that this qualified as proof that all rituals were deceptions.[22] Today, the Lakotas themselves tell stories and jokes about devious individuals posing as medicine men. However, the assumption of these stories is not that the rituals are ineffective, but rather that through their misuse by the unscrupulous their powers are blocked. At times, nevertheless, the ritual proves stronger than the deceiver, as illustrated in this story:

There's two men. They wanted to travel to Rosebud. Nowdays I can get to Rosebud and back in no time. In them days, you have to walk or go on horseback. Both reservations, they don't get to see each other hardly. These two men walked to the other reservation. They weren't medicine men or nothing. One said, "When we get there we're gonna says we're powerful medicine men. We're gonna make money." *Wó'okiye,* that means something to give the medicine man, things to pay him, horses or things. They wanted to collect these things. So they went over.

They had gone to the *yuwípi* and other ceremonies before, so they knew what they were like. They learned there how to do it. One medicine man does the *hablóglaka,* the talk the medicine man gives at a ceremony. One of those two learned from him how to say that just like an auctioneer, talk real fast and still be understood. They learned that and they went to the Rosebud Reservation. They came to these old people's house. These old people had a tame horse and team of horses. These two guys spotted these horses and went at night and stole them and hid them away. Then they came back.

When they arrived, one of them said that he's a medicine man and can find anything that is lost. They walked around and the old man and woman were looking for their horses. The couple heard about the two men so they asked them to help them out. The men wanted dogs and *wó'okiye*—get it ready and we'll look for you. The couple prepared everything and the two did everything like a spiritual man does. They made believe the spirits were talking and kept responding *hó, hó.* Then they told the old couple that the spirits said they'll bring back your horses tomorrow. So the two guys went and got them to bring them back. Early in the morning the horses were back. The two had let the horses loose.

These two, they thought they were really good. They didn't know the real thing would happen. They should have gone home. Another man came up and said that his horse was gone. They didn't know anything about it. They didn't steal it. They had to go through with it because they didn't want to get caught lying. So they made a ceremony. They prayed really hard that the spirits would tell them where the horse was. Here in the roof they saw a hole in the roof and a man with horns looking down. One got scared so he told them to light all the lights up. He was scared but curious. We'll try again, he said. He saw that figure a second time and called for the lights. He was really scared. In the third time, he figured he might as well face it. The man with the horns said: *"Líla ụ̌ši* 'You're really shameful in what you do.' I'll give you my powers and you'll become a real medicine man. You know you're not that kind." So that man became a spiritual man. That's a true story, the *yuwípi* way.

Stories are also employed for the sheer humor of recounting absurd circumstances, again always personalized:

In our sweat my Grandfather, he has one boy. This boy is really crazy. He does things out of the way. When my grandfather goes into the sweat, this boy bothers him. He'll hide all the clothes while they're in the sweat. One day—he has some half-sisters—same mother. One day they said, "We'll help our brother. Take him in the sweat, pray for him, make it really hot. This will help him stop acting out of the way." He didn't want to go in with the women. They said they'd pay him and he'd be a good person if he did it. He gave in because they said they would pay him. They make it really hot so he wants to get out. He starts crying, "Let me go." The sisters hold him down and pour lots of water on the rocks. He starts farting and peeing all over the rocks. That stink really got into the lodge. So he chased all them girls out. The girls said that he's too rough. No way they can help him. He scared them out.

Stories of individuals' foibles are quite common. These stories are often told around or in the sweat, repeated again and again, always with specific individuals mentioned. It is also common for individuals to tell stories on themselves, thus voluntarily leveling themselves with the rest of the group. Individuals demonstrate their own humility, both by praying and by personal narration:

> Once an older man asked me to conduct a sweat lodge ceremony. His duty was to inform the people. It was late spring, the thunder storm season. I started the fire. This older man said he told everyone, but no one was around. I said, "Let's us two do it." The wind was blowing. It was the feeling like just before a storm. The rocks were hot enough to have a good sweat but not that hot. He sang, we both prayed, sang again. The flap was opened and someone came in. It was a good-sized person. I told my partner to make the person welcome. He spoke in Lakota to the person, asked how he was and all the social amenities. That guy who came in just sat there and licked his chops, didn't pay attention to us or say anything. My partner got closer and started talking again, giving him a welcome, this time in English. He moved closer and I heard my partner say: "Hey, cut that out." I said, "I'm going to start the sweat again." My partner closed the door, the first dipper was poured, and then we heard a howling. The door opened and a big black dog ran out. My partner only recalls the black dog but not the words.

The second story goes like this (I have substituted pseudonyms):

> One well-known medicine man called us for a sweat, me and a friend, Mike. We got lost on the way there. We got there an hour late. The sweat was over. Another friend was there, Dave. He said that the rocks were still good. We went in with him. I saw where and how Dave was sitting—he was turned around facing the side of the sweat rather than the pit. When we're in the sweat and ready to pour water in the dark, we tap the rocks with a dipper to make sure we would hit the rocks with the water. Mike went and laid down as soon as he went in. Dave dips some water to pour. Mike's head was close to David's feet. Dave taps Mike's head, thinking it was the rocks, and then pours the water on his head. Mike says, "Thank

you, Grandfather, *háu háu*." Dave did this a few times. Dave says that the
rocks must be really cold because no steam was coming off of them. Then
I realize he's pointing the wrong way and dumping the water on Mike, so I
turned him around. We all laughed and joked about this.

After one round we went out, and here that medicine man and about
thirty guys with braids and shades—they're all glaring at us. Here we were
an hour late and we're laughing around in there.

Another story illustrates both a humbling event and how participants can
amplify the humility:

Once in a sweat, my friend shut the flaps and laid right down. He didn't
even wait for it to get hot but went toward the back. I thought he was sitting
[while, in fact, he was lying down]. I felt something on my shoulder. I
thought it was my friend leaning against me. I elbowed him but nothing
was there. I reached up and it was a little cat on me. My friend makes more
of it and says I said, "Thank you, Grandfather" when I felt something on
me.

Some stories are constituted of personal reminiscences. They allow the
individual to establish himself or herself as ordinary, eschewing any claim to a
sacred or exalted position. In the case of the leaders of the sweat, telling
humorous stories on themselves is in sharp contrast to their initial speech in the
lodge in which they present their spiritual credentials, establishing their right to
run the lodge, and thus returns them to the level of the rest of the group:

I was in the sweat talking about someone when I was hit on the head
through the lodge. It turns out it was a dog jumping against the lodge.

I saw a baby eagle flying around our sweat. I called my husband just to
make sure, and when he saw it he said, "Oh, that's a buzzard."

I was supposed to bring a pup to a sweat, but it was too far to go back to
get one, so I bought a kidney. When I got to the sweat, the spirits said that I
should have brought a dog and that there was an old man with three of them
who would gladly give me one. I went back to that old man, and he gave
me a really big dog, and he said that it would be fine for the sacrifice. When
we tried to strangle it, it kept standing up on its hind legs. Finally we
finished it off, and there was too much meat for us all to eat. Another time
I and a friend applied to the tribe for a buffalo to take to a special
ceremony, and we got it. We had a little six cylinder truck with bald tires
and an appetite for gas. When we drove up to load it, we accidentally ran

over the buffalo's head, and I said, "You just desecrated the sacred cow!" The truck was hung up on the buffalo for a while. Finally we got it loaded and everyone was looking into the truck at the buffalo. When we got there, they had to learn how to cut the meat to dry. My first attempts looked like thick steaks rather than thin strips. We eventually got the hang of it. We fried rather than dried the steaks!

Folks will also tell tales of spectacular occurrences at sweats, especially when they are also humorous. The numinous and the humorous often walk hand in hand:

> We were going to have a sweat one summer evening. Thunder clouds were coming—the earth was yellow. Big thunder was coming. You could hear it. My daughter said, "Mom, look at this cloud." You could see a big sweep—rain or hail. It was just half, going here to here. It looked like a woman with fringes spread like a flying eagle. I couldn't believe it. You could hear the hail. There were two guys at the sweat who were going to come up to the house, but we said to them, "Where's your faith?" They stayed down there. One of them had a cane. When the rains came, they made a dash for their clothes. One man was a cripple and had a hook for a hand. In the confusion the other guy put on his hook. The other, who is very short, put on someone else's long pants and tripped. One guy just had shorts on. Then we had to tow their car up the hill because the rain made the ground slick. As my husband was towing the car, the car jerked and one guy's false teeth were knocked out by the steering wheel. He later said: "My teeth were sitting there laughing at me."

Early stories of the sweat attribute to it miraculous power to create, revive, order, and heal life. In the contemporary era the ceremony is used to recapture that power through intercession with the divine. It is also perceived as a link with the ancient past, a past invested with power. That power is accessed through recreating a structure and a ceremony that is identified today as an ancient and, at times, as the most ancient ritual. Although the oldest stories concerning the sweat are entirely of a serious nature, contemporary stories deal with ambiguity: the sweat lodge ceremony is seen as a source of power, but not everyone can successfully access that power at all times. Stories both reinforce the image of power of the past era and highlight the weakness of the present. Thus, the stories serve as guides in forming the poles of the dialectic that Lakotas use to create tradition. They also serve as Mythic Charters, in Malinowski's terms, which guide and validate present behavior as well as establishing, in part, past practice. Stories also function as important vehicles for negotiating current practice through their indirect reprimands and negative examples. Although stories indeed exercise these functions, they do not determine the entire dialectic for individual inspiration and the constant transformation of stories themselves keeps the system fluid. Thus, no oral—or written—narrative has permanently defined the poles of the dialectic and locked tradition into a single form.

The sweat is the place to exchange weakness for strength, fragmentation for wholeness, disease for health, discord for harmony. Contemporary stories facilitate that transition by universalizing the state of need. Everyone is pitiful. Everyone needs healing, individually and communally. Solidarity is built on common grounds in a fragmented society. The stories bring people together through sharing common experience in their hearing and understanding.

Telling stories back and forth is also a form of social reciprocity. I found the best way to learn stories during my fieldwork was to tell the stories I already knew. Stories themselves are healing both by confirming the power of the spiritual world and by demonstrating that one can indeed access that power. Humorous stories also heal, for they demonstrate the universal fallibility of contemporary existence. Stories are also related for the sheer enjoyment of hearing and telling them. This is particularly true with the Lakotas, who tend to personalize every story with names and situations familiar to their hearers.

The talk within a sweat is quite entertaining, but there are other purposes for conversation: without enforcing uniformity, the stories suggest proper ways of proceeding and provide a mode of legitimation. Stories of the past are incorporated into present needs in the dialectic process that forms tradition.

6

Personal Accounts of the Sweat Experience

Anthropological writing has a tendency to solidify procedure, as discussed in chapter 3. For example, although it is reported in written documents (and, at times, by practitioners) that Lakota sweat lodge structures have sixteen willow stays, one would be hard pressed to find an actual structure that follows that ideal pattern. Writing things down tends to fossilize process, and building ideal structures eclipses variation. Tradition is dynamic—rooted both in the recollections of the past and in the needs of the present. Both poles are dynamic—history grows in depth and is subject to reinterpretation and reconstruction, and peoples' needs change over time.

In order to understand and appreciate how individuals create tradition through combining past with present, one must listen to the voices of the participants. Those voices represent a polyphony, one that is not always in harmony. Clearly, history is important to each narrator, for there are broad consistencies both in procedure and in symbolic analysis. The present is also important, for the narratives reveal a broad range of practices and interpretations of practice based on personal experiences and needs of each participant. As one individual with whom I worked stated, "There's as many opinions about this religion as there are belly buttons."

This chapter examines a variety of interpretations of the sweat lodge and understandings of "Indian religion" expressed by various consultants with whom I have worked. Some individuals say they have always practiced "these ways," whereas others have experienced what can be termed a conversion. The first part of the chapter will concentrate on how individual Lakotas came to participate in the sweat lodge ceremony and made it an essential part of their lives. The second part will examine specific interpretations of the sweat lodge by individual participants. The variety of interpretations demonstrates the rich texture of Oglala symbolic life and the ad hoc flexibility of Oglala ritual in incorporating a variety of individuals, and individual beliefs, into its structure. This is an opportunity to view the dialectic involved in creating contemporary practice. Although this incorporation is, at times, momentary and friable, it demonstrates the essential goal of the sweat lodge: to bring people together and create harmony. At the same time, social fragmentation is also solidified in ritual practice through avoidance of certain ritual events because of disagreement about procedure or disagreement with participants. That fragmentation is equally unstable, for feuding individuals will sometimes appear to participate in rituals, despite denouncing a particular lodge.

Individual Lakotas are quite aware of the broad variations in practice between groups. They hold, however, that there exists a proper form for the ritual and that fidelity to form is important in ritual practice. So an individual, aware of his or her particular way of doing things, will, when speaking of the religious system in general, universalize practice; when speaking of his or her own use of the system, however, the same person will clearly indicate that his or her way of doing things might be unique. This particularization of practice does not insulate individuals from criticism in the realm of ritual behavior. Variations in ritual are both recognized and practiced in some instances, but in other circumstances those variations might be used to disqualify a group or an individual, for there are mechanisms on the reservation to put pressure on people to conform, if their rituals are judged as inauthentic. To date, however, that has never been done through a central authority but rather by self-appointed groups. Nevertheless, those judgments are never definitive, for this mechanism does not stop the practices that are perceived by some as aberrant. There is no central authority governing correct practice. Mechanisms of control are much more diffuse. Gossip and avoidance often isolate individuals or groups whose practice is suspect. Generally, however, no one interferes with another's practice directly. Individuals are fairly free to construct their religious understanding, using available material as they see fit. Certain groups do publicly denounce individuals with some efficacy on and off the reservation. For example, one individual was accused of charging for a Sun Dance. Enough pressure was brought to bear on him that he eventually went on tribal radio to explain himself, to state that he was not in fact charging for the Sun Dance, and to apologize for the misunderstanding.

We are in danger of missing the essence of the sweat lodge if we look merely to doctrine and belief. Although these aspects are important to the sweat, the spiritual, social, physical, and psychological healing that individuals attribute to the lodge are more important. Disagreement, seen as a negative influence, can disrupt the healing process in the lodge, so it is avoided as far as possible. The narratives I collected are consistent in presenting pressing needs that lead individuals to participate in the sweat and other ceremonies available on the reservation. These crises generally involve identity, solidarity, and healing. There is no single attraction to the lodge. Each person's participation has to do with the intimate details of his or her personal history. Individuals who say they have participated in "these ways" attribute persistence of practice to personal needs. Those personal needs are also projected into communal needs for "the people" (meaning primarily the Lakotas, but, through extension, the whole world).

Lakota ritual was interpreted and adapted in public, to make it acceptable to the critical eye of missionaries and agents. We have seen this process take place in the ethnographic literature. Although the unspoken meanings and interpretations cannot be recovered through the ethnographic literature, it is clear that the public face of the ritual changed insofar as it was accessible to outsiders through description by participants. The large flow of outsiders to the sweat today is historically unprecedented before the 1970s, but throughout Lakota history ritual has constantly been adapted to outside influences. Thus, some groups freely use Christian prayers, metaphor, and understandings to present their own view to outsiders but also to extend their own religious symbol set. Ceremonial practice has also widely adapted the worldview and techniques of Alcoholics Anonymous groups. Individuals who have had positive experiences with AA frequently incorporate aspects of that ethos within the sweat. For the most part, that is a conscious adaptation.

Alcoholics Anonymous's approach to theology and philosophy is also congruent with the contemporary approach taken by many sweat lodge practitioners. Because AA groups are formed around common affliction rather than a religious confession, the groups are highly pluralistic with regard to belief. This is compensated for by the group's referring to the divine as a "higher power," thus neutralizing doctrinal disputes. In the Lakota sweat lodge, there is never a confession of faith, but rather a profession of belief in this higher power or powers, called Wakan Tanka, Tunkashila, Ate Wakantanka, or all three. Each word has specific religious meanings, but there is ambiguity in that the words can also be used (and were used, beginning with the missionaries) to indicate God as understood by Christians or, in the case of Tunkashila, God as our grandfather rather than ancestor spirits or the grandfathers. Linguistic unanimity reigns in the sweat lodge because Wakan Tanka and Tunkashila have now attained, in the ceremonial context, a neutral meaning. Note that this meaning represents a compromise. If pressed, individuals would admit differences in conception of the divine, although, in keeping with a pervasive conception on the reservation today, all would agree that there is one God. One frequently hears at ceremonies the statement that we all pray to the same God. This ecumenical attitude, at least in regard to Christian denominationalism, is present in the ethnohistorical data:

> Old Black Bull came to see his granddaughter. To my inquiry: "Do you belong to any prayer (Church)," he answered: "When the Short Coats (congre[gational minister].) have prayer meeting, I go there and pray: Great Spirit have mercy on me and sit down and eat with them. If the Blackrobes have meeting, I also go there and pray and eat with them. And if the White Gowns (Prot[estant]. Epis[copalian]) have meeting, I go also there and eat with them. They all believe in and pray to the same Great Spirit." [Digmann n.d.:107]

Digmann had a less than ecumenical attitude toward the combination of Christianity and Native American belief: "'If the Lord is God,' said I, 'Hold to Prayer: if the Lakota customs are from the Great Spirit, stick to them, but you cannot serve two masters. Do not limp from one to the other'" (n.d.:63).

Narratives of Conversion

The first narrative combines a "conversion" experience with a continuity of sweat lodge practice to maintain the ground achieved. The narrator intertwines what he understands of the philosophies of Lakota religion and Alcoholics Anonymous:

> My drinking became worse. Way back, I had tried different things to sober up—Church, treatment, psychiatrist. I came back to the reservation despondent. I had a warrant for my arrest in Rapid City for DWI. After my wife divorced me, I was in this house, in this room [the room in which this interview took place]. I was laying on the couch with the wood stove

going. I heard an owl outside at midnight. All that the old people taught me came back—a message was transmitted to me. I went to the medicine man and said I needed help. In the 70's, I asked a certain medicine man to help me. He said to put up a ceremony. I invited a priest and some sisters. One particular sister I knew came. They were involved in these things. My auntie and my wife from my second marriage put up the meeting for my drinking. The medicine man told me to go to treatment. I had a very spiritual experience. I went to a big treatment center. I got through with a group meeting and wanted to be alone. I went to the lake to pray.

Eagles came to the ceremony. They said they know my problem. They understood, and they'll help me.

I went to the lake and looked to the west. Some thunder beings were coming up and there was a red cloud above and gray and white—black and red came together. A voice said when the black and red come together, you'll never drink again. They came together. I watched. I had an uplifting feeling.

I then went to bed. There were big windows in this place. I left the curtains open. Around ten or midnight, there was a tremendous thunderstorm. The lightning was like daylight, night and day. I laid on that bed sweating. Then I woke up and visualized a circle of people. I prayed, too. The circle was made up of the grandparents. They were in a circle dancing and praying for me. Thunder was turned into drums. It was an affirmation that I wouldn't drink. I laid like Christ on a crucifix form and cried and thanked God/*Thųkášila* that I was healed. I had my first peaceful sleep in a long time. I woke up and there was a bird sitting outside on my window sill. I went to feed the bird. I thought he'd take off but he stayed there when I fed it. I felt for the first time that I'm OK. The bird didn't fly away. I cried again. I never drank again.

The people at the treatment center told me not to go back to the reservation. I had a dream to make a sweat in the winter and to Sun Dance. I danced four years as a *wóphila* ['thanksgiving'] to *Thųkášila* for taking drink away.

The same narrator later explained a particular dream he had in relation to his use of the sweat lodge:

I was placed in a cave and there was water up to my waist. The cave had two parts. I was instructed to go from one to the other. They [the spirits] put an eagle fan in my hand. When this was placed there, there appeared lots of demons, negative energy. These demons were in motion, coming toward me. I had the feeling that they would overcome me. When I waved the fan, they were pushed back. The fan looked like it was steam. It seemed I had to be on constant alert to keep back the demons. These were two underground domes. When I went into the other dome it was the opposite; everything was peaceful and nothing was coming at me. It's been so long since I had that dream, but it seems what then happened was that I was told to build a sweat lodge. It was January. I asked the medicine man I was following then about it and he said to make it right now. There was three feet of snow. I made it back where it is now. I cleared the snow and burned wood to defrost the ground. I went horseback to get willows. I had to dig for the rocks. On the third day, we had the sweat. It was a difficult time to do it. I didn't ask questions.

Note that the validation was effected in two modes: through a dream and by the consent of a medicine man. The narrator quoted the medicine man's comment that if someone went on the hill and danced in the Sun Dance, then that individual could run a sweat. The narrator qualified this with "This is not a written requirement," thus depriving the injunction of canonical status. Another individual, a member of the Native American Church, renounced the idea that there exist extrinsic criteria for running a sweat, stating that an individual "knows inside" when he should run a sweat lodge ceremony. The majority of individuals, however, would hold that one must complete the Sun Dance and the vision quest to qualify. The person leading a sweat will sometimes state in a narrative at the beginning of a sweat that he or she underwent these ceremonies and thus is qualified to lead the ceremony.

Another important theme present in the narrative is suffering. Imploring the divine because one is pitiful and poor is a consistent theme in Lakota religious practice, observed and recorded since first contact and continuing in the contemporary era. One often hears the phrase "It's hard to be an Indian." That theme is extended to ceremonial practice: *"Lakhól wichóȟ'a theȟí"* 'Lakota ceremonies are difficult.' Each ceremony requires endurance and perseverance. Although the sweat lodge is not meant as an endurance contest (and this fact is often spoken of at the beginning of each lodge and proved in practice, since anyone can have the door opened if he or she is too uncomfortable), there is a concomitant belief that one should suffer in the lodge and that the suffering intensifies the efficacy of the prayers offered. Thus, participants contend that sweats put on for the purpose of healing specific maladies become extraordinarily hot of their own accord. The recovering alcoholic narrator explains how he came to the sweat through the sufferings of his own life and finds that suffering mirrored in the way in which he constructed his own lodge in the adverse circumstances of winter, a time of suffering and want.

In a later interview the same narrator talked about the importance of combining the sweat lodge and the philosophy of AA. He sees both practices as essentially individualistic. He is also critical of some sweat lodge participants who speak one way and act another, reflecting closely the AA injunction "walk your talk."

The private life of an individual is under close scrutiny in Lakota life and ritual practice. When people evaluate the authenticity of individuals, particularly medicine men, they will point to their familial and moral lives. Individuals who practice traditional religion are expected to behave in certain ideal ways. There is a tension between a very high ideal and the struggles individuals face in life. Thus, individuals will condemn and exonerate an individual in the same sentence by stating that so and so does not "walk his talk," and yet "even so-called traditional people [err]. They're human beings." A combination of traditional religion, Christianity, AA, and psychological developmental theory are evident in this statement made by the same narrator:

> My recovery in AA offers more than just sobriety. If I went there just for sobriety I would not go there. Detox can get you sober. AA offered me a place where I can self-reveal in a comfortable way. What is so unique is that the people who go to AA are very accepting—our stories may be different, but we have similar feelings and experiences. AA is a very practical approach, a way of life. That's a similarity with the sweat lodge—a way of life. We can get in trouble by complicating AA and the sweat lodge. AA offers me the opportunity to reveal myself. It takes Carl Roger's steps—understanding yourself. I do this by interacting. This is the same as Lakota—indirect teaching. It is not directed straight at you—AA person tells you his drunkalogue. I can identify with that. That person also found a solution. It might help me. For example, one guy kept falling off the wagon when he went to cash his check at a bar. His sponsor said to go someplace else. The guy did that, and he is still sober.
>
> AA is a spiritual program, but it's very subtle, an attraction rather than a promotion. No one keeps score in there—how many times on the wagon. One day at a time. The Indian way is that way, too. It's a place I can take care of my emotions and thinking. I can talk about how I feel and think. No one is absolutely honest, but you strive to be honest. You need to keep these principles in all your affairs. Talk about your character defects. Use the steps.
>
> In the sweat lodge, you talk about things in there, but it's to take care of spiritual parts. Ever since I sobered up, I have used both AA and the sweat lodge. One of the things I look at—it's easy to talk about letting go—in the

sweat lodge when it's really difficult. I have to let go of my humanness, my trying to let go—I participate in the practice of letting go of fear or pain. For me I need both AA and the sweat in order to maintain some sort of quality recovery. I've seen a lot of Indian people try to stay sober through just the sweat lodge—most of them have relapses. All of them get to a point—you talk about Indianism not alcoholism. In AA, you talk about drunkenness. Guys who go to sweat, they develop a grandiose attitude that they have a direct pipeline to God. They get the idea that they walk alone with God. Lots of that is temporary. They are self-deluded rather than having found the answer. When it appears it's an emotional sobriety. They can stay sober on emotions for a while, or they can stay sober on a religious high. I believe you can. I have seen some people sober up through these religious rituals. You can't measure their intentions. Most guys Sun Dance, have a pipe, sweat, but they don't integrate it in their way of life.

The basic teaching is there, but you don't hear it in the lodge. They pray to symbols—I'm not degrading it—but it's all vicarious, all out there. BUT what you talk about in the sweat you must incorporate in your daily life. Like you should not drink or steal.

It's all theological. The good part about teachings of both AA and the sweat lodge is that—like you tell a story and put yourself in it. It worked for me because metaphorically it has that teaching.

Both ways teach a daily contact and relationship. AA says to continue to pray and meditate. At AA, we don't do that one day a week. When I get up each morning, I turn my life over to God. I learned this through repetition and experience. Symbols in AA and the sweat are important. Some mornings I read the twenty-four-hour-book and burn sage and cedar.[1] I offer the twenty-four-hour-book to the four directions. These guys who come looking for a pure Indian way of life. They'll see this here picture of Christ and they can't understand it. My grandfather had an altar with his pipe and the statue of Mary. There's one God.

We're an animal, and we need arrangements to focus or direct our attention to God. *Thukášila* and God are the same. They're just different words, different symbols.

So I need both.

Everyone in AA works a program different. When you go to a sweat and things are really different. Some do it in one way, others another way. In a way it's dogmatic and in another way it isn't.

The healing effects of the sweat are often focused on drinking and the effects of alcoholism. This healing extends to forming a community of sufferers, those who struggle with alcoholism. Many on the reservation view alcoholism as a disease, an understanding that originated from Alcoholics Anonymous. The sweat is, in all cases, employed to cure or to allow one to continue in recovery from this malady. Often alcoholism is listed with diseases such as cancer and heart disease when discussions turn to what can be cured in the sweat. Those not closely linked with AA groups hold that one can be completely cured of alcoholism in a sweat.

Another individual with whom I worked attributed his continued sobriety to the "spiritual ways of his people." He states, "I would not be the person I am today without these ways." His conversion was a result of his own struggle with alcoholism and the struggle of one of his close relatives:

> I became involved in the sweat through a relative I really love. He saw it as a means to achieve sobriety. He tried many avenues for sobriety. Finally he talked to a medicine man. He had a ceremony to find out how to achieve sobriety. That spiritual man mediated with the spirit world. They knew what he wanted. They told him to make a pipe and stay sober one year before using it. As for myself, I was heavy into drinking and drugs. I eventually went to live with this relative. He told me what was going on. I watched him make the pipe. I realized I had a chemical problem. I went to AA meetings. This relative talked about the pipe way. It gave me a sense of hope and direction. I began talking and reading the literature about the pipe way. I was living away from the reservation then.
>
> I moved back. That was the start. It was a gradual involvement. It went deeper and deeper. I began associating with people who were involved— especially here in Pine Ridge. I was influenced by several medicine men. That's how I got involved over the years. It was a slow incorporation into daily and family life.

The narrator qualified his own views by saying, "This is all debatable; no one agrees on the same thing." At the same time he insisted that ritual practice was not merely a matter of sincerity and good intention but that participants must adhere to specific practices and procedures. He chastised groups who took the easy way out. This individual frequently uses the sweat lodge and is quite candid in his association of the sweat lodge with his path to sobriety. He also links his sobriety to following the Native American Church, Alcoholics Anonymous, and the Christian church:

> I don't limit myself to one single understanding. Christianity is another way of reaching God. It's good. Any way of prayer that helps us lead a good, spiritually guided life is good. You should not compare. What's

good for you might not be good for someone else. I believe I can pray in different ways, Christian, Lakota, Native American Church. We all pray to God. There is only one God. We should not try to incorporate one with the other. In terms of bringing both together into a new way, they are separate and should remain separate. You can incorporate them into yourself. You should not blend them into one way. A Lutheran said that only Christ can save you. Well, I live good ways the same as Christ. "Follow me" means how he lived. You can perform these rituals, but if you don't live it, it doesn't mean it will work. I disagree with incorporation. I don't want to hear Sun Dance songs in Church. I love the Christian way.

At another time the narrator explained why he appreciated the Native American Church ways, saying: "The Native American Church is neutral; it does not have a concrete set of beliefs. It is like AA, since while spirituality is stressed, a specific spirituality is not promoted. The [Native American] Church is a place where you can develop your relationship with God any way you want."

The stress here is on external pluralism and internal freedom—a set of ritual practices should not regulate how a person believes. Nevertheless, ritual practices should be adhered to with care. This individual stresses freedom in respect to belief rather than practice. His assumption is that each group ultimately sanctions the same set of moral behaviors. In belief, however, one should not set up exclusivity, saying that this way is the only way. The tension between doctrinal pluralism and ritual exactitude is mitigated by the principle of freedom: individuals may choose as they wish, but they must behave according to their choices. One may participate in all these systems. The underlying rationale permitting such mobility is that all these systems deal with the same divine being and behavioral requirements. Each system accesses divine power in a different way, but no one system is inherently truer or more appropriate than another, according to this view.

This narrator is also sharply aware of changes in the religious system, and he defends adaptation, even while insisting on exactitude. That is not necessarily a contradiction. He disputes the right of individuals to discredit others with the accusation that certain practices are tainted (much as genetic accusations might be made that mixed-blood individuals are tainted). There is also a defense against accusations made by an outside white audience that certain practices are not authentic. Interestingly, those who endorse adaptation to circumstance are not above criticizing others for the production of spurious ritual behavior. The ultimate criterion of authenticity is based in individual decision and moral behavior, according to this narrator.

Some practitioners incorporate the sweat lodge into a wide variety of beliefs, but others see their incorporation into "Lakota ways" as a conscious break from an extrinsically imposed religious and cultural structure. Thus, another consultant, a middle-aged woman, describes her break from a rather strict Christian past:

> I feared God, felt that he didn't love me. I was afraid of hell. When one of my relatives died, he never went to Church. I wondered, where did he go? I dreamt of him and saw that he was fine. He drank and did this and that. He was pretty old when he died. I have not been to Church for a long time. Now I go to sweats. Here I can see my prayers being answered. In Church, the prayers don't apply; you just say the same thing over and over: the Hail Mary, the Our Father. At the sweats I can go and pray. I can feel the way I want. I can pray and know my answer. Three years ago, I had severe anxiety attacks after a relative died. I had a baby and I had broken up with my husband. This crippled my life-style. I went to sweat and prayed that God would take all that and that I would not be afraid. Here it was gone. I also gave up cigarettes this way. The spirits helped me to quit, and I have never smoked since. I don't even have a desire for it.
>
> I had gone to counseling, and I saw how people held on to grief. Another relative had severe nightmares. I went to see a very well-known medicine man, and that relative never had any nightmares again. The sweat has taken care of really everything. What can't be done in a sweat can be taken care of in a ceremony. I go to sweats to be cleansed, to avoid flu. I have gone for years without a cold or a major illness.
>
> Our whole social life is around the sweat. It is the center of our life. We rarely have a medicine man there to interpret our prayers or to give us answers from the spirits. Lots of people come, and we pray for each other. We have a good support group. It's like a therapy session. The spirits say I'm lucky I have a support group.
>
> Most of our group is single parents—we have a few couples. People can use our sweat. People who have been drinking have come and asked for help. We invite them in and pray for them. Over the last nine years, we have had a stream of people coming in.
>
> One medicine man does everything in the sweat, doctoring and everything. He told us that we did not need to go down there to him all the time. We have our own voice. We don't have to have a medicine man. We'd like to have one, but there is not that kind of money around to help him out all the time.

That consultant emphasizes the efficacy of native religion over Christianity, a system she was brought up in but of which she never really felt a part. She also stresses the direct access to the spiritual realm available through native religion while still acknowledging the valid mediating role of the medicine man. Although the direct experience of spirits is potentially accessible to all, it is the medicine man who acts as interpreter of the messages of the spirits. Some individuals avoid using medicine men or call them in only for very important ceremonies. Some individuals today state that a medicine man is not a necessary component to the sweat but that it is good to have one when available. The narrator also makes a distinction between the generality and repetitiveness of Christian prayers and prayers made in the sweat that are contextualized and speak to the moment. Christianity is seen as an extrinsic imposition by this individual; native religion is integral to her way of life.

> Some people resent white people getting involved in our religion. The religion is just life. Indian religion is like any other: live, respect others, respect the earth, walk as you talk. You can't separate religion from life. It's not a Church. It's a way of life.
>
> I've had nothing to do with the Church for fifteen, twenty years. I only go for funerals. It didn't suit my needs at the time. The Church has changed a lot. It is geared now to the people and to different cultures. As a child, I feared God. The nuns were mean and prejudiced. If we talked in Church, we were punished. I grew up with lots of fears. I was hindered in entering Indian religion because of fear of hell. There is no hell in Indian religion. The Catholic prayers did not mean anything to me, but I said them. I wanted to love God and feel that love in return and not feel guilty about my life. I found this in Indian religion. These nuns did not love me. I disliked nuns and felt that they represented the Church. We were poor. Our family cleaned the Church and took care of it. In summer, we picked weeds and shelled peas for the parish priest. We worked off our tuition and books. No one else had to do it. We were never treated as people.
>
> I got married in the Church and took my kids all the time. My husband was drunk or gone, so I was alone. One priest made me feel better about the Church. He used cedar and water and cared about my family. He adopted my grandmother as his mother.
>
> People I'm around see people for who they are. At some sweats I feel alienated. One spiritual leader says that you can fool the people but you can't fool God.

Although this narrative sets up a dichotomy between white and Indian religion, there is an ambivalence toward both. The narrator experiences prejudice in some sweats because she is mixed-blood and does not speak Lakota; moreover, she has had some positive experiences with Christians, particularly one priest who encouraged her during a difficult time. Her overwhelming allegiance, however, lies with the sweat. Her symbolic interpretation of the sweat is richly laced with examples of its efficacy:

I've seen so many miracles that happen in the sweat. At first I was frightened. I had my pipe, and whatever I prayed for happened. I was amazed. My pipe really worked.

When I first got my pipe, I learned about it for about a year. Then I asked a medicine man to pray for me when I went over there to see him before I had a pipe. He told me to get a pipe. I said I didn't want to. I would have to be good all the time. This was too overwhelming and powerful for me. That medicine man said to go home, turn off all the lights and block the windows and put sage all over the floor and the spirits will bring you a pipe. I didn't do this. I put a pipe on lay-away in Denver at a trading post. Eventually I had one made by a friend's son.

I've seen so many things happen and go good. One month ago, a medicine man told me about a woman who had cancer. She went into the sweat lodge and the cancer disappeared. He gave her some medicine.

There are spirits on the hill and in the sweats. There are numerous miracles in our sweats. Things we pray for happen the next day. Once a woman with long hair came to our sweat and then suddenly disappeared. A man once opened and closed our door and then suddenly he disappeared. We all passed him as we went out of the sweat. We thought it was a medicine man we know, but suddenly he was not there anymore.

Once I could not light my pipe. The medicine man who was there said that the spirits were so happy that they had smoked out my pipe.

The sweat and the pipe are all one thing, a part of my life, the pipe religion. At times I pray every day.

Once I dreamed my son would die in an accident. I saw a medicine man, and he told me to pray for ten days each day. I went to where he was in school to see him and spent four days with him. One day, a bird tried to come into my house, hit the window. The next day, my son was in a wreck. When I came home I found out he was in a wreck. I ran out but said to myself not to panic. He went through the windshield and was cut from the nose to the chin. They sewed him up. He told me that he dreamt he was in a wreck. I saw the same tree in my dream. I had a ceremony in thanksgiving. I have a hard time praying for what I need, as I have already gotten so much.

After those many crises I've had clear sailing for three years. Now I have problems with unemployment and other things. If I didn't pray I'd probably be a drunk, too.

Sometimes people reject me and accept whites [in ceremonies or the sweat]. I just go back to my own sweat. There are lots of problems on the reservation. People treat each other poorly.

A fourth narrative account describes a now elderly woman's breaking away from her Catholic boarding school upbringing and returning to traditional religion. Interestingly, it was through a priest that she was converted to traditional beliefs. This narrator also takes a rather critical view of those participating in the contemporary sweat lodge.

I went to boarding school at Holy Rosary [Mission in Pine Ridge] in the 1930s for ten years. I learned the white man's ways. Three months out of the year I went home. My dad died in the 1960s. Before then he went to a *lowápi* ['singing ceremony'] to sing for a medicine man who doctored. He made tobacco ties. A Catholic priest I know became interested in Indian ways. My dad explained pipe, tobacco ties, which are just like rosaries, and other things to him. This priest visited my dad quite a bit. He would tell me when he visited my dad. When my dad died, that same priest buried my dad. It took me all those years to realize that I'm Indian and that my prayers should be in Indian.

At Holy Rosary, they taught that Indians were heathens, devil worshipers. They took my dad's casket into Church in my home parish. The priest put a pipe on my dad's casket. I didn't know what to think. My heart turned to Indian ways. The priest prayed in the four directions with a pipe. I never went back to the Christian ways. I am an Indian. I got the Bishop's permission from the priest to divorce. Then I took my children to another state. I told them the Indian ways. I taught the boys the sacred songs my dad sang.

I never did and never will go into a sweat lodge. No woman is qualified to go into the sweat lodge. They can't watch their mouths or tempers. Those who go around telling about the sweat lodge, I don't believe them. They want to be the most expert. My grandmother and grandfather did not have to have an audience to go into a sweat lodge. Women don't sweat, only those past menopause sweated. Now women run sweats. I can't stand that. Only sacred women, like my father's mother, should do that. That woman was a medicine woman. We stayed away from her. She had a sweat lodge. I never did a sweat.

A fifth narrator explains her dual participation in Indian and white religion as justified by a vision she received between the rounds of a sweat ceremony. The conflict of belonging to both worlds (the woman is a mixed-blood raised off the reservation) is resolved in the vision by participating in both arenas without living exclusively in either.

> I was removed in spirit from the lodge and was flying with an eagle. It was sunny and green down below. I was beneath a golden eagle (I was sure of the species). I could see its piercing eye. He spoke to me with his eye. He told me to look down. I saw a huge circle on the green. It was divided into four parts, one red and the other white. The third and fourth part were muted, and I could not make them out. I wanted to land there. I started to land in the white and could not. I wanted to land on the red but couldn't. It was OK to land in the middle and to stretch my wings into either area, white and red. I then suddenly took off again and was back into the air and back to the sweat. I prayed for so long trying to discern if I could pray both ways. This was a confirmation that I could do this and that what I was doing was a positive and good thing.

The sixth narrative that helps bring out the pluralism of belief in Lakota ritual structures is presented by a member of the Native American Church. His conversion has to do with dedicated membership to the Native American Church rather than to, as he expresses it, "the *chaŋúpa* ['pipe'] way." That allegiance does not exclude him from participating in sweats.[2] Sweats that he leads focus specifically and exclusively on Christ and the Holy Spirit. Besides the exclusion of spirits natural and ancestral, these sweats were at the greatest variance from the "traditional" sweats in that there was no focus on directionality. It is important to note how familiarity with the actor and his motivations increases toleration in ritual variation. Thus, this consultant's relative said to me concerning him:

> The Native American Church is totally different. My uncle [the narrator under consideration], he calls it a peyote sweat. He did it in his own way. It's more Christian. They talk about Christianity inside there. He preaches to people in there. It's all right, that's what he wants. This is what our country's for. Believe how you want. If it's religion and praying, I have respect.

The sixth narrator's acceptance of his conversion depends on right living, a theme that occurs frequently in his story. He said that he "used to be terrible," smoking and drinking, and that he took really sick and had a fifty-fifty chance of living. He was lying by a window at dawn, and he heard his name shouted out. Then, he said, he picked up a Bible tract that said "I will not turn anyone away who comes to me." That was his conversion point. He explained that until his conversion, he could not read, but then he was able to read the word of God.

The narrator goes on to explain his own involvement in the sweat. Unlike the other narrators, he received the ritual from an elder relative who also belonged to the Native American Church, having learned it from another tribe. Note how the narrator qualifies what he has to say, pointing out that it represents his own understanding and that indeed there are many different approaches to the topic.

> I can tell how I understand it. Some make it up. If it is that way, it's all false. Somebody and older guys think they know everything, but they don't know too much. I get scared at that, so I want to tell the truth of it.
>
> The way it is, I have a grandfather on my mother's side. He's the kind of a man that from the beginning of it was a real good person. He usually goes south among different tribes down there. He went over there among the Osage tribe. That's the story of him, he went down there. When he come back, he started having the sweat. That was before I was born. I'm old now. I don't know what year he got it.
>
> In there he goes in all by himself from the beginning. He prays like he prays in his daily life, and he sings peyote songs in there. Then he was telling me in my younger days when I was fifteen. I got hurt and grew up like that. Had a hard time. He said this sweat will ease my pain. It helps arthritis. That's gonna help him, he says of me. I start going in there with him. He taught me how to run it. This sweat faces east, just like a tipi is made. He was telling me this other way of sweating, all the sweat lodges facing west. The one that runs the sweats is the *yuwipi* or medicine man, the one that pours the water. They sit on the right side, looking in. He was saying that four times they open that door. This is similar to this medicine man way of sweating. He was telling me that there's rules of running a sweat, but that's up to the medicine man. They have different rules, different ways. The way I was taught don't have no rules like that. One medicine man said while bringing the rocks in that one rock should be brought in at a time for the first four rocks. Place them in the four directions: west, north, east, south. While they bring them in, everyone keeps quiet. That was one medicine man; that's the way he does it. If you don't keep quiet, this man pours the whole bucket at once. That's his ways. Keep quiet if you don't want to get boiled.
>
> Others have different ways and rulings. Some count the rocks—don't just heat any amount. It has to be a certain amount.
>
> This is when I don't know. He says when I got this when they brought the peyote drum into the sweat. They done that, sing four songs in the

sweat lodge. But I never did see him [my grandfather] do that part. When I first had my sweat. Where my grandfather lived with us he always had a sweat. He's the only one who goes there. When I started going in, everyone goes in.

Before they go into a [Native American Church] meeting, they always sweat. He said it's better than washing yourself in a tub. You'll be prepared for the prayer service. Your voice will be good.

In that narrative, the speaker's own "way" is set apart from that of the "medicine men." He differentiates himself from that group because he sees himself as Christian and thus different. This is in contrast to others who see traditional belief as intrinsically monotheistic. The narrator takes the view that a long time ago, there was not a monotheistic belief.

The way it was. The understanding I got was Indians long time the way they prayed, they say. Pray toward the west, *thatéya wíyoȟpeyatakiya* ['toward the west wind'] they mention. The medicine men have different kind of spirit, they pray to *thatháka oyáte* ['the buffalo people']. *Thųkášila úšimala* ['Grandfather, pity me.']. To the north *tháȟca oyáte* ['the deer people'], *Thųkášila úšimala*. To the east, *sįtésapala oyáte* ['the black tail deer people'], *Thųkášila úšimala,* south, *hįhá oyáte* ['the owl people'] *Thųkášila úšimala po!* All of them, that one, the understanding I got they're praying to them animals, saying *Thųkášila* to them. To pray in the Christian way, you say Father God—he made all this, so we say Father to him. *Thųkášila,* they pray to animals. Now they say they are praying to Father God.

They want to be an Indian. They say a long time ago they pray like that. But they were praying to animals.

The narrator presents Christianity as an improvement over traditional beliefs, even while insisting that all religions are essentially the same.

In a vision while I had the heart attack, I saw a big dungeon, a gap. Sand went into the gap like that [indicated a pouring motion]. Can't fill it up. The sand was really all the people going into that gap. Some were crying, hollering for help. Some had something in their hands. Some had a Bible in their hands, some had the *chąnúpa* ['pipe'] in their hands. Some were holding these things up, trying to get out. They couldn't do it. They keep on going down. I want to know what this vision is. I had a Bible and believe in God but I'm carrying it the wrong way. Same with *chąnúpa.* They don't obey the rules of carrying. I told them regardless of what you have in your hand, even if it's a stick, ask God to bless it and make it sacred. Use it in the right way.

If you don't have the knowledge of God, you won't understand it. Lot of
times I get to my death bed. I experience God talking to me: "This is the
way you should do it, the way you should go."

Sometimes this narrator sees Christ as the only way and freely expresses
this at meetings of the Native American Church and at Native American Church
sweat lodge ceremonies. And yet, he told me that all religions were worthy of
belief as long as people followed what they prescribed. Thus, he says, "God
does not look at skin color but how you behave" and "It doesn't make a difference if you pray with a pipe or a Bible; if you're not right with God, you will
not make it into heaven." When I first entered his sweat I said, "Mitakuye
oyas'in," and he said, "Oh, you say that." He informed me that they did not say
that in there, as it was a Christian sweat. In fact, when they wanted the door
opened, rather than saying mitakuye oyas'in, they would shout *yuǧá* ['open
up']. At a non–Native American Church sweat I attended with this narrator,
however, he freely used mitakuye oyas'in when entering and in his prayers. He
told me that those who believe in Christ say *Até Wakhą́ Tháka* ['Father God'],
whereas those who believe in the spirits and the grandfathers say *Thųkášila
Wakhą́ Tháka* ['Grandfather God'].

That narrator acknowledged that the sweat is "the ancient Sioux way to
pray" and that it was good, even though his sweat was run differently from
those of the non-Christian Indians. He said that some Indians held that white
churches were no good and that Indians should not belong to them. He believed
that was not so and that it was good for people to believe in different ways.
People should still be united but leave religion out of it, according to him.
People should respect each other's differing beliefs.

The symbolism he applies to the sweat is quite different from what he per-
ceives as belonging to "medicine man" sweats. Consistent with all the sweats
that we have examined, however, he holds that the sweat is a suffering way to
pray and that one should endure the suffering to achieve some good. Using
himself as an example, he points out that a disease left him scarred. The scars
really hurt in the sweat, but he puts up with it.[3] He also holds that the sweat is
our mother's womb, and we come out full of sweat and water just as when we
are born. Again, this is quite consistent with contemporary understanding of the
ritual. He further elaborates his understanding of the purpose and meaning of
the sweat, intertwining Christian notions of forgiveness with traditional notions
of purification.

To me it's the way I was taught, I go in there to purify myself. Get ready
to go into prayer service, Native American Church way. I believe. One

time I was taking medicine early in the morning. I was at a meeting that night. That afternoon I took a sweat. I went in by myself. No one was around. When I was in, I got my body ready. In my mind, I asked what about inside me? I made my confession in there. God through Jesus give me forgiveness. It's good to go into sweat to purify body as well as soul. If you do it right. I always say—I don't care what Church. If you do it right, it will do you good.

There is an important shift presented in this understanding. Whereas most contemporary sweaters see the steam as purifying one both morally and physically, this narrator dichotomizes the process, stressing that moral forgiveness comes through Christ and physical purification comes through the sweat.

Just as with George Sword, the notion of a correct procedure is essential to the sixth narrator's description. In contemporary practice, the focus is on interior attitude—one must have a proper disposition when entering any ceremony. This is not to say that ritual procedure is unimportant, just that it is secondary to an inner disposition. Earlier material, as we have seen, points primarily to ritual propriety rather than inner disposition. In the earlier material there is also more interest in interpreting the efficacy of the ritual rather than in examining the symbolic content.

Many of the individuals with whom I worked presented themselves as new to traditional practices. One individual described himself as a "born again Indian" and made no bones about his recent introduction into belief and practice. Another described herself as a "baby" in "these ways." The seventh narrator became involved in traditional practice through one of her children.

I used to be a Catholic. I went to mission for eight years. My mom was a really strong Catholic. Walked a mile every Sunday to go to Mass at the nearby town. There were lots I didn't like about Catholic religion, but I figured I'd always be that.

When my son was young, he told me that he was going to Sun Dance. I didn't know where he got that. I tried to stop him but couldn't do it. I went over to where the Sun Dance was being held on the last day to see what he was doing. There was no one around. Then I saw him. It was sad—a sad song was being sung. I got there and cried. I thought there had to be something to this. So then I went home and I started looking for material. I read *Black Elk Speaks, The Sacred Pipe,* and *Lame Deer, Seeker of Visions.* I said that this is really good if this is how they believe. Another relative was in jail and had to go to court. He said, there would be a ceremony before I go. I said, I don't believe that way. I went to see the medicine man who was going to lead this ceremony. I said to him I didn't believe in the Indian way. He said: "Fine, pray to your God. I think we pray to the same God." I went in—I was scared. Everyone was making ties [tobacco prayer offerings]. I thought I'd panic. It was summer. It was really hot down in that basement. Lights went off and it was calm. I knew I was home, where I was supposed to be.

That night at the ceremony no one told me anything. I sat in the corner next to my son. It was so nice in there. We were sitting there and I felt like he was going to stand up. I reached over and felt his boot—he was standing in the corner. After the ceremony, that medicine man said one of our relatives came and stood between us—came to help us. I thought that was my son but it wasn't.

I was always so skeptical—I thought the lights were made by the medicine man. I had this doubt. There couldn't be spirits. Then I got convinced. We had sweats and the spirits would come in. I knew the people who came into our sweats wouldn't fake it. They were real.

I'm a strong believer now that I know the spirits help us. After that my kids took me to my first sweat. They told the medicine man that they did not want my mom scared, it's her first time. Then we went to the sweat lodge. I was so afraid, so they said we'd have a cool sweat first and then a hot one. I went in and I liked it. It felt good. When I came out, they went in to their hot sweat.

I know this is the way I wanted to sweat—no distractions, pure dark. In Church you are always looking around at how folks are dressed. In there you feel closer to God, you feel the spirits. They say you're in the mother earth's womb.

I heard of another book, *Fools Crow.* That book was full of good stuff. Someone borrowed it on me and didn't give it back.

You know in your heart what's right and wrong. God tries to show us things. Then when my children learn something good, they tell me. She said, "Mom, have a feast and sweat on a regular basis." In the old days they had a *wóphila* ['thanksgiving'] for all they had and for still living. So we started that, periodic sweats. That was about five or seven years ago.

We lived at a different place when we first came back to South Dakota. That was a while ago. One of our relatives built a sweat there for the family. Other people would come to visit—that was a year of mourning. A relative had died. A lot of them came to sweat with us. Then we moved the sweat. Friends and relatives came to the sweat. There was power over there. Strange things would happen.

When I was growing up, they ignored Indian religion. My mother called it devil's work—told me, don't look. We'd go up on top of the house to see the folks across the way. Those folks were traditional. Their boy had pneumonia and were told by the doctors that he would die. They called the medicine man and he doctored him. We wanted to go up there and see the devil.

The narrator did not provide an extensive explanation of the meaning of the sweat. For her it is a place of prayer. Although many of the people I knew had intricate interpretations of the sweat, others were content just to attend and focused more on the effects of the sweat, the help it gave them in their daily life. Also, her knowledge of Lakota religion was acquired through a variety of sources, including books on the Lakotas. She was not critical of these works, finding them a helpful step in her quest.

Although the symbolism of the sweat is generally explained briefly by the leader when people new to this form of prayer attend, even then the explanation is fairly brief. Intricate analyses come out only in interviews. Even when children are present, they are simply told that this is a place to pray; they are not presented with extended explanations.[4] Children are always welcome to enter the sweat if they themselves make up their mind to attend. They are rarely coerced.[5] Parents who themselves did not grow up using the sweat want their children to be exposed to it early so that they will not misunderstand what it is about or fear it. This consideration was voiced to me numerous times and reflects a strong reaction to the highly negative attitude toward Lakota religion that was imparted in the boarding schools and other circumstances.

Key to the sweat is not depth of knowledge but rather sincerity of participation. I met only one individual who would instruct others extensively about the sweat. When this was done, it was outside of the context of an actual sweat. He, like other Lakotas, took the attitude that the proper pedagogy was simply to allow learners to observe. In my experience the majority of instructions given at a sweat were delivered by white participants who were more familiar with procedures than other whites and tended to see the sweat more as a rigid set of rules and procedures than would seasoned Lakota participants.

An eighth consultant, a locally recognized spiritual leader, states that he and his family have always been part of traditional religion. He has no conversion story but stresses persistence in the face of the unacceptability of traditional practice when he was young:

> When I was young it was unpopular to be traditional religion. We were made fun of. Old men who ran ceremonies were ridiculed, called crazy. This was the attitude of even our own people.

Ever since the coming of AIM [the American Indian Movement] in 1972, AIM leaders were role models to the younger. AIM leaders utilized traditional medicine men. We would see leaders actually participating in traditional ceremonies. This motivates them to participate. This is where it came from in 1972.

When I was growing up, I was teased about helping my grandfather. Lots of kids would watch the Sun Dance. I would be the doorkeeper. My peer group would make fun of me. I felt I had done something really bad. They would pinch my chest and ask where my pierce marks were. They would say my grandfather is crazy, but I loved and respected my grandfather, so I helped him out. Other kids were saying stuff to me, but I still went and helped him out.

Consistent in each account we have reviewed is the deliberate choosing of "traditional ways." Although some select this mode of action as an exclusive allegiance, others freely integrate it with other belief systems, both religious and self-help. The eighth narrator harks back to a time when tradition was criticized and seen as negative. He also posits a radical transformation in this attitude with the coming of AIM and the new consciousness. It is generally agreed by the people with whom I worked that the AIM years did produce an increase in visibility and acceptability of traditional practice. Everyone acknowledges that there are more and more sweats on the reservation. Some see this increase as a religious transformation, whereas others hold that it represents an exploitation of the religious system that was already in place and is now used as a political symbol.

The next account, presented by a full-blood woman, shows clearly the elements both of conversion and of a struggle to maintain oneself in a harsh world. She presented herself to me as "a baby at the sweat." In her narrative she integrates her entrance into traditional belief with that of entering sobriety. We have seen the same motif before with the male consultant who constructed a pipe while he reconstructed his life. Interestingly, she also focuses on the antiquity of the lodge; to return to the ancient past is to purge oneself of contemporary woes. Harmonious interaction and sobriety are both strongly linked to the pristine world before the whites arrived. The narrative also threads through doubts and skepticism and subsequent beliefs and certainties. Note also the consistent theme of individualization of interpretation, "for me." Despite her use of communally utilized interpretations (the lodge as an ancient place, a womb, and a place of suffering as well as of joy and tranquility), those symbols are personalized by the narrator. Each narrator appropriates those symbols and others, integrating them into her or his own personal history. The ninth narrator demonstrates these principles well.

When I first went to a sweat, it was really scary. My thoughts were, do I *have* to do this? The leader of the sweat says: *"Takómni* ['there's no way out'], we *have to* finish it." I don't know if anyone goes in willingly. The sweat was the usual kind. At first I couldn't relate to the almost unbearable heat. Yet, after I came out the first times, being light-headed, I thought, ah, that wasn't so bad after all. You go in expecting all kinds of drastic changes. It doesn't happen. I felt light. The next time I knew that the water was valuable. I knew how I'd feel. I respected the heat more. I talked to the rocks: "Have mercy on us, pity us." Others also pray, "Have mercy, pity on us." That was an experience, trying to talk to some rocks [laughter].

I first started going to sweats in the 1980s. I mostly listened to the prayers that were said. I couldn't find contact, connection with God at the very beginning. It was like going to an AA meeting. First I said, my life changed through AA. When will I change? So too in the sweat, you learn sobriety, humility. You learn to care for kids. I wondered if I would learn that. I enjoyed the singing the most. When the songs happen, the discomfort of the heat and the phobia of enclosure went away. . . .

Then my husband said make your own sweat, so we made one down here. I really admire churches. Catholics have pretty buildings. I looked for the connection between the two structures—this one seems so humble. My brother-in-law and my sister tried to make us attend their church. I'd go there but didn't feel a sense of belonging. I did feel that in the sweat. "Ah, I'm back," I said to myself. The rocks meant more. I could almost touch them—touch God. These rocks were here from the beginning of time. I made connection with God through rocks. My dad gave me my pipe. Now I have a sweat and a pipe. My sisters are afraid when they come around— you're supposed to be very good around a pipe. But I'm a person, I'm human. I really hang on to the pipe for everything. If I felt bad, I'd sit with the pipe. It didn't take care of the problem out there but it gave me peace. I held the pipe as a gift from God. I don't understand why a pipe. For a while I told my friend that I can't relate to the pipe. I feel emptiness, no meaning. You can talk to God without the pipe. There were lots of doubts along the way, lots of mystery and unanswered questions.

Little things happened in my doubtful moments. When the lodge was built, I and my family went in first. It is a family sweat lodge. Two of us lit the sweat, placed the four large rocks like a pyramid. All the wood lit with a match. I figured that if it doesn't burn, I'll get gas. It fired up by itself. At the most doubtful times things like this happen. Still, we got gas just in case.

Sometimes I hear something. I don't know what it is. For example, once I heard a knock under our floor.

If I expect that the sweat fire will start on its own, then it doesn't do that. At times I'd really pray—my total faith there. I would go into a trance. That time my son and daughter were in there. They said that I prayed for one hour [at the first sweat]. I didn't remember. I was disoriented when I came out.

Sometimes I went to several different medicine men's sweats. You can see and hear the spirit helpers. That's a mystery to me. I don't see them that often. If you want to see lights, go to a light show. Here we can talk to God. God doesn't have to show himself visibly and verbally. Through the faith and prayers we put in it, somehow it happens. You get a feeling. I don't know how it happens.

Once I must have been in there with lots of doubts. My brother said "*Thąké* ['older sister'], reach out." I held out my hand and he put a red hot rock in there. It wasn't hot. He did not say why he did that. I really came to accept that, with all the work we do here to keep the sweat ready. You never know when someone will bring *opáǧi* ['an offering'] for a sweat. The sweat is a chore, but it's soothing down there. It's a cozy home place down there.

Every time you go to a sweat it's different. Last time the rocks were red hot. It felt cool but we were soaked. A lady from West Germany picked the rocks. They were popping and exploding in the fire. People got scared. I could have gotten scared too. What if they exploded when we were all in the lodge? I thought I could either get scared but I went ahead—faith. It's almost like a challenge. All we have to take in there is faith. We didn't even hear one crack when they were brought in.

I'm young in this—six years old. It is important learning about the sweat. I didn't know what a sweat was until 1983. I went to treatment before that. I was really faithful to AA. One year later, I had a dream. I was at the hospital floating around. In the lobby was an old lady with a green lizard [liquor bottle]. I went above her and she looked up. It was me. Her eyes were yellow. I saw myself. Then I saw a different place. There was a woman dancing the Sun Dance. It was me. I looked happy. My dad and a lady both said I had to Sun Dance. I was supposed to talk to a medicine man. I didn't.

In the spring, I found a little *íyą* ['rock'] in the house. "The little rock came to you," that was what I was told by my dad, to care for it. I put it in a plant pot. The plant would wilt when we had a problem. I put the rock in the plant, but later I found it in my pocket. I moved to a bigger trailer house. I opened the window, and the rock was sitting there. We didn't honor it.

When I was twelve, we were kicked out of a ceremony, we were fooling around. In another ceremony when I was young they *aphíyą* ['doctored'] my dad, fixed a stroke.

That year every night I was at an AA meeting. Thursday AA, Friday, for four days straight I was drunk. The choice was to go back to treatment or lose my job. I went back. While in treatment, in the third week over Christmas and New Year, there was a young *wašícu* ['white person'] folk singer. The woman had us lay down. She sang about an old Indian man with a life of wisdom willing to give and share. I saw this man. I heard a shrill whistle. It was an eagle shrill (only three of us heard it). She was singing of a well-known medicine man on Pine Ridge. That was the same man I pictured when she was singing.

After the second treatment program I went to, I was really lonesome. It was raining, and I was crying, lonesome. My parents were there. My best friend called me. I was trying to change from a life of partying. She didn't say anything. She drove me to one of the districts. We went to a one-room log house. There were about fifty people there. *"Waná yahí!"* ['Now you're here'] they said when I came in. My friend had just heard of the ceremony, but they all acted like they were waiting for us. I smelled the sage. They closed the door and nailed canvas over the windows. They put sage across the door. I was scared and wanted to go. They *yuwípi* ['tie up'] the medicine man like a mummy, wrap him up and lie him down. They started to sing. They talked about seven spirits. It was really scary. There was a sound like a bolt of lightning at the door. I passed out. I was really crying. My friend held me. Though I was crying, they can't hear me as they were singing so loud. The floor was shaking. Someone was coming through the door. Something hit my knee. I thought they'd go by me,

ignore me. Next there were two hands on my head. I screamed. I had sobbing cries. He stood there, and I finally stopped crying. I touched the
hands; they were long and cold. I touched the head. There was hair on one
side and a braid on the other. There was no body. I tried to touch him. They
spoke through the medicine man. They said they came to pray with us,
"Wakhą́ Tháka echéla thokáhekiya po ['Go first only to Wakan Tanka'']."
It was really soothing word in Indian and a lot of humor. They thought I
was really singing, but I was crying. They called everyone *thakóža*
['grandchild']. The medicine man knew me. He said to have pity on each
other and to love each other and care for each other. What should be scary
is living without prayers.

My best friend is also my [AA] sponsor and said this is my spiritual
awakening. This is how I was introduced into Lakota ways. I went back for
more ceremonies, sweats.

That narrator extends the symbols of suffering and humility to the very
structure of the sweat, comparing it to the Christian churches. Nevertheless, the
sweat, in its simplicity and humility, is represented as home, as the "right place"
to be and a place of consolation. It is there that the narrator finds comfort and
security. The ninth narrator, like others, also emphasizes faith in the sweat
rather than ceremonial precision for efficacy. It is the trust and belief of the
individual rather than the efficacy of the ceremony that brings help and healing.

As with explanations for entrance into the ceremonial world of the sweat,
the interpretation of the sweat lodge itself is carefully individualized by each
narrator. Interpretation, like participation, is seen as a matter of conscious
choice. Most postulate a time in the past when these rituals were universally
practiced. Now an individual consciously chooses to participate. A tenth narrator speaks of the delicate issue of incorporating Christian symbols and beliefs
into the prayers of the lodge:

It doesn't matter how you pray. You can use Christ in there—in certain
lodges. In my friend's lodge, he won't say nothing but it bothers him
afterward if they use Christ. Well, you won't use Christ in his lodge
because you'll be burned up in there.

My view is really hard-core—I know it's prayerful to go to a sweat. You
go there and pray like the forefathers. They did not know Christ. I would
scold someone if they did that. A medicine man I know would scold
someone for doing that. Some sweats are Christian oriented, others are
hard-core.

As previously mentioned, when a sweat becomes particularly hot, it is sometimes interpreted as caused by some breach of etiquette within the sweat. Once a sweat became incredibly hot, and afterward someone explained to me that the spirits dumped the whole bucket into the pit because they did not like how someone prayed. There is no direct interpersonal reprimand—it is conveyed by "the spirits" through the intensity of the heat in the lodge.

An eleventh narrator takes a different view of Christ and Christianity within Lakota religion:

> The medicine man who taught me studied the ways of Christianity. He said Jesus was the greatest of all medicine men. He chose twelve disciples much as there are twelve eagle feathers on the tail, twelve moons in the year. He *hablécheya* for forty days and forty nights. He was tempted with power just as young spiritual leaders are tempted with power. He wore a crown of thorns, pierced, and hung on a tree. There is no contradiction between Lakota and Christian beliefs. Jesus told a young man, in order to gain entry to heaven give up all worldly possessions and follow him. Indians by virtue of our history and beliefs are able to do that.
>
> I see him [the narrator's teacher] as a strong believer in Christ and one who can live up to the ways of the pipe. I said to my teacher that if Jesus were here now he'd come to your ceremonies, because they are the humblest of all. I said this in a sweat.
>
> I suppose in proper anthropology the learned would say our beliefs are tainted by Christianity and external influences. I say yes, just as we incorporated nature, horse, allies, and trade. The outside world is here to stay; we can't make it go away. Adaptations are necessary for us to survive. We can only do that by understanding. Our resistance to understanding the outside world makes us accept mostly the bad.

Interestingly, this narrator turns the argument. In the previous narratives, incorporation brings symbolic chaos (too high a temperature in the sweat), but the tenth narrator claims that by rejecting the incorporation of good from another culture, the bad aspects of that culture (specifically referring to drugs and alcohol) will invade.

Like the choice of whether or not to participate in sweat ceremonies, the choice of whether or not to include Christian or any other symbols is up to individuals and small groups. Although the sweat is a ceremony that promotes consensus, its fragmentary nature itself allows for diversity. If one is not comfortable with how a sweat is conducted or with the symbols employed, one is free to find another sweat or build one. The reverse is also true. One individual told me that he erected a sweat and then received word that a local medicine man wished to sweat with him. He took this as a sign of the acceptability of his sweat and his way of belief. Another individual said that the Catholic formula for the sign of the cross was the same idea as the Lakota prayer mitakuye oyas'in.

One individual based his symbolic interpretation on transformation. Although all would admit that one is reborn when emerging from the lodge, some insist that this rebirth demonstrates itself in a change of lifestyle. At the same time the sweat is meant for a universal transformation; to pray simply for oneself is a mark of selfishness. It is expected that if one prays for the needs of all, his or her personal needs will be met. Nevertheless, on the level of practice, people make very specific prayers for their own needs, as seen in the twelfth narrative, and these are generally not criticized:

> A man goes into the sweat lodge for others, not for himself. He sacrifices himself for others in going to the sweat lodge. Some go because everyone else does it. Don't go in for yourself. *Iníkağa* means being reborn. You have to change your ways.
>
> The lodge represents earth and all the elements, water, smoke, stone. Stone is the creator of the universe. People should know all those. Then there should be no fear. An individual should not go in just because he is sick—do it for all the people. "If I overcome this disease, it is for all the people" should be the attitude. You have to have a good reason to go in. I went for a few years to them. The man I went with, his life never changed. In fact, it got worse. They were playing with it for themselves. I told one holy man that I wouldn't come any more because they were not doing this for the people. That medicine man said the same thing but said that he couldn't turn them down. He made a commitment to help all people. Anyone else can quit if they want. When they talk to me, I don't listen to them fully. Their lifestyle never changes. They do it with the wrong intention. I'll go back if they shape up. They have to change first before I support them. If they have respect for *ini,* it will help them. They are pretending, fooling themselves.

There seems to be no competition over wealth of knowledge, although some individuals are generally acknowledged as more knowledgeable than others. At times symbols are brought forth in prayer, particularly the image of Mother Earth. There may be disagreement over who the truly knowledgeable are. Ultimately, it becomes a personal choice as to whom an individual will follow, whether to become attached to a particular group, what to accept in the belief system, and when and how to explain belief concerning the sweat.

Symbolic Interpretations

His discourse carefully couched in his personal experience, one of the previous narrators explains the meaning of the symbols of the sweat. This individual regularly leads sweats at his home and is careful, when new people are attending his sweat, to explain the ceremony.

With me, what I have, it is a spiritual arrangement to pray and make a conscious connection with the spirits and the Grandfather. They all are one. The rocks represent, it's a symbol of God's creation, and it is one of his first creations. It's using something that was created in the beginning. To me to actually pour water, water is a symbol of life. According to the Lakota, it is also the first medicine. You can't live without it. It's both a physical and spiritual life. To use the hot elements and to pour water is a symbol of purifying mind, spirit, and also body. Not only spiritual—in my knowledge by steaming there are physical medicinal benefits. Spiritual is first, physical secondary.

Darkness is a symbol of, you might say, where I am at as for my lack of knowledge. It shows I have little knowledge of the mysteries of God, *Thųkášila*. Whenever you open the door and light comes in, it represents *Thųkášila* as being light, which is of a spiritual nature. Opening of the door four times honors the four directions. The way I was taught, we first invoke the powers of the west. I place to the west a particular symbol, *Wakįyą*— thunder beings, *wahúpakoza* ['wingeds']. I was taught that that was the first direction created according to the legends. I also use the symbol of the buffalo and bear, interchangeable to that direction. Those symbols aren't Gods. They are symbols of God's creation, everything created. These are the symbols I was taught by two medicine men. One of them gave me the authority to run sweats.

The north represents the power of the elk, *heȟáka oyáte*. Elk represents in the Lakota way the virility, the sexual energies. North also represents the wind and the snow, mostly the wind. In this community, wind most of the time comes from there.

To the east is the black tail deer. That's the direction of the first light. To the south is the *itókaǧa*—my grandparents say that the people came from the south with wind in the face. It pulls back hair and skin. I use the bird nation for that direction.

Sitting in a circle represents the continuity. There's a beginning and end to everything. Sitting on the ground (modest—now no clothes). This is material symbology; we come to the earth and go with nothing. The only thing we take is good deeds.

Ikcé wichášа 'common people' no one higher or lower, all equal.

The sweat never did represent a game—see how hot you can stand it. Some see it as an endurance test. Some say the suffering is for the people. I used to think suffering sucks. *Thukášila* sees you are willing to suffer so your prayers are stronger, more answerable.

Sage is an herb or weed, has a capacity to purify. It clears the air and clears the spirits [negative], gets rid of them. "In the name of Jesus Christ, remove all negative spirits." Sometimes I say that to myself.

My way of running the sweat is very contemporary. I don't claim knowledge of what the spirits do or don't do.

This was passed on, this allows us to center. The circle and rocks represent the fact that God is the center. Rocks are the first, represent God as *Thukášila*. When the sweat begins, it is the center that is reality. You actually see the rocks and feel the heat. Though science can explain it, it is still a mysterious spiritual thing. I believe it becomes a church, a holy place. Reverence and honor. Prayers and songs are important. I believe the old medicine men wouldn't understand this. These songs, what I know of science, have energy and waves. Because God is so pure, we're not allowed to see him. Songs can break through a particular barrier. Songs make me stronger; they make me endure the heat better. More than that, someone said that songs are a natural high. I believe that and go beyond it. We have things to get more in tune with God. Song activates endorphins (someone told me that). I believe it, but it's still a mystery. There are four minds; I don't doubt that either. There are lots of ways to explain. I feel uplifted; purification takes place; I feel a higher power, *Wakhá Tháka.*

Sometimes the sweat lodge can be a womb. This is not my original thinking. Water, being safe. Doesn't totally feel that way but kind of represents that. Sometimes I sweat with a pipe; sometimes I don't. Sometimes I have a feeling to be very meticulous and ritualistic. For example, I'll touch the pipe to each of the rocks, make a circle of cedar and sage, offer cedar and sweetgrass to the four directions. Other times no. When I run a sweat, they are not always the same. Pouring water and other things are consistent, but the other things change.

Some sweats are instructional. Sometimes they are spontaneous. Instructional sweats are very close to theater. There is a lot of theater in these ways. I know that's there. Sometimes there's no theater.

I try to explain that this is not the only way—this is just one way. Some want to drop everything. I say always pray and look for discernment. As humans we can fool ourselves.

We can get caught in ritual and detail and miss the prayer. I'm talking about myself. If the detail's meant as an honor, that's OK, but if details are the most important part, then we can't go beyond it. There's only a couple of times, with the humor part. Someone said he was ashamed of the fact that there was laughter in the sweat. I respect that, but this is our sweat and church, and it is how we do it. We don't do it out of disrespect. When you get your own sweat, you can do it that way. Now respect our ways. Somehow you can tell if laughter is disrespectful. Some sweats are really rigid. I couldn't handle it. Other sweats. This is mine or ours, and no one is going to touch it.

The four colors represent the four races. So you can't discriminate. Some say just Indians, no *ská wicháša* ['white people']. Then they say *mitákuye iyúha* 'all my relatives.' People are humans; they go through that. They change eventually and get OK.

Black is to the west, white to the north, yellow to the east and red to the south. To me they represent the four races. White is for purity, red for life, yellow for evil, and black for spiritual ignorance.

To me, *Thukášila* is a word for God.

This narrator holds for the universality of Lakota symbols. It is no coincidence that I would be invited to sweats in which the prevailing attitude is that everyone is welcome if they are sincere. I believe that attitude represents the majority opinion on the reservation. Whereas some sweats are recognized as "Indian only," sweats are often places of encounter and incorporation of outsiders. White can be a relative term. Just as the term *full-blood* is often used culturally rather than genetically (although the two distinctions are often confused and conflated), so too is the term white used in that way. Although Indians, no matter what tribe, are considered as one group and admissible to ceremonies on the reservation, white is often a designation for an unknown non-Indian. Thus, whites who are known to families are incorporated into ceremonies. The problem is that acceptance by one group does not ensure universal acceptance, and one group's relative-by-adoption is another group's white. It is also true that even particular Lakotas feel unwelcome at certain sweats, a reflection of the sometimes factional nature of Lakota social life.

The narrator also focuses on forgiveness and purification. Sage is a very complete purifier. One uses sage to wipe off the sweat from the body. This individual stated that when sage is used in this way, it also removes sins. He views sin, like sickness, as intrusive and alien. It leaves through the pores and is removed by wiping.

Another narrator expresses his understanding of the sweat using sin as a central reality and orienting the symbols of the sweat around it:

> Sweat lodge is the most common ritual. You use it for the other six rituals. You use it for healing, purification, confession—leave your problems at the sweat and walk out, leave a new man. My consensus is that sweat lodge represents the mother's womb. Before you're born, you're exposed to the elements but not to sin. When you come into this world, the second world, you are exposed to sin. The little mound in front of the lodge represents the ultimate goal. At one sweat I attend there is a little trail leading up to the mound from the sweat made up of rough rocks and sands. *Wašícu* call this the straight and narrow; Lakotas call it *chąkú lúta* 'the red road'. It's hard to walk the road. If you slip off it go into the sweat, pray, and ask to try again. You climb the mound—find purpose of life. When you reach the top of the mound, look back, and you're finished with the second world, ready for the third world. *Thųkášila* is a forgiving God. How many times will he forgive us? You have to ask that.

The central themes here are of striving, failing, and forgiving. The sweat is the point of origin, both as a symbolic womb and as the beginning of the path of life. When one fails, one begins again by returning to the point of origin.

A woman who is a member of the Native American Church says that although she prays and sings freely using Christian metaphors and the name of Jesus, she nevertheless sees the sweat ritual as immutable. She equates change in the ritual with loss of efficacy.

> The rocks go into the lodge, and we enter into *ųcí makhá*'s belly. In the womb of the mother, you can ask the father for anything. The breath of the rocks allows us to leave in there the old and come out with the new. This is the place of connection between heaven and earth; this connects us to *makhá* and *tobtób,* the sixteen spirits. We don't know their names. The lodge is about relationship: commerce and development; our duties as mothers and fathers; relationship to the stars and burial places—you have a place to go to when you die. We also need to understand the star formations, so that we know where we need to be. My grandmother says they used to go to the Black Hills to read the prophecy walls, so that we will know what will happen that year.
>
> Each year, you grow and enter into a new dimension, a new role and existence.

The ritual, the sweat lodge never changes. We always do this the same way. If you add anything on to this, the prayers do not go. You need to be stable in your own way.

Again, note in the following narrative the personalization of the symbols and the continuity of symbolic structure across narratives. There is a great variety of symbolic interpretation present, but there are also constants such as the six directions, constituent elements, antiquity, and purification. At the same time there is significant variation in what parts of non-Lakota belief are permitted inside the lodge and the symbols associated with the directions:

The sweat lodge is basically a rite of purification. In the rite, you use the elements, rock, fire, water, and we use living things—willows to build the frame.

The symbols involved: the four directions. Start with the west, black, thunder people, the thunder the power of cleansing rains that come and give life to earth. Lightning gives life to the earth. North, red, the buffalo. Its strength the power of winter. It comes and cleanses. The cold purifies the earth of sicknesses and disease, germs. The harshness helps us to develop endurance, strength within. Our suffering in the lodge helps other people. When we suffer this little bit, we help others along. This particularly helps the Lakota people. Red also represents introspection, the taking of one's inventory. The east is represented by the color yellow and the elk nation, some say the black tail deer. East, the sun comes up, sheds light and life on all living things. Also the place of the morning star of wisdom and understanding. Greeting the morning star and making prayers, a person can gain a lot of wisdom and understanding. South is represented by the color white, the bird nation, some say the owl, some the great winged ones, the geese. South is the power of the summer; it comes and life becomes fresh and new. It is a happy time; feasting, dancing, prayers, gathering fruit, vegetables, meat. Mother Earth is represented by the *phežúta ȟáka oyáte* ['medicine people']. Earth is our mother and grandmother. It bears all fruit and bears us. The heavens is *Thųkášila*, represented by the spotted elk nation. You can't see the air; you can't see God.

All these six powers are honored in the sweat lodge. All a part of the circle of life. All these powers are necessary. They are harmonized as the four seasons—the circle of life. We sit inside a circle in the darkness. The darkness represents the darkness of our human soul, of ignorance. We know nothing and are nothing as human beings, by ourselves. We acknowledge this to God, place ourselves before him to overcome our darkness and ignorance. There are four rounds; the door opens four times in honor of the four directions. The last one includes the mother and father.

Songs are the same in there, prayers, songs, four directions song, calling the spirits songs and Sun Dance songs (there are lots of those). Not everyone agrees on which songs are appropriate, such as using Sun Dance songs in the sweat. All these songs are spiritual. If you are sincere, honest, there is nothing wrong with it.

These rites are ancient, yet they have adapted to the times and have changed to a certain degree. It is only natural. Look at Christianity. Hasn't it changed? Every religion, every culture changes. Before the horse, the culture was different. Horses changed the culture drastically.

A male consultant was particularly astute in bringing out both psychological and interpersonal dynamics in his evaluation of the symbols employed in the lodge:

We call the life-giving steam our grandfather's breath. The creator can breathe life into us. If we're dead spiritually, we can come back to life. If we're sick at heart, the life-giving steam can restore balance.

There are many who like to sweat for the fellowship involved. Many like the introspection, sit in the dark, return to the womb of the mother—the desire to be comforted spiritually, to receive divine guidance.

What I've discovered is wó'okiye. Wó'okiye is life-giving energy the Creator gives to spiritual leaders. They have an overabundance. They must share this. They can heal, prophesy, find lost objects, confirm marriage and love, deal with all types of emotions, jealousy, hatred, prejudice, fears. I believe that in order to properly conduct a ceremony, a leader must have the proper wó'okiye, positive energy.

We need to get back to the original teaching. The sweat and pipe are for good and wise things. We should respect rather than fear God. We lack wisdom in so many things. There are so many abuses without proper wó'okiye to counsel people. Narcotics, alcohol, domestic violence, sexual and physical and social abuse (such as corruption). I believe the sweat lodge ceremony can fit into contemporary life if we don't forget our original teachings. The sweat and our seven ceremonies restore life, purify, rid us of negative things. The sweat is used most frequently. What impresses is it can humble a person—even if there is no intention to—the darkness, enclosed heat, the sweat lodge makes them humble, they cry out and ask for forgiveness, direction, help. That is in itself good. People take hardships to the sweat.

Since the sweat symbolizes rebirth, the people you enter the lodge with, you become their spiritual brothers and sisters. That's why you feel fellowship. Joking and teasing and stories are said in jest. It is a serious ceremony, but the Lakotas take their sense of humor seriously.

A female consultant describes the meaning of the sweat by juxtaposing her understanding and that of another individual who runs sweats and with whom she no longer sweats on a regular basis. It is not infrequent that people compare understandings of ritual procedures and choose to attend or avoid certain ceremonies based on their feelings about how others conduct their rituals. An individual's moral behavior is also added to the equation. If an individual is perceived as not "walking his talk" (a phrase taken from Alcoholics Anonymous and fairly commonly used on the reservation), then individuals will cease coming to the sweat. It is clear that interpersonal factors also enter here:

One guy's sweat is really complicated. He points out what animals are from what directions. I don't get into directions and things like that, but he does that. You can't go in and pray for what you want. Old, young, orphaned, handicapped are the four things you pray for. If you pray for all those, your prayers will be answered, so he said. Where you sit in the sweat determines what to pray for. He holds that individual prayers are "selfish." He's really a controlling person. If he disagreed with me, he'd try to push me out. After I helped a friend through a Sun Dance that he put on, I never would go back.

For some reason, people don't like me. God gave me a gift to see people as they are. They can't manipulate me. I don't join any groups.

When I go into a sweat, to me it's mother earth's womb. When we come out we're new, we have new life. We're washed clean. The rocks are the grandfathers. They have spirits. Water is life, steam is God's breath. He purifies us. Fire is sacred, as it is an element as is water. Our sweats are simple. The one who is running the sweat prays to God, gives thanks for the sacred ceremonies, and sings the songs we know. Then everyone prays. Four rounds are just part of the ritual. Sometimes we have more rounds, sometimes six if the rocks are hot, there is lots of water, and people just want to relax. It is important to keep the sweat neat and clean. This is our prayer; we want God to recognize it. We keep it free of trash. We don't want people to be afraid, so we are not strict. We bring in little kids, wrap them in a blanket, and put them in the back. At one ceremony a little kid complained that it was cold in there when we all were really hot. God protects them.

One medicine man says a girl is pure until she has her moon. There is no need for kids to participate in the sweat. We want our kids to know the sweat, so we include them if they want to go in. I take kids in during the flu season. People criticize our sweat for being open. Kids are pure until puberty. We believe this too, but we want them to know and respect it. We had to learn about our religion. We came from other religions, so we had to learn.

Sometimes we have morning sweats and cook breakfast down there. Of course, we make a second fire.

Sometimes you go in the sweat and you feel you're all alone on top of the hill. It's you and God. That is the purpose of darkness in the ceremony. Sometimes you see the stars in there. Even though I'm sitting inside the sweat, I am really outside sometimes. It is something immense.

Another individual who runs quite a few sweats and ceremonies gives about the most expansive explanation of the symbol system that I have collected. He also tends less to bracket this information as his own knowledge. On the other hand, he freely acknowledges the internal pluralism that exists in the religious system as he experiences it:

A long time ago, fire was sacred. The *ochéthi šakówį* ['seven fire places', the original seven groups of the Lakota alliance]. There was only one *ochéthi* ['fireplace']. The sweat has the symbolic meaning of *ochéthi. Phéta ohákešni* 'the everlasting fire', it was one of the earliest ceremonies. It was earlier than the seven rites. The oldest sacred object was the fire. They carried it from camp to camp wherever they went. The sweat is like the camp/fire place. It is not a political symbol.[6] No one knows how far back it goes. The sweat has lots of meanings. The lodge, *thuká thi'ógnake ki* ['the dwelling that contains the rocks'], is the spirits' lodge. You go in and cleanse your body, spirit, soul. It is like being reborn again. You go into the womb of mother earth. *Iníkaǧa*, make new, make the breath of life over again. The sweat is the mother's womb, and you are reborn in there. The steam is the breath of God, and when you go in there, your life is renewed and you come out a new person. The rocks inside the sweat, *tunkan oyate* ['the rock people'], the ancient ones, ancient spirits. Rocks are spirits, living beings. When you heat up the rocks, you bring the life back to that spirit when it was created. You doctor yourself with the elements of first creation, water, fire.

There are lots of different types of sweat ceremonies, old times sort of ritual ones. There were certain steps you had to do. No one broke the rules. You always enter on the left side. You couldn't go across where the altar is. Once the pipe is loaded, only the leader goes in on the right. He goes directly in, no crossing.

The pipe rack, *chanúpa ógnak,* buffalo skull mound, *owáka* ['altar']. The mound is the altar for the sweat lodge. From the pit to the mound to the fire is the road of life. The mound is the peak of your spirituality, like the summer Sun Dance. The spirits sleep in the winter. The mound is the summer months, fast, Sun Dance, then you go back down. He goes to fast on the hill, which is represented by the mound. The mound represents a hill, a place for visions and also a place for death, for the scaffold.

The altar put beside the mound represents the heaviness of life. You fill the pipe and rest it on the rack. You carry your hardships for so long, and then you fill the pipe to relieve you of those hardships. That's what the pipe represents.

The doorman is supposed to work in a circle. The doorman goes around six times clockwise, putting in rocks. The first six (six is a sacred number) are laid in a special way. The first is laid either on the east or west, for example, east, south, west, north. Two stones are placed in the middle, one on the bottom, one on top, representing the heavens and the earth.

The fireman is working in a circle. Every year has changing seasons. It is also the year of your life. It's a continuous circle. The tobacco offerings and the filled pipe represents the people's prayers. They make flags and fill the pipe. This represents prayer. Sometimes they lay the ties on the mound by the pipe rack or put them inside the sweat lodge. Some put a willow staff in front of the sweat lodge and tie them to the staff. The staff is called the staff of life, *sagyé* 'cane'. The staff belonging to an individual has their sacred things on them, like those things used in the *hablécheya* 'vision quest'. If there's one there, the people can bring their offerings. Some tie an eagle feather and leave it there. When they bring in those six rocks and there's a filled pipe in there, they concentrate on why the sweat is being held: healing, fasting, death, anything that comes up. It's a serious matter when they fill the pipe, not just for nothing. Therefore the people are quiet, respectful for the pipe and for those rocks. Everyone is quiet until the pipe goes out again.

Even the fireman, when he's working with the rocks, nobody bothers him. They leave him alone. That fireman is doing the work for that prayer. He's working with that spirit, that rock. He's doing something sacred, so no one bothers him at that time.

Sweat's like the beginning of time. This body is a piece of the earth. It's like going back to creation when the first breath of life was blown into our bodies. These rocks, when they are heated, are like the beginning of time when rocks were lava, I guess. Fire is the most important symbol in the sweat, it's a sacred energy, one of the first sacred things they had since the people began.

The buffalo skull represents all the beings of the earth that are not human, the four-legged. The buffalo skull represents all of life on the earth that passed on already. The feather represents all the birds. This is really what the sweat is all about; this is going back to creation, all these animals and birds. A long time ago *hukáka wóglake* 'the old fables', *hukákiya* 'the ancient ancestors', the people lived in the earth long ago, guided by rock spirits. They had no sight, as it was completely dark. All the animals lived there too. When the people came out of the earth, a scout saw a hole with light coming in. It was too bright for him, but then he got used to the light and looked around and saw a country, saw the sun and the earth. He wandered the earth for a while and then went back in. It took time to get used to the earth. There were no living things on the earth. The scout told the buffalos and the people about it. The buffalos were greedy, so they went charging out. The scout said to go slow because the light will hurt your eyes. The buffalos came out anyway, and that is why the buffalo are blind.

When they first came out of the earth, the Great Spirit gave them fire. This was his first gift to the people. That's kind of a creation story.

There are no stories that I know of for how they got the sweat.

The sweat is all by itself. As far back as people can remember they had it, thousands of years, even more, millions.

Women when they fast, they talk to them that they'll be in their mother's womb again, so they put them in the sweat lodge and make it completely dark in there. The woman sits there two to four days. The sounds she hears are like the sounds a child hears in its mother's womb. Long time ago, old ladies used to go into sweat and fast. Women never did go on the hill like the men. In the old days, usually the men sweated themselves. Sometimes they had family sweats, man and wife and daughters. Sometimes they had matters they had to pray about. Ceremonial sweats separated men from women. Warrior societies had medicine bundles that can't be brought around women, so just the men would sweat. Sometimes they use the steam to purify sacred objects or offering ties. They use the steam to purify you, *ap'óya* ['to steam']. Mostly the sweat lodge is for cleansing. You can clean your body with the incense as well as the steam. You purify the body to its newborn state. Everyday life has a contaminating nature—women on menses, people's thoughts *(thawáchj)*, jealousy, envy. Not your own thoughts. Murderers are considered like a sick woman. His aura around him is bad. When you come into contact with a person like that and shake his hand or talk, you have to purify yourself. Those who are preparing to doctor someone also take precautions. No woman in her menstruation time or one not in the right frame of mind should come near. For example, this includes drunks and people who don't believe in the Indian ways.

At the sweat lodge, it's like a release of everyday life. It gives you power to continue again, strengthen the mind, spirit, the body. You let them [concerns and troubles] go to the Great Spirit in the sweat lodge.

The reason they darken the lodge or ceremony is so that spirits can communicate that way. Some people are scared to pray—their spirit is so *ohų́kešni* ['weak']. The total darkness frees their spirit to communicate with God. It's like a blind-from-birth individual. He relies on his senses and his trust. When it is dark, you cannot see physical things. When we pray together I have to use my senses. It blocks out all the things that deceive us with eyesight. I see you with my eyes but I'm not seeing the real you. Two spirits communicate in prayer.

It has to be dark for the spirits to come in. It goes way back to the old-time stories. We lived below the earth. There was no light there. Spirits took care of us. We had to trust them for food. They took us to places for food. When you're in the dark, you're in ancient time. The door opening represents going out onto the earth. When people first came out, they were pure. You are prejudiced if you see people [by their skin color]. In the sweat it's dark; you can't see them.

The sacrifice of the heat, you're teaching that person to have awareness of their spirit—that they'll make their personal prayer. Lots of things are too easy for us. When we pray, it's in the time of need. We have to clear our mind, have to go through hardship—that hardship is the heat. Newcomers, teach them to be patient. You have to suffer to be heard.

The east side of the sweat is the entrance. You begin construction of the sweat with the four quarters. Put them first, tie them together. You unite the whole universe, the two east and two west willows join, and the two north and two south willows join, and these meet and cross over at the top.

The narrative above provides a variety of thematic understandings of the sweat. I have reproduced it as a continuous narrative to show how those themes are developed and explained. The narrative also highlights central symbols that are consistent among sweat lodge users. One of them is that of the return to original times. The narrator also emphasizes the most consistent contemporary association of the sweat: rebirth. The sweat is the mother's womb. At the same time the sweat lodge is a place of suffering and struggle. It is through the suffering that the sufferer is released, and it is through hardship that prayers are answered. The security of the womb forsaken for the rigors of the world seems reversed in Lakota symbolism, for here the rigors of the womb (the sweat lodge is seen as a suffering place) are endured in order to gain a secure life outside. Thus, the sweat lodge itself has two associations, the warmth and comfort of the womb and the suffering and ignorance from which one escapes when the door is opened. Finally, the narrator stresses respect and care in performing the ritual. Despite his strong opinion on the matter, I have never seen this individual directly reprimand anyone during a sweat. There is a general belief throughout the narrative that in the old times all rituals were conducted properly and that today the practice has weakened.

One particular consultant spoke to me in the context of a difficult life. By holding onto the pipe and the ceremonies, that individual manages to survive the difficulties of the reservation. In all these narratives, local consultants see themselves as surviving intense suffering, both in their personal lives and in a difficult world. The consultant admits that the external situations may not alter, but nevertheless she has strength to endure the suffering. The sufferings of the sweat, unlike those in the world, can be selected and regulated. In the sweat, sufferings are transcended, giving strength for the participants to do likewise in their lives when they emerge.

The same individual ran a sweat for other women. In describing how she ran the sweat lodge, she explains both the symbol system and its levels of meaning for her and the participants. Note how she tries not to interfere with others' understandings of the lodge:

Sometimes I feel it's not me in there. I heard a tapping in my eardrum when it was my turn wówahokukhiya ['to give counsel, instruct']—it was like a preaching. I talked one hour and didn't remember it.

The only time I ran a sweat was at the Sun Dance. You know I'm really new at this. For me, I see it almost like as if it is a cycle of learning. What I learned is through my own experience. I ran the sweat lodge for the women. I had to respect their experience even though I understand the Sun Dance is only for men. These women may go through the same experience. I keep my thoughts on the prayers for understanding and strength for these women and prayers for their prayers. In the Sun Dance, we were given seven rocks. That was the only time that these Sun Dancers could drink water. After we all got in the sweat lodge, there was respect for the rocks, thuká oyáte ['rock people']. They're there to help us through. Fire, heat, water, and steam are there to purify and strengthen us. Because at the Sun Dance, the inside of the circle is so sacred they have to be purified before and after. They have to be purified as they go into a wakhá ['holy'] place.

So I used the sage when all the ladies get in the sweat. I give each one sage that they chew on first and then I sage the rocks. Then I sprinkle water on the rocks. Then we close the door and pray. In my prayer, I admit I don't understand, but I give thanks that I'm there. For some reason I'm there and have been asked to help. I give thanks and ask only that our prayers be heard. I give thanks naming each direction and spirit connected to each direction, and I acknowledge what each season brings. From the west, the thunder, is the coming of spring, the natural new year for the Lakota people. The directions, they don't exactly bring the following seasons. Then I go towards the north, the *thatháka oyáte* ['buffalo people']. I see these whenever the winter storm-clouds are like buffalo. I learned this through the elders: *Waná thatháka oyáte khichíkšą* ['now the buffalo people play around'], *ukíye* ['come back']. They bring back the white blanket of snow for *µcí makhá* ['grandmother earth']. The east is the *sµtésapala* ['black tail deer'], the spirit animals. East brings power of first light of the morning star, *wicháȟpi ithókabya ki*—light before the morning star. *Wicháša zi'íc'iya* ['man painted yellow']. This brings the summer— the way I understand. The fall is the south. The south, *itókağatakiya*— through *hµhá oyáte* ['owl people'], *wanáği oyáte* ['ghost people']—people who have gone on before, left, died—that resembles the fall season. The leaves, grass die out in the fall.

If I look, the seasons are crisscross—that's the only place I know that the four directions cross each other.

The fifth direction is *µcí makhá* ['grandmother earth']. She remains the same, endures all these changes and still provides for life: plants, animals, *ikcé wicháša* ['common or Indian people']. She provides water. The sixth direction is *Wakhą Tháka,* the greatest mystery of all. I relate *wąblí wąkátakiya* [' eagle above'] to that.

All these spiritual powers and directions, they are not Gods, they are helpers. They are there to help us pray to God. Interpretations will say—*tókhaš hé hóyechiciciyį kte,* I will send a message for you to God.

Hóyemiciciya yo 'Send a message to God for me'.

As I hear interpretations, there is one supreme being. That's why the *wó'µye*—offerings, tobacco ties, relate to these spiritual beings. We give offerings. There are times when we have direct relations to God. Most times in formal prayer, we ask spiritual beings to help us pray to God. They know God.

That's how I can really respect Christianity in the sense that they have like the pope, preachers, fathers—here in human flesh and blood to be messengers to God. That shows that I respect it. Once I was totally Christian, and then I went totally towards the sacred pipe. I thought I found a direct contact with God. Later I saw I needed to pray through spiritual leaders and Christianity. I learned my lesson well. I got big-headed— thought I didn't need anyone. I could go straight to God. This had a devastating effect on me.

Once I acknowledged all the directions, then I ask each Sun Dancer to pray: *waná lená naniȟ'µkte, waná lená óniciyįkte* 'They listen to you, they help you pray.' That's how I acknowledge the four directions, the spiritual beings. Then I tell them that their prayers will be taken. Each says their prayer.

We open the door four times. First door is when I ask the four directions. One teacher involved with alcohol recovery says there's a seventh direction—yourself, your spirit. Then there are prayers and a song. . . . Sometimes the Sun Dancers will make tobacco ties or flesh offerings at the sweat. They sweat the air they breathe, the new purification. We ask God to come after all these offerings—whatever form they might be. *Thųkášila lená k'eyá hiyó'uye yo!* 'Grandfather, come after all these that we offer!' *Thųkášila lená k'éya chic'ú ye.* 'Grandfather, I give you all these.' *Wó'ųyąpi ki lená yuhá hóyemiciciya yo, waníkta cha lená k'éya chic'uye.* 'Grandfather, these offerings, call these spirits to take these offering that I might live.' *Hóyemiciciya yo* 'Talk for me.'

We use the rocks because they represent the beginning of creation. They are one of the oldest forms of creation, the grandfathers of time. We use the fire brought by the *wakįyą* ['thunder-beings'] to purify, for purification. Rocks go through purification themselves; for them to help us they are purified through the fire. We use the water as it is. It comes naturally from *ųcí makhá* ['grandmother earth']. We use it as a form of purification on the rocks. When it provides steam, we are purified. The rocks urc purified in order to purify us.

The sweat lodge is built the way it is from natural willows. I don't know why we use willow, maybe because it can bend. I'm sure there's a reason why we use willows.

The lodge represents to me the womb that we come from. Sometimes inside the sweat I feel like I felt this before. I can almost feel a heartbeat on the ground. The drum stands for the heartbeat. It represents the heartbeat. The sage is used at Sun Dances. I think sometimes they use cedar for healing. Sage is for strength.

Bear root is generally used by the medicine man. Someone is given that. *Sįkpétha* is a bitter root for healing, numbing.[7] You can take it as is or boil it. It is used for purification and if you are having a hard time. You can also wash your hair with it.

The four colors represent the four types of people: black, white, red, and orientals. That's what they represent. They forget that and say no white people can be here. There are no colors for upwards, downwards, and the seventh direction.

A brief evaluation of the symbol system is also provided by this female consultant. Again, the emphasis is on rebirth, the most consistent symbol used for the sweat lodge. Note also that the antiquity of the ceremony is underscored:

The sweat lodge is one of the original sacred ceremonies of the Lakota people. It's older than the pipe. You come to the sweat to pray. You leave anger and resentment at people at the door. Almost all sweats face west. You sit like in a tipi. The middle of the sweat is the center of the universe. Seven rocks are brought in, and a pipe is used to bless the rocks and pray with them. They represent the seven sacred grandfathers. The rest of the rocks are then brought in, a minimum of twenty-eight. You also bring ties and tobacco to pray with—these are offerings. Tobacco is a spirit food. They carry dreams faster to the spirit world with tobacco.

It's like sitting in a womb, returning to mother earth. The leader is on the right; he pours water, prays to the directions, prays special prayers to *Thųkášila.*

The altar has a buffalo skull and cherry stick. The four directions song is sung as well as Sun Dance songs, sending home song—the spirits are going home.

Thųkášila is the creator, the *tákuškąšką* ['that which moves']. The fire pit and the altar and the door are in line with the west. West is the direction everyone is using now. It used to be east for the morning star. Lakota people were called the morning star people. The four directions are represented in the sweat lodge. In some sweats, people sitting in those directions pray for specific things. In the four directions is also the life cycle (also in the medicine wheel and the circle). You begin with the west in the life cycle. The red road goes east/west, north/south, I can't remember what that is. The spirit road that takes them home, I think.

The rocks are our grandfathers, created in the first day. The lodge is the womb of grandmother earth. It's like returning, rebirth, going back to mother. Sage is a purifier, a cure-all like aspirins. Sweet grass also heightens smell and brings the spirits. Water is first medicine, before there was medicine.

Another Lakota consultant, who is heavily involved in the New Age movement, provided this representation. Note that certain elements, such as the dipper, are emphasized, whereas others are reinterpreted along New Age patterns:

We pray from the beginning. Each force has a vital essence, provided by Mother Earth. The rocks have a sacred life force continuum. The pit, altar, and lodge are equivalent to the body chakras. To go into the sweat is to return to your mother's womb. It is an ideal pregnancy—total acceptance of the life force that is in there. This is not the case with some women. The womb is *ųcí iná* ['grandmother mother']; you can be totally open and you won't be judged. When you're in there, you share it. When you go into the sweat, the sacred life force continuum is focused in the lodge. The path between the pit and the altar is the path to *Thųkášila*. Water is a healing aspect. It comes from the feminine aspect. Healing comes from it. If you use it in the right way, there are unbelievable healings manifested. You need to "do it in a good way." If you're really open and pray from your heart and make ties, you know you are reborn. This changes your daily ways—you see the sacred life force continuum in everyone you have interactions with. The four rounds are equivalent to the four ages [stages of growth] of people.

My grandfather has shown me these things and continues to show me. According to him, it has to do with the buffalo. One aspect is spiritual, the second is physical, the third is the integration of the spiritual with the physical, and the fourth is the return to the spiritual. This sends energy out. My grandfather says you need to live in a good way.

The dipper symbolizes the star people. We all come from the stars. We are energy. The dipper interchanges energy with the water in the sweat just as we interact with the water. The dipper exchanges energy with the people. The dipper mingles the higher energy with the earth energy.

The red willow or cherry branches are placed in a specific way. This aligns with the meridians of the earth. By going inside, this realigns your own meridians. This is healing and uplifting.

The lodge is effective because it sits right on the earth. I don't like to sit on carpets. You sit on *ųcí* and feel the love and existence. This, to me, is close to symbols, but it is a reality or state of being.

The spirit rocks have a sacred life force continuum. Each comes to do a certain thing. They can do individual healing. Place the rocks in the four directions and center. You do this to honor the *Thųkášila*s in the four directions and in the center and also to honor our deceased relatives who are there.

When I went with one friend to sweats, they used hides. Now they use tarps. The buffalo is so sacred. All of the buffalo is used. The insides were eaten raw, lots of protein and enzymes. This is part of life. It was important to use a hide now—the essence of using the hide. Now almost everyone uses tarps from the National Guard in Rapid City.

A male member of the Native American Church expresses the intrinsic curative properties of the sweat in his symbolic exposition. Ritual as cure is also essential to Native American Church ritual, where peyote acts as both a teacher and a healer. In this narration, each symbol focuses on origins—the center of the world and the beginnings of the world. In addition to the cleansing qualities of the sweat, equal weight is given to pollution factors, here expressed in menstruation. At the same time women have a prominent role in this man's sweat lodge:

> All you do, face west. Face the door to the west; that is where the thunder comes from. The wind starts from there. You're sitting in there a long time. Pray all directions, inside there, really getting hot. That is the center of the earth, hot. Takes out worries, your mind, everything out. It can cure you; take sickness in with you, and you can leave it in there. Don't bring it out. This is traditional way you believe. If you'll take a sweat and purify your mind, don't be among women, some of them sick, don't even get close to them. They'll ruin feelings and power you have. Today even when we go to the grocery store, I can't go in there. The women might be sick.
>
> The sweat lodge is the womb. The woman have authority in the lodge. A woman brought the peace pipe. Women make the lodge, make food. Women don't go into the lodge or touch the peace pipe, according to tradition. But my grandfather said that women can do those things. That's all I know, maybe someone knows more. Many people have different interpretations.

A final interpretation is provided by an individual who has had formal training in Christian spirituality. The symbols in this particular narrative are interpreted along the lines of both spirituality and psychological self-help. The point made here is not to debate the essential meaning of a symbol but to express symbolism as part of one's own autobiography. Part of that autobiography is interaction with a preexisting and predetermined tradition, but individuals readily transform ceremonial participation from external experience into interior insight. Thus, individuals stress that meaning is "for them" rather than universal.

> Christ's experience of suffering. When I suffer, I think of that. The Sun Dance. Christ died of pierces. We do a little of that suffering *for the people.* Christ spent forty days fasting in the desert. We only do a little of that—four days. Christ said we'll be reborn again as little babies. The sweat lodge, we're reborn in that. You can see the burning bushes if you believe enough. Sweat lodge is to me a three-fold purification realm: physically, mentally, emotionally, spiritually. In fact, it's maybe a fourfold realm. It's a purification of the human values. This is the end result of coming out of the sweat. The sweat lodge is a symbol of mother's womb, Mother Earth—representation of womb of the grandmother and mother—

holistically feeling secure within your mother as a child. My mother would hold me and pray. Also the understanding of the inner child. We need security—we need to touch home base. When I prepare myself to go to the sweat, this is what I look at. When I get there, for me, it starts with the fire, the openness, to sit in fellowship, to share stories, feelings, whatever we're going to pray about. Our selves, community, family—not done in sacredness, as humans—smell of fire, glow of evening star—smell of the freshness of ash, wood, feel the warmth of the wood. See someone clearing out the sweat—hear the rocks clinking as they are taken out of the sweat from the last time.

Talking—this is very relaxing. Then you hear the leader say get ready. Everyone is busy getting ready—undress, take pitchfork and get the rocks ready. I've led the sweat a couple of times but don't feel ready. I prefer to be an active participant. Then you bring in the rocks. Depends on your understanding of who the grandfathers are—four or seven. The seven grandfathers were here from the beginning of time—they have the hidden knowledge of the world. In the sweat, they release some of that—they give us knowledge. Sage is put on the rocks. That's the blessing of the rocks. Woman blessed the rocks, purifies them for coming of people.

After the rocks are in, the people come in—they enter into a different world—a sacred one, not the one out there. Medicine and everything comes together. They're related to everything around. Things make sense and belong to everything around. People come in and sit around and talk. Rest of the rocks come in—fifteen to thirty. You use every rock. None of them should be left in the fire. You don't waste. Water brought in. Water is medicine, life, purification. The pail of water is put over the rocks—this is what is brought to the grandfathers. This is what will help us.

The last person comes in and closes the door. Door faces west, *heyókha*s face east. Coming from the west clockwise is the cycle of life, how it begins. The door is then closed, and the leader says get used to the heat. Alter your breathing, remember why we're here. Sit in meditation. Then the four-directions song is sung. Before that the leader will greet everyone there and say what we're here for—the purpose of the sweat. This keeps the people intact. The four-directions song is sung. Just the way the sound goes, high and low pitch, starts to generate something in you. You're into prayers; they become real; you appreciate yourself. Each round is a direction. Prayers go out with the steam. You see things, hear things; you hear the spirits sing and talk. These are the rocks and other spirits which are called in. To me they are like guardian angels—animals are like angels.

You *experience* heat and sweat. Your experience deepens your prayer, your faith. You feel fortunate you're here. Old people can't be here. Pray for them. When my mind slips away I remember those who want to be here, the unfortunate. I can experience and pray. We love and respect and have compassion for our people, so we are there. In other rounds only a small part of our prayers are for ourselves; most are for the people. In winter and summer, the elderly and children suffer the most—extreme. So now we pray for the children and elderly. We pray for each other as well in the sweat lodge. There are mystical happenings in there.

Last door is opened, coming to the end. You never prayed for yourself but you did something for yourself. It might have been a hard day and you feel negative towards life, but you come out positive. Go in feeling far from God, come back out close to God. For me, it's like coming out from a hug—I feel better about myself. Lots of prayers are *wóphila* 'thanks' for how God has done some things. Now we're out of the sweat, and we greet each other with a handshake. It's the same as the sundance and *hablécheya;* people thank you for praying for them. That's what you do. You pray for the elderly, children, orphans, handicapped. These are all the people in the world. We can be this spirituality. This is what the sweat lodge means to me—gets me through the feeling of inner child within—child given its positive strokes. Also I feel purified. After last round, inside or outside, someone packs the *chaŋúpa* ['pipe']—load it before sweat, out on the altar. In the fourth round, you smoke it inside or outside. The smoke goes into the universe. The sweat shows God as ominous [*sic*].

I began this work with the suggestion that tradition can be usefully viewed as the result of a dialectical process combining historical understandings of past actions with present needs. These narratives provided by Lakota participants of the sweat bring out both a respect for the historical past and a lively awareness of present needs and suitable ways to address those needs ritually. This individual level of creating tradition is then, as we shall see in the next chapter, validated or disqualified in various communal and interpersonal contexts.

Although the basic understandings of the sweat are consistent, and there is a uniformity of central symbolic images, there remains a highly personal inter-action with the ceremony, expressed through diverse and sometimes conflicting symbols. It is not surprising, given the intensive cultural disruption precipitated by the reservation system, that the current trends are spoken of as a "return" to tradition. The freedom of individual interpretation is essential to this religious system, as is the communal evaluation of ritual activity. Overt coercion for conformity is never acceptable. If, however, one disagrees with interpretations and beliefs, there is always recourse. In the next chapter we will also look at acceptable forms of the social interactions that provide ways of dealing with potential conflict.

7

Harmony and Alliance versus Discord and Separation

The functionalist school of anthropology has made much of ceremony as an integrative mechanism. Although Lakota practice certainly supports that position, the analytical possibilities for ceremony are not thereby exhausted. Ceremony may also serve as either the source or the structural representation of disharmony and contestation, either in its practice or in disagreement over procedures and between participants. Tradition, which is a dialectic combining historical precedent and contemporary need, is not immutable but is itself a matter of debate and contention. It is precisely in the manipulation of historical representation and contemporary practice that solidarity and factionalism are represented and/or created.

Harmony and Alliance

Participants acknowledged harmony and healing as important aspects of the sweat lodge ceremony. So often is the sweat understood as bringing families closer together that it is proclaimed by some as a family ritual. Family can be genetic or fictive in that reference: one friend referred to herself as part of a "sweat clan," a group of people bonded together through participation in the sweat. It was clear throughout my fieldwork that individuals consistently sweated with one another both to symbolize and to intensify their bonds of kinship and friendship. The sweat also serves as a place for creating and enhancing new relationships. These social groups had fairly stable cores. Occasionally, new groups formed and old groups dissolved, and more often one or two individuals would enter or leave particular groups. When I was invited to sweat, it was generally stated as an invitation to sweat with a group: "Come sweat with us." Often the one inviting would mention who else would be at the sweat. This both encourages one to attend as a social outlet and provides warning in case there were any conflicts with individuals mentioned in the list.

Today, the kinship unit is often the nucleus around which a sweat group forms. The sweats are usually located on land belonging to one of the members. One leader began a sweat by stating that he was the head of this particular household and therefore had the right to lead sweats for his own family and those who wished to join with them. Thus, kinship legitimates both practice and leadership. The relationships established through communal prayer and suffering are strong ones, because to suffer with people (and for others, if you are in the lodge in behalf of other people) is to form a deep bond with them. The sweat lodge provides both symbolic and actual suffering, as well as refreshment and recreation. The testimonies given in previous chapters point to the socially integrative function of the sweat ritual and the self-consciousness of the process. So, to join with someone in sweating is to establish potential kinship with that person, to be "reborn" with her or him as a sibling.

As much as participants view the sweat lodge as socially integrative, they also see the ceremony as personally or psychologically integrative. The sweat is a safe place for psychological and emotional reconstruction, and many people are motivated to attend a sweat because of inner feelings of disquiet or anxiety. Several times friends have stopped by and invited me to go sweat with them, simply explaining, "I need a sweat." There are often multiple motives for seeking a sweat. Seeing the sweat only as psychologically therapeutic severely limits its dynamic. What is essential is that if an individual needs to use the ceremony in a therapeutic way, it is always possible to access that potential. The many functions and interactions within the sweat account for its continued importance. In addition, one sweats not only in one's own behalf but in behalf of others who are in need. Suffering by proxy is found throughout Lakota ceremonial practice. One can be cured through the spiritual power of the lodge without actually being present, even though all recognize that there are concomitant physiological benefits from attending the actual ceremony.

Despite the solid communal nature of the sweat, I was surprised by how many participants express the sense of being alone in the sweat and the personal benefits of this ceremony: "*Thiyópa awáyąke* ['doorkeeper'] closes the door. It's pitch dark in there. Make sure it's pitch dark. Then you feel that loneliness—you're all alone. All things come into your mind. You're alone on Mother Earth. *Thųkášila* is there. Water on the hot stones makes you aware you are human."

This aloneness is paradoxical, for it is always in the context of the presence of other beings, both human and spirit. The same narrator continues: "In going to different sweats, the medicine man has spirits. You see and hear them. It is a good feeling; you are not alone. They tell you to pray. They'll *hóyeniciyį kte* 'answer your prayers'. If someone wants healing for someone in the hospital, they go over there and come back." The benefits of personal healing clearly extend beyond the physical action of the sweat through the ability of spiritual beings to aid others.

Contemporary stories concerning intertribal encounters express the potential for harmonious relations within the ceremonial context. Several of my consultants maintain that in the old days when a sweat was in progress, or while any ceremony was being performed, the tribe was protected from enemy attack. One individual said, "If an enemy tribe came up on a ceremony, instead of fighting, they join in on it. No one stops them because they are an enemy. The Plains tribes all practice this. They understand each other by ceremony and ritual. They take part in it." Note how in this story integration is extended to mean incorporation of outsiders into the group. It is the inclusive motif, here portrayed on a ceremonial level, that is an essential dynamic of the sweat.

It is generally accepted that political concerns are not to be broached in a sweat, for politics may cause controversy and threaten harmony. I was once in a sweat where people were joking about the Mni Wichoni [*mní wichóni* 'water of life'] project, which is a project to bring Missouri River water to southwestern South Dakota.[1] As we were seated and rocks were being brought into the sweat, someone asked how people were voting on the bill. Someone else quickly stated that there should be no politics in the sweat. Then someone suggested that he would vote for the bill if the pipe ended in the sweat so he could pour the water on directly. Everyone laughed at that, easing the tension over the initial question. The sweat then began with a song. After the sweat, the leader mentioned to me that he had started a song because he did not think it was a good idea to talk about those things in the sweat.

Although people will pray about how they have personally been made to suffer because of politics on the reservation, I have not heard political issues bandied about within the sweat lodge. Once, at a reservation sweat that was run by a white person with all-white participation, I heard the Mni Wichoni project explained and participants encouraged to intervene in the matter. This would be uncharacteristic of Lakota practice within the confines of the lodge. This is not to say that the sweat is not used in conjunction with political functions or that political issues are unimportant. If there were political consensus among a group sweating, such issues could be freely examined, for there would not be the danger of creating enmity; thus, political concerns can bring people together for a sweat. One friend said that when he was at Wounded Knee during the occupation in 1973, there were sweats going on all day, every day. Sweats have been erected at political rallies, particularly in the Black Hills. A sweat lodge was also erected near a roadblock protesting the proposed supervision of roads on the reservation by state police. That reflects a strong contemporary tendency to place political issues within a religious context. It also shows that controversial issues can be broached in forums where there is consensus. What is essential is not the nature of the issue but its potential for disrupting harmony. Ultimately, politics is seen as potentially divisive, disharmonious, and dangerous. In my experience, even when politically like-minded people gather for a sweat, there is no mention within the ceremony of political stands or programs. Reservation politics are generally factional and potentially volatile, and thus they are carefully avoided during a ceremonial enactment. Nevertheless, politics can shape the groups that come together to sweat.

The large contemporary following that the sweat lodge has garnered is due in part to the bracketing of symbols within the lodge. By bracketing I mean the purposeful ambiguity of symbols and meanings within the sweat lodge. Thus, symbols are primarily apprehended as open to personal interpretation and not as doctrines that one must assent to as a requirement for inclusion.[2] There is generally no compulsion to accept a set of symbols or a single interpretation of those symbols.

Symbols are integrated into the sweat lodge ceremony by the individual. Because of the heterogeneity of belief on the reservation and the ideal of harmonious interactions, the symbols are selectively employed and rarely interpreted to exclude other meanings. Public argument over meaning is avoided. The multiplicity of sweat lodges represents, over and above the physical limitations on the number of participants, another mechanism to keep argument at a minimum. The refrain "as I understand it," continually used in the interviews I conducted and in the sweat lodge ceremony itself, provides an entrée to individuals with differing beliefs to participate in a common sweat. This diminishes religious differentiation in favor of social cohesion. It also allows the leader to avoid setting him- or herself up as an authority, a position that invites criticism and repudiation. Because tradition is produced in a dialectical manner, there is room to incorporate ambiguity and compromise in its constitution.

The symbols used in the sweat are not entirely personal and individualistic, however. Within individual sweats and across sweats, there is a commonality of symbols and symbolic expression that arises from a basic belief and confidence in the spiritual world and in a set of symbols generally associated with the physical elements of the sweat: rocks, water, the cardinal directions, the natural world, the earth and the heavens, and suffering and release. The precise nature of spiritual existence is not defined other than to affirm the existence of one God, who is worshiped in different ways by all peoples. The key symbol remains the relatedness of all creation, a universalism that permits and promotes integration along kinship lines. The commonality of interpretation is created through selective integration of particular individuals into certain lodges.

Like language, itself a symbol system, symbols used in the sweat are learned and exchanged. Each sweat allows individuals to employ their personal sets of symbols, which are generally part of the larger set employed within the sweat lodge; that is done primarily through prayers and speeches. Individuals are selective in displaying their own set of symbols, for the sake of harmonious relations—one of the implicit goals of the sweat. This noncoercive opportunity for representation allows individuals to hold back those symbols that others might judge inappropriate in a particular context. The personal displays of symbols allow others to add to their own symbolic repertoire of songs, images, gestures, and interpretations. The opportunity is also created to forge deeper relationships with the members of the group by sharing common symbols. Thus, there is a language of symbols assembled through an ongoing dialectical process that permits and prohibits certain symbolic conjunctions. Because some groups have a greater range of interpretive tolerance than others, individuals seek sweats where their symbolic language will be accepted as proper.

Those with broad understandings of Christian symbolism interlock those symbols with the ones used in the sweat lodge. Others see themselves as Lakota purists and will consciously exclude any reference to Christianity. Others bifurcate symbols, using those that they perceive as relevant to each observance, whether traditional, Christian, or Native American Church, but only within

those particular domains. In practice, however, this division is not strictly maintained. Instead, individuals judge the appropriateness of employing particular
symbols based on the participants at a particular lodge rather than the necessity
to profess a specific ideology.

Generally, individuals who have fairly harmonious relationships with each
other gather around particular sweat lodges. They will also invite potential
friends as a way to broaden relationships. When someone requests a sweat
lodge for a specific need, he or she seeks out a leader who is an amicable relative or someone whom he or she trusts. Thus, by the time a ritual actually takes
place, people have sorted themselves out into compatible groupings.

Accessibility is a minor factor in selecting a suitable sweat. Although some
individuals use sweats near their homes, others drive over an hour to sweat. Of
course, this depends upon the availability of transportation. People will travel
great distances for sweats that have been planned in advance for significant
occasions.

Kinship is also factored into the equation, with most people preferring to
sweat with someone from their own extended family. Often bonds of fictive
kinship are drawn and reinforced in instances when one is attached to a leader
not from one's own family. As Ella Deloria has demonstrated, kinship is the
dominant metaphor in Lakota culture and the central guide to both social
structure and behavior.[3] DeMallie (1978a:244) further refines this analysis by
demonstrating that there was (and is) a fluidity of kinship based on behavior
and choice. Thus, individuals can freely incorporate themselves into genetically
unrelated groups as full family members.

A few of the sweats in which I participated were gatherings based on a
shared interest in alcohol recovery programs rather than on genetic kinship,
although kinship behavior was extended among these people. Another sweat I
attended was "put up" for several days for the use of Vietnam veterans, Indian
and non-Indian.[4] The majority of the sweats I attended were also attended by
individuals related by blood. These groups are generally supplemented by
friends, Lakota and non-Lakota, who are sometimes adopted into the family.

Often, compatible groups include "outsiders," a term difficult to define on
the Pine Ridge Reservation because of the heterogeneity of the population itself
and because the term, used on the reservation, is rather situational. An outsider
could be someone who does not belong to one's particular extended family,
someone from another district, someone from another tribe, a non-Lakota, or a
non-Indian. The designation of full-blood and mixed-blood might, in different
situations, qualify individuals as insiders or outsiders. One individual expressed

his opinion to me that a lot of mixed-bloods were more sincere about participation in the Sun Dance and sweats than some full-bloods. The underlying assumption was that, by nature, the full-bloods should be more observant because they are more Indian (this individual defined himself as full-blood). This shifting series of identifications is further complicated by the fact that those adopted into family groups, through a formal ceremony or informally through the exchange of kinship terms, are also considered in certain contexts insiders, whether they are whites or Lakotas or members of other tribes.

As I have mentioned before, just as full-blood and mixed-blood are cultural rather than purely genetic designations, the term *white* and the judgment that whites should be excluded from the sweat are often applied to outsiders rather than to known friends. Once on the tribal radio a tribal member said that no whites should be allowed inside a sweat lodge. I asked someone about that, and he said he agreed with the man on the radio. I then pointed out that I sweated with him, and he replied that that was different. The issue revolves around the qualification of persons to sweat rather than a simple genetic judgment. Thus, strangers should not enter sweats. At the same time the sweat can transform potential enemies into actual friends and allies. On the other hand, one group's allies are another group's strangers, thus generating intergroup suspicion and separation.

Stressing the power of thought, contemporary participants hold that one should neither demonstrate nor bear any malice toward other coparticipants in the sweat. Open conflicts are not appropriate in the sweat lodge. The lodge is designated as neutral territory. It is a neutral zone for both escaping and, through prayer and suffering, remedying conflicts. This bracketing of conflict is both ideal and real. In actual practice, conflicts during ceremonies are kept to a minimum, particularly in relation to the higher incidence of conflictual interactions outside of ceremonial practice. To avoid conflict, individuals generally avoid hostile others by not participating in their ceremonies. This was eloquently expressed to me by one individual:

> Lakota by tradition don't argue. This is out of mutual respect. Like, if I go to a sweat I won't openly criticize you. I just don't go back. It's not the style. Out of respect, Lakota don't have constructive criticism. You go to someone respectful and ask him to pass it on [your observations]. When that happens, families will follow along—don't go to that lodge.
> Internal disharmony among families or within a family starts in there and goes out from there. *Onábleca* means you cause to scatter: political, spiritual, family. It starts from inside like firecrackers in a sweat.

This desire for harmony extends beyond the internal practice of one's belief to getting along with people of other beliefs. One consultant stressed to me the importance of not letting religious pluralism divide people:

> He then told me that some Indians say that the white churches were not good and that people should not belong to them. He said that this was not so and that it was good for people to believe in different ways. People should still be united but leave religion out of it. It should not be a point of contention but of unity. People should respect each other's religious beliefs.

Identity through Alliance

To say that the sweat lodge is a place to affirm one's identity is a commonplace. From interviews I have conducted, it is clear that the ceremony accomplishes this in a highly self-conscious fashion. As seen in chapter 4, a large group of people approach incorporation into the sweat ceremony using the idiom of conversion. They see the lodge as a place to regain or intensify their identity as Indian and Lakota. The sweat is not, however, the sole source of identity for the Lakotas. It is believed, particularly by outsiders, that to be authentically Lakota one must participate in "traditional" ceremonies and speak, as one white friend put it, "the ancient language." Although identity is increasingly tied to religious practice for some Lakotas, many base their identity on multiple interactions focused on kinship allegiance, on values such as generosity, and on community participation and cooperation, all of which are considered by many essentially Lakota. These actions are invisible or less visible to the outside world, however. Thus, ceremonial practice has grown in importance as the place to assert and validate identity.

The use of the sweat as an expressive form is consistent with the general Lakota trend to translate their culture for the outsider into understandable and acceptable terms. Expression of identity has intensified in an area that holds a fascination for the outside world. Specific Lakota groups use the sweat to close and open boundaries between the outside and inside worlds.[5] Ultimately, those boundaries are fuzzy, situational, and relative. This permeability of boundaries, in keeping with the incorporationist tendencies of the Lakotas, is balanced against localized factionalism, defined primarily by kinship group, as well as a growing nationalism, defined by tribe and nation, over and against the world surrounding the Lakotas.

Cultural identity and cultural resistance have consistently been the analytical foci for understanding of contemporary Lakota ceremonial practice.[6] Identity established through resistance is multidirectional and as dependent on incorporation as on exclusion. Inclusion is the other side of the coin, which other analyses have ignored or underemphasized.

Religion and ceremonial practice are sometimes viewed as the primary bastions of cultural resistance for the Lakotas. However, just as factionalism is a paradoxically vital component of consensual societies, so too incorporation is an essential component of cultural resistance. Opposition and alliance are effected through highlighting contrary, similar, and identical beliefs in careful combinations. Although religion is used to resist assimilation, it is also used to garner alliances through counterassimilation. Opposition, for the Lakotas, is situational and not unilateral. Incorporation of allies allows for a more successful opposition of perceived enemies. The designation of allies and enemies (*Lakhóta* and *thóka*) is fluid and does not always parallel the categories Lakota and non-Lakota. Alliance ultimately is based on social interaction rather than racial or national identification.

Interaction with the outside world is an essential factor for understanding the constitution of the sweat lodge ceremony. History and practice fold foreign elements into tradition, elements that may eventually be transformed so that they are perceived as entirely from the Lakota past. This is particularly so because of the geographic diffusion of the ritual off-reservation by both professional and lay visitors to the reservation and by out-migration of the Lakotas themselves. Although the sweat lodge could be found at the time of European contact throughout North America, this contemporary diffusion, whose source is the Lakota reservations, brings with it many specifically Lakota elements. Sage is used in sweats in Wisconsin, and the Navajos use two forms of sweats, earth huts and Lakota-style blanket-covered lodges. The Lakota phrase mitakuye oyas'in has become a standard prayer in the sweat as well as a prayer in general for non-Lakotas and non-Indians.[7]

Historically, Lakota society has had several highly developed mechanisms for the incorporation of outsiders. Theirs was and continues to be a permeable society. For instance, Black Elk considered the Cheyennes to be one of the bands of the Lakotas (DeMallie 1984:140). Before the coming of the whites, that alliance pattern was motivated through trade and warfare. At contact, it was motivated by and expressed in trade relationships.[8] With the disappearance of the fur trade and the alienation of a land base suitable for a subsistence economy, along with the deliberate slaughter of game, the Lakotas entered a period of unequal relationship with the U.S. government.[9] Nevertheless, the Lakotas adroitly allied themselves with sympathetic easterners who would assist in advocating their position. The fame of the Lakotas was spread through vivid newspaper accounts, wild west shows, popular literature, and ethnological exhibits. This pattern of alliance structuring continues today throughout the United States and Europe. Interestingly, some advocacy groups actively criticize groups that focus on Lakota spirituality, holding that the Lakotas are best aided through political means.

As seen in the previous chapter, the Lakotas desire to control the representation and presentation of their religion, which is seen by many as the last remnant of the "true" Indian culture. I have frequently heard Lakota people encourage each other in speeches to hang onto the religion because it is the last thing they have left. This was heard among people who considered themselves traditional as well as at Native American Church gatherings. The Lakotas maintain the unique character of Lakota belief, but they also insist on the universal nature of this belief and its conjunction with the beliefs of the Euramericans through such statements as "We all worship the same God" and "The four colors represent the four races of mankind, and they are all present in any Lakota ceremony." Exclusivity is quickly and consistently merged with inclusive metaphor.

Interpersonal alliances are rarely formed around the nucleus of the "tribe"; as with most interactions among the Lakotas, this process takes place on a familial level.[10] In my fieldwork it was common to attend ceremonies with other whites. We were made to feel quite welcome there. People told me there were some sweats that were for Indians only. This seems to have been the exception rather than the rule. Obviously, those who exclude whites from their ceremonies are beyond the scope of this research. The people with whom I worked frequently leveled the accusation of lack of authenticity at those who excluded whites, stating that, if the four colors represented the four races of people, then no one could be excluded from a ceremony on the basis of race.[11]

Another factor concerning alliance clearly came out in many of the interviews I conducted. Because of intricate and sometimes agonistic familial relationships, some individuals stated that their relationships with whites were less problematic and more satisfying than relations with local Lakotas. Acutely aware of the criticism leveled against them by some for associating with whites, these individuals contended that the incorporation of whites into family groupings was universal on the reservation. In the words of two of those interviewed:

> [Local] people treat us bad. The white people are more friendly. I don't have just anyone as a friend. Mostly [white] professional people were friends, even though I did not have that kind of job.
>
> I probably have more white people that I trust and the friendship has been long and square. I can honestly say that my prejudice was very limited. I only sometimes when I was drinking acted prejudice because I was with friends who were prejudiced. I'm not all Indian. I'm part white. My dad and mom never talked about whites in a bad way. Probably prejudice because someone raised hell. Or if there was prejudice, they didn't do well with it, accept it.
>
> Under stress and criticism, I associate with some whites. Almost every person on this reservation has some connections with whites. They are honest and trusting relations. I was criticized for being with whites by a certain person. Then that person got pigs and a tractor from the whites.

Thus, whites who are viewed as capable of promoting a harmonious environment within a specific sweat are acceptable ceremonial companions. This stance is weighed against the potential social disharmony created within the local community by criticism of the practice of admitting whites and suspicion over profiting from the ceremony. Incorporation has many benefits, both for the ceremonial sponsor and for his or her potential friends. The sponsor provides access to ceremonies and Lakota life in general, while the potential friend legitimates the sponsor's position and enhances his or her own position and system of supports. Both sides also establish bonds of mutual aid—spiritual, emotional, and economic. This is not the selling of religion but the establishment of an interdependent relationship analogous to and often built along the lines of kinship. It is a two-edged sword, for association with whites may also diminish one's reputation. I avoid using the classic paradigm of broker and client, for these relations are based on much more than material advantage and utility. This is not to discount the economic significance of the relationships, but emotional and social factors prevail over the economic, according to participants in such relationships.

I recall one instance in which an individual was criticized for having whites at his sweat lodge. The one who leveled the criticism claimed that his lodge was for Indians only, and yet I sweat with this second individual, as do several other whites I know. When I first sweated with the second individual, he expressed the importance of his lodge by explaining that whites from far-off states would drive out to attend his sweats. By pointing out his alliance with other whites in one instance, he demonstrated to me both the validity of his ceremony by the range of people welcome at his lodge (white people from far distances came to his lodge) and the fact that I was welcome in that place (other whites sweated with him). By later claiming to exclude whites, he demonstrated to his Lakota relative the validity of the sweat as shown in the range of individuals welcome at his lodge (people who were relatives, i.e., Lakotas). This is not duplicity, for whites who do sweat are generally reclassified by the members of the group with whom they sweat.

The growth in the use of sweat ceremonies today for rites of incorporation demonstrates the intensification of the social utility of the sweat. I have witnessed several instances of this in the course of my research. On a formal level, sweats are sometimes used to seal relationships. For instance, names may be given in sweats with the accompanying ritual of tying an eagle feather onto the hair of the one being named. This was done for outsiders to make them part of the group. One sweat I attended was used by a Lakota family as a vehicle for a formal adoption. The ceremony, held within the lodge, formalized the kin relationship established between two whites and a particular Lakota family. Other adoption ceremonies I have seen did not involve the sweat in any way. Walker himself mentions that those taken in adoption were expected to help prepare sweat ceremonies, but that the sweat was not intrinsic to the hunka [*hųká* 'adoption'] itself. This is also true for Black Elk's description (in Brown 1953: 101–15) of the hunka. In discussing the hunka ceremony, Walker (1917:127) explains that if one of the hunka partners should take a sweat bath or seek a vision, the other should support him and help pay the shaman. A contemporary spiritual leader explained adoption in the sweat in this manner:

> You can do an adoption at a sweat because you're purified, cleansed by the stone people. Steam, *iyáp'ochiya* ['steam'] and water and steam purifies you. You do it this way, it's forever. Anything you do before God, he accepts it. *Osúthųyąpi* 'hard as a rock', can't be broken, that's the quality of adoptions in the sweat.
>
> They do the adoption in the third round either inside or outside the sweat. You bring them out to stand there and you pray with a feather. Tell how you'll adopt them—mother, father, son, daughter. Then complete all that— you go back in and you both pray. Adoption prayer—pray for him, for his future, spiritual and financial. Pray for each other so you never forget what went on there.

Just as some individuals hold that only certain songs are appropriate within the sweat, certain individuals disagree as to whether the sweat is an appropriate (or, as it is often framed, "the traditional") place to effect an adoption. There is no central authority to decide this issue. Because of the extreme decentralization of the sweat and the lack of control other than individuals and their social circle, particular adaptations to needs and circumstances are easily effected.

Incorporating the Outside

The most striking feature of the sweat, beyond the actual experience of the ritual itself, is its broad-based participation. One reason is clearly the increased availability of sweats and the willingness of individuals to conduct the ceremony, but it goes beyond that. The sweat in particular and ceremonies in general have become the primary meeting ground for personalized encounters by the Lakotas dealing with the outside world. Although clearly there are other forums—legal, economic, and social—for these interchanges, it is ceremony that most clearly allows the Lakotas to encounter others securely on their own ground (literally and, off-reservation, figuratively), using their own symbols and metaphors. Since Lakota ceremonial practice is not centrally regulated, it more faithfully duplicates earlier social and political patterns than do contemporary governmental agencies and imposed reservation structures. The dialectical nature of tradition also allows for rapid adjustment to new needs while retaining a valued link to the past.

It is evident that some whites have had a deep interest in Lakota ceremony, both from the popularity of written works on the Lakotas and from the significant attendance by whites at ceremonies conducted by Lakotas, both on and off the reservation. This interest is of long historical duration. Even missionaries who condemned such beliefs and practices were quite interested in Lakota religious practice. One historically significant transformation that took place was when many churches desisted from an antagonistic posture toward Lakota ritual. This happened quite some time after the government stopped interfering in the religious practices of the tribes under the Collier administration in the 1930s. When I first went to Pine Ridge in 1976, there already were Jesuit priests actively participating in sweat lodge and other ceremonies. In fact, it was a priest who first brought me to a sweat lodge. Two priests whom I know themselves ran sweat lodges. One provided these comments concerning his own sweat:

I spiritually needed to have a sweat bath once a week while on the reservation. I had my own lodge behind my church or I would go over to other people's lodges. When I was in one parish, there were about ten young fellows with whom I would sweat. I have sweated with some well-known native leaders. I was welcome at all their places. There was only one place I was not welcome at Sun Dance time when the AIM group was there. I was turned away at the gate. I have sweated with those folks at other times though. I felt a spiritual calling to do it. It came naturally. I didn't have any trouble with it. I also invited medicine men to my sweat lodge. They came and appreciated it. A group of medicine men were all there once and getting ready for a sweat. I asked whose pipe they would use and they asked me if I had a pipe and they told me to get it. I then asked who should fill the pipe. I wanted one person to do it as he was my spiritual grandfather or, if not him, the oldest one there. The oldest said: "It's your pipe, you fill it." I then asked who should lead the sweat lodge and they said "Well, you filled the pipe." I felt humbled by these religious leaders allowing me to lead a sweat bath for them.

When one medicine man first came to my lodge, he was very skeptical. Another medicine man told him to come along. There were also six young fellows there. The skeptical medicine man was scoffing at first, assuming I did not know what I was doing. At the end, he commented on how hot it was. He thought he would be let off the hook and it would be an easy sweat because I would not know what to do. It was what is referred to as a strong sweat.

The liminal position of non-Indians participating in sweat lodge cere-monies and especially running them is clear in this interview. The narrative is an approbation text, validating the practice of this priest, who himself is a recognized officiant at Catholic ritual. The position of a priest is unique and potentially provides validating force on both sides of the exchange. The general assumption brought out in this narrative and elsewhere is that a Lakota is more qualified to perform the ritual than a white. The narration implies, however, that sincerity is the more important qualification, and thus the lodge is not bounded by physical type. As we have seen in the previous chapter, however, that cri-terion is not settled; some would object to a white person, even or especially a priest, leading a sweat. But ethnic membership alone is not sufficient either, for some Lakotas voice opposition to certain other Lakotas leading sweats.

I once attended a lodge on the reservation that a white person, who was not a priest, conducted. He began by apologizing for his unworthiness, which is not unusual even among Lakotas. He carried his unworthiness to the ethnic level, however, which would not be done by a Lakota. The more liminal, it seems, the more insistent the apology becomes. He then went on to apologize that he could not speak the "ancient language." Finally, he apologized for any mistakes that he might make, saying that he was doing these things with a good heart. He concluded by explaining that there was no one else who was willing to conduct the ceremony and that was why he was in that position.

During my work I encountered many whites who came to sweat with native people.[12] It is generally acknowledged that when a native person is available, he or she is always the more appropriate person to conduct the ceremony. Nevertheless, there are whites who are deeply involved in sweating and other Lakota practices. I worked with one white individual who was acutely aware of his liminal position in dealing with Indian religion. He became involved in Lakota religion as part of a quest for identity: "Part of the attraction of Indian medicine for me is that I'm historyless. I'm Irish. My grandparents are dead. I don't have a cultural history and a sense of who I am. Hanging around the Sun Dance has made me a better Catholic, too."

This individual felt that although he is white, he still had legitimacy in participating in and performing ceremonies. A Lakota spiritual leader asked him after a ceremony one evening to serve as his assistant. He traveled around with that leader setting up his altar and, when the leader was traveling abroad, running a sweat lodge in his absence. Such high visibility, in the social climate of the 1970s, caused some conflict between this man and certain militant Indians. Although he was authorized in the performance of his duties by the spiritual leader, some Indians and he himself felt that he was out of place. He analyzed the experience as an opportunity for a deeper understanding of what it means to be Indian:

> I understand now that it is hard to be an Indian. People make a lot of demands on your time. The medicine man I worked with really helped people. At a big doings with militants, I tended the sweat fire and he was the medicine man. I was the only white there. Many Indians were pissed off at this. I was at one place a month. I experienced racism there. This was good because I now know how Indians feel.

He is also rather precise in stating that it was the mixed-bloods, rather than full-bloods, who caused him grief. In his account the true tradition (represented by the true inheritors, the full-bloods) is faithful to its universality (the four colors representing all the races), whereas the mixed-bloods adulterate the tradition through their exclusivity. This view is not universal, but the trichot-

omy of full-blood, mixed-blood, and white accurately represents local taxon-
omy symbolized in race but generally ascertained through behavior. In the prac-
tical order, questions of propriety have more to do with relationship than with
race.

While recognizing himself as genetically extrinsic to Lakota practice, the
white interviewee nonetheless sees himself as part of a mainstream tradition.
This is particularly brought out in his discussion of New Age people who
frequent sweats in certain areas:

> When the New Age people come into a sweat I have to say that this is a
> religion, therefore you need to pray in this way and not to use crystals or
> things like that. There is a certain amount of friction about that. They will
> come and heal the Indian people, so they think. They think they are pure
> channels of light. I'm pretty judgmental of them. They see the pipe as
> another form of crystal. Just another thing to be used for healing.
>
> Their way of proceeding is the same as with fundamentalists—they think
> that their belief is more correct. These New Age people shoot crystals at the
> medicine man. I saw someone do this with one medicine man. The
> medicine man didn't say anything. You aren't supposed to say anything,
> just shut up. The New Age people come out to Bear Butte and do the same
> things. Another Indian who set himself up as a medicine man used to bring
> a lot of New Age people around. He'd combine his things with theirs. It
> was like a game show. They are all vegetarians. After a sweat you eat dog,
> kidney, the belly of a cow. This is traditional food and part of the ritual.
> They'd sit there and eat an apple—they're incredibly insensitive. They'd
> say we can't eat meat because it is too impure.
>
> The New Age people would come to doings and leave their giveaways
> [things they had been given after the sweat ceremony as a show of generos-
> ity] behind. The Indians were hurt by this. I hated those people. They
> always caused trouble. It wasn't intentional. They had a good heart. They
> just did not understand. The New Age people tell me I was an Indian in a
> former life. I don't believe in reincarnation.

The speaker considers himself a follower of the traditional path. Some
white people identify themselves as New Age believers, although this is a rather
ambiguous term for a rather heterogeneous group. The New Age people I met
on the reservation were interested in a combination of Native American beliefs,
various self-help programs, and crystal use. One white individual told me that
New Age people are reincarnated Indians.[13] Another explained to me that the
contemporary Indians are the soldiers who persecuted the Indians in the

preceding century: New Age people are reincarnated Indians whose task is now to return the true native belief to the Indian people so that they, the Indian people (who actually were white soldiers), might be released. Such people sometimes created some tension in participating in sweats. While some of these outside individuals were critical of what they perceived from their reading as ceremonial imprecision and laxity, they also contended among themselves over what is the "true" Lakota observance. The Lakotas generally showed a broad tolerance for these people. One Lakota with whom I worked had this to say about New Age believers, expressing admiration for some and disdain for others:

> There is a similarity between the New Age and the Lakota way. I have a satellite dish out there with my channels. New Age is like this—some good channels, some questionable. One person likes certain animals so has all kinds of pictures, hides, earrings, rings depicting these animals. There's nothing wrong with that but too much credence, all the symbols that are supposed to have all the answers.
>
> They're like spiritual workshop junkies. A lot of them have unreasonable imaginations, and most of them are connected with astrological teaching. A lot of them study dreams, astrology, space ships, pyramid energy, astro-travel. I think most of them are searching for power, an instant power so they can show off. Some of them can get some bad power and get fooled. Some become Godlike. They think they have big heavy answers.
>
> Some New Age people I really like. They're honest. They're misdirected by unscrupulous teachers. They're really vulnerable. Most I come into contact with have a misnomer [sic] and romanticize the Indian.
>
> There's a lot of people exploiting this field. Lot of them became disenchanted with organized religion. Most women are feminists. There's ten to one women to men. I never figured that out. Seems like they're all rebelling against something—organized religion.
>
> The ones I come in contact with really walk their talk on that. Sometimes they're extreme and not practical, but they try.
>
> Most of them come from an alcoholic home. They display a placating, patronizing, martyr attitude. They experience a lot of guilt. They always want to help someone. There's nothing wrong with that.
>
> There's some good things. They don't want to dirty a religious ceremony with money. Some do think you can buy religion.

One white person with whom I worked spent a long time with a Lakota spiritual leader and himself would conduct sweats in the absence of the medicine man. As in a previous example, this is seen by all as second best to having an authentic practitioner. At the same time, he holds for the legitimacy and authenticity of his substitution. He frequently refers to his teacher to authenticate his own leadership, another common Lakota device of legitimation. Such legitimating by linking interpretation to a Lakota antecedent is characteristic of many whites who practice Lakota ritual. Lakotas themselves, as we have seen, generally particularize interpretation by insisting that this is "how I see it" rather than linking interpretations to other Lakota antecedents. But some Lakotas also refer to those who taught them to run a sweat; others hold that by virtue of being Lakota, or because they participated in the Sun Dance or the vision quest, they are the proper leaders of the ceremony. Whites are more likely to mention permissions or mandates in explaining why they run or participate in sweats. In all cases the leader characteristically devalues his or her own position as leader, stating that he or she is not worthy, while at the same time giving credentials for worthiness based in ceremonial participation and success with healing. Whites are less likely to base their worthiness on individual experience, emphasizing instead permission from a Lakota.

The white consultant who discussed his rootlessness states this about the interpretation of the sweat lodge ceremony:

A sweat is a very sacred thing. You may not understand what I say about it, but you have to respect it. All is done in a clockwise manner. The circle of life, all is in a circle. We begin and end as a baby, in diapers and in need of help. We complete the circle of life. The medicine man whom I assisted taught me about the sweat. The pit is in the center of the lodge. The line of earth to the altar, this represents the path of the mole. The mole hears the prayers in the sweat and then carries them out to the pipe. The mound represents the earth. The circle in the middle is the circle of life. The rock boys are spirits when offered. The sticks holding up the sweat are ribs. The sweat is the womb. We pray for the people in the sweat. We pray for the big picture in the sweat, and then we get more specific. Finally you pray for yourself, but only so that you will be a better person, to help the people. You don't make selfish prayers—you pray to be a better person, to be a better helpmate.

You walk around the sweat lodge before coming in. This walking around is different from the way some medicine men do things. A *heyókha* does things as he likes. I have run sweats and cared for the door at the same time. I sit in the southwest, a neutral position. You can go in and go out and you don't screw up the circle. When I get in, I talk about being in the womb of the mother. I pray. I talked about praying for a while and the sacred way to do things, the way of the first dwellers of this island. When you're here, you need to respect this way.

I run a sweat pretty much the way I was taught by him [his mentor]. The west is represented by black: the mystery of life, thunder, and the spotted eagle. There are two roads; one runs east to west and is black. The whites walk this road. It is darkness and destruction. The red road runs from north to south. The spirit world is in the south. You go there when you die. Though you walk to the north, you face the south. This represents praying to the spirit world. In the east is the buffalo. Your pipe goes to the next generation. The road of life has a beginning but not an end. The pipe has to be from your family, from father to son. The boarding schools screwed this up. In the south are all dead things. The owl represents the spirit world. The owl clan has spirit persons in it who are psychic. While the Ojibway hate the owl, which is a harbinger of death, the Sioux see it as good luck.

Indian culture was pretty rigidly defined by rights and privileges. It got screwed up with the reservation and families. For example, one clan was pipe makers. Another family became medicine people. There were fairly well defined roles—the anarchy now is even more pronounced. Societal pressures don't work anymore.

The four directions represent the four colors of people. The east represents wisdom and enlightenment. For that reason, we all come out facing east. The direction moved west because we are in disharmony. I heard this from some medicine men. My mentor holds that the four directions are really only one direction—the direction of the Great Spirit. You walk the road trying to make harmony. The four colors are only one color. All four colors live on this island. There are more here than on any other island. The Great Spirit wants us to be harmonious. My mentor doesn't like white people, but they are welcome at his ceremonies. He became a medicine man because the spirits told him to do that. He's a traditional medicine man because of his family line. The woman makes the family. The man stands between the two worlds and interprets. The woman has all the power. Men help women live their life in a good way, and to do this, he must live a good life. The medicine man, his life belongs to the people.

When my mentor runs a lodge (and I run my lodge after his fashion), the first seven rocks are brought in and then he tells about the sweat lodge. The first rock is placed in the west, cedar is put on it, it is touched by a pipe, and then the prayer *mitákuye oyás'į* is said. The rocks, they're relatives, rock boys. The second rock is placed to the north, the third to the east, and the last to the south. A rock is also placed in the northeast for the sky, to the southeast for the earth and the center for the Great Spirit. My mentor used only seven rocks. In the winter, he used twenty-one, so people could warm up. He used the same seven rocks for all of the four rounds. There is also a "wipe down" sweat, or when there are several sweats being run (for a crowd of people), the sweat might go for one round.

The four-round sweat is for doctoring. Whoever was being doctored sat in the east, in the position of honor.

Next they bring in the bucket and pass it around the circle. It is then set in the center of the one who is running the sweat and the doorkeeper. They sit and talk for a while. The pipe is smoked before the sweat starts. The pipe represents truth. You speak the truth from your heart. The pipe is then placed at the altar. You close the door and pour water on the rocks. The leader prays first, and then they pray around the circle. The medicine man prays again, last.

They use the four-direction song as the first song to call the spirits. During a doctoring, they sing the doctoring songs and the sick person prays. You pour water on the rocks as you see fit. You have to use *all* the water. There is no drinking of water in my mentor's sweat. In a doctoring ceremony there is no eating all day until the sweat is over. When it is over you go and eat meat soup, fry bread. That's a traditional meal.

Everyone has their own way. They operate the sweat by their own vision or according to whoever taught him.

The spirits are stronger than my lack of faith. They appeared to me. At first, I used to laugh at ceremonies. I didn't believe in them. Later I could see that my mentor was snoring at his altar while the spirits moved around.

This narrative establishes both a line of transmission, from mentor to narrator, and an orthodoxy—there were rigidly defined roles and successions to those roles, according to the narrator. This further explains the narrator's reserve in taking a ceremonial position, because he is not related by blood to any of these families. But he also introduces a second theme of direct transmission of ceremonial power by mentioning that his mentor's commission was received directly from the spirits. Legitimation of the mentor serves to legitimate the student.

A white woman living on the reservation became involved in the sweat lodge through people with whom she worked. She participated in all-women sweats. This group prioritized gender over race, so she was quite welcome there. For her the practice of the sweat was not a conversion in the sense of a shift of allegiance or membership, but rather in valuation of experience. The sweat was an experience remarkably stronger than any she had experienced in her own religious tradition:

> In my experience of Catholic religion, there is no prayer ceremony as intense as a sweat. Mass is different. You're sitting there in a sweat in darkness. You hear the rocks and steam, smell the cedar and sage, hear the songs and prayers. It's a very positive, overwhelming experience. It brings you to such a level of introspection. I don't know, just the most intense prayer experience I ever had. If someone has a drum, your heart falls into sync. Even if you don't understand the songs, you learn to pray with them. They become familiar. The sweat is a common ground for common people to get together, Indians, priests, non-Indians, nonbelievers. You ask for support, support each other. The more it becomes part of your prayer life, the more you miss it. It's such an intense experience. Once you have a positive experience, you don't want to leave it.

In addition to personal experiences of conversion and transformation, there are stories told of other non-Lakotas whose lives are changed through the sweat lodge. Much of this is associated with healing. As we have seen from the narrations above, outsiders sometimes come to the reservation seeking Indian spirituality. Although they are seen by some Lakotas as intrusive, others welcome them. This story told by a female Lakota consultant typifies the second type of situation:

> Three years ago, a twenty-one-year-old European girl came to us. We met her out of the blue sky. She came back. I saw her at our village. A week later, she came back there. She told me she was to go to a certain place. She stayed with us a whole month. We had sweats about four times. In the first sweat she told us she was drawn clear across the sea to a Native American home to find God. She didn't believe in prayers in her country. That made her feel real good. She wants to return in five years. She told us we had a beautiful culture and the people are beautiful and powerful. She learned to pray in the sweat.

Disharmony and Contention

The sweat clearly creates social solidarity both within the existing group and by incorporating others into the group. This is accomplished on the ceremonial level through intense interaction and mutual suffering—both sharing life's sufferings and undergoing the symbolic and real suffering in the sweat. The ceremony can also serve to differentiate and to solidify distinctions between individuals and groups. One of my most startling realizations came at the end of my fieldwork. I had hoped to put on one big dinner for all the people with whom I had prayed and worked. When I proposed this plan to several friends, it was met with little enthusiasm. Although no one directly challenged my plan, it was clear that people were not interested in a large gathering. One friend indicated the futility of my plan in a roundabout way by telling me the story of how he had had a ceremony to which he invited several medicine men. He said that as it turned out none of the medicine men were there at his place at the same time. As one would leave, another would come. He explained that they did not get along well with one another. By example, he was explaining why such a dinner would not work. Although all shared the commonality of the sweat lodge ceremony as an important aspect of their lives, that did not serve to bind them all together across groups. In fact, tensions within certain lodges served sometimes to separate individuals, causing them to move to other lodges where they felt more comfortable. That was the most common reason offered to explain why an individual would change lodges. Part of the popularity of the lodge lies in its perceived ability to create harmony in a social structure that the Lakotas admit is disharmonious. The multiplication of lodges indicates the extent of the factionalism and at the same time allows for successful integration by not straining the system with impossible combinations of people. Individuals both integrate and differentiate themselves through the particular sweat lodge in which they participate.

On another level, people who sweat differentiate themselves from those who abstain from sweating. There is no sharp differentiation of these individuals and groups, however, in normal social interaction. Everyone is expected to interact harmoniously on a public social level. In normal social relationships, conflicts should neither be kindled nor displayed. But this ideal is sometimes breached. Although I was consistently told that anyone is welcome at any sweat as long as he or she has good intentions, people would deliberately exclude themselves from certain sweats, stating that they felt unwelcome. This is generally due to interpersonal conflicts that are not evident on the surface. The prevalent choice in Lakota interaction when faced with discord on a public level is to exclude oneself from the arena of potential conflict.

I attended a sweat at one place where many different people were invited both to participate and to conduct the sweat. At times, one individual would be selected or reluctantly offer to officiate, and then, with the arrival of other individuals, that person would defer leadership to whomever was considered more qualified to run the sweat. For example, one night a woman was asked to run the sweat. When a man acknowledged as a traditional leader arrived, leadership was passed to him. Two women objected (much later and quietly) that women could run a sweat as well as men. The two women began absenting themselves from the sweat. They never broached the question within the context of either the sweat or the socializing that occurs before and after but retained their criticism for a later time. The women were close friends of most of the participants, so a breach was never opened. They eventually returned to regular participation. An example of a split over impropriety was provided in this interview:

> I used to go *thi'óle* ['show up and enjoy another's hospitality'] sweat at one place. The preparation was really something. How they put the rocks in. I wondered if that made a difference. I was going *thi'óle* sweat but after four times I felt uncomfortable. There was something missing. I didn't want to go there any more. I had a funny feeling. One other lady quit, too. She had a bad feeling. I found out that the men drank beer after the sweat.

The main motivation for participatory differentiation is explained by the fact that certain people cause disquiet or disharmony within a particular individual, and thus he or she cannot enter the sweat lodge with the proper predisposition. This differentiation is carried down even to the family level. I encountered certain instances of individuals excluding themselves from sweats because of an ongoing conflict within the family. I was told by those excluding themselves that they could not generate the proper predispositions because of the unresolved conflict. With the resolution of the conflict, these individuals returned to sweating with their extended family. Interestingly, when I was told this in an interview, I stated that I would not write it down because of the personal nature of the conflict. Both narrators insisted that I include the information because they felt that it was essential for understanding how the sweat really is. People on the reservation enter the sweat carrying a long history of interaction, both individual and family.

Exclusion is not the only solution for conflict, for despite underlying hostility, there is a strong motivation to maintain group harmony, particularly on the familial level. In the instance above, the basic thrust of the story was this: the family does not get along, and there is hostility; therefore it is inappropriate to join together in a sweat lodge ceremony at this moment. The sweat lodge, at the same time, is seen as capable of healing division. Nevertheless, there were times when family members would avoid each other or absent themselves from ceremonies because of underlying hostilities. As one woman told me, "When you go into a sweat lodge, you have to have a good mind. You should not go in if you are mad at anyone. My relative had a big disagreement with me and then she goes into the sweat lodge!"

Nevertheless, this family would band together to put on various other ceremonies; underlying hostilities were passed over in order to accomplish the task at hand. Thus, the ceremony did serve to bond the family closer for the time of its preparation, execution, and celebration (the meal afterward), even though some individuals excluded themselves from the actual ceremony. I met one of my friends in the sweat of the family with whom he had said that he would never participate. When I asked him later why he was there, he explained that he was around at the time, so they invited him. To turn down a direct invitation would disgrace the family.

Another cause for separation of individuals who sweat together regularly was disagreement about the manner in which a ceremony was conducted. This was again balanced against the expressed ideal of group solidarity and family fidelity. More often than not, individuals would participate in a sweat lodge despite their misgivings about the nature of the ceremony. Family loyalty motivated individuals to participate in ceremonies they would ordinarily not attend. Another motivating factor was that people did not want relatives to be shamed by their obvious absence from a ceremony. When a person was directly invited, refusal to attend a lodge would embarrass the family member who had issued the invitation. Sometimes the invited parties agree to attend and never show up.

Avoidance as a standard way of dealing with social conflict holds for the sweat also. The extreme of avoidance is hiving off, the process of effecting a permanent separation and setting up a duplicate polity. This hiving off, motivated by disagreement or a simple desire to be apart, is an important part of Lakota social structure and is utilized today in the realm of ritual. As Bad Bear phrased it around the turn of the century,

> When a man was not pleased with his camp or his people, he set up his tipi far away from the camp. He was the chief of his own tipi and all who lived in it. His friends would come to his place and set up their tipis there, and they would acknowledge him as their chief. If there were not many who went to his camp he did not amount to much. But if many joined him he became a chief of influence. [in Walker 1982:25][14]

Conflict on the reservation sometimes occurs on the spiritual level through the system of cursing. Although I encountered some people on the reservation who felt themselves victims of curses or saw the effects of cursing, I never encountered anyone who would admit to cursing anyone. I was once told that someone used a sweat lodge for throwing curses. The individual who told me was present at this sweat and did not know what was going on at the time. He did not approve of the action. Later he experienced a tragedy in his life and attributed it to his presence at the sweat. Curses are leveled at individuals, who therefore must protect themselves. Sweats and other spiritual practices such as prayer meetings are used to neutralize the effects of curses. At one sweat I attended, several of the rocks exploded while they were being heated in the fire. Someone said that the reason the rocks exploded was that someone was trying to put a curse on that family.

There are a variety of views of cursing on the reservation today. Some hold for its actuality and power, but others feel that it does not really exist. Such people hold, however, that if you do believe in cursing, it will be effective. They also feel that jealousy and interpersonal enmity cause the problem. Cursing is not discussed much publicly. It is seen as both a product and a cause of interpersonal conflict. Jealousy is often cited as the motivating force for cursing. Often singers and dancers at powwows and other public performances are the target of curses, as are spiritual leaders and their relatives.[15] There are few references to cursing in the contemporary literature.[16]

There was only one extensive reference I could find in the contemporary literature, quite outside the anthropological corpus, to anything resembling cursing. Barbara Adams from Pine Ridge presents in a work aimed at a New Age audience a ritual that she terms "kumuga" [*ȟmúǧa*]:[17]

> The medicine man uses this ritual on "someone who has no ears," someone who pays no attention or is disrespectful. The medicine man asks for a hair from the head of a menstruating woman. He puts this hair on his palm, and he blows on it. The hair goes directly to its target's knees, no matter how far away that person is. He immediately feels it. His knees buckle. He has to participate in a sweat lodge before he can walk again. [1990:55]

I have heard the term "no ears" used on the reservation, and there are definite negative effects believed to result from contact with a menstruating woman, but I have never heard of this ceremony. In my experience on the reservation, cursing on the reservation is considered a hostile and not a pedagogical act as expressed above. Nevertheless, Adams's testimony, which represents one voice, is readily available to Lakota and non-Lakota readers and thus has a relevance.

Control of the Sweat

There is a growing disquiet on the part of Lakotas over the alienation of their symbols and rituals. Many perceive interpretation of their culture by non-Lakotas (or Lakotas with whom they disagree) as part of this alienation. Lakotas are also very sensitive to the context in which their symbols are used by non-Lakotas. Some approve of the Catholic Church's wide use of Lakota symbols in its rituals, whereas others feel that their symbols do not belong there. There is controversy also over the often stated contention that Lakota religion and symbols are universal and therefore for everyone. This is particularly true as Lakota religion is cast more and more in the mold of an ecological spirituality. Thus, some Lakotas object to ceremonies performed for and sometimes by non-Lakotas. Lakotas object most when ceremonies are performed for money. The New Age movement is another area in which some Lakotas feel that their symbols are alienated from them and then exploited. The Lakotas do not provide a unified front in this regard, for some Lakotas actively promote such integrations as necessary and beneficial.

The attempt to regulate religious practice within Lakota groups and outside the reservation is considered pressing by some Lakotas as well as some non-Lakotas, but there also exists an ambivalence toward canonization of ritual. The ambivalence lies in the basic independence of Lakota ritual practitioners regarding whom they choose to teach and include in rituals, balanced against the opinion that Lakota religion is the sole provenance of the Lakotas, that it should not be usurped or exploited, and that it needs to be protected. It is here that participants attempt to regulate the process of dialectical creation and representation of tradition. The complication is that there are no universally shared or consistent criteria for leadership and participation in the sweat lodge or any other ceremony. Nor are there clear and consistent universal procedural rules. Unlike other Plains groups, Lakotas have no system of ownership and transference of ceremonies. Also there are no mechanisms for enforcing rules universally. Although a group of generally consistent protocols are practiced at the sweat, none take the form of hard and fast rules.[18] This allows for an important dynamism and adaptability of the content and context of sweats, but it creates problems if sweats do not have a consistent clientele based in a local community where gossip, selective participation, and ostracism are efficient means of control—particularly when individuals practice ceremonies away from the reservation and beyond the reach of face-to-face social control. The importing of individuals into the ceremony from outside the reservation community also vitiates the effect of the internal controls. Thus, even though Lakotas will avoid certain individuals' sweats, those people can still develop a clientele from other reservations or among a larger white population.

It is important to keep in mind that there is a dual tendency toward, on the one hand, decentralization in Lakota polity and spiritual activity and, on the other hand, nationalism and central control of religious practice. Although people consistently remark that there should be supervision of Lakota religion and its practitioners and that there should be rules regulating ritual procedures, people are pretty much on their own in deciding the appropriateness of ceremonial behavior. The sweat lodge is a small-scale operation both by sheer physical limitations and also by social-structural choice. This social-structural fragmentation is a vehicle for consensus, creating smaller groupings, which are more likely to arrive at mutually agreeable decisions.

Aaron Two Elks, a Lakota, summed up the problem accurately when he stated, "The bad thing is, there are no Lakota People here to challenge them [questionable practitioners]" (Avis Little Eagle, *Lakota Times,* July 2, 1991, A2). Andy Smith, a Cherokee woman, a cofounder of Women of All Red Nations and an outspoken critic of New Age appropriation of native spirituality, takes a similar stance:

> Moreover, white women want to become Indian without holding themselves accountable to Indian communities. If they did, they would have to listen to Indians telling them to stop carrying around sacred pipes, stop doing their own sweat lodges, and stop appropriating our spiritual practices. Rather, these New Agers see Indians as romanticized gurus who exist only to meet their consumerist needs. Consequently, they do not understand Indian people, or our struggles for survival, and thus they can have no genuine understanding of Indian spiritual practices. . . . This trivialization of our oppression is compounded by the fact that, nowadays, anyone can be Indian if she wants to be. All that is required is that a white woman be Indian in a former life or that she take part in a sweat lodge or be mentored by a "medicine woman" or read a "how to" book. [1991:74, 75]

In criticizing a certain non-Lakota pretender to spiritual leadership, Avis Little Eagle states: "Mary Thunder has regular vision quests, pipe and sweat lodge schedules and circuits she follows. Mainly on the East Coast and in the Southwest where there are no Lakota to challenge her" (*Lakota Times,* July 24, 1991, A2).

Most telling in contemporary attempts to regulate and restrict the sweat are the accusations of "selling" sweats. During my research this was the most consistent accusation against individuals who run sweats on the reservation. Although just about everyone I knew was accused of this practice at some time or other, I never witnessed financial transactions at any sweat. Nor was my own research contingent upon monetary remuneration. I was once told that a certain Lakota put on a sweat for a group of white people and charged them each three hundred dollars to attend. I attended that particular sweat and, to my knowledge, no money changed hands; the participants were, in fact, mostly Lakotas. Most accusations are leveled at Lakotas who leave the reservation and travel around putting on ceremonies and seminars. People on the reservation generally claim that such people earn astronomical amounts of money. Accusations abound concerning these "wandering shamans," but actual cases have also been documented.[19] The accusations themselves have important functions, representing both a protest against the alienation and sale of cultural property and an attempt, through publicly shaming accused and potential abusers, to extend control of such behavior off the reservation.

A more far-reaching mechanism for social control is pan-Indian groups, which extend control of practice beyond the local level. Various groups claim authority in religious matters, citing as their source of legitimation "the elders." This again is met with ambivalence because, though control is more effective off-reservation through these groups, control is at the same time taken away from local reservation groups. The pan-Indian groups are quite specific in their denunciations. For instance, an AIM resolution dated May 11, 1984, states this concerning the use of sweat lodges:

> Whereas there has been a dramatic increase in the incidence of selling of Sacred ceremonies, such as the sweat lodge and the vision quest . . .
> A non-Indian woman going by the name of "Quanda" representing herself as a "Healing Woman" and charging $20.00 for sweat lodges;
> Wallace Black Elk and Grace Spotted Eagle, Indian people operating in Denver, Colorado, charging up to $50.00 for so-called "Sweat Lodge Workshops." [reproduced in Churchill 1990:97]

Churchill (1990:96, 98) portrays AIM as significant in policing the misuse of traditional ceremonies, mainly through statements made by Russell Means.

Other groups cited as investigating questionable spiritual leaders are the International Treaty Council, based in California (Avis Little Eagle, *Lakota Times,* July 2, 1991, A1), and the Center for the Support and Protection of Indian Religions and Indigenous Traditions (SPIRIT) (Taliman 1993:10).

Another attempt at control has been through the printed text. A plethora of information sheets have been produced by native groups, reservation and urban, denouncing various practitioners of Indian religion. This textual mode of attack has moved into the news media, particularly papers owned and operated by Indians and the Internet. A series of articles appearing in the *Lakota Times* chronicles the activities of some of these "plastic medicine men" (according to the current parlance). One report claimed that a certain lodge on the Pima reservation charged $250 per person, and that caviar, wine, and cheese were served afterward (Avis Little Eagle, *Lakota Times,* July 24, 1991, A1). Concerning Lakota sweats, Little Eagle quotes individuals who state that sweats are sold by certain individuals for $1,200 and in Germany for $90. There is also an organization run by two Lakotas that will provide seminars nationally and overseas titled "Understanding the Sweat Lodge" (Little Eagle, *Lakota Times,* July 17, 1991, A2, A1).[20]

Some Lakotas interpret the universal dimension of Lakota belief to include universal participation. They see ceremonies restricted to Indians alone as a violation of the universality of Lakota religion. However, it is clear by such opposition that some groups contend that Lakota ceremonial practice should be used only by Lakotas or other Indian groups. This ideological conflict has not been resolved. Generally, it is felt by groups that invite non-Lakotas that they are acting correctly but that other sweat groups have to make up their own minds on the matter. The eschewing of segregation is also brought out in the media. Avis Little Eagle begins an article concerning pretender medicine men:

> Lakota spiritual beliefs and ceremonies were given to the Lakota freely by *Wakantanka,* "the holiness of all that is." They must, in turn be shared freely. . . . The way of the Sacred Pipe was a gift given to the Lakota and was meant to be taught to all races so they too could find a close relationship with all of creation. [*Lakota Times,* July 31, 1991, A1]

This article denounces the use of Lakota ceremonies for profit, stating that true spiritual leaders would neither brag about their position nor use it for financial gain. The authority of Frank Fools Crow is also invoked to legitimate the incorporation of whites into Lakota ceremonies: "Mr. Fools Crow told him [Baptiste Dubray] if they did not allow non-Indians to learn spiritual ways, then the Lakota no longer had *wausila* [*wa 'yśila* 'pity'] for other human beings" (Avis Little Eagle, *Lakota Times,* July 31, 1991, A2).

New Age representation of Lakota religion, written primarily for white audiences, also emphasizes the importance of free universal participation of sincere individuals. William Lyon, transcriber of Wallace Black Elk's narratives, states:

> What Nick Black Elk failed to do in his lifetime, Wallace Black Elk attempts to achieve in his—to bring the sacred mystery powers back into the hands of the people and to see the Tree of Life Bloom again on Earth. Wallace, however, extends his scope beyond the realm of the Lakota Nation to include all human beings. He believes that the power of the Sacred Pipe is for everyone. Wallace noted long ago that when the spirits do appear, they never claim to a racial identity. In fact, Lakota prophecy speaks of the Sacred Pipe as going out to all nations. Shamans need only follow the sacred rules for handling (carrying) a Sacred Pipe. . . . Wallace's attitude may irritate those who think whites are stealing the Indian's religion, but he sees this world view as not simply his personal philosophy but as part of the sacred teachings themselves. In his Earth People philosophy, power is seen as a gift from the Creator for all human beings. [Black Elk and Lyon 1990:xiii–xiv]

The works of Ed McGaa (1990, 1992) and Barbara Means Adams (1990) also present invitations for all to save Mother Earth through understanding and participating in Lakota philosophy and ceremony. McGaa states: "I hope that the reader will attempt to do some ceremony in order to carry on that position of stewardship, even if it is a simple holding of a stone to the rising dawn in recognition of the earth wisdom that comes with each new day" (1990:41; see also Marshall 1992:88).

Non-Lakotas have also entered the debate over ritual authenticity, a controversy that has been taken up through the media of journals and papers. Some academics have voiced opposition to the white appropriation of native ceremonies. Let me provide but one example.[21] Kay Koppedrayer, an instructor at Wilfrid Laurier University in religion and culture, denounces the New Age use of native spirituality as "spiritual pornography" and critiques its appropriateness by highlighting its inaccuracy. It is instructive to note that her critique is based on her own Indian sources, particularly the "elders," thus employing the classic validation pattern used by the Lakotas, as well as the very people she is criticizing, since New Agers generally claim that they conduct ceremonies at the behest of spiritual leaders and elders themselves:

The vision quest, marketed in the ads in the back of the magazine is an example. For all my conversations with Lakotah on the Pine Ridge and Rosebud reservations out in South Dakota, I have never heard any of them talk about a vision quest. For sure, many have recounted to me stories of "going up the hill," their fasting, their *hanbleceya*. Women have told me what it was like when they went up 35 years ago: some told me what they can recall of their grandfathers and uncles going up in the early decades of this century. I have heard people joke about recent times up the hill, but, as far as I can recall, no one has ever used the expression "vision quest." At any given time there may be people thinking about *"hanbleceya,"* but the only people who vision quest on the reservations are white. . . .

In contrast, the "vision quest" that is sold in the back of New Age magazines twists the meaning all around. A "vision quest" is performance-orientated; it represents power and the type of kicks usually associated with the use of illegal drugs. [*Lakota Times,* Jan. 16, 1991, 5][22]

The debate over white participation is, at least in the present time, less intense than the argument over the exportation of ceremonies by Lakotas from the reservation and the appropriateness of non-Lakotas performing Lakota ceremonies. Lakota exporters frequently are charged with selling the religion.[23] This area is difficult to maneuver in, for to designate an individual as a "wandering shaman" is to make a negative value judgment about his or her practice. Nevertheless, this is done frequently on the reservation and in cities with large Indian populations, both verbally and through circulated sheets of paper listing people who are considered charlatans. Some of these spiritual leaders do leave the reservation to present teachings to people across the country and into Europe (Feest 1990). Feest states:

> One characteristic of the old and continuing relationship of Europeans with the "Indian" is, indeed, the perpetual willingness to accept their own centuries old expectation that the Indian has a worthwhile "message" for everyone. Frenchman or German, nationalist separatist or conservative industrialist, all are ready to listen to the most absurd statements if validated by an association with Indianness. [1990:330]

The popular press has taken up the issue of legitimate practitioners. Ward Churchill observes:

> Since 1970 there has also been a rapid increase in the number of individuals purporting to sell "Indian wisdom" in a more practical way. Following the example of people such as the "yogi Ramacharaka" and "Maharaji Ji," who have built lucrative careers marketing bastardizations

of East Asian mysticism, these new entrepreneurs have begun cleaning up
on selling "Native American Ceremonies" for a fee. [1990:94]

Churchill goes on to cite various Indian authorities in the matter and to name
names concerning misuse of spiritual traditions.

I avoid making judgments on the validity of each practitioner with whom I
worked since even Lakota consultants vary on whom they consider to be legitimate practitioners. The general rule is that if you are satisfied with a ceremonial
leader, then you should stay with that person; if not, find another leader and join
another group. What is vital is that evaluation itself is an issue and that there are
neither consistent criteria nor universally accepted representatives responsible
for judging the validity of practitioners. There is, however, lively discussion
over the necessity for such a group and for set criteria.

Thus, the diffusion of the sweat lodge ceremony is not something that
always sits well with its primary practitioners. Although opinion is universally
against the exploitation of this or any other ceremonies through sale and appropriation by non-Lakotas, the universality of the symbols used in the sweat is
sometimes mobilized to legitimate universal practice. Degrees of participation
become the finer distinction in this debate. Furthermore, the incorporative
nature of the ceremony is a far-reaching one, universal in its outreach yet particular in its articulation, for sweat lodges on the reservation are basically
kin-related, through blood, adoption, or common interest that binds individuals
together. This essential kinship element, with its social controls, weakens as the
ceremony becomes more and more removed from the geography and the
population of the reservation itself.

The main issue here is legitimacy and authority, which has been broached
in chapter 3. Most would agree that non-Lakotas who are known to and accepted by the Lakota participants may participate in sweat lodge ceremonies.[24]
The consistent stance is that Lakotas themselves, however, are the only proper
keepers and leaders of specifically Lakota ways. They are the legitimate opera-
tors of the dialectic of tradition. An ancillary issue is the extent to which whites
may participate in Lakota ceremonies taken as a group. One leader with whom
I sweated allowed whites at his sweat but did not think whites should be
permitted to dance in the Sun Dance. With study and exploitation (some would
say study itself is exploitation) of ritual, the center of authority and legitimacy
shifts away from the Lakotas on the reservation to texts and individuals who are
beyond the local control of reservation participants.

Some individuals claim authority to teach Lakota spirituality by reason of their adoption. Thus, according to another article in the *Lakota Times*, Mary Thunder, a woman who teaches Indian spirituality,

> claims to be an adopted Lakota and says she was trained by Chief Leonard Crow Dog and Wallace Black Elk, as well as others. . . . Mary Thunder, who is part Irish, also claims to be part Cheyenne and to have been adopted by elders of the Lakota Sioux. She said the elders taught her many Indian ways and gave her permission to teach others. . . . She claims she was named a peace elder by Grandma Twylah Nitsch of the Seneca Nation. Ms. Thunder told Mr. Phalon the Lakota elders who adopted her encouraged her to spread knowledge of Indian ways to other people in need. [Avis Little Eagle, *Lakota Times,* July 24, 1991, A1, A2]

Oh Shinnah Fast Wolf, another controversial spiritual leader, "also occasionally passes herself off as a Lakota medicine woman, adopted by the late Matthew King's family in Kyle" (Avis Little Eagle, *Lakota Times,* Aug. 7, 1991, A1). Matthew's son Dennis states that she was indeed adopted by his father because of her kindness to Lakota elders. Dennis does not mention whether she may legitimately conduct Lakota rituals. One of Oh Shinnah's coworkers at Four Directions, Inc., defended her spiritual practice on the basis that "she had ties to the Lakota because she was adopted by the family of the late Matthew King. Oh Shinnah calls Matthew King, 'Pop'" (A2). These credentials proffered by adopted spiritual leaders employ a *hablóglaka* in the sense that they legitimate one's position as a spiritual practitioner. Interestingly, legitimacy is based on genetic incorporation through adoption. Although Lakota spiritual leaders will sometimes refer to their past teachers, legitimacy is also focused on experience. Mary Thunder goes on to include spiritual experiences, but when presenting her credentials, her initial focus is on genetic (adoptive) legitimacy.

Just as tales of power and weakness are told to explain the reality of the Lakota world, temporal and spiritual, such stories are also told with regard to these questionable leaders. Avis Little Eagle quotes this tale:

> He [Arval Looking Horse, the keeper of the sacred calf pipe] said a longtime friend called him recently and told him she saw Wallace Black Elk and Mr. Sun Bear on a Caribbean cruise. They were doing sweat lodge ceremonies for the voyagers.
>
> Mr. Looking Horse said he laughed when his friend told him there had been one point at which there was great fear the ship might sink. The friend

told how Mr. Sun Bear practically climbed on top of women and children to get to the life boat, saying, "I'm a medicine man I must be saved." [*Lakota Times,* July 17, 1991, A2]

Such stories, originally part of oral tradition, have been transferred to the news media, thus paralleling the expansion of spiritual practice itself into the national forum.

Lakotas have also taken to the newspapers to confront directly what they perceive as abuse of the sweat lodge (and other ceremonies). The most available paper on the reservation and nationally is the *Lakota Times.* Letters to its editor and commentaries provide a wealth of opinion on these matters. Martina Looking Horse attacked misuse of the sweat lodge (and those who conduct the ritual) on two fronts: the inappropriateness of white participation and the insincerity of certain pipe carriers (practitioners of Lakota religion). Note that the paper states that these views and opinions "do not reflect the opinion or attitude of the Keeper of the Pipe or the Looking Horse family":

> First of all I would like to say that our spiritual way of life is being exploited. Many people are hungry for spiritual knowledge, and there are many people cashing in on that. Now there are many non-Indians who are Pipe carriers, even though they don't know anything about the "Pipe. . . ."
>
> Thanks to a few token Indians who think our religion is for sale, we have many people who don't understand our ways becoming Pipe carriers. No! It's not all right to go out, buy a Pipe, then say you're a Pipe carrier. . . .
>
> The white man took our land, destroyed whole races of indigenous people, took Indian children away from their parents, stuck us under the rule of the BIA, and Tribal Councils, (who took us for what little we had left) and now they want the last thing we have left—our religion.
>
> Beware, my people, because this is where they can really sap us. More white people practice our religion, but they have changed the rules to fit their needs, so they use our religion against us. The four colors *do not* represent the four races. The original four colors were: green, red, yellow and white. Do you see any green men walking around?
>
> There are a lot of spiritual men who go around saying, "The white people are pitiful. Have pity on them and teach them our ways."
>
> Well! How about us Lakota? We are at the rock bottom. Who is going to pity us, and teach us our ways. . . .
>
> Somehow, they brought our religion down to their mentality, which is pornographic in nature.
>
> [N]ow our religion is tainted by greed and lust. It used to be so pure, simple and basic. . . .

We should close our ceremonies to non-Indians until we become stronger as a race of people. . . .

Now we even have white people who are experts in our religion, and seem to think they know more than we do.

They even write books, and have retreats, and go on speaking forums on our religion. So who is benefitting from all this? [*Lakota Times*, January 29, 1991, A6].

In another letter, which begins by quoting an article in an Iowa paper, the use of the sweat by non-Indians is again directly attacked. Note the accusation of selling religion and the cosmic consequences of using this ceremony inappropriately:

Death in a sweat lodge moves reader to say "wannabes must desist"

In Iowa, Dec. 20, 1988, there appeared the following Associated Press article: "Man dies in sweat lodge."

IOWA CITY - A Fairfield man, Steven Gordon Hauring, 39, died Sunday at University Hospital, Iowa City, after collapsing in a "sweat lodge" makeshift sauna patterned after devices used by American Indians in purification rites.

Cedar County Sheriff's officers said the incident occurred at the Cedar Valley Stables near West Branch where several people had erected the sweat lodge. Hauring was Vice-President of Ritan Corp., a Fairfield firm that makes electronic games and components.

[End of article citation—Beginning of *The Lakota Times* article]

Suggested caption to the above article: In spite of warnings expressed by the Indian news media, (*The Lakota Times*) some traditional Indian people and others, "wannabes" continue to exploit the very sacred Lakota spiritual/cultural practices and way of life.

Now the situation has taken a grim turn of events. There has been and are ongoing numerous situations where non-Indians and some Indian people continue blindly to self-destruct. I imagine Sitting Bull, Crazy Horse, Gall and others have turned over in their graves several times in view of such ludicrous practices.

Also, in the past several weeks a non-Indian who for the past few years made futile gestures at practicing Indian medicine, simply because a Lakota encouraged him to do so also died. This last person had a significant following of "wannabes" and even some native Americans who were strong advocates and followers of his way, even after others warned him against his practices.

The bottom line to all this is, whites no longer need Indian people to advise them, they have learned enough by picking the brains of Indian people, they now can forge ahead on their own, conduct ceremonies, seminars, and teach Indian culture in schools and of course exact exorbitant fees for their services, such as might be. Nothing could be further from the truth and these latter statements and the thought of aspiring "wannabes" in their reckless and wayward journey through life.

It is imperative that "wannabes" and their advocates cease and desist from the dangerous venture they have embarked upon! Remember, these are the very ways our Lakota ancestors lived and died of. Why do others think the Lakota people are locked into a bitter struggle over our sacred "Paha-Sapa" today?

/s/Ken Bordeaux, Lincoln, Neb. [*Lakota Times,* Feb. 28, 1989, A5]

The social dynamics originally contextualized within the sweat extend far off the reservation because of both the influx of whites to observe and participate in these ceremonies and the migration of Lakotas into urban areas to teach and conduct Lakota rituals. Although the observation of certain ceremonies has been documented for the early reservation period (the Indian agent V. T. McGillycuddy was present at certain Sun Dances in the later 1800s), it is only recently that non-Lakotas participated in the ceremonies themselves. Finally, the textualization of Lakota practice has for some time provided another source of diffusion for these practices, particularly as texts shifted from scholarly analyses and descriptions of the ceremonies to "how to" works.

The Lakotas increasingly attempt to control the production of tradition, which continues to spread beyond the geographic and cultural boundaries of the reservation, but it is clear that the essential dynamic of the dialectic creates variation as many different people (including today non-Lakotas) conceptualize tradition through the dialectical process. The dynamic of hiving off also contributes to the multiplicity of lodges. That the sweat lodge can only accommodate a certain number of people at one time is not a sufficient explanation for the multiplicity of lodges—during the Ghost Dance era single and dual lodges were used in a communal manner to purify large numbers of participants. To argue that the multiplication of lodges is merely a result of the increased numbers of people sweating is to miss an essential social dynamism favoring decentralization of ritual. Though large lodges can be and sometimes are constructed today, particularly at Sun Dances, people usually build their lodge with the number of people they wish to include in mind. Thus, the physical constraint of the lodge is deliberately taken advantage of in order to regulate interaction.

The lodge operates on a microlevel as a locus for reconciliation, just as it operates to differentiate larger group composition and allegiance. Generally, social tolerance needs to be established before individuals sweat together, for there is a constraint on entering the sweat lodge with bad feelings toward another. It is clear, however, that sweats serve not only to solidify bonds between participants, but also to articulate social distance through ceremonial structure and stricture. Thus, the sweat lodge has become a vital incorporative ritual while at the same time continuing to allow for and be part of a dynamic of social differentiation.

The issue of ceremonial control has become pressing today as Lakotas witness the rapid spread of their traditions and symbols around the world. The strength of Lakota tradition, a strength that whites have observed but not always appreciated since the early 1800s, is that it is highly decentralized and heterogeneous. That strength has become a potential weakness as Lakotas more and more attempt to reassert their own authority in the production and representation of their ceremonial practice. Thus, issues of who may establish tradition, where it may be represented, and who may legitimately officiate and participate in ceremonial practice are increasingly crucial and, at times, increasingly divisive.

Leaving the Lodge

This work has considered the interrelation between history and contemporary needs, which are combined to create the living tradition of the *inipi* ritual on the Pine Ridge Reservation that I participated in between 1988 and 1990. I have highlighted several features of this ceremony that interface with basic Lakota values and needs. The sweat lodge, though historically retaining its fundamental structure both in physical appearance and in the ritual actions carried out within the sweat, has undergone a broad transformation in thematic content. That change has been partially in response to the radical social transformations in Lakota lifeways imposed by government agencies and missionary groups. Equally importantly, individual participants have actively altered the sweat ceremony by creative symbolic interpretations and innovations in response to both personal inspiration and contemporary needs. History and present experience form the poles of the dialectic, as do formulations of the past that interact with individual and group creativity to guide and shape contemporary practice.

The construction of tradition, as I have shown throughout this work, is one point of contestation in Oglala life. Tradition is not simply a combination of past and present but an individually and communally acceptable combination of these elements. It is clear that this combination, given the fact that the Oglalas have little centralized authoritarian religious control, produces different results when created by different groups. The final appeal, however, remains to the past. As a result the sweat lodge has been a very consistent ceremony over time and has provided grounds for debate in the present.

Chapter 7 of this work shows that the contest over tradition has moved beyond the scope of the Oglalas themselves. The sweat lodge was and has reemerged as a pan-Indian ceremony, one that today has taken on a Lakota form

252

in many areas. It has moved beyond its original practitioners and examination by anthropologists and missionaries to examination by and utilization for individuals outside of the Lakota people who seek spiritual enlightenment and ecological integrity through Native American rituals.

The construction of tradition, adapting the past to the needs of the present, is not merely an intellectual exercise or an expression of ethnic identity. The sweat lodge remains a vital social and personal institution in Oglala life. Because of its malleability, the ceremony has become a bridge, one that is frequently crossed, to what is perceived as the world of the past—a world of harmony and power, of success and strength. At the same time the ceremony is firmly rooted in present reality—familial, social, economic, and religious. In crossing this bridge, individuals are better prepared to return anew to the present world with regenerated strength and optimism. The sweat lodge ceremony provides a forum for solutions to contemporary problems by facilitating the creation and strengthening of relationships and social interactions. When one enters the sweat, one is both reminded of and brought into the pristine world of the ancients. The sweat becomes, in the classic Geertzian sense, a model of and for a meaningful universe that recovers the power of the past in the present (Geertz 1973). Lakota ceremonies are eminently pragmatic, focusing on contemporary concerns and invoking aid for immediate problems. Every person I have worked with presents the lodge as an aid in coping with and transforming harsh realities; harshness clearly is reflected in the "suffering way" of praying, and transformation is seen in the humor and harmony the lodge creates. At the same time, its meaning cannot be fully exhausted by simply understanding its function. Not only does it *do* some things, but it also *is* many things.

Although the actions of the ceremony and the structure of the lodge are perceived as ancient (and the ethnohistorical evidence bears this out), the prayers are personal, stressing individuals' problems, sufferings brought about through poverty, division, alcoholism, and unemployment. The return to the ancient is also pragmatic rather than rigorous: foreign materials such as pitchforks and black plastic are used in the "ancient" lodge without any sufferings of conscience. It is not a precise form that must be recreated, but a sense of the past, which goes beyond gestures and structures to the principal goal of harmony, within the group and throughout the universe. Thus, tradition makes use of historic forms not with the goal of precise reenactment but to intensify the power of the contemporary ceremony.

Despite my obvious personal zeal for the subject, the sweat lodge is neither the linchpin nor the cornerstone of Lakota society. The adaptability and mutability of the ceremony is not without limits. I have shown how both the Lakotas themselves and others have attempted to control ceremonial behavior when either participant, Lakotas or whites, oversteps perceived bounds of ritual propriety. These boundaries themselves are variable, set by individuals and groups engaged in the sweat ceremony. When conflict arises and cannot be resolved, the recourse is hiving off. The resulting multiplicity of forms and practices is a source of debate. Multiplication of lodges is sometimes motivated by the desire to avoid conflict and promote harmony. The variety of lodges both structurally duplicates, on the level of ritual practice, the prioritization of familial (genetic and fictive) alliance over national identification and structurally reduplicates preexisting factionalism.

Conflicts over the sweat are generated by the same elements that establish the ceremony as an increasingly viable social and religious phenomenon: its heterogeneity and permeability. Despite variability, there is an assumption both on and off the reservation that there exists one ideal set of norms and procedures because the past is often idealized and compressed into a heterogeneous whole. From the time of George Sword, around the turn of the century, participants in the sweat lodge have insisted that there is a proper way to perform the ceremony. History remains a real and essential guide to behavior in the present. On the reservation this causes conflict over who may use the ceremony and how it should be properly conducted. Textual reproduction of the ceremony is, at times, perceived as alienation of cultural property. At other times it is used as a viable way of approaching the past. As we have seen, ethnognosticism is sometimes used in order to demonstrate the spuriousness of what is known by outsiders and to validate and protect the authority of insiders. The extent of the permeability of the lodge, both cognitively and experientially, continues to be a subject of debate and contention.

Conflict over the sweat, as we have seen, has moved to a national level. Both Indians and whites have set themselves up as arbiters in the conflict, with firm opinions about what is ritually appropriate and correct. Interestingly, other Indians and anthropologists have chosen another Lakota strategy for dealing with conflict: saying nothing. Some engaged in the sweat will give opinions when asked, but their general stance is that what other people do is "up to them," and what is important is how we do it here. More and more, however, use and control of the sweat ritual has entered the realm of public discourse on a national as well as the local level. The Declaration of War against Exploiters of Lakota Spirituality is a clear indicator of this new trend (Churchill 1994:273–77). Regulation of the sweat (and other ceremonies) is often discussed, but no definitive united action has been taken. Different groups vie for spiritual authority, whereas many continue to hold that spiritual practice is inherently individual and thus should not be regulated. All parties in the debate appeal to tradition to authenticate their claims.

This is not to say that the sweat formerly was without regulation. The eth-nohistorical data makes it clear that in each era there was a sense of ritual pro-priety. At the turn of the century, that sense was so strong that it seemed enough to say that there were proper procedures but not to specify them, for it was assumed that they were common knowledge. Today, regulation parallels the production of ritual and is carried out by individuals, kin lines, and com-munities in which the individuals live. With the expansion of the sweat off-reservation and with individuals coming to the reservation to participate in the sweat, a concomitant expansion in regulatory attempts has become necessary, and various strategies have been attempted.

Although many participants characterize the sweat as a rite of physical and spiritual purification, prayer, speech, song, and back-channeling are also vital to the inner workings of the lodge. Not only are physical and moral impurities extruded through sweat, but social problems are also purged within the context of intense interaction with the elements of the ceremony. This experience binds people together through the powerful dual bond of communal suffering and liberation. Thoughts, which for the Lakotas have an efficacy in the world, are voluntarily exposed and transformed. Negative thoughts are purged and positive ones promoted.

It is no coincidence that the sweat lodge was foregrounded in the Lakota Ghost Dance, a movement, from the Lakota perspective, to purify their world from foreign contamination. This process continues in the contemporary sweat, where participants sometimes recreate a ritual universe symbolically purged of foreign elements. For some groups this involves an exclusion of whites, but for most, non-Lakota persons and certain foreign elements are selectively included and transformed into familiar and acceptable elements of Lakota life. Although such inclusions, whether persons or paraphernalia, may at first appear to violate the integrity of the constructed Lakota universe, it is the sweat lodge that symbolically transforms alien persons and objects into allies and kin.[1]

Just as the sweat lodge is mutable, so is it permeable. Individuals both symbolically and physically move, spatially and socially, from the outside into the inside. Many Lakota individuals did not grow up with the ceremony but in adulthood have found there a spiritual and social home. The persistent image of rebirth reveals the symbolic investment in the transformative nature of the sweat. Everyone and everything potentially can be born Lakota. When familial, ethnic, and geographic outsiders are incorporated into a sweat group, the transformation expands and potentially enriches Lakota society itself. Lakotas present themselves in these situations in their own terms, careful to translate who they are for the initiate and, at the same time, attentive in making the rigorous ceremony comfortable through humorous stories, jokes, teasing, and affable social interaction.

The social dimensions of the sweat allow not only incorporation of individuals but also exclusion and differentiation. This is generally not accomplished through direct confrontation. Rather, the fragmentary nature of the sweat lodge allows individuals the freedom to select or create situations that they feel are comfortable and harmonious. More often than not, sweating groups are defined by kinship, although families will split over certain issues or situations. Life experiences, gender, and common interests are also foci around which groups gather. Thus, the construction of tradition is contingent upon the sweat group, its purpose, and the experience of individuals within the group.

The flexibility of the content of the sweat ceremony lies in how lodge symbols are used. The shape of the ceremony has as much to do with the people present, their immediate needs, and their relationships, familial and social, within the group as it has to do with idealized structures of past performances available to the leader and the participants. Knowledge of the past is valued and essential for the conduct of the sweat, but so is a sensitivity to present needs. Leaders carefully create each ritual anew, selecting from a range of available symbols and guided by persistent but also flexible ritual forms. This is often done so skillfully and effectively that it is not surprising that many Lakotas critique Christianity for its tendency to depend primarily upon written texts in ceremonial interactions. Criticism is also leveled at anthropological texts for not "correctly" representing or interpreting what happens in the ceremony. Thus, individuals will say that all the elements are present in texts and yet something is missing. That something is the vitality of the present, an element that text is incapable of capturing, for it inevitably displaces the present into the past. There is an irony here, for the past is mined in order to enliven the present. Texts do not have a final authority in Lakota thought, although they are growing in importance, abundance, and availability. Despite the popularity of the Black Elk texts, they have not become liturgical guides on the Pine Ridge Reservation; they may have achieved that status elsewhere, however.

As the sweat lodge is a heterogeneous phenomenon, so too are motivations for engaging in it. Its popularity cannot be traced to a single cause—social restructuring, revitalization, identity transformation or reinforcement, social alliance, physical healing, psychic succor, or cultural resistance. It is precisely because the sweat lodge can be readily adapted to so many different individual and communal uses and interpretations that its efficacy is secure.

The heterogeneity within the sweat ceremony is not simply a series of free variations. The ceremony is a highly adaptable element of a cultural system and, as we have seen, exhibits remarkably consistent patterns in its structure and enactment. A dominant metaphor for the sweat lodge, one that remains operant, is kinship. People who sweat together more likely than not are related to each other by birth or through adoption. Birth, as symbolized in the lodge, represents a symbolic and experiential validation of kinship.

The importance of fictive kinship with whites can be traced historically. Before the outbreak of the Minnesota Rebellion in 1863, many white friends and adopted relatives of the Dakotas were warned of the impending danger. The first recorder of a Dakota sweat lodge ceremony, Louis Hennepin, remarked that he had been adopted into the family that brought him to the lodge to be cured. Florentine Digmann, S.J., observed in the late 1800s that the diocesan priest who preceded him on the Rosebud Reservation, Fr. Craft, was an adopted member of Spotted Tail's family and used kinship terms in addressing them. Ella C. Deloria (1944) evaluated kinship and its concomitant obligations as the very core of Lakota life. This reality endures today.

Throughout the literature on the Lakotas, particularly regarding ceremonial behavior, there has been a tendency to regularize data in order to present Lakota culture as a single, coherent system. Although all observers have recognized that there are wide variations in ceremonial behavior and interpretation, the significance of this feature of Lakota culture has generally been overlooked. The missionaries to the Santees attributed the heterogeneity they saw to the moral turpitude of the Dakota religious system; Walker felt that the lack of writing promoted variation. I have shown that heterogeneity is, at root, the essential feature of the sweat lodge and accounts for its continued and ever widening use. At the same time I have presented as comprehensively as possible for one observer (with the aid of the records of many observers over time) the variety of symbols and actions contained in the sweat lodge and their ramifications for the lived world of the Lakotas. I have attempted to let texts and participants speak for themselves while responsibly drawing out conclusions from what I have learned and experienced.

Tradition is neither past nor present; it represents an ongoing dialectical process that unites in ever-new ways the structures of past performance (and the needs that generated those structures) and present needs (and the past structures that influence the construction of present ritual solutions). Although tradition is sometimes a point of contention, it is primarily a point of unity for the Lakotas. The sweat lodge performance represents one such conjunction of past and present created through ceremonial action. The exact character of tradition remains elusive because of its constructed nature, but its importance continues as both a unifying and a differentiated force, on and off the reservation. Just as Lakota terms for the divine may be employed without being debated, so too the designation of traditional itself, given to a variety of manifestations, is employed as a source of unity and common purpose.

When I was leaving the Pine Ridge Reservation at the end of my fieldwork, I went to the hospital to visit an elderly woman whom I had known for eighteen years. While I was speaking with her, she told me that her grandsons had visited her the day before. She then looked up and said, "You're my grandson too, you know."

I realized then that I had grown so close to many people on Pine Ridge that I sorely regretted leaving. The sweat lodge was a key element in that process of bonding. The lodge was both a place to grow closer to people and an expression of those connections. Interacting with people who had become family and friends also involved me in some painful situations. Life on the reservation has its difficult and harsh moments as well as its pleasant and comforting ones.

I have tried to present what I was taught, what I observed, and my personal interpretations in as respectful, sensitive, and fair a way as possible. I have also kept my sources anonymous in order to make a point about contemporary practice—it is not invested in a single expert or a single "traditional" community, for these designations are value judgments that, although necessarily made by participants, are a potential source of bias if made by an outside observer seeking to understand the entire system. I do not contend that every representation of tradition is "valid" but that there is a process for creating and evaluating tradition. I have also sought to protect the privacy of my friends who generously shared this material with me and, more significantly, prayed and suffered with me, consoled me when my father died during my fieldwork, and made a place for me in their lives.

I know there will be some debate over the very presentation of these data and my analysis, for this is the nature of the dialectic of tradition. In examining this dialectic I have refrained from creating and authenticating my own view of tradition or who may authentically participate in its production. Instead, I have attempted to show the variety of sweats over time in order to demonstrate that the ceremony has never been totally isomorphic. Nevertheless, history remains a guide, which helped produce a ceremony with remarkable consistency over time. The sweat lodge represents a series of variations on historical forms as they are understood today. This is not a flaw but an essential dynamic of Lakota religious and, ultimately, cultural processes. I have tried neither to legitimate one form over another nor to judge any form inadequate. I have tried to examine the structure and importance of the construction of traditional practice as exemplified in the sweat lodge without making any individual or group, or my own work, the central authority for the practice. It is clear that, to date, there is no central religious authority in Lakota ceremonial practice, but as the religious system continues to transform and expand, and as it is assailed through exportation and exploitation, such an authority may someday be put in place. Although some individuals and groups on the reservation would claim definitive authority, ritual practice remains part of familial practice, controlled along family lines, be they genetic or fictive.

I was encouraged by many Lakota people to continue this study, throughout my work on Pine Ridge from 1988 to 1990. The topic, particularly the early accounts of the ceremony, was interesting to them. They felt I had an interesting perspective, since I was always going *thi'óle* ('showing up to enjoy another's hospitality') to many different sweats. They also believed that I had been in school far too long and that I really should finish up and get out of there and maybe come back to the reservation. Ultimately, they generously responded to my request, one made in prayer as well as social contexts, *Ómakiya po!* 'Help me out!' For these people and their generosity, I am indeed grateful.

Notes

Entering the Lodge

1. This phrase does not refer to the actual building of the sweat lodge structure but rather to calling together people to sweat on a specific occasion.
2. At times the filling of the pipe is done in front of the lodge as a public ceremony.
3. For an explanation of the treatment of Lakota words and translations, see below, "Constructing This Text."
4. The songs reproduced here might be sung in actual sweat lodges. I was taught several versions of them outside of the sweat by friends, and one individual told me that it was acceptable to write them down because they did not belong to anyone in particular but were used for prayer. Other songs were told to me that belonged to individuals. I was asked not to reproduce them in this book, and I have honored that request.
5. The west is consistently associated with the thunder-beings, but the animals associated with the other directions are not the same for all practitioners. The directional symbols are learned from teachers or generated through personal vision experience. See W. K. Powers (1986:138–40) for a semiotic analysis of the use of animal, seasonal, and directional symbols in relation to sacred numbers.

6. Honoring the often spoken and generally understood dictum used in the sweat: "What is said in here remains in here" (a statement also used by Alcoholics Anonymous), I do not reproduce anyone's specific prayers or speeches. Instead, I describe the ritual process of a sweat, placing it in the context of an actual sweat ceremony.

7. For commentaries on continuity see White 1974 and Schusky 1970.

8. The sweat lodge ritual has also increased in importance on other reservations and in urban areas, prisons, and alcohol and drug treatment centers. I restrict my analysis to the geographic boundaries of the Pine Ridge Reservation for this work.

9. For a description of Oglala religion, see W. K. Powers 1975, and for a work on religious pluralism on the Pine Ridge Reservation, see Steinmetz 1980.

10. The Bureau of the Census reported in its 1990 Census Profile for November 2–June 1991 that there were 11,200 American Indians living on Pine Ridge, the second largest American Indian reservation in the United States. American Indians, Eskimos, and Aleuts comprised 7.3 percent of the total population of the state of South Dakota (Bureau of the Census 1991:6). The data for the 1990 census are questioned in many circles. Race is determined by self-ascription, so the statistics may not be totally accurate. Verbal reports of population on Pine Ridge set the figure as high as 19,000.

11. I use the term *Lakota* rather than *Sioux* because it has come into more general usage. The tribe is incorporated under the title "Oglala Sioux Tribe"; the college calls itself Oglala Lakota College. Although the term *Native American* is used more and more, people on the reservation generally refer to themselves as *Indians* when speaking English.

12. For histories of the Lakotas, see Ewers 1938, Mekeel 1943, Hyde 1957, and Olson 1965.

13. The stereotypes of anthropology and anthropologists both humorously and highly critically portrayed by Vine Deloria Jr. (1969:83–104) continue to hold currency on the reservation.

14. According to a letter to Franz Boas from Ella Deloria: "The interpreter must have changed it [a bawdy element in the story of "The Wizard and His Wife"] so as not to offend Dr. Walker. Of course, it was right to do so" (in Jahner 1983b:20).

15. He was told the story of the White Buffalo Cow Woman, and the fact that one of the two young men who encounter the woman has lustful thoughts for her was omitted (Little Shield in Buechel 1978:238–41).

Chapter 1

1. For a discussion of continental and international distribution and possible origins of the sweat lodge, see Krickeberg 1939, Lopatin 1960, and Driver 1975:132–33. See also Driver and Massey's map charting the distribution of both direct fire and water vapor sweating in North America and Mesoamerica (Driver 1975: map 20). For more popular accounts of the Native American sweatlodge and European sauna, see Bruchac 1993 and Aaland 1978. Bruchac's work includes legends of various Native American groups regarding the sweat, as well as an interpretation of the elements of the sweat that relies primarily on Lakota material. Aaland also provides a history of bathing throughout the world.

2. This text is from the second London issue of 1698. For a full description of Hennepin's publications and a discussion concerning his credibility, see Winsor 1884, Paltsits 1903, and Delanglez 1941. Thwaites says of Hennepin's reliability: "The pages of our adventurous friar abound in exaggeration and self-glorification; although his geographical and ethnographical descriptions are excellent, and add much to our knowledge of the North American interior during the last third of the seventeenth century" (1903, 1:xxxiii).

3. Hennepin mentions that these groups live along the rivers branching off the river eight leagues above the Falls of St. Anthony on the "River of the *Issati* or *Nadoussians*" (the Rum River) (1903, 1:223–24). They consist in the *"Issati,* the *Nadoussians,* the *Tintonha* or *Inhabitants of the Meadows,* the *Ouadebathon,* or *Men of the Rivers,* the *Chongasketon,* or *Nation of the Wolf* or the *Dog,* for *Conga* signifies either of these Creatures. There are also several other Nations, which we include under the general Denomination of *Nadoussians"* (1903, 1: 225).

4. The nineteenth-century chroniclers attempted to record the lives of the people in their aboriginal form, but radical changes were already taking place in their society. Nicolas Perrot had established a trading post among the Dakotas in 1685. The Santees sided with the British in the War of 1812. In 1819 construction was begun on Fort Snelling in an attempt to secure final dominance of American interests in the area. Although Samuel Pond (1908:77) decries the myth of the unspoiled savage, he consciously attempts to present a picture of natives untouched by white civilization,

despite this long history of contact, both military and commercial: "My main object has been to show what manner of people the Dakota were as Savages, while they still retained the customs of their ancestors" (3). Pond wrote this account between 1865 and 1875, trying to portray the "untouched natives" as they were in 1834, the year he and his brother arrived at Lake Calhoun to work among the Dakotas.

5. For a description of the early missionary work of Thomas Williamson, Samuel and Gideon Pond, and Stephen Riggs, see Willand 1964 and Anderson 1986.

6. For information on ritual painting of stones, see Lynd 1864:169–70. For types of prayer addressed to the stones, see Lynd 1864:196 and Prescott in Parker 1966:206.

7. Father Ravoux, who first came among the Dakotas in 1842 and who was a contemporary of Stephen Riggs, recorded this similar prayer made by a Dakota while holding his hand upon a large boulder tinged with vermilion: *"Tunkanshidan, unshimadawo! [Thųką́šidą ųšimada wo!]* My Grandfather, have mercy on me" (1890:37).

8. Riggs states concerning the inner structure of the ritual: "This [sweat ceremony] consists in washing and steaming one's self four times over hot stones, accompanied with singing, etc." (1890:200). He provides another similar though shorter description of a sweat lodge ritual (1869:82–84).

9. According to Stephen Riggs (1880a:110) Lynd had an outstanding command of the language. Lynd's marriage to two Indian women, according to Riggs, although "censurable," gave him an advantage over even the missionaries in learning about Indian life (111). He worked for some time on a manuscript concerning the history, legends, language, and religion of the Dakotas. Most of this document was damaged or lost during the Minnesota Uprising, but a portion of chapter 6 of the manuscript, concerning the religion of the Dakotas, was recovered.

10. Stephen Riggs (1869:82) lifted these sentences word for word, changing only the Dakota orthography, for his description of the sweat lodge, indicating his dependence on Lynd as an ethnographic source.

11. Philander Prescott, an interpreter for the U.S. Army, discounts the frequent use of the sweat lodge by the Dakotas, but he had more limited contact with the Santee Dakotas, and his is the only dissenting voice on this issue. He filled out a questionnaire designed by Henry Rowe Schoolcraft and

distributed by the Indian Bureau, which specifically asked, "Do they employ vapor-baths efficaciously for the health of their patients?" (Prescott 1852:181).

12. Thus, Samuel Pond states: "It is natural for those who write about Indian superstitions to wish to furnish the public with some regular system of mythology. If they do not question too many of the wakan-men, they may think they have found what they are seeking for; but if they extend their researches too far, their system will all crumble to pieces, and they will find themselves surrounded by chaotic fragments. If anyone wishes to construct a consistent system of Indian mythology, such as will be satisfactory to the public, the best way for him to do it is to form a theory of his own, adopt some Indian notions, reject others, invent some himself, and not ask the Indians too many questions" (1908:92). His brother Gideon concurs: "For little can be obtained from these [medicine] men concerning it [the Dakota divinities], except by stratagem; and that which they do disclose is often exceedingly confused and contradictory. One will affirm, another deny, and a third, perhaps, inform you that both the others are wrong" (Pond 1857:648).

13. For the vision quest see Lynd 1864:165–66 and Riggs 1893:225; for the Sun Dance see Lynd 1864:167, Riggs 1893:225, 231, and Dorsey 1894:452; for initiation into the mysteries of the society of the sacred dance see Riggs n.d.:8 and Riggs 1893:228; for the raw fish feast see Pond 1866:230–31; for other sacred ceremonies see Lynd 1864:167; for general religious rites see Pond 1866:244; for sacrifice to takuxkanxkan [*tákuškąšką*] see Pond 1854:645, 1857:651; for worshiping haokah [*heyókha*] see M. Eastman 1849:158; for its curative power see M. Eastman 1849:158, Williamson 1851:250, Prescott 1852:182, and Pond 1866:251; for ritual purity see Williamson 1851:255 and Riggs 1890:200; for killing eagles see Riggs 1890:200; for war see Pond 1854:648, 1857:654, Lynd 1864:161–62, and Dorsey 1894:444; for stealing horses see Lynd 1864:170; for communicating with spirits, invoking their aid, and learning of the future, see Riggs 1893:101.

14. Williamson never spoke Dakota with a great facility (Riggs 1880b: 375), but it is clear that as a medical doctor he paid particular attention to native remedies.

15. For specific instances of this concern, see Prescott 1854:71; Lynd 1864:154, 159, 168–69, 170, 173–74; Pond 1866:250–51; and Ravoux 1890:37. Dr. Williamson denounced the worship of stones in one of the

first hymns he composed in Dakota: "Wakantanka wanji [*Wakháthąka wąží* 'There is one God']; Jehowa eyapi [*Jehówa eyápi* 'Called Jehovah']; Tuka tona witkotkopi [*Tukhá tóna witkótkopi* 'But those who are fools']; Inyan wakandapi [*Íyą wakhádapi* 'Worship stones'] (Riggs 1880c:20).

16. See Pond 1854:645, 1857:651, 1866:250–51, Riggs 1869:60, and Pond 1908:87. Stephen Return Riggs (1890:445, 536) states that *tákuškąšką* is one of the Dakota gods, the moving god or god of motion. It can also mean a familiar spirit and thus has the same connotation as the word *wašíčų*. These familiar spirits (described by Riggs as forces or beings) have the ability to communicate with men. Lynd (1864:156) specifies the nature of some of these spirits as those of the dead from whom information can be elicited.

17. For a detailed biography see Miller 1976 and Wilson 1983. Wilson is rather uncritical in his treatment of Eastman's works. There has been a resurgence in interest in Eastman, indicated by the reissuing of many of his works. Those currently in print are listed in the bibliography.

18. Charles Eastman critiques the divergence of white civilization from its Christian ideal while at the same time justifying his own entrance, ambivalent as it is, into white society and culture (C. A. Eastman 1916:192–94).

19. There are several descriptions of the actual ceremony available in the nineteenth-century Teton material, including Digmann n.d.:11–12; Clark 1885:365; Mooney 1896:822–23; Humfreville 1899:145; Curtis 1908: 66–70; Walker 1917:66–68; Sword in Walker 1980:78–79; Thunder Bear in Walker 1980:130–32; Tyon in Walker 1980:152–53, 154–55. All these descriptions are directly attributed to native consultants except for those of Digmann, Curtis, Humfreville, and Walker 1917. Since Digmann so strongly objected to the sweat lodge as a superstitious practice, it is doubtful that he ever attended as a participant observer. Humfreville (1899:145) is at variance with all other descriptions in stating that the lodge was constructed directly over the heated rocks (a practice among some North American peoples but never before or after described for the Sioux) and that the bath was used for dry heat, the sick party placing a blanket or buffalo robe directly over the rocks and lying thereupon. Mooney (1896: plate 94, facing p. 823) provides a sketch of a Sioux sweat house and sacrifical pole. John Anderson took several photographs of sweat lodges on the Rosebud Reservation. One depicts a wood house with women jerking beef in front of it. Between the women and the house are two sweat lodges,

rather conical, and a tepee. That photograph was copyrighted in 1893 (Hamilton and Hamilton 1971:112; Dyck 1971:190). The second photo, dated 1898, shows men inside a sweat lodge with the cover half drawn away from the frame and a bucket visible inside the lodge (Hamilton and Hamilton 1971:225). A third photo shows a sweat lodge located near a tepee with a winter dance lodge in the background (Dyck 1971:177). Another shows Left Hand Bull making ceremonial arrows next to a sweat lodge frame (Dyck 1971:311).

20. Sword (in Walker 1980:92) states that medicine men administer medicine to their patients by swallowing, smoking, or steaming.

21. This point was corroborated by Two Runs and Elk Head in 1931 in reference to the sweat used by the keeper of the sacred pipe and all other sweats (Mekeel 1931–32:45).

22. Walker, in the introduction to "The Oglala Sun Dance" remarks, "As should be expected of a people who had no literature, no ceremony was invariable, but it was required that in each ceremony each rite should be performed always in the same manner as nearly as the circumstances would permit" (1917:58). Although his basic insight is correct, his causal reasoning is wanting. Ceremonies are variable not because of an inability to stabilize them through written texts but rather because their essential nature is malleable according to individual leaders, participants, and circumstances. Variability does not represent a lack of control over procedure (a cognitive deficiency similar to the theological deficiency ascribed by the early missionaries) but a central dynamic of ritual.

23. Some of those contexts are as follows: undertaking anything of importance (Walker 1917:66; Sword in Walker 1980:78), ensuring success in the chase (Clark 1885:365; Walker 1982:81), seeking abundance for the people's needs (Clark 1885:365), so that a holy man can locate a buffalo (Walker 1982:75), finding lost items (Digmann n.d.:92), as a preliminary to any ceremony (Walker 1917:66; Sword in Walker 1980:78, 100), prayers (Tyon in Walker 1980:155), a Sun Dance (Bushotter in Dorsey 1894:451), during the Sun Dance itself (Curtis 1908:98; Walker 1917:66–68; Tyon in Walker 1980:176), before and after the vision quest (Curtis 1908:65; Sword in Walker 1980:81, 85, 86; Thunder Bear in Walker 1980:130; Tyon in Walker 1980:151–53), the Buffalo ceremony (Collins 1902:829; Walker 1980:243), use by a medicine man (C. A. Eastman 1916:123), use by mourners (Clark 1885:368; Tyon in Walker 1980:163–64), to refresh oneself (Walker 1917:66; Sword in Walker 1980:78, 81, 100), to cure

illness (Digmann n.d.:10, 11; Humfreville 1899:145; Collins 1902:829; Walker 1917:66; Sword in Walker 1980:78, 100; Tyon in Walker 1980:154–55), to promote longevity (Clark 1885:365), to strengthen the life *(ni)* or ghost (Sword in Walker 1980:78, 81, 100), and to purify the body (Sword in Walker 1980:78, 100). Use of the sweat is also documented for martial purposes (Clark 1885:365; Tyon in Walker 1980:155), for protection in peace (Clark 1885:365), for inflicting illness (Tyon in Walker 1980:162), for amorous redress (Tyon in Walker 1980:155) to compel someone to marry (Tyon in Walker 1980:162), for release from a vow (Sword in Walker 1980:78), and for moral purification (Mooney 1896:823; Collins 1902:829; Sword in Walker 1980:84).

24. James Mooney (1896: 823) makes the first explicit mention of the sweat lodge morally purifying a person, although Sword states (in Walker 1980:84) that the lodge will remove all that causes a man to think wrongly. Sword focuses this "inner cleansing" on present mental dispositions, whereas Mooney uses the more Christian understanding of purification from past actions. It is important to recall that the Ghost Dance, which Mooney was investigating at the time, had strong Christian elements.

25. Henry W. Henshaw (1910:662) states that there were three reasons for sweats: religious, medicinal, and recreational. Concerning the Sioux, he cites Boller: "The Sioux, after severe exertion on a hunt, resorted to the steam bath as a means of invigorating their tired bodies" (662). Henry Boller's work (1959:240) does mention a sweat lodge, but he is speaking of Gros Ventres (Hidatsas) rather than the Sioux.

26. Mary Collins states, in opposition to a generally positive view of the healing powers of the sweat at that time, "On coming out of this hot bath the person often rolls in the snow, or cold water is poured over him, so that death sometimes results, often immediately" (1902:829). Mary Collins was a missionary with the American Missionary Association and worked on Pine Ridge. In some instances sweat lodges were used by various tribes during smallpox epidemics with devastating effects, but there are no records for the Lakotas or the Dakotas of death resulting from ordinary usage.

27. Alfred Riggs states: "They [the Santees] believe strongly in witchcraft. If trouble comes, some enemy is shooting them from a distance with his magic" (1912:7). He does not associate the sweat lodge with this practice.

28. Sword, in addition to being the captain of the Pine Ridge Police, was an Episcopal lay reader. This description would be more acceptable to an

outsider than one focused on the operations of spirits. See Ella C. Deloria (quoted in Jahner 1983b:20) for a parallel tendency for Lakotas to alter mythological accounts to suit specific hearers.

29. Aaron McGaffey Beede, an Episcopal priest who worked among the Lakotas of Standing Rock Reservation, states in reference to the mind power of the Lakotas: "They say that some men can hear such things [as a dance eighteen miles away] more than a hundred miles, and can hear them at any distance however far, if they are in the sweat booth with the hot stones and water on them. This process they say puts the men's mind into a holy state ('wakan state,' 'mysterious state'). Such phenomena are not regarded by Indians as miracles, but as a normal human capacity" (Beede n.d.:1:118 [iv, 2]).

30. George Sword also stresses in the vision quest his power of thought for effecting desired results. A faster must "think continually about the vision he wishes" (Sword in Walker 1980:85; see also 79, 81).

31. James Owen Dorsey groups *mniwátu, wamnítu,* and *mní wašícu* together. They are horned monsters with four legs that cause waves on the water and drownings. Dorsey (1894:440–41) further states that the *mniwátu* or water monster is still in the river (according to contemporary Teton reckoning) and that it causes the breakup of the ice. The monster is of a quite visible size (Dorsey 1889:135). This is a divergence from Sword's more microbiotic conception of these creatures. It should be kept in mind that Walker agreed with the Oglala intrusive theory of disease but rejected "their trick with the worm" (pretending to suck out the disease) and demonstrated to them the cause of tuberculosis by showing them bacilli through a microscope (DeMallie and Jahner 1980:10–11). This is probably the source of the diminutive water monsters mentioned by Sword.

32. Tyon, Garnett, Thunder Bear, Sword, and Blunt Horn state: "The sky was the first created. The earth was the second thing created" (Walker 1980:100).

33. Bushotter's autobiography can be found in Bushotter 1887. For a biographical sketch of him, see DeMallie 1978b.

34. Digmann (n.d.:23) also mentions that the Ghost Dancers used the sweat, as do Walker's consultant Short Bull (in Walker 1980:143), Curtis (1908:52), Elaine Goodale Eastman (1978:28, 32), James McLaughlin (1910:204), and Warren K. Moorehead (1891:162).

35. George Sword (in Walker 1980:81) states in one instance that the pipe is used along with the sweat lodge in the vision quest ceremony, but he does

not indicate whether the pipe is brought into the lodge or not. It is only in Walker's synthesis of the Sun Dance and other ceremonies of the Oglalas that he specifically connects the pipe and the sweat lodge. He seems to be referring only to a sweat used in preparation for a vision quest. Otherwise, pipes are not mentioned in connection with the sweat for the early period.

36. For the vision quest see Densmore 1918:184, 188, 274, 275; Buechel 1978:270; for the Sun Dance see Densmore 1918:98; for death and mourning see Buechel 1978:270; for forms of prayer see Buechel 1978:270, 271.

37. This comparison of ties with a rosary is frequently made by the Lakotas in the contemporary era. I suspect that Ruby picked up the metaphor from his consultants.

38. I discovered on a trip to the Crow reservation in 1989 that this remains the custom there.

39. There is only one other definite reference to this practice in the historical literature (Spindler 1955:116).

40. Stephen Riggs describes a *wo´-ke-ya* as "a shelter, a cover, a booth" (1890:590). He also states that *i-ni´-wo-ke-ya* is a sweat house (200). A *wa-ke´-ya* is a skin tent, a Dakota lodge (512). Finally, *ke´-ya* means sloping, like a roof (275). Buechel describes a *wok'éya* as "an Indian dwelling made of straw, psa, grass, peji, etc. Some tribes live in such houses. Waȟpe wok'éya ['leaf lodge' or bower], [is] a certain lodge used in the Sun Dance" (1970:602).

41. Although the simplicity of the ceremony might indicate that the participants did not intend an elaborate ritual (a full sweat lodge was and continues to be commonly conceived of as comprising four rounds [Riggs 1890:200]), the fact that a dog was consumed after the sweat indicates a strong ceremonial disposition among the participants because dog is the ritual meal par excellence. It is also a meal generally associated with heyoka and yuwipi ceremonies, rather than sweats.

42. In his dissertation on the Crow Tobacco Society, Peter Nabokov (1988:151ff.) points out that this spiritual arrangement represents a transaction on the part of the supplicant based in an assumed reciprocity. The Crows utilize the mechanism of adoption, but the Lakota transaction is based in convincing the grantor that the petitioner is truly suffering and needy.

43. For references to the sweat and the Sun Dance, see Hilger 1946:168 and Milligan 1969:16; for vision seeking see Beckwith 1930:421–22, Standing

Bear 1931:159, Mekeel 1931–32:59, and Deloria 1944:62. For finding lost property see Standing Bear 1934:11–12; for the capture of eagles see Standing Bear 1934:80; for seeking a vision to become a medicine man, see Standing Bear 1931:159.

44. Brown (1953:xiii) first met Black Elk in the fall of 1947, but I have chosen to place this material in the decade of the 1950s because that is when it was made available to the general public.

45. Brown states in a later work concerning the sweat lodge, "Each of the materials in the lodge has its symbolical value, as does every detail of design and ritual usage" (1964:23).

46. For a comprehensive cultural assessment of Black Elk's life, see the introduction in DeMallie 1984 and see Steltenkamp 1987.

47. This is not to say that there is no mention of moral good in the nineteenth-century and early-twentieth-century writings. However, it does not seem to have been an overwhelming preoccupation at that time.

48. For the latest entry into the Black Elk allegiance debate, see Holler 1995:204–23.

49. To prepare for his first vision quest, when he was eighteen, Black Elk went to the sweat lodge to purify himself before going out to lament (Black Elk in DeMallie 1984:227). After he was done, the old men brought him to the sweat lodge and had him smoke the pipe to the four quarters, above, to mother earth, and all, before entering the lodge (231). The earth is also referred to as "mother" here (231) for the first time in an ethnographic text in connection with the sweat lodge ceremony. See Gill 1987 for an in-depth analysis of the origins of the concept of mother earth.

50. See Black Elk in Brown 1953:43 for its use as a preparatory rite, for its gender inclusiveness, and for its access to power. For its use in conjunction with other rituals, see Black Elk in Brown 1953:46, 48–56, 60–66, 81–84, 99–100, 117 and in DeMallie 1984:243, 215, 227. For its use after mourning, see Neihardt 1951:197 and Black Elk in DeMallie 1984:382; for its use for ritual cleansing, see Black Elk in DeMallie 1984:391–92; and for its use to receive warnings of danger, see Black Elk in DeMallie 1984:157–59.

51. In the contemporary sweat the rocks are laid upon the platform created as a base, and then slats of wood are piled around the platform vertically to form a tepee-shaped structure. The manner of first building the entire wood structure and then placing the rocks on that, as described by Black Elk, seems an impossibility. The rocks would have nothing to support them if

placed on the vertical slats representing the tepee. Perhaps Black Elk meant that the rocks were inserted into the structure through the slats. It is not clear from his description.

52. Note that in Black Elk's story of the two murderers (in DeMallie 1984:391), the door of the sweat lodge faces south.

53. Generally today the four elements of earth, air, fire, and water are cited by native participants as the original components of the universe. Interestingly, rock is not singled out as the first created or as having special powers or status in this fourfold classification.

54. Black Elk does not explain this, but today it is viewed both as discourteous and, more importantly, a break in the physical connection between the petitioner and the object of consideration (the center or the rocks).

55. Normally, present and future tenses are used in Lakota song lyrics; the rest of the song is in the present tense, so the past tense seems odd. This is how Brown transcribed the song.

56. The winged One is the white goose, and the giant is *Wazíya,* the personification of the north (DeMallie 1984:117 n. 9).

57. I use "inclusion symbol" to indicate that the symbol itself acts as a container that is "filled" with other symbols. Both sweat lodge and pipe, as described by Black Elk, are receptacles that can be filled with other symbols and themselves represent various symbols. Black Elk does not make this analysis himself. Both are "filled" with the directions and various spirits and animals. We shall see a greater elaboration of this in contemporary practice.

58. Black Elk's description of the sweat used at this time stresses four rounds but does not give particulars, such as directionality for each round.

59. The publication of *The Sixth Grandfather* was essential in this regard, for the transcripts from Neihardt's conversation are the closest we have to Black Elk's original words (he spoke in Lakota, his son Ben translated, and Neihardt's daughter transcribed). Unfortunately, there are no transcripts available from Brown, nor has the author ever discussed the mechanics of creating *The Sacred Pipe.*

Chapter 2

1. For the sweat as a religious rite, see Feraca 1961:156, Nurge 1966: 106, Erdoes 1972b:174, Lewis 1972:46, and W. K. Powers 1982:x; for its use

for purification, petitioning, and thanksgiving, see Steinmetz 1980:55; for its use in conjunction with other rituals, see Feraca 1961: 155, Nurge 1966:106, Lewis 1972:46, Erdoes 1972b: 174, Henry Black Elk in Theisz 1975:25, Amiotte 1976, Mails 1978: 124–29, and W. K. Powers 1982:x. For use of the sweat for contemporary needs, see Mails 1978:91, 153, 207; W. K. Powers 1982:28; and Stolzman 1986a:44, 1986b:13–14; and for its use for healing, see Lame Deer in Erdoes 1972b:174, Mails 1978:124–29, W. K. Powers 1982:x, Stolzman 1986a:44, and Rendon 1993.

2. See M. Powers (1991) for a description and analysis of a contemporary hunka ceremony. I would add to the analysis that the extension of relationships (as well as the solidification of relationships and affirmation of the culture, as mentioned by Powers) is essential to the hunka ceremony.

3. An old man named Twin, from Standing Rock, first told them about the sweat lodge (Laubin and Laubin 1957:106). Their principal informant for the entire work was Chief One Bull of Standing Rock, along with the people of both Standing Rock and Pine Ridge reservations (xi).

4. This is the only mention of this feature I have discovered. Perhaps they are extrapolating from the practice of virgins making the initial cut on the Sun Dance tree.

5. DeMallie demonstrates that the political structure of the Dakotas and the Lakotas is ideally based on the number seven, although, on the ground, this reality was not always present (DeMallie 1986:21).

6. Spindler (1955:77), W. K. Powers (1975:134), and Mylott (1980:41) also hold that sweat lodges "mark" the presence of traditional homes.

7. As Murray and Rosalie Wax (Wax, Wax, and Dumont 1964) have demonstrated, *full-blood,* although a genetic designation connoting ancestry, generally refers to behavioral patterns (see also Daniels 1970).

8. Tyon states (in Walker 1980:154) that everything within the sweat is done with reverence. This is within the context of a ceremonial sweat. Again, the fact that humor is not referenced to the sweat in early accounts does not necessarily exclude the phenomenon. Nevertheless, it is surprising that there is no mention made at all of the use of humor in the ceremony in these early accounts, considering how pervasive humor is in contemporary sweats.

9. The use of back-channeling has been consistently referred to throughout the literature (Digmann n.d.:11; Black Elk in Brown 1953: 35, 53, 87; Ruby 1955:62; Feraca 1961:157; W. K. Powers 1975:91; Mails 1978:92; Brave Dog in Buechel 1978:271; Stolzman 1986b:21, 56).

10. With the exception of Mooney (1896:822), no commentator up to this point mentions the use of a buffalo skull in connection with the sweat lodge ceremony.

11. Black Elk (in Brown 1953:111) also associates ceremonial painting of a person with change and new birth.

12. Walker published his Sun Dance article in 1917 in the *Anthropological Papers* of the American Museum of Natural History, but this would clearly be less accessible to the Lakotas in general and young readers in particular.

13. The influence of Joseph Epes Brown's Black Elk material extends to other authors. Vinson Brown, a white author who studied under Kroeber and Lowie, wrote a rather romantic work concerning the spirituality of American Indians so that whites might learn from native Americans. He bases his writings on both anthropological literature and experience (he mentions a *lowápi* he attended with Frank Fools Crow). He writes in chapter 11 of a fictionalized youth, Dawn Boy, who seeks a vision with the medicine man named Sees-beyond-the-lightning. The description of the sweat lodge ceremony he undergoes prior to his vision quest is based largely on Joseph Epes Brown's material in *The Sacred Pipe* (V. Brown 1976:111–14), which he cites in his bibliography. See also Falarzik n.d.:20–31 for a description of the sweat lodge (and Lakota religion in general) almost entirely dependent on Joseph Epes Brown's material; Erdoes (1990:20) also utilizes this material as well as his own interviews with Lame Deer; see Brown 1964:22–24 for a rendition of Indian religion and the sweat, again highly dependent on his earlier material. McGaa (1990, 1992) and his followers also extensively utilized Black Elk's image and written materials. One of his followers and he himself saw Black Elk during one of their sweats (McGaa 1992:94, 98).

14. Jackson also includes a description of the sweat lodge, without attributing the passage to any author or describing the sources. That passage gives a standard description of lodge construction and use. It also states, "Many people still practice the Rite of Purification," which "cleanses people of sin" and is also used for healing and in conjunction with "*Uwipi* [*yuwípi*]," Sun Dance, and vision quest (Jackson 1978:90).

15. There is an illustration of this fireplace in Mails 1978:86. The fire pit is actually drawn with a circular embankment around the pit. There are several contemporary sweats with pits encircled in this manner. See also Mails 1978:65, 66, 67, 89, 98, 209, 242, 254–60, 262, 263, 289, 298 for other illustrations of the fireplace, the lodge, and the sweat lodge ceremony

itself. Pete Catches states that the fire pit for his sweat "signifies an old man" (Catches 1997:80).

16. Fools Crow does not give a specific reason for not using these materials. In contemporary practice some say that they represent white man's technology and thus should be excluded. Often in the same lodges, however, carpet is laid on the ground and a pitch fork is used to carry hot stones from the pit to the sweat lodge. This technological purity, though clearly stated as an ideal, is thus rarely consistently carried through. On a more pragmatic level, one individual told me that wire should not be used because it will heat up and burn someone.

17. Like Thomas Mails (Mails and Chief Eagle 1979:4) in his relationship to Fools Crow, Richard Erdoes (1972b:275) was told by Lame Deer that it was foreordained that he write this account of Indian religion. Erdoes provides a brief autobiographical sketch, portraying himself as an exile and a seeker (267–83).

18. By first-person I specifically mean written by the narrator himself. With the exception of Amiotte's and Bordeaux's, all accounts are filtered through an editor-coauthor.

19. For other examples of both Lakotas and Jesuits drawing these comparisons, see Steinmetz 1970 and 1984b and Stolzman 1986a.

20. Mails, himself a minister, engages in this process when he reflects on the meaning of killing the Sun Dance pole as an enemy: "So the [Sun Dance] Tree, like Christ on the cross and in the tomb in the Christian concept, represents the lull between the casting off of the old—of the past, ignorance, sin, hopelessness, and, at the end of the four days of ritual, the bursting forth of the new growth—of future, knowledge, forgiveness, and hope" (1978:200).

21. Prescott (1852:182) states that four sticks were used for sweats as a matter of course. Most sources indicate that twelve to sixteen sticks were normally used (Black Elk in Brown 1953:31, 48; Laubin and Laubin 1957:106; Lame Deer in Erdoes 1972b:177; W. K. Powers 1975:49, 90; Mails 1978:95; Tyon in Walker 1980:154; Stolzman 1986b:14).

22. Mails (Mails and Chief Eagle 1979:201–4) utilized material from his Sun Dance book, in this instance specifically concerning the sweat lodge ceremony, for his narrative biography of Frank Fools Crow (124–26).

23. Black Elk expresses this symbol in a prayer form, "May we be as children newly born!" (in Brown 1953:40). The symbol of rebirth is much more explicit in the works describing the thought of medicine men in the

twentieth century. Black Elk never specifically equates the sweat lodge with a womb.

24. Black Elk states, "O Rocks, you have neither eyes, nor mouth, nor limbs; you do not move, but by receiving your sacred breath [the steam], our people will be long-winded as they walk the path of life; your breath is the very breath of life" (in Brown 1953:37). Although there might be precedent in tradition for these images, the wording of the sentiments is remarkably similar. Whether Erdoes included this material in Lame Deer's narrative or Lame Deer himself assimilated the concept, it seems to have derived from the Brown text, further pointing to the text's importance as a paradigm for ritual practice and interpretation. Given Rice's findings (1994), it is clear that Erdoes incorporated literary materials into his narrative well beyond the knowledge of Lame Deer.

25. In my dissertation I was less attentive to the many parallels between the Erdoes's sweat lodge description in *Lame Deer—Seeker of Visions* and that of Black Elk in *The Sacred Pipe*. Thanks to a critical reading of my text by Robin Ridington in which he invited me to be more critical of the Erdoes corpus, and after a rereading of Rice's article (1994), I see that much of Erdoes's text can be found in Brown's work and am now more inclined to state that Erdoes created much of this text from the Black Elk material. Interestingly, when Erdoes is faced with the fact that on the reservation most sweat lodges face west and Black Elk in Brown is insistent that it faces east, we suddenly have the voice of Lame Deer, at a time when more anthropological sources on the Lakotas were difficult to access, asserting that they are wrong and he is right.

26. Sage is used to cover the floor of the lodge (Mooney 1896:822; Brave Dog in Buechel 1978:272; Fools Crow in Mails and Chief Eagle 1979:121; Tyon in Walker 1980:154, 176), to please the spirits (Ringing Shield in Walker 1980:113), to expel evil (No Flesh in Walker 1917:163), and for participants to wipe themselves (Old Buffalo in Densmore 1918:275; Bordeaux 1929:155; Beckwith 1930: 422; Standing Bear 1934:12; Ruby 1955:49; Milligan 1969:12; Lame Deer in Erdoes 1972b:181; Amiotte 1976:40; LaPointe 1976:8; Mails 1978:90). In none of these descriptions does the extrusion of sweat have a connotation of removing moral impurity. This seems to be unique to Black Crow's conceptualization.

27. Powers cites the works of Dorsey (1894), Wissler (1912), Walker (1917), Densmore (1918), Neihardt (1932), and Brown (1953), although he is not specific as to which author provides what information, what information

was gathered from consultants as part of memory ethnography, and what came from direct observation and participation.

28. Powers provides several descriptions of the contemporary sweat lodge (1975:134–36, 1982:25–33; see also 1969:126–31, 1982:19–32). Consistent with the Lakota viewpoint, he states that the ritual has not changed over the years.

29. Feraca (1961:157) places this prayer before the individual smokes a pipe.

30. Powers (1969:126–31) provides a detailed description of his first sweat lodge ceremony, which was conducted by George Plenty Wolf in 1966.

31. See Steinmetz 1967, 1980, 1984a, and 1984b (also see 1969, 1970); Steltenkamp 1982 (see also 1987); Stolzman 1986a and 1986b; and Zeilinger 1986. Other works on Lakota stories published by the Catholic press include Big Crow and Sansom-Flood 1987, Zeilinger and Charging Eagle 1987, and Black Bear and Simms 1987.

32. Pete Catches also states that Good Lance told him that "these rocks that you call tunka, have no eyes, have no ears, and have no mouth, but it is through these that we pray to the Great Spirit. When we enter a sweat lodge, these same rocks see us; they hear our prayers; they implore the Great Spirit to receive our prayer" (Catches 1997:85–86).

33. At variance with Stolzman is an account by a Catholic Sister: "The sweat lodge is a ceremony of purification and prayer, perhaps more similar to the Asperges [sprinkling with holy water] before the Catholic Mass than the Sacrament of Reconciliation, since Indians do not see the sweat lodge as a place where sins are forgiven" (Mylott 1980:62). This would, in fact, be the case for some Lakotas, although others, as we have seen, strongly see the ritual as intended for moral transformation and expurgation of sin. Suffering is deliberately undertaken for some perceived good such as the health of a relative or the group, rather than as a reparation for some past moral transgression. One suffers in behalf of another rather than in reparation for personal sins. So too, in Lakota cosmology one's relatives might suffer as a result of one's transgressions.

34. There are other books that give instructions for preparing and conducting sweat lodge and other Lakota ceremonies (McGaa 1990, 1992). See also the World Wide Web (links last tested as valid in August 1997): http://mato.com/~redhawk/buildlge.html for building the sweat lodge and http://mato.com/~redhawk/ceremony.html for conducting a sweat lodge.

35. This is not to say that Catholic priests, or some whites in general, did not cause controversy through their participation. See McGaa (1990:88–90)

for a denunciation of Paul Steinmetz's participation at Frank Fools Crow's Sun Dance and Churchill (1990) for a generalized statement about authentic leadership in native ceremony.

36. Stolzman sets up a progression of attitudes toward the sweat lodge based on age and experience: "There is a common pattern in the different Lakota attitudes and approaches to the sweatbath. Beginners frequently come because of family associations, friendship, or curiosity, rather than deep faith. . . . Secondly, adolescents usually are searching for an Indian identity through their participation in a sweatbath. . . . Thirdly, more mature individuals are steadier. They see this ceremony in the context of all other ceremonies. They understand the role these ceremonies have in reference to the life of one's family and relatives. . . . Finally there are the prayerful old people. They avoid noisy group sweatbaths, preferring them alone. The welfare and the health of the people are definitely in their prayers, and they spend hours in the sweatbath close to God and the spirits. They are frequently tempted to despair for their people and for themselves, but they continue in patience and perseverance, developing a more personal relationship with the spirits" (Stolzman 1986a:59).

37. William Schweigman (Eagle Feather) was an active participant in the dialogues held by Stolzman with the Rosebud Medicine Men.

38. On the importance of mental disposition in Lakota ceremony see Laubin and Laubin 1957:114; Lame Deer in Erdoes 1972b:178; Fools Crow in Mails 1978:202, 204; Sword in Walker 1980:79, 81; and Crow Dog in Erdoes 1990:23. For cleansing of the mind see Beede n.d.:1:118 (iv, 2); Walker 1917:156; Standing Bear 1931:80; Black Elk in Brown 1953:32; Lame Deer in Erdoes 1972b:181; Sword in Walker 1980:85; W. K. Powers 1982:24; and Erdoes 1990:19.

39. The exception to this rule is when the sweat is utilized as a preparation for another ritual, such as the vision quest or the Sun Dance. In the case of the vision quest, the quester is isolated from other participants through ritual silence. In the Sun Dance, participants usually sweat only with other participants and the Sun Dance leaders. Sometimes others are invited to sweat after the dancers and officials finish.

40. See Paul Steinmetz 1980 for a discussion of multiple ceremonial participation among Oglalas.

41. The one exception that I encountered was a sweat utilized by members of the Native American Church. Another sweat lodge that some of these same members used had a rather elaborate altar in front of the lodge.

42. In one case I know of an old pit was utilized, which had aligned with a former lodge but was completely out of line with the currently used structure.

43. Sometimes the stones are simply loaded without ceremony into the lodge by the leader before the participants enter.

44. This image is not universal among participants, but it is prevalent. Some Lakotas hold that the past was much more difficult and less enlightened than the present. Those who expressed this view stated that they would never say it in public because such an opinion would cause controversy. Nevertheless, the sweat ceremony is understood by all as originating in the past and as having been practiced by the "old timers." The eligibility of certain individuals to lead or practice the ceremony may be put into question, but the ceremony itself, though not practiced by all, is generally respected by Lakotas.

45. For articles concerning the use of sweat lodges in alcohol treatment programs throughout the United States, see Hall 1985 and 1986 and Bill McAllister's article "Dances with Demons: A New Old Way to Fight Alcoholism among Indians," *Washington Post National Weekly,* June 17–23, 1991. The healing and rehabilitation paradigm is also extended to prisons. See *Indian Inmates of the Nebraska Penitentiary v. Gunther,* No. CV72-K-156 (D. Neb., filed May 19, 1987); Grobsmith 1994; Waldram 1997; Richard Seven's "Ritual of Rebirth," in the *Seattle Times,* Jan. 24, 1988, K1–K2; Gordon Hanson's "Warden Praises Sweat Lodges," in the *Rapid City Journal* of Nov. 23, 1988, 5; "Trial Nears in Religion Suit by Indian Inmates," *New York Times,* Dec. 11, 1988, sec. 1, p. 38; and "Sweat-lodge Rehabilitation," *Lakota Times,* Apr. 25, 1989, 4, for discussions on this topic.

46. W. K. Powers states: "One must believe, because if he does not the rituals will not be effective; the spirits will refuse to enter a dwelling where skeptics are present" (1982:98).

47. It is important to note that others believe misuse or even simple mistakes have detrimental personal or cosmic consequences. For example, several people were convinced that the severe weather in the summer of 1993 was caused by the abuse of traditional ceremonies.

48. For an example of controversies over who should be admitted to sweats and other Lakota religious rituals that has reached the level of tribal government, see K. Marie Porterfield's "The Selling of the Sun Dance," *Indian Country Today,* July 28–August 4, 1997, A1, A6.

Chapter 3

1. See Hobsbawm and Ranger 1986 for a comprehensive presentation of this phenomenon.

2. Vine Deloria himself admits this in an introduction he wrote to *Black Elk Speaks:* "The most important aspect of the book, however, is not its effect on the non-Indian populace who wished to learn something of the beliefs of the Plains Indians but upon the contemporary generation of young Indians who have been aggressively searching for roots of their own in the structure of universal reality. To them the book has become a North American bible of all tribes. They look to it for spiritual guidance, for sociological identity, for political insight, and for affirmation of the continuing substance of Indian tribal life, now being badly eroded by the same electronic media which are dissolving other American communities" (1988:xii-xiii). He later claims that Neihardt's *Black Elk Speaks* and *When the Tree Flowered* and Brown's *The Sacred Pipe* "now bid fair to become the canon or at least the central core of a North American theological canon" (xiii-xiv). Alice Kehoe contends that the formulation of Lakota ritual in *The Sacred Pipe* "was instrumental in establishing Black Elk's version of Oglala supernaturalism as *the* Indian religion, just as nineteenth-century Lakota costume has become *the* Indian dress" (1990:197, emphasis in original). These same observations were made earlier by DeMallie, who characterizes the Black Elk corpus, for some, as "a blueprint for religious revitalization." DeMallie accurately contends that these materials, on a macro level, "appear to be evolving into a consensual American Indian theological canon" (1984:80).

3. Chief Archie Fire Lame Deer (1994) and Helene Sarkis put together a set of these cards along with an explanatory booklet.

4. A rather glaring example of this phenomenon can be found in the introduction to the controversial novel *Hanta Yo*. Ruth Beebe Hill's "consultant" Chunksa Yuha states: "I am Chunksa Yuha, one of eight Dakotah boys to whom the old, old men of the tribe taught the suppressed songs and ceremonies, material suppressed for two hundred years, suppressed until now, until this book *Hanta Yo*. . . . But I remain Indian in thought, word and act. The grandfathers intended that I so live. For of the eight children chosen to perpetuate the ceremonies and songs, I alone am alive" (Chunksa Yuha 1979:11). And finally, in direct address to anthropology: "That remarkable woman Frances Densmore had produced

an analytical study of Indian music, but the grandfathers had withheld from even the best of her Indian informants that which could be misinterpreted and corrupted" (13).

5. The early work of Powers states that "boundaries of ethnicity are synonymous with the boundaries of religious belief" (1975:xv). He dichotomizes identity according to "full-bloods and native religion" and "mixed-bloods, non-Indians and Christianity" (129). In this work he overemphasizes religious belief and practice as constituting traditionalism; moreover, he ultimately defines religious belief and practice himself, using an amalgam of consultants, structuralist theory, and ethnohistorical documents. Some native people would take exception to this analysis, as do some anthropologists. Concerning the Lakotas living on the Rosebud Reservation, Elizabeth Grobsmith states, "There are many different styles of Indian life, even within one reservation community" (1981:44). She discounts distinctions of traditional and acculturated in ethnographic description, believing that they do not reflect the contemporary situation, which is one of internal pluralism (admixtures of traditional and modern). I hold that this is true also for the Pine Ridge Reservation. Powers links traditionalism with tribal membership and belief in what he characterizes as "Oglala Religion" (1987:119–20). Though recognizing other modes of being Oglala, Powers consistently attributes valid (read authentic and true) identity to participants in Oglala religion, thus entering himself and his views into the Lakota discourse on legitimacy. I consider religiosity to be one of many avenues to constitute identity, albeit one that has grown in significance in the contemporary era, with ramifications beyond the religious. Other avenues of identity are traditional behavior, such as generosity, loyalty to family, simple living, powwow participation, and association with "traditional" people. But Indian identity is not restricted to tradition. Systems of action such as rodeo, tribal government, activism, and membership in other religious groups are perceived (at least by some groups) as valid ways of constituting and communicating Oglala identity.

6. See Allan Hanson (1989) for an analysis of the effects of anthropological writings and politics upon the Maoris and the equal effect of the Maoris on anthropology. See also the work of Hobsbawm and Ranger (1986) for a discussion of innovation in traditional practice.

7. I heard this joke told several times on the Pine Ridge Reservation, but I have also heard it repeated elsewhere in Indian gatherings. It has become a pan-Indian piece of humor. I have no idea of its origin. On Pine Ridge, an

individual's name is often appended to the joke, the corpus of the joke itself then used to describe that particular individual.

8. In an earlier work Powers confirms Walker as a competent field-worker despite the fact that Ella Deloria was unable to corroborate some of his findings among her contemporaries: "However, Walker is considered by other Sioux specialists (DeMallie 1971; Hassrick, 1964) as a good ethnographer who used capable informants" (1975:66). He goes on to say that Walker's material does, indeed, match that provided by Sword and other Oglalas without examining the adequacy of these individuals as consultants.

9. His writings were reproduced, in part, as a school textbook for use on the reservations (Frerichs and Olson 1979).

10. Eastman's works in print are *Indian Boyhood* (1902), *Red Hunters and the Animal People* (1904), *Old Indian Days* (1907), *Wigwam Evenings: Sioux Tales Retold* (coauthored with his wife, Elaine Goodale Eastman) (1909), *The Soul of the Indian* (1911), *Indian Scout Talks* (1914), *The Indian Today* (1915), *From the Deep Woods to Civilization* (1916), and *Indian Heroes and Great Chieftains* (1918). All have been reprinted (see the bibliography).

11. Powers further elaborates this dichotomy: "We must question those beliefs founded and fostered by the young generation of religionists who, on so many reservations, in so many Indian communities, and in so many cities, use native religion as an implement of politics and economics, and perhaps—something that is most vehemently eschewed by old timers—for self-aggrandizement" (1987:153–54).

12. This represents a Lévi-Straussian principle of transformation of bipolar opposites: publish and perish!

13. Powers, in this footnote, gives two different criteria for validity of medicine men: "They are to be revered and followed only as long as they demonstrate their power through healing and their ability to mediate between Indian and white cultures" (1986:226). So the medicine man acts as the mediator between the Lakotas and the spirits, rather than between two cultural groups. After stating in one work that Fools Crow and Chips are highly ranked among the people whom they serve, Powers later says, "Hierarchical ranking of medicine men, is, again, antithetical to Lakota thought" (1990a:148).

14. The individual most active in presenting a singular Lakota tradition and defending it against all comers is Julian Rice (1991).

15. Ceremonial precision and the reluctance to reveal ceremonial practice are particularly salient in the works of Alice Fletcher (1883, 1884).

16. Humfreville (1899:145) claims that the sweat was built over the fire pit once the rocks were heated and the embers were cleared, and that the patient was laid directly on the heated stones. There is no other record that the Lakotas or the Dakotas utilized the *inipi* as a dry bath, nor are there any indications that the lodge was ever built directly over the fire pit.

17. This sweat belonged to a member of the Native American Church. I have sweated with other Native American Church members, and their sweats do have altars in front of the door.

18. Whether or not Lame Deer was conscious of the enthnographic material, it is instructive that this statement has gone so long unchallenged and that Erdoes, if in fact he invented this section of the work, saw fit to place this opposition in the voice of Lame Deer rather than to present it based on his own experience with Lakotas and specifically with Lame Deer.

19. For texts on directionality in the sweat lodge, see Walker 1917:67; Ruby 1955:63; Laubin and Laubin 1957:107; Feraca 1961:156; Lame Deer in Erdoes 1972b:178; W. K. Powers 1975:90; Amiotte 1976:31, 39; Schweigman in Mails 1978:89; Fools Crow in Mails 1978:202; Black Crow in Jackson 1978:96; Fools Crow in Mails and Chief Eagle 1979:202, 95, 121, 125; and DeMallie 1984:393.

20. In his work, Powers (1975:186) demonstrates that the alignment of the sweat is consistent with that of other ritual and domestic structures.

21. Although there has not been any systematic medical research done on native American sweat lodges, there have been extensive writings on saunas, particularly in Finland. For a collection of articles, see Teir, Collan, and Valtakari 1976 and Vuori and Vapaatalo 1988. Aaland (1978: 249) also has a short bibliography concerning medical research on the sauna. For both physiological and psychological reflections on the sweat lodge by a white participant, see Weil 1982. See also Ross 1989:37 for a discussion of the physical and psychic benefits of the sweat lodge. Jordan Paper (1990:88–90) discusses the physiological and psychic effects of the sweat lodge ceremony in relation to communal trance.

22. One consultant stated that when she had a flu she went into the sweat, said all her prayers in the first two rounds, and then used the rest of the sweat to get rid of her sickness. Lakotas do separate the physiological effects of the

sweat from the spiritual, at least cognitively, but they see the one as dependent on the other, particularly in cases of serious illness.

23. For an example of a polemic against native religion, see *Presbyterian Quarterly Review* 1861. Stolzman 1986a is the clearest attempt at a rapprochement. See also Zeilinger 1986.

24. These data can be found in Digmann's diary (n.d.).

25. For a description of native discourse (in this case Cree) utilized in opposition to white narrative, see Schwimmer 1972.

26. See Talal Asad (1988) for a parallel discussion of changes in Western conceptions of ritual. Asad juxtaposes ritual as symbolic with activities outside of ritual that are instrumental (73). I do not think this dichotomy holds up under analysis of either mundane or sacred action. Rather, the symbolic and instrumental permeate all actions to a greater or lesser extent. It is a question of degree rather than exclusivity.

Chapter 4

1. Whereas Riggs is ambiguous as to whether the fourfold structure is an essential part of all sweat lodges or only those that are sacred, Buechel specifies that for the bath to be wakan, one uses the fourfold structure and singing, and so forth. George Sword (in Walker 1980:83–84) explains the ritual by means of its physiological effects rather than its formal structure.

2. For nineteenth-century terms for the sweat, see Digmann n.d.:92; M. Eastman 1849:158; Williamson 1851:250; Pond 1866:230–31; Mooney 1896:822; Humfreville 1899:145; Walker 1917:66, 67; 1983: 375; and Sword in Walker 1980:81. For terms in contemporary literature, see Black Crow n.d.:4; Bordeaux 1929:154; Black Elk in Brown 1953:38, 48, 56, 81; Catches 1997:77; Laubin and Laubin 1957:113; Lame Deer in Erdoes 1972b:174; LaPointe 1976:8; Jackson 1978:90; Mails 1978:87; Black Elk in Lyon 1990:56; and Holy Dance in Lewis 1990:127.

3. In some sweats water is referred to as *mni wichóni* 'water of life' and is proclaimed as the first medicine as it is distributed between rounds.

4. Riggs (1890:340) defines *ní* as 'life', as does Buechel (1970:362). Sword states: "The *ni* of a Lakota is that which he breathes into his body and it goes all through it and keeps it alive. When the *ni* leaves the body of a

Lakota, he is dead" (in Walker 1980:100). Powers (1987: 64–66) defines *ni* as one of four souls that represent a phase or mode of existence in a continuing series of reincarnations.

5.   The Black Elk material has the most intricate recording of prayers utilized in a sweat lodge (Brown 1953:31–43, 53–56, 83). Contemporary records also include prayers used by spiritual leaders (Mails 1978:88–95; W. K. Powers 1982:27–29, 80–83).

6.   W. K. Powers (1982:26–32, 80–83) provides a highly literary reproduction of two sweat lodge ceremonies that captures the rhythms of this practice.

7.   In his comments concerning what is prayed for in the contemporary sweat, Powers focuses on the role of a sacred person as spokesperson for the group: "The sacred person prays to the spirits of deceased men, animals, birds, and other cosmological forces, addressing them as *Tunkašila,* Grandfather. He prays for the welfare of the people, for participants' special concerns such as financial needs, family and health problems, and important decisions that have to be made with reference to business transactions with the federal government. The sacred person addresses the spirits and is addressed by them" (1975: 136; see also Stolzman 1986b:22, 1986a:44).

8.   See Densmore 1918:59–60 for a discussion of compositional origins of Chippewa and Lakota music.

9.   The one exception is at Native American Church meetings. Their songs are freely recorded and played afterward. There have been some movies and documentaries made with scenes of sweat lodges in them. These remain controversial.

10.   Powers (1986:73) holds that the same songs employed in sweats are found in yuwipi and vision quest rituals. Both Powers (224, chap. 3 n. 2) and Steinmetz (1980:55) recognize a contemporary sharing of elements between the sweat lodge and yuwipi.

11.   Powers (1986:70–102) suggests the utility of tracing the structure to the yuwipi ceremony through the various songs employed. The narrative given here was constructed by the speaker without, to my knowledge, referring to Powers's work.

12.   Thomas Mails (1978:109) quotes this song. It is not entirely clear from Densmore whether it was sung by people participating in the sweat as they entered the lodge or by singers outside the lodge.

13. Densmore provides two other songs in the context of a Sun Dance that refer to life: *Oyáte wą wakháyą yąkápi* 'the tribe sitting in reverence'/ *niwáchįpi* 'they wish to live' (Densmore 1918:121); and *Thųkášila* 'Grandfather'/ *wani kte lo* 'I will live'/ *ephé lo* 'I have said it' (131). She also provides two other songs employing this key concept, one is an honoring song sung by a woman: *Wakhá Tháka* 'Wakan Tanka'/ *o'úšimalaye yo* 'pity me'/ *letáhą* 'from henceforth'/ *théhą wani kte lo* 'for a long time I will live' (135); the other is a curing song: *Táku wą* 'something'/ *hehákas'e/thathákas'e* 'elk like/buffalo like'/ *wąláke cį* 'you behold'/ *yanípi kte lo* 'you will live' (255). (Lakota words retranscribed.)
14. Walking Bull (n.d.:10) presents a similar song.
15. John Around Him has recorded a song similar to this: *Thųká úši'ųlapiye yo!* 'Spirits have pity on us!'/ *Thųká úši'ųlapiye yo!* 'Spirits have pity on us!'/ *Hé mitákuye ób* 'with my relatives'/ *wanikta cha* 'I shall live'/ *lená chic'u welo* 'so I give you these offerings' (Around Him and White Hat 1983:15, Lakota words retranscribed).
16. Powers records a similar song: "*Wąkátakiya hóyewaye lo/ Chąnúpa kį yuhá hóyewaye lo/ Mitákuye ób wani kte cha lechámų welo/ Eyáya Thųkášila čhéwakiye lo.* 'I send a voice above./ With the pipe, I send a voice above./ I do this because I want to live with my relatives,/ Saying this over and over, I pray to Grandfather'" (1975:136, Lakota words retranscribed).
17. There are other examples of this sentiment in sweat lodge songs (Brown 1953:84; Around Him and White Hat 1983:15), Sun Dance songs (Mails 1978:124); yuwipi songs (W. K. Powers 1986:70, 87), and Ghost Dance songs (Walking Bull n.d.:6 [This song is mistranslated in English to say "we wish"—Lakota says "I want"]; W. K. Powers 1990b:20, 21, 24, 30, 37, 41, 56, 57). Note the grammatical switch in Ghost Dance songs from first person singular (*wani* 'I live') to second person singular and plural (*yani* and *yanípi* 'you [singular and plural] live'). Black Elk's songs also stress that the people continue to live (Brown 1953:54, 65–66).
18. There are also published songs using this phrase in reference to the yuwipi ceremony (W. K. Powers 1986:84, 85, 94, 97) and the sweat lodge (W. K. Powers 1982:28, 30, 83) and combining a prayer for the individual and the group, in the context of the woman's-first-menses ceremony (Walker 1980:250).

19. The rhythm of prayer when the door is shut and speech when the door is open can be found in the literature (Lame Deer in Erdoes 1972b:181; see also Stolzman 1986b:24, 28; 1986a:55–56).

20. For discussion of qualifications for running a sweat lodge (or other ceremonies) see (Amiotte 1976:32, 40).

21. There are other instances of dialogue in the sweat regarding instructions to one seeking a vision and subsequent interpretation of the vision (Walker 1917:68, 1980:134–35; Densmore 1918:184, 188; Mekeel 1931–32:59; Brown 1953:60, 64, 81–82; W. K. Powers 1975:92; 1982:26–31, 80–83); Amiotte 1976; and Thunder Bear in Walker 1980:130–32. Speeches are also given in the sweat as part of the Sun Dance ritual (Brown 1953:84, 99–100).

22. W. K. Powers (1982:31) gives an example of negative consequences for improper actions.

23. Arthur Amiotte (1976:32) presents an instance of this; see also Mails and Chief Eagle 1979:97–98.

24. Bill Schweigman discusses how individuals may speak during certain rounds of the sweat about their experiences or problems (Mails 1978:93).

Chapter 5

1. Charles A. Eastman (1911:78) claims that the sweat lodge is the oldest ritual practiced by the Dakotas, whereas Lynd (1864:166–67) claims that the Sun Dance, which is always accompanied by the sweat lodge, is in fact the Dakotas' most ancient ceremony. The vision quest and the sweat lodge are considered the first rituals of the Lakotas, predating the sacred pipe, but some assert that the sweat lodge is the oldest ritual (Feraca 1961:156; Lame Deer in Erdoes 1972b:174; Henry Crow Dog in Erdoes 1976:115; Tyon, Garnett, Thunder Bear, Sword, and Blunt Horn in Walker 1980:104; W. K. Powers 1987:3; Catches 1997:77). The sweat lodge today is universally recognized as a very ancient ceremony and often cited as the first ceremony of the Lakotas.

2. There are few references to covering the sweat lodge with green boughs in the literature (see chap. 1 for other instances). To my knowledge this procedure is never used today, and hide, usually buffalo, is acknowledged as the original covering used for the sweat lodge by the Lakotas. Because

the Dakotas lived in a more wooded area than the Plains, it is conceivable that that readily available material was utilized for a covering.

3. This account concurs with Sword's treatment of disease as explicated in chapter 1. Sword further legitimates the medicinal use of the sweat and his own etiology of disease in this narrative that was extensively edited by Walker.

4. Charles and Elaine Eastman (1909:64–69) also tell the story of the badgers and the bear. They omit any reference to the sweat lodge, stating that the avenger sprang from a drop of innocent blood (not saying whose innocent blood). The avenger chases away the bear, and the badger regains his home. Riggs's version was reprinted in a textbook on Santee history and culture (Frerichs and Olson 1979:17–22).

5. This line of analysis was suggested to me by Raymond D. Fogelson (personal communication). I amplify the idea in the latter half of the paragraph.

6. A version of the same story was provided by Horn Cloud: "An adopted child, for example, had this ceremony [*hųká*]. It has corn in it, from an old story of a couple who couldn't have children. They tried everything. They were given a corn to plant and it grew and became their son" (in Lewis 1990:82). No mention of the sweat lodge is made in this version. Black Elk states that Matohoshila [*Mathó Hokšíla* 'Bear Boy'] had a great vision about corn and later found some growing just as in his vision when he was traveling in the southeast. He brought the corn back to his people. Black Elk (in Brown 1953:102) sees corn as properly belonging to the Rees (Arikaras) rather than the Lakotas. It was utilized to make peace between these two groups when it was returned to the Rees as part of the *hųkápi* ceremony.

7. Jahner's article on Stone Boy (1983a:171–78) provides an introduction for the poetics and meanings of this persistent story. She states that, consistent with the thematic content of the whole story, the uncles' transformation from death to life in the sweat lodge consists in crossing boundaries, in this case the structure of the lodge itself (175).

8. Versions of this story have been recorded by C. A. Eastman (1902:126–37), Wissler (1907:199–202), Taopi Sica [*Tha'ópi Šíca* 'Bad Wound'] (in Walker 1917:193–20), Frerichs and Olson (1979: 69–75), and Sword (in Walker 1983:89–100); see also Sword in Jahner 1983a:179–85 for another, poetic version of the Sword version; and see Marie

McLaughlin 1916:179–97; Ella Deloria 1932:87–95; Lame Deer in Erdoes 1972b:174–76; Blue Thunder in Theisz 1975: 58; Crow Dog in Erdoes 1976:108–16; Old Man Walker in Buechel 1978:53– 58; Bad Yellow Hair in Buechel 1978:53, 56–57; Two Bulls in Thalhuber 1981:34; Walker 1983:140–53; Adams 1990:111–15; Bruchac 1993:111–13. Several versions, Wissler 1907:199–202, E. Deloria 1932:87–95, and Sword in Walker 1983:89–100, combine two stories with similar plots and structures.

9. The story of Iron Hawk told by Left Heron bears some resemblance to the stories of Hakela and the four uncles. An old woman who has the power to kill by pointing her walking stick kills four men. Iron Hawk shatters her spine with an arrow and then lifts each of the four men by the arm, and they come back to life (Beckwith 1930:382). No mention is made of using a sweat lodge in that tale.

10. In Erdoes's version (1976:106), she actually is their sister. There are, in different versions, three (Two Bulls in Thalhuber 1981), four (McLaughlin 1916; Bad Wound in Walker 1917; E. Deloria 1932; Walker in Buechel 1978; Bad Yellow Hair in Buechel 1978; Sword in Walker 1983), five brothers (Lame Deer in Erdoes 1972b), or ten (C. A. Eastman 1902).

11. In various versions she throws a pebble into the water (McLaughlin 1916), swallows a stone in an attempt to commit suicide (Erdoes 1972b), or puts a pebble in the bosom of her dress (C. A. Eastman 1902) or in her mouth so she can use her hands to work (Erdoes 1976: 110).

12. See Wissler 1907, Bad Wound in Walker 1917, E. Deloria 1932, Walker in Buechel 1978, Two Bulls in Thalhuber 1981, and Sword in Walker 1983.

13. See Wissler 1907, Sword in Walker 1983, McLaughlin 1916, Deloria 1932, Lame Deer in Erdoes 1972b, Henry Crow Dog in Erdoes 1976, Bad Yellow Hair in Buechel 1978, and Two Bulls in Thalhuber 1981.

14. See McLaughlin 1916 for the version in which he stands outside. Two versions state that he enters the lodge (Wissler 1907; Lame Deer in Erdoes 1972b). The other stories are not clear on this point.

15. Barbara Means Adams's contemporary version of Stone Boy (1990:111–15) is the one most similar to Eastman's, although in her version Stone Boy saves all the people by returning their hearts rather than destroying them.

16. In a contemporary work, Allen Chuck Ross claims that the sweat lodge itself duplicates the origin story: "I mentally reviewed the sweat lodge

ceremony and realized it was a genesis story. The sacred fire used to heat the rocks represents the eternal fire that burns at the center of the universe. The red-hot rocks are Inyan, the Creator. They are passed into the sweat lodge in a sacred manner, then placed in the center. The sacred water is brought in and the flap closed. It is pitch-black in the sweat lodge, expressing the beginning of time. All that existed at that time were the spirits. The ceremony begins by calling in the Wakinyan Oyate [Thunder Nation]" (1989:132).

17. Ella Deloria (1932:ix) states that Stone Boy and other *ohúkaką* stories (tall tales), were related only after sunset. Neihardt (1951:85, 153) corroborates this, stipulating that one will grow curly or long hair on one's backside if this rule is violated.

18. Digmann reworked these stories and placed them at the beginning of his journal, stating: "Here an example of how shrewd medicine men abused the credibility of the poor people" (n.d.:11–12).

19. Powers also bears out this point: "In modern times, when the influence of the white man prevails, rituals become an intense focal point of the Indian Way, a time to recapture the old times, the 'sacred' times when the power of the Indian was strong and in no way diminished by white contact" (1982:97).

20. H. David Brumble (1990:39–41) points out that educational narratives are a common feature of native American discourse. They are told about third parties. Lakota stories often instruct by means of counterexample, as in the case of *Iktómi* 'trickster' stories.

21. Such stories are extended to Christian clergy as well as native spiritual leaders. One frequently told tale is of the priest who is shaking hands at a powwow and saying "Peace to you." One old man who is a Lakota speaker (and thus speaks English using Lakota vowel qualities, in which *ea* sounds like a short *i*) replies, "Peees on you too, Father."

22. For a similar view of native religious practice as deception see Goll 1940:14–16.

Chapter 6

1. *24 Hours a Day* is a book of daily meditations very popular with people in Alcoholics Anonymous.

2. Note that there are two groups of Native American Church members on the reservation today, Half Moon and Cross Fire. This narrator belongs to the Cross Fire group, which is overtly Christian. See Steinmetz 1980:79-87.

3. This is also a consistent theme in Native American Church meetings, that this way of praying is difficult and a suffering way. The medicine (peyote) is acknowledged as difficult to eat, as is the difficulty of remaining attentive through the night-long ceremony. So, too, "putting up" a meeting is difficult because of the time and expense involved.

4. This seemed to be a generalized pedagogical pattern on the reservation. When I expressed interest in learning about the sweat to one family, they suggested I move in with them for a while. Another woman told me that her father would help me, but it would be best just to listen to him and not ask a lot of questions. She assured me that he would eventually get around to what I needed to learn.

5. The only exception to the noncoercion rule that I encountered was when a mother held a healing sweat for her young son and requested he attend at least the first round. Despite his reluctance, he complied with her wishes. He was free to leave after that and did so.

6. I inquired whether this could be interpreted politically, since it referred to the symbol used for Lakota unity within the group and among the alliance. The negative answer has more to do with the modern use of the sweat for political purposes, which, as for all Lakota rituals, is considered an abuse, rather than potential symbolic links.

7. *Sįkpé thawóte* 'muskrat food', calamus or sweet flag (Buechel 1970:454).

Chapter 7

1. On November 14, 1989, there was a referendum vote on the reservation to determine whether there was popular support for the bill. The referendum failed. The project has since moved ahead although it remains controversial in some quarters.

2. This flexibility of the ceremonial system is much in keeping with the flexibility of the kinship system. Alliance is a priority, so kinship terms are manipulated through adoption and within the context of ceremonial practice to allow wide incorporation into both kinship and belief structures.

3. See E. Deloria 1944:17; see also McLaughlin 1910:24.

4. The veterans felt that the Indians had a strong warrior tradition and therefore that the Indians appreciated them more than the larger American society did. There is a growing number of nonreservation veterans, particularly from the Vietnam war, becoming involved in reservation activities, particularly veterans' powwows.

5. Van Gennep's framework (1969:15-40) of rites of passage as essential to territorial transitions and adoptions provides a useful paradigm for these instances. The sweat lodge is often utilized today as a rite of social passage, one in which individuals are incorporated into specific groups. Because the sweat is normally located near the owners' home, it is also a point of spatial as well as social transition. The sweat is usually situated in a secluded area rather than, as in Van Gennep's model, guarding an entrance, but its situation is nevertheless appropriate, for the sweat provides access into more personal relations and is generally not a first move in establishing an alliance.

6. For works that focus on culture as a vehicle of identity, see C. A. Eastman 1911; Brown 1953, 1976; Wax, Wax, and Dumont 1964; Daniels 1965, 1970; Kemnitzer 1969; W. K. Powers 1969, 1975, 1986, 1987; Erdoes 1972a, 1972b, 1990; Grobsmith 1974, 1979, 1981; White 1974; Schusky 1975; Talbert 1976; Mails 1978; Mails and Chief Eagle 1979; Mylott 1980; Roos et al. 1980; Medicine 1981, 1987; Bolz 1984, 1986; Rice 1984, 1989; M. Powers 1986; Stolzman 1986b; McGaa 1990. Works that prioritize resistance include W. K. Powers 1975, Medicine 1981, and Bolz 1984, 1986.

7. This diffusion is not always successful. When I sweated with a group on the Crow reservation, one man told me that he refused to attend a sweat put up at a Sun Dance by a Lakota medicine man on the Crow Reservation because the door was facing west. See W. K. Powers 1987:147–68 for a discussion of the impact of Indian religion and culture on contemporary society.

8. The Lakotas were never enlisted as a group to fight other native groups. Individuals were utilized by the United States as scouts, and the Lakotas were part of the regular army in World War I.

9. The peak of the buffalo slaughter in the Dakota territory was 1882, when two hundred thousand hides were obtained from that region and Montana. The next year saw only forty thousand hides shipped to eastern markets. The last shipment of robes east took place in 1884 (Dary 1974:119).

Ecological changes such as fences, railroads, and replacement of native grasses also played a significant role in the diminution of the buffalo.

10. Although the Oglala Sioux Tribal Council is the federally recognized governing body of the Oglala Sioux Tribe, Inc., many on the reservation do not place ultimate authority in this body. Groups on the reservation organize and gather resources independent of the tribal council. This is situational, for in some instances individuals deal with the "tribe," as the governing body is termed, and at other times the same people organize and act independently. Control of the tribal council is in the hands of different groups at different times.

11. At times I thought that accusations of exclusivity were much like accusations of selling the sweat, part of a symbolic interaction that did not, in most cases, generally present itself on the level of practice. One sweat that was reputedly all Lakota was attended by a white woman I knew. I suspect that personal interaction would supersede racial restrictions in almost all cases. Perhaps symbolic exclusion through peripheral inclusion (or symbolic inclusion through central exclusion) might be established, as in the case of whites who help out at Sun Dances by lighting sweat fires and inspecting cars that enter the area.

12. For texts describing white use and justification for usage of sweat lodge ceremonies, see Weil 1982, Smith 1991, and Gray 1992.

13. In a letter to the editor of the *Lakota Times*, David Kir presents this view: "There are many whites looking for these [Lakota spiritual] teachings. There is good reason for it. You red people told my white great-great-grandfathers that one day all these dead red children would come back through the white children of the future. We're back!" (1992, A4).

14. *Thųwáyapi* is the term for forming a camp (Walker and Garnett in Walker 1982:16). See also Antoine Herman and Walker in Walker 1982:17; Charles Garnett in Walker 1982:24.

15. As one person explained it to me: "*Waȟmúǧa* ['a curse', literally a buzzing or humming—sound or an object thrown at a person], lots of dancers get *iȟmúǧa* by *waȟmúǧa* people—they have to be purified again. A person shoots medicine and they cause a feather to fall or a dancer to trip. They play with it. *Wichóȟ'ą yuhá škáta*—'He's playing with his power.' Kind of like disrespectfully doing a ceremony."

16. For examples of this see Grobsmith 1981:78 and M. Powers 1986:96.

17. She states that the names in the creation stories were spelled "to reflect the original Olakota dialect in which the stories were told" (Adams 1990:165). I assume that this holds true for the rest of the vocabulary utilized in the work.

18. For instance, there is a general prohibition of menstruating women's participating in or even being in the vicinity of a ceremony. Some individuals, however, will allow menstruating women to view ceremonies or even participate. General protocols such as reverence, disposition, and interactional expectations are consistently maintained.

19. See Avis Little Eagle's work for examples of documenting these accusations (*Lakota Times,* July 2, 24, 31, Aug. 7, 14, 1991; January 21, 1992; January 14, 1993); see also Bob Young, *Casco Bay Weekly,* March 11, 1993, 11).

20. Accusations of marketing Indian religion are by no means restricted to sweat lodges. I focus on this aspect to keep within the bounds of this work.

21. For a scholarly article critiquing white appropriation of native culture and ceremony by a non-Lakota Indian, see Green 1988; for a non-Indian scholar's criticism, see Kehoe 1990. Although not condemning non-Indian use of the sweat lodge, Bruchac provides a critique of abuses. For another commentary on the situation, as well as a listing of other scholars, Indian and white, who have raised objections to the exploitation of Indian religion, see Whitt 1995.

22. Alice Kehoe (1990) also bases her critique of misappropriation of ceremonies on inaccuracy.

23. Alice Kehoe quotes extensively from a pamphlet advertising the spiritual activities of Wallace Black Elk, a Lakota from Rosebud who is not genetically related to Nick Black Elk from Pine Ridge (he claims a spiritual relationship): "He [Wallace Black Elk] toured the continent in 1983 accompanied by an anthropologist, William S. Lyon, and in 1986 he joined Lyon in advertising seminars on Indian shamanism featuring an 'enactment over a five-day period of the Lakota *inipi* ("sweat-lodge") purification ceremony.' Lyon promises Wallace will also perform 'routine shamanic duties such as shamanic healing via the "sacred pipe," precognitive experiences, the leading of traditional ceremonies, and other such normal shamanic activities'" (quoted in 1990:201).

24. The reader should keep in mind that this text reflects attitudes observed during my fieldwork between 1988 and 1990. A return visit to Pine Ridge

in summer 1997 revealed that the participation of whites in Lakota ceremonies is more controversial than it was and has become more divisive. See K. Marie Porterfield, "The Selling of the Sun Dance," *Indian Country Today,* July 28–August 4, 1997, A1, A6.

Leaving the Lodge

1. W. K. Powers refers to this process in his own works as Lakotaization.

References

Aaland, Mikkel
  1978   Sweat. Santa Barbara: Kapra Press.
Adams, Barbara Means
  1990   Prayers of Smoke. Berkeley: Celestial Arts.
Amiotte, Arthur
  1976   Eagles Fly Over. Parabola 1(3):28–41.
  1982   Our Other Selves: The Lakota Dream Experience. Parabola 7(2):26–32.
  1987   The Lakota Sun Dance: Historical and Contemporary Perspectives. *In*
          DeMallie and Parks 1987, 75–89.
Anderson, Gary Clayton
  1986   Introduction to The Dakotas or Sioux in Minnesota as They Were in 1834,
          by Samuel W. Pond, vii–xxi. St. Paul: Minnesota Historical Society Press.
Around Him, John, and Albert White Hat
  1983   Lakota Ceremonial Songs. Rosebud, S.Dak.: Sinte Gleska College.
Asad, Talal
  1988   Toward a Genealogy of the Concept of Ritual. *In* Vernacular Christianity,
          edited by Wendy James and Douglas Johnson, 73–87. New York: Lilian
          Barber Press.
Beckwith, Martha Warren
  1930   Mythology of the Oglala Dakota. Journal of American Folk-Lore 43:
          339–442.
Beede, Aaron McGaffey
  n.d.   Typed extracts from manuscript diary. North Dakota Historical Society.
          Bismarck.
Big Crow, Moses, and Renee Sansom-Flood
  1987   A Legend from Crazy Horse Clan. Chamberlain, S.Dak.: Tipi Press.
Black Bear, Ben, and Thomas Simms
  1987   Otokahekagapi (First Beginnings): Sioux Creation Story. Chamberlain,
          S.Dak.: Tipi Press.

Black Crow, Selo
    n.d.   Mystic Warrior—Some Cultural Errors. Unpublished paper. Wanblee,
             S.Dak. Copy from Dowel Smith, Oglala Lakota College, Kyle, S.Dak.
Black Elk, Wallace, and William S. Lyon
    1990   Black Elk: The Sacred Ways of a Lakota. San Francisco: Harper and Row.
Bleeker, Sonia
    1962   The Sioux Indians. New York: William Morrow.
Boller, Henry A.
    1959   Among the Indians: Eight Years in the Far West, 1858–1866. Chicago:
             Lakeside Press.
Bolz, Peter
    1984   Ethnic Identity and Cultural Resistance. *In* North American Indian Studies,
             edited by Pieter Hovens, 2, 204–24. Ghttingen, Ger.: Edition Herodot.
    1986   Ethnische Identitat und kultureller Widerstand. Frankfurt, Ger.: Campus
             Verlag.
Bordeaux, William J.
    1929   Conquering the Mighty Sioux. Sioux Falls, S.Dak.
Brown, Joseph Epes
    1953   The Sacred Pipe: Black Elk's Account of the Seven Rites of the Oglala
             Sioux. Norman: University of Oklahoma Press.
    1964   The Spiritual Legacy of the American Indian. Pendle Hill Pamphlet 135.
             Lebanon, Penn.: Sowers Printing.
    1976   The Roots of Renewal. *In* Seeing with a Native Eye, edited by Walter
             Capps, 25–34. New York: Harper and Row.
Brown, Vinson
    1976   Voices of Earth and Sky. Happy Camp, Calif.: Naturegraph.
Brumble, H. David
    1990   American Indian Autobiography. Berkeley: University of California Press.
Bruner, Edward
    1986   Ethnography as Narrative. *In* The Anthropology of Experience, edited by
             Victor W. Turner and Edward M. Bruner, 139–55. Urbana: University of
             Iliniois Press.
Buechel, Eugene, S.J.
    1970   A Dictionary of the Teton Dakota Sioux Language. Edited by Paul Man-
             hardt, S.J. Pine Ridge, S.Dak.: Holy Rosary Mission.
    1978   Lakota Tales and Texts. Edited by Paul Manhart, S.J. Pine Ridge, S.Dak.:
             Red Cloud Indian School.
Bureau of the Census
    1991   Race and Hispanic Origin. U.S. Department of Commerce, Economic and
             Statistics Administration. Washington, D.C.
Bushotter, George
    1887   Lakota Texts with Interlinear English Translations by James Owen Dorsey.
             Manuscript 4800, National Anthropological Archives, Smithsonian
             Institution. Washington, D.C.

Catches, Pete, Sr.
    1997   Oceti Wakan (Sacred Pireplace). With Pete Catches, Jr., and Robert Holden. Pine Ridge: Oceti Wakan.
Chunksa Yuha
    1979   Introduction to Hanta Yo, by Ruth Beebe Hill, 11–14. Garden City, N.Y,: Doubleday.
Churchill, Ward
    1990   Spiritual Hucksterism. Z Magazine, December, 94–98.
    1994   Indians Are Us? Monroe, Maine: Common Courage Press.
Clark, William Philo
    1885   The Indian Sign Language. Philadelphia: L. R. Hamersly.
Clifton, James
    1990a   Introduction: Memoir, Exegesis. In The Invented Indian, edited by James Clifton, 1–28. New Brunswick, N.J.: Transaction.
    1990b   The Indian Story: A Cultural Fiction. In The Invented Indian, edited by James Clifton, 29–47. New Brunswick, N.J.: Transaction.
Collins, Mary C.
    1902   Religion of the Sioux Indian. Missionary Review of the World, November 25, 827–31.
Confederation of American Indians, New York
    1986   Indian Reservations: A State and Federal Handbook. Jefferson, N.C.; McFarland.
Curtis, Edward S.
    1908   The North American Indian. Vol. 3. Reprint, New York: Johnson Reprint, 1970.
Daniels, Robert E.
    1965   Cultural Identity among the Oglala Sioux. Master's thesis, University of Chicago.
    1970   Cultural Identities among the Oglala Sioux. In The Modern Sioux: Social Systems and Reservation Culture, edited by Ethel Nurge, 198–245. Lincoln: University of Nebraska Press.
Dary, David
    1974   The Buffalo Book. Chicago: Swallow Press.
Delanglez, Jean, S.J.
    1941   Hennepin's Description of Louisiana: A Critical Essay. Chicago: Institute of Jesuit Study.
Deloria, Ella C.
    1932   Dakota Texts. Publications of the American Ethnological Society 14. New York: G. E. Stechert.
    1944   Speaking of Indians. New York: Friendship Press.
Deloria, Vine, Jr.
    1969   Custer Died for Your Sins: An Indian Manifesto. New York: Macmillan.

1988   Introduction to Black Elk Speaks: Being the Life Story of a Holy Man of the Oglala Sioux, by John G. Neihardt, xi–xiv. Lincoln: University of Nebraska Press.

DeMallie, Raymond J.

1971   Teton Dakota Kinship and Social Organization. Ph.D. diss., University of Chicago.

1978a   Pine Ridge Economy: Cultural and Historical Perspectives. *In* American Indian Economic Development, edited by Sam Stanley, 237–312. The Hague: Mouton.

1978b   George Bushotter, Teton Sioux, 1864–1892. *In* American Indian Intellectuals, edited by Margot Liberty, 91–104. St. Paul: West.

1980   Change in American Indian Kinship Systems: The Dakota. *In* Currents in Anthropology: Essays in Honor of Sol Tax, edited by Robert Henshaw, 221–41. The Hague: Mouton.

1986   The Sioux in Dakota and Montana Territories: Cultural and Historical Background of the Ogden B. Read Collection. *In* Vestiges of a Proud Nation, edited by Glenn Markoe, 19–64. Burlington, Vt.: Robert Hull Fleming Museum.

1988   Lakota Traditionalism: History and Symbol. *In* Conference on Native North American Interaction Patterns, edited by Regna Darnell and Michael Foster, 2–21. Hull, Quebec: Canadian Museum of Civilization, National Museum of Canada.

DeMallie, Raymond J., ed.

1984   The Sixth Grandfather: Black Elk's Teachings Given to John G. Neihardt. Lincoln: University of Nebraska Press.

DeMallie, Raymond J., and Elaine A. Jahner

1980   James R. Walker: His Life and Work. *In* Walker 1980, 3–61.

DeMallie, Raymond J., and Douglas R. Parks, eds.

1987   Sioux Indian Religion: Tradition and Innovation. Norman: University of Oklahoma Press.

Densmore, Frances

1918   Teton Sioux Music. Bureau of American Ethnology Bulletin 61. Washington, D.C.

Dent, Fredrick Secretary

1976   Federal and State Indian Reservations and Indian Trust Areas. Washington, D.C.: U.S. Department of Commerce.

Digmann, Florentine, S.J.

n.d.   History of St. Francis Mission, 1886–1922. Manuscript, Archives of St. Francis Mission. Saint Francis, S.Dak.

Dooling, Dorothy M., ed.

1984   The Sons of the Wind: The Sacred Stories of the Lakota. New York: Society for the Study of Myth and Tradition.

Dorsey, James Owen

1889   Teton Folk-Lore Notes. Journal of American Folk-Lore 2:133–39.

1894   A Study of Siouan Cults. Eleventh Annual Report of the Bureau of American Ethnology, 351–544. Washington, D.C.

Driver, Harold
1975   Indians of North America. 2d ed., rev. Chicago: University of Chicago Press.

Dyck, Paul
1971   Brulé: The Sioux People of the Rosebud. Flagstaff, Ariz.: Northland Press.

Eastman, Charles A.
1902   Indian Boyhood. New York: McClure, Phillips. Reprint, Williamstown, Mass.: Corner House, 1975.

1904   Red Hunters and the Animal People. New York: Harper. Reprint, New York: AMS Press, 1976.

1907   Old Indian Days. New York: McClure. Reprint, Lincoln: University of Nebraska Press, 1991.

1911   The Soul of the Indian. Boston: Houngton Mifflin. Reprint, Lincoln: University of Nebraska Press, 1991.

1914   Indian Scout Talks. Boston: Little, Brown. Reprinted as Indian Scout Craft and Lore, New York: Dover, 1974.

1915   The Indian Today. Garden City, N.Y.: Doubleday, Page. Reprint, New York: AMS Press, 1975.

1916   From the Deep Woods to Civilization: Chapters in the Autobiography of an Indian. Boston: Little, Brown. Reprint, Lincoln: University of Nebraska Press, 1977.

1918   Indian Heroes and Great Chieftains. Boston: Little, Brown. Reprint, Lincoln: University of Nebraska Press, 1991.

Eastman, Charles A., and Elaine Goodale Eastman
1909   Wigwam Evenings: Sioux Tales Retold. Boston: Little, Brown. Reprint, Lincoln: University of Nebraska Press, 1990.

Eastman, Elaine Goodale
1978   Sister to the Sioux: The Memoirs of Elaine Goodale Eastman, 1885–91. Edited by Kay Graber. Lincoln: University of Nebraska Press.

Eastman, Mary
1849   Dahcotah; or Life and Legends of the Sioux around Fort Snelling. New York: John Wiley.

Erdoes, Richard
1972a   The Sun Dance People. New York: Knopf.
1972b   Lame Deer—Seeker of Visions. New York: Simon and Schuster.
1976   The Sound of Flutes and Other Indian Legends Told by Lame Deer, Jenny Leading Cloud, Leonard Crow Dog, and Others. New York: Pantheon.
1990   Crying for a Dream. Santa Fe: Bear.

Ewers, John C.
1938   Teton Dakota: Ethnology and History. Berkeley, Calif.: U.S. Department of the Interior, National Park Service.

Falarzik, Dagman, ed. and illustrator
    n.d.   Unnipi—We Live: An Introduction to the Spiritual Way of the Sicangu
            Lakota (Brule Sioux). Bremen, Ger.: Overseas-Museum.
Feest, Christian
    1990   Europe's Indians. *In* The Invented Indian, edited by James Clifton, 313–30.
            New Brunswick, N.J.: Transaction.
Feraca, Stephen E.
    1961   The Yuwipi Cult of the Oglala and Sicangu Teton Sioux. Plains Anthro-
            pologist 6(13):155–63.
Fletcher, Alice
    1883   The Sun Dance of the Ogalalla Sioux. Proceedings of the American As-
            sociation for the Advancement of Science (1882) 31, 580–84.
    1884   Indian Ceremonies. Separate reprint from Report of the Peabody Museum
            of American Archaeology and Ethnology, vol. 3, nos. 3 and 4, 260–333.
            Salem, Mass.: Salem Press.
Foster, Morris
    1991   Being Comanche: A Social History of an American Indian Community.
            Tucson: University of Arizona Press.
Frerichs, Robert, and Paul Olson, eds.
    1979   A Few Great Stories of the Santee People Told by Many Nineteenth
            Century Santee and by Edna Peniska and Paul Robertson of the Modern
            Santee. Lincoln: Nebraska Curriculum Development Center.
Geertz, Clifford
    1973   The Interpretation of Cultures: Selected Essays. New York: Basic Books.
Gill, Sam
    1987   Mother Earth. Chicago: University of Chicago Press.
Goll, Louis, S.J.
    1940   Jesuit Missions among the Sioux. St. Francis, S.Dak.: St. Francis Mission.
Gray, Spaulding
    1992   Gray's Anatomy. New York Times Magazine, May 17, 42–48.
Green, Rayna
    1988   The Tribe Called Wannabe. Folklore 99:30–55.
Grobsmith, Elizabeth S.
    1974   *Waku"za:* Uses of *Yuwipi* Medicine Power in Contemporary Teton Dakota
            Culture. Plains Anthropologist 19:129–33.
    1979   The Lakhota Giveaway: A System of Social Reciprocity. Plains
            Anthropologist 24:123–31.
    1981   Lakota of the Rosebud. A Contemporary Ethnography. New York: Holt,
            Rinehart, and Winston.
    1994   Indians in Prison: Incarcerated Native Americans in Nebraska. Lincoln:
            University of Nebraska Press.
Hall, Roberta
    1985   Distribution of the Sweat Lodge in Alcohol Treatment Programs. Current
            Anthropology 26:134–35.

1986   Alcohol Treatment in American Indian Populations: An Indigenous Treatment Modality Compared with Traditional Approaches. *In* Alcohol and Culture, Annals of the New York Academy of Sciences 472, 168–78.

Hamilton, Henry W., and Jean Tyree Hamilton

1971   The Sioux of the Rosebud: A History in Pictures. Norman: University of Oklahoma Press.

Handler, Richard, and Jocelyn Linnekin

1984   Traditions, Genuine or Spurious. Journal of American Folklore 97:273–90.

Hanson, Allan

1989   The Making of the Maori: Culture Invention and Its Logic. American Anthropologist 9:890–902.

Hassrick, Royal B.

1964   The Sioux: Life and Customs of a Warrior Society. Norman: University of Oklahoma Press.

Hennepin, Louis

1903   A New Discovery of a Vast Country in America. Edited by Reuben Gold Thwaites. 2 vols. Chicago: A. C. McClurg.

Henshaw, Henry W.

1910   Sweating and Sweat-houses. *In* Handbook of American Indians North of Mexico, edited by Frederick W. Hodge, Bureau of American Ethnology Bulletin 30, part 2, 660–62. Washington, D.C. Reprint, Totowa, N.J.: Rowman and Littlefield, 1970.

Hilger, Inez

1946   The Narrative of Oscar One Bull. Mid-America, n.s., 17:147–72.

Hobsbawm, Eric, and Terence Ranger

1986   The Invention of Tradition. New York: Cambridge University Press.

Holler, Clyde

1995   Black Elk's Religion: The Sun Dance and Lakota Catholicism. Syracuse, N.Y.: Syracuse University Press.

Humfreville, James

1899   Twenty Years among Our Hostile Indians. New York: Hunter.

Hyde, George E.

1957   Red Cloud's Folk: A History of the Oglala Sioux Indians. Rev. ed. Norman: University of Oklahoma Press.

Jackson, Loretta

1978   Pute Tiyośpaye (Lip's Camp): The History and Culture of a Sioux Indian Village, Written and Complied by the Students and Faculty of Crazy Horse High School in Wanblee, South Dakota, on the Pine Ridge Indian Reservation. Albuquerque: Sloves-Bunnell.

Jahner, Elaine A.

1983a   Stone Boy: Persistent Hero. *In* Smoothing the Ground, edited by Brian Swann, 171–86. Berkeley: University of California Press.

1983b   Introduction to Walker 1983, 1–40.

Kehoe, Alice
    1990   Primal Gaia: Primitivists and Plastic Medicine Men. *In* The Invented
            Indian, edited by James Clifton, 193–210. New Brunswick, N.J.: Trans-
            action.
Kemnitzer, Louis
    1969   Whiteman Medicine, Indian Medicine and Indian Identity on the Pine
            Ridge Reservation. Pine Ridge Research Bulletin 8:12–23.
Krickeberg, Walter
    1939   The Indian Sweat Bath. Ciba Symposia (April):19–26, Summit, N.J.: Ciba
            Pharmeceutical Products.
Lame Deer, Archie
    1994   The Lakota Sweat Lodge Cards. Rochester, Vt.: Destiny Books.
LaPointe, James
    1976   Legends of the Lakota. San Francisco: Indian Historian Press.
Laubin, Reginald, and Gladys Laubin
    1957   The Indian Tipi: Its History, Construction, and Use. Norman: University of
            Oklahoma Press.
LaViolette, Gontran, O.M.I.
    1944   The Sioux Indians in Canada. Regina, Sask.: Marian Press.
Lewis, Thomas
    1972   The Oglala (Teton Dakota) Sun Dance: Vicissitudes of Its Structure and
            Function. Plains Anthropologist 17:44–49.
    1990   The Medicine Men: Oglala Sioux Medicine and Healing. Lincoln: Uni-
            versity of Nebraska Press.
Lopatin, Ivan
    1960   Origin of the Native American Steam Bath. American Anthropologist 62:
            977–93.
Lowie, Robert
    1913   Dance Associations of the Eastern Dakota. American Museum of Natural
            History, Anthropological Papers 11 (2). New York.
Lynd, James
    1864   The Religion of the Dakotas. Minnesota Historical Collections vol. 2, pt. 2,
            150–74. Second edition, 1881.
Lyon, William
    1990   Black Elk. New York: Harper and Row.
Macgregor, Gordon
    1946   Warriors without Weapons: A Study of the Society and Personality Devel-
            opment of the Pine Ridge Sioux. Chicago: University of Chicago Press.
Mails, Thomas
    1978   Sundancing at Rosebud and Pine Ridge. Sioux Falls, S.Dak.: Center for
            Western Studies.
Mails, Thomas, and Dallas Chief Eagle
    1979   Fools Crow. Garden City, N.Y.: Doubleday.

Marshall, Kathryn
  1992   Searching in the Sacred Universe. American Way, March 1, 56–90.
McGaa, Ed (Eagle Man)
  1990   Mother Earth Spirituality: Native American Paths to Healing Ourselves and Our World. San Francisco: Harper and Row.
  1992   Rainbow Tribe. San Francisco: Harper and Row.
McLaughlin, James
  1910   My Friend the Indian. Reprint, Lincoln: University of Nebraska Press, 1989. Page references are to the reprint edition.
McLaughlin, Marie
  1916   Myths and Legends of the Sioux. Reprint, Lincoln: University of Nebraska Press, 1990. Page references are to the reprint edition.
Medicine, Beatrice
  1981   Native American Resistance to Integration: Contemporary Confrontations and Religious Revitalization. Plains Anthropologist 26:277–86.
  1987   Indian Women and the Renaissance of Traditional Religion. In DeMallie and Parks 1987, 159–71.
Mekeel, H. Scudder
  1931–32 Field Notes Summer of 1931 and 1932. White Clay District, Pine Ridge Reservation, South Dakota. Archives of the Department of Anthropology, American Museum of Natural History. New York.
  1943   A Short History of the Teton-Dakota. North Dakota Historical Quarterly 10:137–205.
Miller, David Reed
  1976   Charles Alexander Eastman: One Man's Journey in Two Worlds. Master's thesis, University of North Dakota, Grand Forks.
Milligan, Edward
  1969   Sun Dance of the Sioux. Bottineau, N.Dak.
Mooney, James
  1896   The Ghost-Dance Religion and the Sioux Outbreak of 1890. Fourteenth Annual Report of the Bureau of American Ethnology, pt. 2. Washington, D.C.
Moorehead, Warren K.
  1891   The Indian Messiah and the Ghost Dance. American Antiquarian and Oriental Journal 12:161–67.
Mylott, Patricia
  1980   Lakota Medicine Men. Master's thesis, St. Louis University.
Nabokov, Peter
  1988   Cultivating Themselves: The Inter-Play of Crow Indian Religion and History. Ph.D. diss., University of California, Berkeley.
Neihardt, John G.
  1932   Black Elk Speaks: Being the Life Story of a Holy Man of the Oglala Sioux. Reprint, Lincoln: University of Nebraska Press, 1988. Page references are to the reprint edition.

1951   When the Tree Flowered: The Story of Eagle Voice, a Sioux Indian. Reprint, Lincoln: University of Nebraska Press, 1991. Page references are to the reprint edition.

Nurge, Ethel
1966   The Sioux Sun Dance in 1962. Proceedings of the Thirty-Sixth Congress of Americanists, 105–14. Sevilla.

Olson, James
1965   Red Cloud and the Sioux Problem. Lincoln: University of Nebraska Press.

Paltsits, Victor
1903   Bibliographical Data. *In* Hennepin 1903, vol. 1, xlv–lxiv.

Parker, Donald Dean, ed.
1966   The Recollections of Philander Prescott: Frontiersman of the Old Northwest, 1819–1862. Lincoln: University of Nebraska Press.

Paper, Jordan
1990   Sweat Lodge: A Northern Native American Ritual for Communal Shamanic Trance. Temenos 26:85–94.

Perrot, Nicolas
1911   Memoirs on the Manners, Customs, and Religion of the Savages of North America. *In* The Indian Tribes of the Upper Mississippi Valley and Region of the Great Lakes. Edited and translated by Emma Blair, vol. 1, 25–272. Cleveland: Arthur H. Clark.

Pond, Gideon H.
1854   Power and Influence of Dakota Medicine-Men. *In* Historical and Statistical Information respecting the History, Condition and Prospects of the Indian Tribes of the United States, edited by Henry R. Schoolcraft, vol. 4, 641–51. Philadelphia: Lippincott, Grambo.

1857   Religious and Mythological Opinions of the Mississippi Valley Tribes. *In* Historical and Statistical Information respecting the History, Condition and Prospects of the Indian Tribes of the United States, edited by Henry R. Schoolcraft, vol. 6, 648–57. Philadelphia: Lippincott, Grambo.

1889   Dakota Superstitions. Collections of the Minnesota Historical Society, vol. 2, pt. 3, pp. 215–55. Reprint; first published 1860–67.

Pond, Samuel
1908   The Dakotas or Sioux in Minnesota as They Were in 1834. Reprint, St. Paul: Minnesota Historical Society Press, 1986. Page references are to the reprint edition.

Powers, Marla
1986   Oglala Women. Chicago: University of Chicago Press.

1990   Mistress, Mother, Visionary Spirit: The Lakota Culture Heroine. *In* Religion in Native North America, edited by Christopher Vecsey, 36–48. Moscow: University of Idaho Press.

1991   Lakota Naming: A Modern-Day *Hunka* Ceremony. Kendall Park, N.J.: Lakota Books.

Powers, William K.
   1969   Indians of the Northern Plains. New York: G. P. Putnam's.
   1975   Oglala Religion. Lincoln: University of Nebraska Press.
   1982   Yuwipi: Vision and Experience in Oglala Ritual. Lincoln: University of Nebraska Press.
   1986   Sacred Language: The Nature of Supernatural Discourse in Lakota. Norman: University of Oklahoma Press.
   1987   Beyond the Vision: Essays on American Indian Culture. Norman: University of Oklahoma Press.
   1990a   When Black Elk Speaks, Everybody Listens. In Religion in Native North America, edited by Christopher Vecsey, 136–51. Moscow: University of Idaho Press.
   1990b   Voices from the Spirit World. Kendall Park, N.J.: Lakota Books.
Presbyterian Quarterly Review
   1861   Paganism and Demon Worship. Presbyterian Quarterly Review 10:353–80.
Prescott, Philander
   1852   Contributions to the History, Customs, and Opinions of the Philander Dacota Tribe. In Historical and Statistical Information respecting the History, Condition and Prospects of the Indian Tribes of the United States, edited by Henry R. Schoolcraft, vol. 2, 168–99, vol. 3, 225–46. Philadelphia: Lippincott, Grambo.
   1854   Manners, Customs, and Opinions of the Dacotahs. In Historical and Statistical Information respecting the History, Condition and Prospects of the Indian Tribes of the United States, edited by Henry R. Schoolcraft, vol. 4, 59–72. Philadelphia: Lippincott, Grambo.
Ravoux, Augustine
   1890   Reminiscences, Memoirs and Lectures. St. Paul: Brown, Treacy.
Rendon, Varcie
   1993   A Journey to Life: Native People with HIV Disease and Traditional Healing. Seasons (autumn):2–8.
Rice, Julian
   1984   How Lakota Stories Keep the Spirit and Feed the Ghosts. American Indian Quarterly 8:331–47.
   1989   Lakota Storytelling: Black Elk, Ella Deloria, and Frank Fools Crow. New York: Peter Lang.
   1991   Black Elk's Story: Distinguishing Its Lakota Purpose. Albuquerque: University of New Mexico Press.
   1994   A Ventriloquy of Anthros: Densmore, Dorsey, Lame Deer, and Erdoes. American Indian Quarterly 18:169–96.
Riggs, Alfred
   n.d.   Religion of the Dakotas. Manuscript no. 3453, National Anthropological Archives, Smithsonian Institution. Washington, D.C.
   1912   What Does the Indian Worship. Santee, Nebr.: Santee Normal Training School Press.

Riggs, Stephen Return
  1869   Tah-koo Wa-kań; or, The Gospel among the Dakotas. Boston: Congrega-
           tional Sabbath School and Publishing Society.
  1880a   Memoir of Hon. Jas. W. Lynd. Collections of the Minnesota Historical
           Society, vol. 3, 107–14.
  1880b   Memoir of Rev. T. S. Williamson. Collections of the Minnesota Historical
           Society vol. 3, 372–85.
  1880c   Memorial Discourse on Rev. Thomas S. Williamson, M.D., Missionary to
           the Dakota Indians. New York: American Tract Society.
  1890   A Dakota-English Dictionary. Edited by James Owen Dorsey. Contribu-
           tions to North American Ethnology 7. Washington, D.C.
  1893   Dakota Grammar, Texts and Ethnography. Edited by James Owen Dorsey.
           Contributions to North American Ethnology 9. Washington, D.C.
Rood, David S., and Allan R. Taylor
  1996   Sketch of Lakhota, a Siouan Language. In Handbook of North American
           Indians, vol. 17, Lanugage, edited by Ives Goddard, 440–82. Washington:
           Smithsonian Institution.
Roos, Philip, Dowell Smith, James McDonald, and Stephen Langley
  1980   The Impact of the American Indian Movement on the Pine Ridge Indian
           Reservation. Phylon (March):89–99.
Ross, Allen Chuck
  1989   Mitakuye Oyasin: We Are All Related. Ft. Yates, N.Dak.: Bear.
Ruby, Robert H.
  1955   The Oglala Sioux. New York: Vantage Press.
Schusky, Ernest L.
  1970   Culture Change and Continuity. In The Modern Sioux: Social Systems and
           Reservation Culture, edited by Ethel Nurge, 107–22. Lincoln: University
           of Nebraska Press.
  1975   The Forgotten Sioux: An Ethnohistory of the Lower Brule Reservation.
           Chicago: Nelson-Hall.
Schwimmer, E. G.
  1972   Symbolic Competition. Anthropologica, n.s., 14:117–55.
Shils, Edward
  1981   Tradition. Chicago: University of Chicago Press.
Simard, Jean-Jacques
  1990   White Ghosts, Red Shadows: The Reduction of North-American Natives.
           In The Invented Indian, edited by James Clifton, 333–69. New Brunswick,
           N.J.: Transaction.
Smith, Andy
  1991   For All Those Who Were Indian in a Former Life. Women of Power 19:
           74–75.
Spindler, Will H.
  1955   Tragedy Strikes at Wounded Knee. Reprint, Vermillion, S.Dak.: Dakota
           Press, 1972.

Standing Bear, Luther
   1931   My Indian Boyhood. Reprint, Lincoln: University of Nebraska Press, 1988. Page references are to the reprint edition.
   1934   Stories of the Sioux. Reprint, Lincoln: University of Nebraska Press, 1988. Page references are to the reprint edition.
Steinmetz, Paul
   1967   Experimental Handbook. Holy Rosary Mission, Pine Ridge, S.Dak. Mimeographed.
   1969   Explanation of the Sacred Pipe as a Prayer Instrument. Pine Ridge Research Bulletin 10:20–25.
   1970   The Relationship between Plains Indian Religion and Christianity: A Priest's View. Plains Anthropologist 15:83–86.
   1980   Pipe, Bible and Peyote among the Oglala Lakota. Stockholm Studies in Comparative Religion 19. Stockholm: Almqvist and Wiksell International.
   1984a   The Sacred Pipe in American Indian Religions. American Indian Culture and Research Journal 8(3):27–80.
   1984b   Meditations with Native Americans—Lakota Spirituality. Santa Fe: Bear.
Steltenkamp, Michael F.
   1982   The Sacred Vision: Native American Religion and Its Practice Today. New York: Paulist Press.
   1987   No More Screech Owl: Lakota Adaptation to Change as Profiled in the Life of Black Elk. Ph.D. diss., University of Michigan.
   1993   Black Elk: Holy Man of the Oglala. Norman: University of Oklahoma Press.
Stolzman, William, S.J.
   1986a   The Pipe and Christ: A Christian-Sioux Dialogue. Pine Ridge, S.Dak.: Red Cloud Indian School.
   1986b   How to Take Part in Lakota Ceremonies. Pine Ridge, S.Dak.: Red Cloud Indian School.
Talbert, Carol
   1976   The Resurgence of Ethnicity among American Indians: Some Comments on the Occupation of Wounded Knee. In Ethnicity in the Americas, edited by Frances Henry, 365–83. The Hague: Mouton.
Taliman, Valerie
   1993   Sioux Declare War on "Wannabe" Indians and New Age Hucksters. Indian Trader (courtesy of the Navajo Times) 24(7):1, 9–10.
Tedlock, Dennis, and Barbara Tedlock, eds.
   1975   Teachings from the American Earth: Indian Religion and Philosophy. New York: Liveright.
Teir, Harald, Yrjo Collan, and Pirkko Valtakari
   1976   Sauna Studies. Papers read at the Sixth International Sauna Congress in Helsinki, August 15–17, 1974. Helsinki: Bammalan Kirjapaino Oy.
Thalhuber, Pat
   1981   Even the Eagle Dies. Pine Ridge, S.Dak.: Shannon County Schools Supportive Services.

Theisz, Ron, ed.
    1975   Buckskin Tokens. Aberdeen, S.Dak.: North Plains Press.
Thwaites, Ruben Gold
    1903   Introduction to A New Discovery of a Vast Country in America, by Louis
              Hennepin, edited by Reuben Gold Thwaites, vol. 1, ix–xliii. Chicago: A. C.
              McClurg.
Van Gennep, Arnold
    1969   The Rites of Passage. Chicago: University of Chicago Press.
Vuori, Ilkka, and Heikki Vapaatalo
    1988   Annals of Clinical Research. Special issue on Sauna. Helsinki: Finnish
              Medical Society Duodecim.
Waldram, James B.
    1997   The Way of the Pipe: Aboriginal Spirituality and Symbolic Healing in
              Canadian Prisons. Peterborough, Ont.: Broadview Press.
Walker, James R.
    1917   The Sun Dance and Other Ceremonies of the Oglala Division of the Teton
              Sioux. Anthropological Papers of the American Museum of Natural His-
              tory 16(2). New York.
    1975   Oglala Metaphysics. In Tedlock and Tedlock 1975, 205–18.
    1980   Lakota Belief and Ritual. Edited by Raymond J. DeMallie and Elaine A.
              Jahner. Lincoln: University of Nebraska Press.
    1982   Lakota Society. Edited by Raymond J. DeMallie. Lincoln: University of
              Nebraska Press.
    1983   Lakota Myth. Edited by Elaine Jahner. Lincoln: University of Nebraska
              Press.
Walking Bull, Gilbert
    n.d.   Chanupa Prayers and Songs in the Lakota Traditions. Saugerties, N.Y.
Wallis, Wilson
    1919   The Sun Dance of the Canadian Dakota. American Museum of Natural
              History, Anthropological Papers 16(4), 317–80. New York.
    1923   Beliefs and Tales of the Canadian Dakota. Journal of American Folk-Lore
              36:36–101.
Wax, Murray, Rosalie Wax, and Robert Dumont
    1964   Formal Education in an American Indian Community. Supplement to
              Social Problems 11(4).
Weil, Andrew
    1982   The Indian Sweat. American West 19(2):42–49.
White, Robert A.
    1974   Value Themes of the Native American Tribalistic Movement among the
              South Dakota Sioux. Current Anthropology 15:284–89.
Whitt, Laurie Ann
    1995   Cultural Imperialism and the Marketing of Native America. American
              Indian Culture and Research Journal 19(3):1–31.

Willand, Jon
  1964   Lac Qui Parle and the Dakota Mission. Madison, Minn.: Lac Qui Parle
          County Historical Society.
Williamson, Thomas
  1851   Dacotas of the Mississippi. *In* Historical and Statistical Information
          respecting the History, Condition and Prospects of the Indian Tribes of the
          United States, edited by Henry R. Schoolcraft, vol. 1, 247–64. Philadel-
          phia: Lippincott, Grambo.
  1869   Dakota Medicine. *In* Riggs 1869, 435–50.
Wilson, Raymond
  1983   Ohiyesa: Charles Eastman, Santee Sioux. Urbana: University of Illinois
          Press.
Winsor, Justin
  1884   Father Louis Hennepin. *In* Narrative and Critical History of America,
          edited by Justin Winsor, vol. 4, 247–56. Boston: Houghton Mifflin.
Wissler, Clark
  1907   Some Dakota Myths. Journal of American Folk-Lore 20:121–31, 195–206.
  1912   Societies and Ceremonial Associations in the Oglala Division of the Teton-
          Dakota. Anthropological Papers of the American Museum of Natural
          History 11(1). New York.
Zeilinger, Ron
  1986   Sacred Ground. Chamberlain, S.Dak.: Tipi Press.
Zeilinger, Ron, and Tom Charging Eagle
  1987   Black Hills: Sacred Hills. Chamberlain, S.Dak.: Tipi Press.
Zitkala-Ša
  1901   Old Indian Legends. Reprint, Lincoln: University of Nebraska Press, 1985.

Index

In *Studies in the Anthropology of North American Indians*

The Four Hills of Life:
Northern Arapaho Knowledge
and Life Movement
By Jeffrey D. Anderson

The Semantics of Time:
Aspectual Categorization in
Koyukon Athabaskan
By Melissa Axelrod

Lushootseed Texts: An
Introduction to Puget
Salish Narrative Aesthetics
Edited by Crisca Bierwert

People of The Dalles:
The Indians of
Wascopam Mission
By Robert Boyd

The Lakota Ritual of the
Sweat Lodge: History
and Contemporary Practice
By Raymond A. Bucko

From the Sands to the
Mountain: Change and
Persistence in a Southern
Paiute Community
By Pamela A. Bunte and
Robert J. Franklin

A Grammar of Comanche
By Jean Ormsbee Charney

Northern Haida Songs
By John Enrico and
Wendy Bross Stuart

Powhatan's World and
Colonial Virginia:
A Conflict of Cultures
By Frederic W. Gleach

The Heiltsuks: Dialogues of
Culture and History on the
Northwest Coast
By Michael E. Harkin

Prophecy and Power among
the Dogrib Indians
By June Helm

Corbett Mack: The Life
of a Northern Paiute
As told by
Michael Hittman

The Canadian Sioux
By James H. Howard

The Comanches:
A History, 1706–1875
By Thomas W. Kavanagh

Koasati Dictionary
By Geoffrey D. Kimball
with the assistance of
Bel Abbey, Martha John,
and Ruth Poncho

Koasati Grammer
By Geoffrey D. Kimball
with the assistance of
Bel Abbey, Nora Abbey,
Martha John, Ed John,
and Ruth Poncho

The Salish Language Family:
Reconstructing Syntax
By Paul D. Kroeber

The Medicine Men: Oglala
Sioux Ceremony and Healing
By Thomas H. Lewis

A Dictionary of
Creek / Muskogee
By Jack B. Martin and
Margaret McKane Mauldin

Wolverine Myths and Visions:
Dene Traditions from
Northern Alberta
Edited by Patrick Moore and
Angela Wheelock

Ceremonies of the Pawnee
By James R. Murie
Edited by Douglas R. Parks

Archaeology and Ethnohistory
of the Omaha Indians: The Big
Village Site
By John M. O'Shea and John
Ludwickson

Traditional Narratives of the
Arikara Indians (4 vols.)
By Douglas R. Parks

Native Languages and
Language Families of
North America
(folded study map and
wall display map)
Compiled by Ives Goddard